# SINGER OF THE LAND OF SNOWS

Traditions and Transformations in Tibetan Buddhism

DAVID GERMANO AND MICHAEL SHEEHY, EDITORS

# SINGER OF THE LAND OF SNOWS

## Shabkar, Buddhism, and Tibetan National Identity

Rachel H. Pang

**University of Virginia Press**
Charlottesville and London

University of Virginia Press
© 2024 by the Rector and Visitors of the University of Virginia
All rights reserved
Printed in the United States of America on acid-free paper

*First published 2024*

1 3 5 7 9 8 6 4 2

Library of Congress Cataloging-in-Publication Data

Names: Pang, Rachel H., author.
Title: Singer of the land of snows : Shabkar, Buddhism, and Tibetan national identity / Rachel H. Pang.
Description: Charlottesville : University of Virginia Press, 2024. | Series: Traditions and transformations in Tibetan Buddhism | Includes bibliographical references and index.
Identifiers: LCCN 2023036410 (print) | LCCN 2023036411 (ebook) | ISBN 9780813950655 (hardcover) | ISBN 9780813950662 (paperback) | ISBN 9780813950679 (ebook)
Subjects: LCSH: Zhabs-dkar Tshogs-drug-rang-grol, 1781–1851. | Lamas—China—Tibet Autonomous Region—Biography. | Yoginis—China—Tibet Autonomous Region—Biography. | Tibetans—Ethnic identity. | Buddhism—China—Tibet Autonomous Region. | Religion and politics—China—Tibet Autonomous Region. | Nationalism—China—Tibet Autonomous Region.
Classification: LCC BQ986.A38 P36 2024 (print) | LCC BQ986.A38 (ebook) | DDC 294.3/923092 [B]—dc23/eng/20230823
LC record available at https://lccn.loc.gov/2023036410
LC ebook record available at https://lccn.loc.gov/2023036411

*Cover art:* Photo HenrysPhotography/shutterstock.com; ornament mr_owlman/shutterstock.com

*For my parents and teachers*

# CONTENTS

| | |
|---|---|
| Acknowledgments | ix |
| Conventions and Translations | xiii |
| Introduction | 1 |
| 1. "Tibet" and "Tibetans" in Shabkar's Autobiography | 21 |
| 2. Mapping Tibet's Buddhist Geography | 42 |
| 3. Vernacularizing the *Namtar* Genre | 63 |
| 4. Reviving and Adapting Two Foundational Myths | 87 |
| 5. Imagining a Community Based on Buddhist Values and Practices | 109 |
| Epilogue: The Deep Historical and Religious Roots of Tibetan National Identity | 135 |
| Appendix: Locations Mentioned in Shabkar's Autobiography | 151 |
| Notes | 167 |
| Bibliography | 197 |
| Index | 213 |

# ACKNOWLEDGMENTS

This book is the result of the joint effort of many people. Although my name is on the cover, it would not exist without the collaboration and assistance of a great number of individuals who contributed to the causes and conditions that made this book.

First and foremost, I would like to thank my parents. From a young age, my mother and father nurtured a deep love for learning within me and supported me through innumerable challenges. It was also they who first taught me the meaning of unconditional love. Words cannot express my gratitude to them.

I have had the great privilege to study under some extraordinary Tibetan Buddhist teachers who embody wisdom and compassion. I would like to thank the V. V. Thrangu Rinpoche, Khenpo Karthar Rinpoche, Lama Tashi Dondrup, Yongdzin Lama Nyima, Lama Chopel, Changzö Yontan Gyatso, Lama Ajo, Lama Sonam, Khenpo Chonyi, Lama Jikmé Tshultrim, Lama Nyima Gyaltsen, Khenpo Losel, Lama Rigdzin, Lama Yonden, Ani Kelsang, and Palden Dondrup. Their presence informs the way that I read and engage with Tibetan Buddhist texts.

This project began over a decade ago at the University of Virginia (UVA). I am grateful to my main doctoral advisor, David Germano, as well as my dissertation committee and professors for giving me a strong foundation in graduate school: Paul Groner, Kevin Hart, Karen Lang, Francis Aaron Laushway, Kurtis Schaeffer, John Shepherd, and Nicholas Sihlé. I am also indebted to the kindness of Laura Troutman and Elizabeth Smith. UVA is where I laid the foundations for the study of Tibetan language. I am grateful to Gen Tsetan, Gen Tinley, Khenpo Ngawang Dorjee, Nicholas Tournadre, Sonam Yangkyi, Tsering Wanghcuk, Steven Weinberger, and Eric Woelfel and for their kindness and masterful instruction. In Amdo I also had the honor of studying with some wonderful teachers and am grateful for the assistance of some dear friends, including Gergen Tashi Drolma, Gergen Namlha, Gergen Kunga, Gergen Dawa Lodri, Chen Laoshi, Yang Laoshi, Liu Ke, and Norbu Drolma. This journey began at the University of Toronto, and I am grateful to Frances Garrett for her kindness throughout my academic career.

I express my gratitude to the editors Eric Brandt, David Germano, and Michael Sheehy at the University of Virginia Press. Thank you for believing in this project and giving it an opportunity. I am grateful for your wise and generous counsel as you shepherded this manuscript through the publication process. Thanks also to Fernando Campos, Bridget Manzella, Enid Zafran, Ellen Satrom, Wren Morgan Myers, Clayton Butler, and their team for producing this book with such expertise and enthusiasm.

The unconventional direction of this book began with my curiosity about the relationship between religion and national identity. Thanks to Sienna Craig, Holly Gayley, Lama Jabb, and Mark Turin for their generosity and constructive feedback in my first foray into this topic in an article published in *Himalaya*. Matthew Walton hosted a conference at Oxford University on Buddhist nationalisms that put me into conversation with authors and texts that shaped the course of my inquiry. Thanks to Matt as well as Besir Ceka for sharing their expertise on nationalism. Katia Bowers, Ellen Tilton-Cantrell, and Audra Wolfe also contributed to this project from its initial stages. In particular, I am grateful to Katia for her generosity and advice and Ellen who helped to clarify my argument, build a narrative arc, and revise the manuscript. I am fortunate to have the friendship and support of Katia, Amy Krings, and Jungmin Lee during the writing process. Andrew Quintman and two anonymous reviewers from the University of Virginia Press also played a crucial role in improving this manuscript. I express my deep gratitude to them for their incisive feedback and encouragement. Geoffrey Barstow, David DiValerio, Trent Foley, Matthew King, Bill Mahony, Gerardo Marti, and Karl Plank also helped me to revise the proposal and general direction of this project in a significant way. I am grateful for their wisdom and kindness.

A number of librarian collaborators helped me to locate many of the sources in this project. I am grateful to Nawang Thokmey at the University of Virginia; Jean Coates, Cara Evanson, Joe Gutekanst, Jayme Sponsel, and Trish Johnson at the Davidson College Library; Lauran Hartley at Columbia University East Asian Library; Élie Roux and Travis DeTour from the Buddhist Digital Resource Center; Tsering Wangyel Shawa from Princeton University Library; and Kristina Dy-Liacco at Latse Library. Thanks also to Nat Case for producing the excellent maps in this book.

As I worked on this project over the years, many scholars and friends contributed as interlocutors as I explored ideas in Shabkar's writings. Some of them include Gregory Alles, Naomi Appleton, Christopher Bell, Kin Cheung, Gabriele Coura, Brandon Dotson, Piko Ewoodzie, Douglas Duckworth, Thomas Espenchied, Christopher Jones, Amelia Hall, Hsiao-Lan Hu, Nancy Lin, Klaus-Dieter Mathes, Matthew Orsborn, Matthieu Ricard, Geoffrey Samuel, Abraham Vélez de Cea, and Nicole Willock. There are also the anonymous reviewers of numerous articles that I wrote who helped improve my ideas. Thank you for the important conversations and feedback that helped to shape the ideas in this book.

Over the past decade, as I worked on this project, I had the privilege of writing in the supportive environment of the Religious Studies and East Asian Studies Departments at Davidson College. Thanks to Jason Blum, Graham Bullock, Trent Foley, Rocky Hoffman, Jaya Jha, Rosaline Kyo, Fuji Lozada, Andy Lustig, Bill Mahony, Melanie McAlpine, Amber MacIntyre, Karl Plank, Greg Snyder, Dáša Mortensen, Gladys Newport, Doug Ottati, Lynn Poland, Shelley Rigger, Miffy Tsai, Anne Wills, and Rizwan Zamir. Wendy Raymond also played a fundamental role in supporting many aspects of this project early on. Mary Murchane, Rachael Murdock, and Trish Tilburg helped to clarify and improve this project as I worked on grant applications. I would also like to thank the conveners of the Faculty of Color Caucus—Helen Cho, Laurian Bowles, Melissa González, and Amanda Martinez; I am grateful for their advocacy work and inclusive community building at the college. Davidson College also generously provided a subvention grant for the publication of this book.

A significant part of working at Davidson is teaching. I had the privilege of working with some wonderful students over the years. In particular, I would like to thank Sarah Aziz, Christina Brown, Yeeva Cheng, Sarah Fink, Ben Haden, Clare Harbin, Elise Lankiewicz, Morgan Mercer, and Buer Su for their illuminating contributions and making teaching energizing and a joy.

Finally, I express my gratitude for my brilliant siblings Renée and Ernest who are the most kind and honest intellectual conversation partners. Thanks also to YL Yee, Sam Sook, Uncle Norman, BEE, and 嬷嬷 for their generosity and kindness—especially during my travels in Asia. Last but not least, I am grateful to Passang for filling my life with love and laughter. You are the best travel companion both in the Himalayas and in life.

# CONVENTIONS AND TRANSLATIONS

In this book, most Tibetan terms have been translated into English. In places where the original spelling of the Tibetan word is useful for specialists, I provide the Wylie transcription in parentheses. Tibetan is the default second language of the book. For languages other than Tibetan, the foreign word in parentheses is preceded by "Ch." for Chinese, "Skt." for Sanskrit, and "M." for Mongolian. When Tibetan terms are left untranslated, I use the Tibetan Himalayan Library's (THL) phonetic system to convey them. The exception is in instances of proper names that are already well-established in the literature that use a non-THL phonetic system. Prominent examples include "Shabkar" (which is rendered as "Zhapkar" in THL phonetics), and "Milarepa" (which is rendered as Milarépa in THL phonetics). In such cases, I have opted for the well-established phonetic rendition of the name. Generally, Tibetan book titles are translated into English, followed by the Tibetan title in Wylie in parentheses on the first occurrence. The full bibliographic information is supplied in the footnote and bibliography. The exception is once again for well-established titles such as the *Maṇi Kabum*.

The research in this book is based on the Shechen edition (2003) of Shabkar's collected works. The Shechen edition is based on images of the original woodblock prints of Shabkar's collected works. The Qinghai edition (1985) edits many of the typographical errors of the Shechen edition, but omits some passages present in the original woodblocks. In general, I cite only the Shechen edition of Shabkar's autobiography. This default mode of citation does not include the publication date: Zhabs dkar, *Snyigs dus*, 1: 345.2. In places where I consult both the Qinghai edition and the Shechen edition, I differentiate between the two editions by including their publication date. In such cases, the Shechen edition appears as Zhabs dkar, *Snyigs dus* 2003, 1: 345.2 and the Qinghai edition appears as Zhabs dkar, *Snyigs dus* 1985, 2: 353.2.

The passages from Shabkar's collected works that appear in English translation in this book are my own. In cases of material where passages exist in alternate translations, I include the page numbers of them for the readers' reference.

# SINGER OF THE LAND OF SNOWS

# Introduction

If you visit the Repgong Valley in modern-day Qinghai Province in the People's Republic of China, villagers and herders will recount tales of a local Tibetan Buddhist master called Shabkar Tsokdruk Rangdröl (1781–1851). Many residents of the Repgong Valley believe Shabkar to be the reincarnation of Tibet's beloved poet-saint Milarepa (1052–1135). Shabkar is known by several epithets, including "Singer of Tibet, Land of Snows," "Self-Liberation of the Six Senses," and "White Feet."[1] Defying sartorial conventions of the time, he wore his hair in the topknot of tantric yogis but cloaked his body in the saffron robes of monks. His eclectic manner of dress was an expression of his impartial (*phyogs ris med pa*) outlook, which was based on his experience of spiritual awakening (Skt. *nirvāṇa*). Shabkar's impartial attitude and nonsectarian approach to religious difference characterized the religious activities that made him famous, including his thousands of spiritual songs, his advocacy of vegetarianism, and his extensive travels across the Tibetan plateau. Shabkar is widely considered one of the great Buddhist luminaries of nineteenth-century eastern Tibet.

Tibetan literary sources remember Shabkar for both his spiritual and literary legacies. The *Oceanic Book* (*Deb ther rgya mtsho*), a religious history published a couple of decades after Shabkar's death, remembers him for his role as the caretaker of Trashikhyil Hermitage and as author of an autobiography and dharma texts.[2] Some seventy years after Shabkar's death, Gendün Chöpel (1903–1951)—Tibet's first modernist, who was born in the same valley as Shabkar—saw Shabkar as a representation of the Buddhist bodhisattva of compassion Avalokiteśvara, and as having the ability to convey profound Buddhist ideas in an easy-to-understand manner.[3] Hum Chen's *Collection of Histories of Repgong's Tantrists* (*Reb kong sngags mang gi lo rgyus phyogs bsgrigs*) highlights Shabkar's extensive pilgrimages, abstinence from sinful foods, protection of animals, generosity toward the destitute and ill, teaching activities, and restoration of Buddhist monuments, as well as his large collected works.[4] A modern history of the Amdo region commends Shabkar for his pilgrimages, teaching legacy, and collected works.[5] Döndrup Gyel, one of the fathers of modern Tibetan literature, uses Shabkar's songs as examples of the songs of spiritual realization (*mgur*) genre in his survey of Tibetan song.[6]

One relatively unexplored aspect of Shabkar's life and works is the robust way in which his autobiography and collected works imagine Tibet. This theme is apparent in one of his epithets, the "Singer of Tibet, Land of Snows" (gangs can bod kyi glu dbyangs mkhan). He received this epithet from Machen Pomra, the resident deity of the holy mountain Anyé Machen, in a dream vision in 1809. Shabkar describes the experience follows:

> A white-[colored] man came and called me. I followed him to a large, magnificently beautiful tent at the center of hundreds of white tents. When I went inside, there was a great king seated upon a lofty throne. In front of him, to the right, was a throne upon which he instructed me to sit. When I sat down, he stood up and gave me a long immaculate white silk scarf and a splendid hat. He said, "It is wonderful that you emulate the life stories of past masters, and sing dharma songs of spiritual realization. I bestow upon you the name "Singer of Tibet, the Land of Snows." It is kind of you to leave behind your *Collected Songs* in Tibet; in the future, it will be of immense benefit to faithful disciples. Please continue to engage in the essence of practice and benefit the teachings and beings with your meditative accomplishments. At the same time, express the meaning of the Buddha's teachings through song. Hereafter, I promise to assist you in all your dharma activities."[7]

Prior to this vision, Shabkar would usually say that he was from Repgong,[8] with only sporadic references to being "of Tibet."[9] After this vision, however, Shabkar would frequently refer to himself as "the Singer of Tibet" in his *Collected Songs* (*Mgur 'bum*). Whereas the epithet "Singer of Repgong" conveys a localized identity, "the Singer of Tibet" communicates a pan-Tibetan one. "Singer of Tibet" also evokes the memory of Milarepa, the poet-saint whom Shabkar and his disciples considered Shabkar to be an emanation of.

When we consider the figure who gave Shabkar this title, the idea of Shabkar as Tibet's spokesperson takes on an even greater significance. Machen Pomra is "master of the territory" (*sa bdag*) of the Golok region in Tibet's northeastern province of Amdo and the resident deity of Anyé Machen, a mountain in the region.[10] And Pomra's significance transcends the local. According to some Buddhist sources, Pomra was one of the nine mountain deities who were initially evoked as witnesses for the establishment of Buddhism as state religion by the Emperor Trisong Détsen in the eighth century.[11] These nine mountain deities were the guardians of their respective territories and formed a mountain cult that has "an important bearing on the ethnic identity of the Tibetans."[12] Indeed, many people from Amdo refer to Anyé Machen as "the soul mountain of snowy Tibet" (*bod gangs can gyi bla ri*).[13] The term "soul" (*bla*), which is also translated as "subtle life essence," refers to a Tibetan folk belief that humans, animals, sacred lakes, mountains, and trees have a "subtle life essence" within them.[14] Tibet's nine mountain deities in addition to the soul of the king of Tibet were thought to have a "soul of the body" (*sku bla*) in it.[15] As the soul mountain of Tibet, Anyé Machen is connected to the ideology of the ancient Tibetan kings and attracts pilgrims from all over the plateau, serving as a source of national cohesion.

Thus, Pomra represents both the embodiment of the local land as well as the cultural memory of the Tibetan Empire, which once encompassed the entire plateau. It is difficult to think of a figure who could have had greater authority than Pomra for bestowing such a title upon Shabkar. Shabkar's genealogical links to Pomra made this especially true; Shabkar was from a clan whose main local deity is a part of Anyé Machen's retinue.[16] Thus, when Shabkar calls himself "the unprecedented eloquent singer of Tibet" who sings songs "for the benefit of Tibet," the approval expressed by Pomra lends authority to Shabkar as Tibet's spokesperson.[17]

In Shabkar's autobiography, the theme of Tibet's national self-imagination is evident in his representation of Avalokiteśvara, the Buddhist bodhisattva of compassion and the patron deity of the Tibetan people. Shabkar was intimately connected to Avalokiteśvara. In addition to self-identifying as Avalokiteśvara's reincarnation and seeing visions of the deity,[18] Shabkar practiced and composed contemplative manuals (*sgrub thabs*, Skt. *sādhanā*) associated with the deity and taught his followers to worship Avalokiteśvara through the recitation of the six-syllable mantra. Shabkar's intimate connection to Avalokiteśvara is not unique to Shabkar; the deity plays a key role in the lives of some of his spiritual predecessors. For instance, the Third Karmapa, Rangjung Dorjé (1284–1339), was another emanation of Avalokiteśvara who saw the deity frequently in visions. However, Rangjung Dorjé's interactions with Avalokiteśvara were religious in nature, and he did not refer to Avalokiteśvara as Tibet's destined deity.[19] Kelden Gyatso (1607–1677), one of Shabkar's main spiritual role models, also saw Avalokiteśvara in visions and wrote contemplative manuals on the deity.[20] Kelden Gyatso's biographer even recounts an episode in which Gyatso saw the Dalai Lama as an emanation of Avalokiteśvara.[21] However, unlike Shabkar, Kelden Gyatso did not emphasize Avalokiteśvara's role as Tibet's patron deity, but rather considered him solely from a spiritual perspective.[22] In contrast to his predecessors, Shabkar made frequent references to Avalokiteśvara as "Tibet's destined deity" (*bod kyi lha skal*) and portrayed the Dalai Lamas as his incarnation.[23] In one of

Shabkar's visions, Avalokiteśvara self-identifies as "Tibet's destined deity" and gives instructions to "the people of Tibet" (*bod khams mi rnams*).[24] Thus, in comparison to many of his spiritual predecessors, Shabkar's portrayal of Avalokiteśvara has an unmistakable national dimension to it.

The strong association between Avalokiteśvara and Tibet is found in a couple of texts by authors from Amdo contemporaneous with Shabkar. In the *Detailed Explanation of the World* (*'Dzam gling rgyas bshad*), Tenpo Nomönhen refers to the "country of Tibet" as "the land tamed by Avalokiteśvara."[25] Similarly, in the *Oceanic Book,* Drakgön refers to Tibet as "the country of the land of snows tamed by Avalokiteśvara."[26] Shabkar's autobiography along with these two texts suggest that the nationalistic side of Avalokiteśvara as Tibet's destined deity was important alongside the deity's role as the bodhisattva of compassion for some authors from Amdo in the nineteenth century.

Shabkar's autobiography and songs present a multidimensional portrayal of Tibet and the Tibetan people, map Tibet's territory, incorporate vernacular elements of Tibetan literature, and depict Buddhism as a coalescing force for Tibet. Altogether, these characteristics signal that Shabkar's autobiography and songs are significant texts for Tibet's national self-imagination in the early modern period. The question of what constitutes the early modern period remains a subject of debate among scholars. Most definitions of the early modern period have tended to cluster around 1450 to 1800 CE.[27] In particular, there is much disagreement about whether or not that concept can or should be applied to non-European contexts. In this book, I interpret the early modern period to be the period "roughly correspond[ing] to the development of Tibetan self-consciousness of its political and cultural position vis-à-vis other powers in the region."[28] I use Janet Gyatso's definition because it allows for the inclusion of both the Later Transmission Period (tenth through twelfth centuries) and the nineteenth century—both periods that were key to developing Tibet's concept of itself and its relationship to the rest of the world—in the definition.

Until now, the nineteenth century has been characterized as being "largely moribund" within the history of the idea of "greater Tibet."[29] Shabkar's autobiography and songs, in conjunction with other geographical texts from nineteenth-century eastern Tibet such as Drakgön's *Oceanic Book* and Jamgön Kongtrül's *Twenty Five-Sites of Khams* (*Mdo khams gnas chen nyer lnga*), demonstrate that this era was an important one in what Martin Mills refers to as Tibet's "developing biographical narrative of state."[30] Thus, in this study, I read Shabkar's autobiography and songs not within their original spiritual context, but from the perspectives of the study of cultural nationalism and modern Tibetan literary studies, in order to understand the role of Shabkar's portrayal of Tibet in the history of the idea of Tibet.

This book attempts to strike a delicate balance between understanding Shabkar's portrayal of the concept of Tibet on its own terms while also addressing the significance of this portrayal through the framework of cultural nationalism. Shabkar's autobiography reveals an alternative conception of identity, community, and territory rendered invisible by contemporary state-centric definitions of nations and nationalism. In his autobiography, Shabkar articulates a concept of Tibet that we might call a Buddhist imagined community. He does so by incorporating vernacular literature, providing a narrative mapping of the Tibetan plateau, reviving and adapting the myth of Tibetans as Avalokiteśvara's chosen people, and promoting shared Buddhist values and practices. This Buddhist imagined community exhibits aspects of modern cultural definitions of nation, but largely exists outside of the Westphalian state-centric concept of nation. Shabkar's concept of Tibet contributed to the opening up of a discursive space for the articulation of modern forms of Tibetan nationalism.

Although Shabkar was neither the first nor the only author to articulate a Tibetan national identity in early modern Tibetan literature, the way he articulates such an identity through this particular combination of five features is distinctive. This study is limited to a close reading of a single source. It is my hope that it will open up inroads for the exploration of how a collective identity was conceived and articulated in Tibet's early modern literature.

## The Story of the Idea of Tibet

In contemporary parlance, the term "Tibet" (*bod*) has different meanings. Sometimes "Tibet" refers to the Tibet Autonomous Region (TAR) (Ch. *xizang zizhiqu*), the southwestern province in the People's Republic of China (PRC). The term TAR does not correspond to traditional Tibetan divisions of space. It was created by the PRC and imposed upon the Tibetan landscape. The TAR roughly corresponds to the Tibetan province of central Tibet (*dbus gtsang*) and a section of Kham Province. Other times, "Tibet" refers to the "three provinces" or *chölka sum* (*chol kha gsum*, M. *chölge*) of Tibet as a whole: Amdo, Kham, and central Tibet.[31] This concept of Tibet corresponds to the point of view of the Central Tibetan Administration (CTA), also known as the Tibetan government-in-exile. The CTA's territorial claim of Tibet also roughly corresponds to what Tibetologists call "cultural Tibet" or "ethnographic Tibet." In order to make clear what one is referring to, scholars of Tibet have found it helpful to distinguish between "political Tibet" and "cultural Tibet," with the former referring to the TAR and the latter referring to "the wider realm of Tibetan culture."[32] "Cultural Tibet" is also sometimes referred to as "greater Tibet" (*bod chen po*, Ch. *daxizangqu*).[33]

The term "greater Tibet" is a controversial one. The CTA maintains that the term represents a deliberate misrepresentation by the PRC of the Fourteenth Dalai Lama's proposal to transform the culturally Tibetan areas of China into a "de-militarized Zone of Peace" as part of his Five-Point Peace Plan.[34] Journalists and academics have also criticized the term for failing to capture the vicissitudes of Tibet's historical borders and the internal divisions that exist in Tibetan society.[35] There is, however, historical precedent for the term "greater Tibet": the term *bod chen*, which can be translated as either "great Tibet" or "greater Tibet." The term "great Tibet" appears in the Chinese-Tibetan Treaty of 821–22, the writings of the Fifth Dalai Lama, and the writings of Jamgön Kongtrül, for instance. In each of these cases, the meaning of the term is context dependent. This topic is explored in more detail in chapter 1.

Nevertheless, although there may be controversy surrounding the term "greater Tibet," the *idea* of Tibet encompassing areas beyond central Tibet is an ancient one with roots in the Tibetan Empire. Beginning in the seventh century CE, Tibet's Yarlung dynasty unified much of the Tibetan Plateau through military conquest. No single Tibetan ruler would ever replicate this feat. Despite the fall of the Tibetan Empire in the mid-ninth century, the concept of Tibet as encompassing the entire Tibetan Plateau remained a steadfast trope in Tibet's collective consciousness. Subsequent generations of Tibetans would look back at the imperial period with nostalgia, reviving and adapting the notion of a plateau-wide Tibet for the next millennium.

According to traditional histories, in the tenth century, Tibet emerged from the "dark period" that followed the fall of the Tibetan Empire. During this period from the tenth to the twelfth century, which is traditionally called the Later Transmission Period, Tibet experienced a renaissance of Buddhist teachings.[36] Beginning in the twelfth century, there is textual evidence of a newfound sense of collective identity for Tibetans across the plateau. George Dreyfus characterizes this as a "proto-nationalism" that "arose as an aspiration to recapture the lost might of the Tibetan empire" through the revelation of treasure objects hidden away during the imperial period by the Indian tantric master Padmasmabhava and his associates.[37] At the nucleus of this collective identity was the idea that Avalokiteśvara was Tibet's patron deity and the Tibetan emperor Songsten Gampo his earthly incarnation. This topic is explored in detail in chapter 4.

The next noteworthy period for the history of the idea of a pan-plateau Tibet was the period of Mongol rule from the mid-thirteenth to mid-fourteenth centuries. According to traditional Tibetan Buddhist histories, on the eve of invading Tibet, the Mongol chief Kublai Khan summoned one of the greatest Tibetan Buddhist teachers of the day, Sakya Paṇḍita, along with his nephews, to his camp. The khan was so impressed with them that instead of invading Tibet, he converted to Tibetan Buddhism and began what is known as a patron-priest (*mchod yon*) relationship between the patriarchs of the Sakya sect and the Mongol khans. Eventually, the khan gave the three administrative regions of Tibet, the *chölkha sum* to Sakya Paṇḍita's nephew Pakpa as an offering.[38] Around a century later, the scholar Sakyapa Sönam Gyeltsen (1312–1375) would connect the *chölka sum* to the geographical extent of the Yarlung dynasty, Avalokiteśvara's cosmological power, and the Tibetan people, in his classic history of Buddhism in Tibet, *The Clear Mirror of Royal Genealogies (Rgyal rabs gsal ba'i me long)*.[39]

The rise of the Ganden Podrang government under the Fifth Dalai Lama in the mid-seventeenth century marked the next substantial revival of the idea of a plateau-wide Tibet. In 1642, the Mongol chief Gushri Khan assisted the Géluk sect in winning the civil war in central Tibet.[40] The Khan presented the conquered territory as an offering to the Fifth Dalai Lama. Drawing from the myths of Avalokiteśvara as Tibet's patron deity and Tibet's first Buddhist king Songsten Gampo as his earthly incarnation, the Fifth Dalai Lama further solidified the connection between the reincarnate lineage of the Dalai Lamas and Avalokiteśvara through literary compositions, rituals, and architecture. For example, he built his Potala Palace on the site of an Avalokiteśvara Temple on Marpori that dated back to the time of the seventh-century Emperor Songsten Gampo.[41] The Fifth Dalai Lama also suggested that the Ganden Podrang government in central Tibet had "ritual responsibilities for the protection of the wider land of Tibet far beyond its effective political borders."[42] In this way, the Fifth Dalai Lama evoked symbolic mastery over "greater Tibet" without his government having any actual control beyond central Tibet.

In contemporary times, the territorial claims of the Central Tibetan Administration (CTA) also take part in the history of the idea of a plateau-wide Tibet. The CTA maintains that Tibet consists of the provinces of Amdo, Kham, and Wü-Tsang, which correspond to the Tibet Autonomous Region and the Tibetan Autonomous Prefectures found in the Qinghai, Gansu, Sichuan, and Yunnan provinces of the PRC.[43] This concept of the geographical basis of Tibet as consisting of the three provinces of Kham, Amdo, and Wü-Tsang exists not only at the government level, but is "deeply embedded in the political culture of the Tibetan diaspora."[44] Although the *chölka sum* or three administrative regions are interpreted as the three provinces of Kham, Amdo and Wü-Tsang in contemporary times, other historical iterations of the idea include central Tibet, Upper Tö, and Lower Tö or central Tibet, Ngari, and Dokham.[45]

In contrast to the Later Transmission Period or the reign of the Fifth Dalai

Lama, the nineteenth century has been characterized as "largely moribund" within the context of the history of the idea of "greater Tibet."[46] This is of no surprise when we consider the history and context of this period. The nineteenth century was a period characterized by conflict, internal fragmentation, and colonialism in inner, east, and south Asia. India was subjugated by the British, the Qing dynasty was struggling to fend off European colonial aggression, and central Tibet had lost much of its previous power, both political and military. Nevertheless, as I demonstrate in this book, the concept of a plateau-wide Tibet was not moribund, but rather, undergoing a creative reformulation in eastern Tibet during the nineteenth century.

During this period, as Lhasa and Beijing were beleaguered by their own struggles, the eastern Tibetan provinces of Amdo and Kham, located on the borderlands between China and Tibet, rose to prominence. These regions had a long history of being fiercely independent, resisting centralized rule from both Lhasa and Beijing.[47] It was within this context of the rise of eastern Tibet and the waning of centralized power in Lhasa and Beijing that authors from eastern Tibet mapped their territories and reimagined their significance within the Tibetan Buddhist world. Prominent examples of such texts include Drakgön's *Oceanic Book*, Tenpo Nomönhen's *Detailed Explanation of the World*, Chokgyur Lingpa's *A Brief Inventory of the Great Sites of Tibet* (*Bod kyi gnas chen rnams kyi mdo byang dkar chags*), Jamgön Kongtrül's *Twenty-Five Great Sites of Khams*, and Shabkar's autobiography.[48] In particular, in addition to mapping large sections of the Tibetan plateau, Shabkar drew from and adapted Tibet's classic textual tradition to reimagine a grand vision for the Tibetan civilization as Avalokiteśvara's chosen people on the cusp of its modernity. Shabkar's re-imagining of Tibet was part of a greater context of flourishing geographical thought in eastern Tibet during the period.

A final note on vocabulary. In this book, I use the word *Tibet* (*bod*) in a way that is consistent with Shabkar's usage of it. When Shabkar says *Tibet*, he is referring to the plateau-wide version of the concept—namely, of Tibet comprising central Tibet, Ngari, Amdo. Kham plays an insignificant role in Shabkar's portrayal of Tibet. Shabkar does not use the term *greater Tibet* (*bod chen*) to describe this concept but rather simply *Tibet* (*bod*). In turn, in contrast to the way that many early modern and modern Tibetan authors use *bod* to refer to central Tibet, Shabkar uses *Wü-Tsang* or *Wü* (*dbus gtsang* or *dbus*) to describe central Tibet. In keeping with Shabkar's usage, in this book, *Tibet* will refer to the idea of "greater Tibet" while *central Tibet* will refer to the province of Wü-Tsang.

## The Theoretical Framework of Cultural Nationalism

Shabkar does not use the modern Tibetan word for "nation" (*rgyal khab*) to refer to Tibet. When referring to the Tibetan Empire of the seventh to ninth centuries, he uses the word for "country" or "kingdom" (*rgyal khams*). When describing the Tibet contemporaneous to him, he uses the words "Tibet" (*bod*), "land of Tibet" (*bod yul*), or "realm of Tibet" (*bod khams*). Because Shabkar does not use the word *nation*, it would be anachronistic to impose the word onto his description of Tibet. Nevertheless, juxtaposing Shabkar's concept of Tibet with Euro-American academic tools such as the study of Tibetan literature, the comparative study of Buddhist societies, and the study of cultural nationalism sheds light on specific aspects of Shabkar's portrayal of Tibet. The main methodology of this book is to understand Shabkar's concept of Tibet on its own terms while using modern Euro-American academic frameworks to illuminate the significance of specific aspects of Shabkar's portrayal of Tibet.

One important lens for thinking about Tibet has been the nation-state.[49] With the plight of the Tibetan people and the nation-state being the dominant mode of international organization, it is of no surprise that this is often the main perspective through which many view this issue. And yet, the concept of nationhood is historically contingent. Our contemporary understanding of a nation and state as being conterminous has its origins in the Westphalian notion of nation that arose within the specific historical context of eighteenth-century Europe and the Americas.[50] In other words, the concept of the nation-state is but one historical form of the concept of nation. When we impose state-centric definitions of nation on different cultures and time periods, this renders alternative conceptions of identity, community, and territory invisible. Specifically, some have argued that the Westphalian state-centric notion of nation represents a "straitjacket in which the preexisting diversity of systems had no place and the accommodation to which Asian polities had been accustomed was absent."[51] Using the framework of the nation-state is not always helpful for understanding polities across space and time because the framework can obscure indigenous concepts of identity, community, and territory.

The Tibet that Shabkar describes lies outside of the concept of nation-state but shares common elements with non-state-centric cultural definitions of nation. Anthony Smith's non-state-centric definition of nation is as follows: "a named and self-defined human community whose members cultivate shared myths, memories, symbols, values, and traditions, reside in and identify with a historic homeland, create and disseminate a distinctive public culture, and observe shared customs and common laws."[52] Another non-state-centric definition of nation is Steven Grosby's. He defines nation as "a territorial community of nativity" that "requires a relatively extensive, bounded territory or an image of such a territory, the existence of which usually involves the following: a self-designating name, a center (with institutions), a history that both asserts and is expressive of a temporal continuity, and a relatively uniform culture that is often based on a common language, religion, and law."[53] Shabkar's portrayal of Tibet is in accord with both Smith's and Grosby's definitions. Chapter 1 engages in a detailed comparison of Shabkar's concept of Tibet with Smith's and Grosby's definitions. When I use the word "nation" in this book, I use it in the non-state-centric sense of the word, in accord with Smith's and Grosby's definitions.

Because of the affinities between Shabkar's concept of Tibet and non-state-centric definitions of nation, the theoretical framework of cultural nationalism is a promising one from which to examine Shabkar's concept of Tibet. The study of cultural nationalism allows us to appreciate the concept of nation beyond the state-centric model. This approach focuses on the role that literary, philosophical, and cultural forces play in the formation and sustenance of a national consciousness. While nationalism studies has largely concentrated on the roles that historical events and societal developments such as industrialization have played on the establishment of nations, scholars of the cultural approach to the study of nationhood have shown how literary, cultural, historiographical, and cartographical sources all play a role in forming the idea of a nation before it actually develops into a political institution.[54] In other words, the historical development of the concept of a nation can form the foundation upon which the institution of nation is later established.

In this book, I draw from the work of theorists of cultural nationalism. Joep Leerssen outlines an approach where we "trace nationalism as something that emanates from the way people view and describe the world—in other words, as a cultural phenomenon, taking shape in the constant back-and-forth between material and political developments on the one hand, and intellectual and poetical reflection and articulation on the other."[55] This book shares Leerssen's approach, in that I analyze the ways in which literature, cartography, myth, and religion play a role in shaping Shabkar's concept of Tibet. Within the field of Tibetan studies, this book owes much to Lama Jabb's study on modern Tibetan literature, which "highlights the role of culture in the perpetuation and reinforcement of Tibetan national consciousness."[56] Building on both Leerssen's and Jabb's approaches, I examine the role that Shabkar's autobiography plays in the history of the idea of Tibet. From the field of cartography, I draw from the work of Richard Helgerson, Christian Jacob, and Michael Wintle. These authors have demonstrated the critical role that maps play in the formation of national consciousness all over the world. My approach to studying the role of myth in the formation of Tibet's national consciousness is informed by Anthony Smith's ethno-symbolist model of nationhood. Smith identifies four ethnic building blocks of nationhood: "ethnic origin myths, beliefs in ethnic election, the development of ethnoscapes, the territorialization of memory, and the vernacular mobilization of communities."[57] I adapt Smith's theory slightly because Shabkar's main basis for Tibetan unity is not ethnicity, but rather Buddhism. Finally, Lotte Jensen's multidisciplinary approach to understanding how national cultures in Europe were shaped between 1600 and 1815 influences the way in which I have chosen to focus on a variety of cultural forces: literature, cartography, myth, and religion.

## A Buddhist "Imagined Community"

In Shabkar's portrayal of Tibet, Buddhism is what holds the imagined community together. Shabkar's portrayal corroborates multiple Tibetologists' observations that Buddhism was the most significant unifying force for Tibetans in the early modern period.[58] Religion is an aspect of nation, nationalism, and national identity that many contemporary theories of nationalism do not take into account. Anthony Smith has observed that for scholars who consider the nation to be a modern phenomenon, "religion is a residual category in the modern world, and is inversely related to nations and nationalism."[59] And yet, as some scholars have observed, religion was "the most powerful and all-pervasive mass medium of the *premodern* 'imagined community.'"[60] Indeed, Buddhism is so important in Shabkar's portrayal of Tibet that Tibet as depicted in his work can best be described as a *Buddhist* imagined community. Other elements that form essential building blocks of nationhood, such as shared territory, myths, language, and so forth, are depicted in Shabkar's autobiography as well, but they lie in the background. Buddhism is Tibet's central coalescing force as portrayed by Shabkar in his autobiography.

The term "imagined community" was coined and developed by Benedict Anderson to analyze nationalism. He defines "nation" as "an imagined political community—and imagined as both inherently limited and sovereign."[61] Anderson's concept of the nation describes the modern state-centric notion of nation that arose in Europe and the Americas in the late eighteenth to early nineteenth centuries. For Anderson, the nation is "imagined" because all its members understand that they are a part of a "nation" with others whom they do not know personally; it is "limited" because there are boundaries to the nation, and it is "sovereign" because the legitimacy of the nation is not derived from divine sanction, but rather from the state itself. According to Anderson, "the convergence of capitalism and print technology on the fatal diversity of human language created the possibility of a new form of imagined community, which in its basic morphology set the stage for the modern nation."[62]

Although I borrow the term "imagined community" from Anderson to describe Shabkar's Buddhist imagined community, there is not much continuity between the way that I am using the term and the way Anderson uses it. The main point of similarity is in the "imagined" part of Anderson's definition. This is to say that all members of Shabkar's Tibet do not necessarily know each other, but Shabkar nevertheless imagines them to be members of a greater entity known as "Tibet" under the patronage of the deity Avalokiteśvara. However, Shabkar's Tibet is not as "limited" as Anderson's concept of the imagined community. This is because even though Shabkar's imagined community of Tibet is specifically Buddhist, he sees both non-Tibetans and non-Buddhists residing in Tibet as being part of this imagined community. Finally, unlike the "sovereign" aspect of Anderson's nation, which derives its legitimacy from the state rather than divine sanction, the source of legitimacy for Shabkar's Tibet is Buddhism. The term "imagined community" is also particularly apt for this study because it captures the way in which the idea of nation is hinted at in Shabkar's portrayal of Tibet, but never explicitly mentioned.

Anderson's concept of the "imagined community," despite being extremely influential, has not been without its critics. The political theorist Partha Chatterjee, for instance, has put forth a postcolonial critique of Anderson's theory. Chatterjee asks, "If nationalisms in the rest of the world have to choose their imagined community from certain "modular" forms already made available to them by Europe and the Americas, what do they have left to imagine?"[63] Anderson's theory denies groups outside of Europe and the Americas the agency that allows them to imagine their own relationship to territory, identity, and community. Although Chatterjee's analysis mainly addresses anticolonial nationalisms, it reminds us that we need to take heed to the possible limitations of applying Anderson's concept of "imagined community" uncritically to other times and places outside of Anderson's case studies.

One of the limitations of Benedict Anderson's idea of the "imagined community" is that it does not take into account the role that religion plays in the formation of polities outside of modern Euro-American contexts. Other models of Buddhist governance in premodern Asia may be more helpful for understanding Shabkar's Buddhist imagined community on its own terms. Shabkar's Tibet was a part of what Timothy Brook, Michael van Walt van Praag, and Miek Boltjes term the "Tibetan Buddhist world," Tibet's unique model of international law from the thirteenth through the early twentieth century. The Tibetan Buddhist world was interwoven with two other separate but interrelated bodies of international law: "the Mongol Chinggisid world" and "the Sinic world."[64] As its name implies, one of the characteristics of the Tibetan Buddhist world is the way in which the Buddhist and secular realms were intertwined. Unlike the Mongol or Chinese states, which were based on territory or military might, there was no single ruler who united culturally Tibetan areas from the thirteenth through early twentieth centuries. Instead, the various political factions within Tibet were interlinked in a series of relationships that were upheld by "overarching religiopolitical concepts, principles, and constructs."[65] Buddhism was one of these main concepts, from which Tibet derived both its political structures and sense of self-worth. Shabkar's autobiography gives us a sense of how an individual figure might live out his life within the context of the greater "Tibetan Buddhist World."

The imagined Buddhist community that Shabkar articulates is also closer to models of other early modern Buddhist societies in Asia than it is to modern definitions of the nation-state. For example, as will be explored in chapter 1, the idea of Tibet that Shabkar portrays shares many characteristics with concepts such as the *sasana*—the Buddhist community and its teachings—and "moral community" of Theravāda Buddhist societies in Burma and Sri Lanka in their precolonial periods. Both the *sasana* model and Shabkar's portrayal of Tibet as an imagined Buddhist community lie outside of the ethnostate model, which centers ethnicity as the main criteria for belonging to a nation-state. These models recenter religion as a coalescing force for communities, reminding us of alternative conceptions of identity, community, territory that lie outside of the nation-state model. The contemporary Buddhist nationalisms of Sri Lanka and Burma, which emerged out of the context of colonialism and are ethno-religious in nature, do fit into the ethnostate model—but not so these earlier pre-colonial examples.

By recentering religion as a major force that unifies an imagined community, Shabkar's concept of Tibet (as well as concepts such as the Theravāda Buddhist idea of *sasana*) may help us understand one of the reasons why nations persist. Anthony Smith observes that the process by which a nation's key cultural resources become sacred is modeled after religious traditions.[66] In the case of Tibet (as well as Burma and Sri Lanka), the sacrality of the nations is not modeled after religious tradition; it *is* the religious tradition. Smith also observes that in many premodern civilizations, ethnicity is rarely separated from religion."[67] In Tibet, Buddhism is linked to genealogy and ethnicity, albeit in different ways. Over the centuries, layers upon layers of myth have been woven together about Avalokiteśvara as the patron deity and father of the Tibetan people, the Dalai Lamas being the embodiment of Avalokiteśvara, and the idea that Buddhism is Tibet's main asset. Understanding how myths, territory, literature, and religion are interwoven to form the imagined Buddhist community of Tibet in Shabkar's autobiography helps us to begin to understand how the roots of the Tibetan nation are deeply intertwined with Buddhism.

## Autobiography's Role in Tibet's National Self-Imagination

Modern Tibetan literature plays a critical role in Tibet's national self-imagination. In his study of contemporary Tibetan popular songs, poems, and novels, Lama Jabb observes that "the modern Tibetan literary text is itself national."[68] Popular music and creative writing represent "the tentative formation of an embryonic public space within which Tibetans are expressing their common concerns and collective identity under difficult political circumstances" and in which they "imagine themselves as a nation" and "reinforc[e] [a] Tibetan national consciousness."[69] An important twentieth-century Tibetan Buddhist autobiography that is a cornerstone for Tibet's national self-imagination is the Fourteenth Dalai Lama's *My Land and My People*. In the text, the Dalai Lama tells his life story against the backdrop of the PRC's annexation of Tibet.

Still, is it appropriate to examine Tibetan Buddhist autobiographies from the early modern period for their significance in Tibet's national self-imagination? Although Shabkar's concept of Tibet fulfills non-state-centric definitions of nation, he does not use the word "nation" to describe Tibet in his autobiography. Moreover, there is the issue of genre. Shabkar's autobiography belongs to the broader genre of the Tibetan Buddhist life story, or *namtar (rnam thar)*. Literally translated, the term *namtar* means "complete liberation"; works in this genre tell the story of an enlightened master's spiritual journey. Traditionally, the *namtar* genre functioned to generate faith in its audience about a Buddhist master's spiritual qualities and to provide an exemplum to be emulated. Shabkar composed his autobiography with these traditional goals in mind. Unlike some examples of *namtar* from the contemporary era, Shabkar had no intention of fostering a nationalistic consciousness in his autobiography. Would we be distorting Shabkar's text to read it using the frameworks of Euro-American literary studies and the study of cultural nationalism?

*Namtar* is a well-studied genre in Euro-American scholarship. There have been various academic studies of important *namtar* that have approached the genre using nontraditional frameworks. For example, Janet Gyatso's groundbreaking study, *Apparitions of Self* (1998) placed the autobiography of Jikmé Lingpa in conversation with autobiography studies. Sarah Jacoby's

*Love and Liberation* (2014) examines one of the few extant autobiographies by a Tibetan woman, Séra Khandro, mainly from the perspective of gender and sexuality studies. Amy Holmes-Tagchungdarpa's study of the lineage of Tokden Shākya Shrī, *The Social Life of Tibetan Biography* (2014), uses the concept of "networks" to illuminate how Shākya Shrī's community used his biography to create religious authority in east, inner, and south Asia. These three examples illustrate how placing *namtar* in conversation with different academic fields can illuminate aspects of the genre that have been heretofore overlooked. In this study, I read Shabkar's *namtar* from both the perspective of literary studies and the study of cultural nationalism. The spiritual and literary qualities of Shabkar's *namtar* are well known; reading the text from these additional theoretical perspectives allows me to consider this text's contribution to Tibet's national self-imagination in the early modern period.

## Shabkar's Autobiography and Songs

Shabkar Tsokdruk Rangdröl was born Ngakwang Trashi, in the Tibetan village of Nyengya in the Repgong Valley of eastern Tibet in modern-day Qinghai Province in 1781. The inhabitants of the Repgong Valley call their valley "the golden region" (*gser mo ljongs*) because of the way the wheat and barley fields that encompass the area turn a brilliant golden color during harvest time. It was into this farming community surrounded by high mountains that Shabkar was born. As with the birth of many Buddhist saints, Shabkar's conception and birth were accompanied by auspicious omens such as his mother having dreams of sacred objects. A highly intelligent child with deep faith in Buddhism, Shabkar spent his youth among the tantric *ngakpa* (*sngags pa*) communities of Repgong, studying with various Buddhist masters. At the age of twenty, Shabkar renounced worldly life and was ordained as a monk by a prominent Géluk master from the region, Arik Géshé. Shabkar subsequently left Repgong and sought the spiritual guidance of Chögyel Ngakgi Wangpo near Qinghai Lake. The latter teacher would become Shabkar's main teacher.

After mastering his teacher's spiritual instructions, Shabkar emulated the itinerant lifestyle of past meditation masters. He spent the rest of his life in meditative retreat, on pilgrimage, teaching Buddhism, and giving charity to the destitute. By his mid-twenties, Shabkar had become a famous singer of songs of spiritual realization and was given the epithet "Singer of Tibet, the Land of Snows" by the resident deity of the sacred mountain of Anyé Machen in Amdo Province. Even over 170 years after Shabkar's death, throughout the Repgong Valley and beyond, people still remember Shabkar for the countless songs that he sang all over the Tibetan plateau. Most local histories of the Amdo region or Repgong contain an entry about Shabkar.[70] Shabkar is best known for his autobiography, songs, extensive pilgrimages across the Tibetan plateau, advocacy of vegetarianism, and nonsectarian attitude.

Shabkar left behind a large collection of writings, totaling fourteen volumes. Shabkar's collected works includes writing in a variety of genres, including autobiography and biography, songs of spiritual realization, elegant sayings, dharma discourses, spiritual advice, letters, liturgies, and "emanated scriptures." In addition to being revered in the Tibetan cultural world, Shabkar's writings have received considerable interest in Tibetan Buddhist communities worldwide. The first volume of his autobiography, some of his songs, and some of his writings on vegetarianism and his *Emanated Scripture of Mañjuśrī* (*'Jam dbyangs sprul pa'i glegs bam*) have all been translated into English.

Shabkar is most famous for his autobiography. At just over 1,500 folios and replete with exquisite poetry and evocative prose passages, Shabkar's autobiography is revered as one of the great masterpieces of the Tibetan *namtar* genre.[71] I translated *namtar* as "complete liberation" above, but the word can also be translated as "story of complete enlightenment," "autobiography," "biography," "hagiography," or "life writing." In traditional contexts, Tibetan Buddhist practitioners read these texts telling the story of a spiritual master's journey toward enlightenment in order to increase their faith and to learn how to live an ideal spiritual life. At its heart, Shabkar's autobiography is a spiritual work, and his autobiography has been enjoyed in that capacity by Tibetan Buddhist audiences for almost two centuries.

Shabkar's *Collected Songs* serves as a repository for the songs that did not make it into his autobiography. At just under 1,200 songs enshrined in a three-volume collection, Shabkar's *Collected Songs* is one of the largest extant collections of songs of spiritual realization in Tibetan literature. Like *namtar*, songs of spiritual realization are religious works. These songs are composed and performed extemporaneously by spiritually awakened figures and are meant to convey their enlightened state to their audience. Despite their spiritual provenance, Shabkar's *Collected Songs* contribute to the robust portrayal of Tibet found in his autobiography. The Tibetan collective identity that the songs embody comes across in Shabkar's intention for compiling them: he intended his song collection "to benefit future generations of Tibetan people."[72] The chapter structure of Shabkar's *Collected Songs* also reinforces the view of Tibet as a Buddhist imagined community from a geographical standpoint. Its chapter structure roughly mirrors the chapter structure of Shabkar's autobiography, which is organized mainly according to the sacred sites that Shabkar visited on the Tibetan Plateau. In this way, the *Collected Songs* reinforces the emphasis on Tibet's sacred geography that we find in

Shabkar's autobiography's organizational structure. Finally, although they are primarily spiritual in terms of content, some of the songs contribute to the robust representation of Tibet found in Shabkar's autobiography. For these reasons, Shabkar's autobiography, along with his *Collected Songs*, serves as the primary material upon which this book's central argument is based.

Shabkar kept records of his life and songs at the insistence of his disciples.[73] Based on these records, he composed his autobiography and compiled his *Collected Songs*. As is common for the *namtar* genre, Shabkar did not write the first volume of his autobiography, but rather, he composed and dictated it to his disciple Sangyé Rinchen.[74] In contrast to the first volume, however, he wrote down the second volume of his autobiography.[75] Shabkar intended for his autobiography and *Collected Songs* to be widely disseminated. As early as 1808, he described sending manuscripts containing a thousand of his songs to his disciples.[76] A few decades later, in 1840, he sent a manuscript of his autobiography to disciples in central Tibet.[77] In 1847, he gifted forty xylographs of the first volume of his autobiography and his *Collected Songs* to his disciples in central Tibet.[78] In 1848, he gave a set of his *Collected Works*, which included his autobiography and *Collected Songs* to a reincarnate lama in Golok.[79] Finally, Shabkar described giving the second volume of his autobiography to his disciples Gurong Trülku and Sangyé Rinchen to publish and disseminate right before his death.[80]

The main literary model for Shabkar's autobiography and *Collected Songs* is *The Life of Milarepa* by Tsangnyön Heruka (1452–1507). This is of no surprise. When most Tibetan Buddhists hear the name "The Singer of Tibet," the figure who probably comes to mind is Milarepa. Although Shabkar was born seven centuries after Milarepa, he was nevertheless intimately associated with the eleventh-century figure. From a young age, Shabkar emulated Milarepa's peripatetic lifestyle, devoting himself to a life of meditative retreat far removed from the din of towns and cities. Like Milarepa, Shabkar had the ability to sing songs of spiritual realization extemporaneously. The nearly two thousand songs that Shabkar left behind in his *Collected Works* greatly outnumber the extant songs from Milarepa's collection. Indeed, statues and *tangkas*, or scroll paintings, of Shabkar depict him in the same traditional singing posture of Milarepa, with his right hand cupped at his ear and left hand holding a ritual skull cup. Both Shabkar and his disciples believed that he was the reincarnation of Milarepa.

There are many similarities between Shabkar's autobiography and Heruka's *The Life of Milarepa*. For instance, the opening of Shabkar's autobiography imitates the opening of Milarepa's biography, where his disciples make multiple requests to the teacher to tell his life story. Shabkar also modeled many of his songs after those of Milarepa. For example, Shabkar's "The Song of the Six Remembrances of the Lama" (bla ma dran drug gi mgur) alludes to Milarepa's famous song of the same title.[81] However, it is not just the similarities between Shabkar's autobiography and Heruka's *The Life of Milarepa* that are noteworthy, but also the differences between them. Traditional Tibetan society was a highly conservative one where authority and value were derived from the degree to which one adhered to previous tradition.[82] In some historical instances, innovation (*rang bzo*) was even punished, as in the notorious case of Tibet's first modernist, Gendün Chöpel.[83] Thus, when a Tibetan Buddhist author departs from tradition, they are deliberately going against society's expectations; it is worth paying attention to such instances.

Shabkar's autobiography departs from Heruka's *The Life of Milarepa* in three main ways: it has a more robust portrayal of Tibet than its predecessor, it adopts an organizational structure that emphasizes Tibet's Buddhist geography, and it incorporates the influence of folk literary genres. Chapter 1 of my book analyzes the robust manner in which Tibet is portrayed in Shabkar's autobiography. Chapter 2 focuses on Shabkar's multifaceted portrayal of Tibet and the way his autobiography emphasizes Tibet's Buddhist geography. The influence of folk literature on Shabkar's autobiography is the subject of chapter 3.

One of the main reasons that I suggest we need to pay attention to Shabkar's robust portrayal of Tibet in his autobiography is because Tibet's portrayal by Heruka in *The Life of Milarepa* falls flat in comparison. This is not to say that Heruka's *The Life of Milarepa* was not important for the history of the idea of Tibet. Milarepa's life story was the first to place Tibet on the Buddhist map in a substantial way, as Andrew Quintman has demonstrated.[84] The various versions of Milarepa's life story also played a critical role in shaping the significance of the Tibetan landscape over several centuries.[85] Heruka's *The Life of Milarepa* is important in the history of the idea of Tibet because it established the idea of Tibet as a center of Buddhism through the scene of Nāropā's famous prophecy about Milarepa, in which he declares, "In the gloomy land of Tibet lives a man like the sun rising over the snows," and proceeds to bow toward the north three times.[86] In this quotation, Tibet is "gloomy" because Buddhism had not spread widely there yet. In comparison to Heruka's portrayal of Tibet in *The Life of Milarepa*, Shabkar's portrayal of Tibet is more multifaceted. Shabkar portrays Tibet as a flourishing civilization with its own territory, language, history, religion, and system of law and governance that are unified by the divine patronage of the bodhisattva of compassion, Avalokiteśvara.

Thus, although Shabkar's activities are much more wide-ranging than the theme of Tibet, for the reasons above, I think it is justified to highlight and further explore what might seem like a marginal aspect of Shabkar's autobiography according to traditional Tibetan Buddhist conventions. It is impossible to say for sure if Shabkar was intentional about—or even conscious of—this dimension of his oeuvre; his main aim was clearly to benefit the spiritual lives of his audience. Nevertheless, I hope to demonstrate that his contribution to the history of the idea of Tibet is significant.

## Chapter Structure

In this book, I explore the roles that myth, literature, cartography, religion, and the idea of Tibet play in the formation of the Buddhist imagined community of Tibet as portrayed by Shabkar in his autobiography and songs. Chapter 1 of the book examines Shabkar's idea of Tibet on its own terms through an analysis of Shabkar's usage of the words "Tibet" (*bod*) and "Tibetans" (*bod kyi mi*). Shabkar's concept of Tibet has much in common with cultural definitions of nation, while also including a strong religious dimension that is not present in those definitions. The religious dimension of Shabkar's concept of Tibet is better understood through comparisons to the concepts of *sasana*, moral community, or galactic polity in precolonial Theravāda Buddhist societies such as Burma or Sri Lanka. Shabkar's establishment of a robust idea of Tibet in his autobiography is crucial because a nation can only exist if the idea of a collective imagined community exists in the first place.

Another essential aspect of a nation is its territorial basis. Chapter 2 of the book explores the spatial concept of Tibet that is created through a narrative mapping of Shabkar's pilgrimage sites in his autobiography and songs. The mapping of a landscape has profound significance for the formation and maintenance of nations. Theorists of cartography in early modern Europe have demonstrated that the visualization of a nation through mapping can serve as an essential stage in acculturating the broad populace to the idea of belonging to the imagined community of a nation based on a delimited territory.[87] Here, the term "map" need not be an image, but can also take the form of a narrative, as in the case of chorography. In his autobiography, Shabkar provides a detailed chorography of the Amdo region, central Tibet, and areas of southwestern Tibet and Nepal. Prior to the nineteenth century, the Amdo region was not always included in maps of Tibet. Shabkar's autobiography plays an important role in establishing Amdo as an essential part of Tibet. Moreover, Shabkar's narrative mapping of large areas of the Tibetan Plateau articulates a distinctly Buddhist, animate, and multidimensional sacred space that is intimately linked to the spiritual practice of its inhabitants.

The presence of a vernacular literature plays an important role in the origins and perpetuation of a nation. Literature can predict and establish the foundations of the imagined community of a nation before the actual institution of the nation arises, as has been demonstrated in both early modern and ancient literatures.[88] Chapter 3 explores the significance of the merging of the *namtar* genre with vernacular genres such as folk song and Tibetan opera in Shabkar's autobiography. Because of his respected stature as a spiritual teacher, this merging of these genres elevated popular literature, making a national literature based on the vernacular a possibility. Thus, the fact that Shabkar's writings are both elite and based on the vernacular is another way in which they have contributed to the idea of Tibet as a nation.

The concept of being a chosen people continues to sustain some of the oldest nations in human history. For almost a millennium, the Tibetans have believed that they are the chosen people of Avalokiteśvara, the Buddhist bodhisattva of compassion. Chapter 4 explores how Shabkar revives and adapts the myths of Avalokiteśvara and Padmasamabhava to reinforce and develop the idea of Tibet as a Buddhist imagined community and Tibetans as Avalokiteśvara's chosen people. By reviving and adapting this myth, Shabkar takes part in a centuries-old tradition of giving the Tibetans what Anthony Smith calls "a heightened sense of collective distinctiveness and mission."[89] Myths of ethnic election play an important role in the long-term survival of an ethnic group. However, in contrast to versions of the Avalokiteśvara myth that emphasize Tibet's imperial past, Shabkar's revival of the myth is forward-looking and imagines a Tibetan present and future under the leadership of the Dalai Lamas and other historic-mythic figures.

Finally, historically, religion played an important role in holding together nations across the world. This is easy to forget because a concept of the secular nation-state, divorced from religion, is currently the international norm. However, as Anthony Smith has argued, "it is impossible to grasp the meanings of nations and nationalism without an understanding of the links between religious motifs and rituals and later ethnic and national myths, memories, and symbols."[90] Chapter 5 explores how Buddhism is depicted as one of the most important forces that holds together the Tibetan nation in Shabkar's autobiography and songs. This is apparent by the way he frequently evokes Avalokiteśvara as the patron deity of the Tibetan people and the way in which he self-identifies as Avalokiteśvara's incarnation while promoting Buddhist practices across the Tibetan Plateau. In particular, by promoting a vegetarian diet, nonsectarianism, and pilgrimage as a natural outflow of Buddhist practice, Shabkar opens up the discursive possibility of Tibetans being united by quotidian acts inspired by Buddhist values.

# 1

# "Tibet" and "Tibetans" in Shabkar's Autobiography

Before Shabkar was known as "Shabkar," he went by many other names. At birth, he was called Ngakwang Trashi, meaning "Auspicious Lord of Speech."[1] Later, when he began training with the tantric community of Repgong, they referred to him as Tséring Trashi, meaning "Auspicious Long Life."[2] Upon ordination, Shabkar received the name Jampa Chödar, which means "Loving One who Spreads the Dharma."[3] Later, when he engaged in Dzokchen training, his guru gave him the tantric initiation name Tsokdruk Rangdröl, meaning "Self-Liberation of the Six Senses."[4] In addition to these official names, Shabkar referred to himself using various epithets in his autobiography and *Collected Songs*. Common examples include "singer," "renunciant," and "yogi."

Shabkar often included a place name in conjunction with his various epithets. Early in his career, he would identify himself in reference to his hometown, as in the case of the "singer of Repgong" (reb gong glu ba).[5] During this period, he also showed hints of embracing a pan-Tibetan identity, such as when he referred to himself as "Tsokdruk Rangdröl of Tibet" (bod kyi tshogs drug rang grol) or "I, the unprecedented eloquent singer of Tibet" (sngon med bod kyi glu pa kha bde nga).[6] In 1809, Machen Pomra's bestowal of the title of "Singer of Tibet, Land of Snows" (bod kha ba can kyi glu dbyangs mkhan) onto Shabkar marked an important shift in how Shabkar represented himself. Following that event, Shabkar would refer to himself as "Singer of Tibet," gesturing to his preference for this pan-Tibetan identity over his local identity. During his stay on Tsonying island between 1806 and 1809, we have the first evidence of someone describing Shabkar as "White Lotus Feet" (zhabs pad dkar).[7] "Lotus Feet" is a common Tibetan honorific term used to refer to Buddhist teachers. But it would not be until 1818—while travelling in southern Tibet—that Shabkar would fully embrace the epithet "White Feet."[8] In doing so, Shabkar took the commonly used term of "White Lotus Feet," shortened it to "White Feet," and adopted it as his own epithet. The overall pattern that we see with regard to Shabkar's geographical identification is that he began with a strong local identity early in life, shifted to a pan-Tibetan identity in his early twenties, and then shifted to a universal identity that transcended place in mid-life. Throughout this process, there was no contradiction between Shabkar's local and pan-Tibetan identities—he embraced both.

When Shabkar identified as the "Singer of Tibet," what exactly did he mean by "Tibet"? In this chapter, I examine Shabkar's representation of Tibet on its own terms. My goal is to uncover an indigenous concept of Tibet as portrayed by an author who styled himself as the Singer of Tibet. Shabkar uses the term "Tibet" (*bod*) to refer to an area that includes central Tibet, western Tibet, and Amdo. He hints at the inclusion of the Kham region, but does not describe it in detail, as he does the other regions. Shabkar's concept of Tibet roughly corresponds to large regions of ethnographic or cultural Tibet. Although language, history, and so forth are present in Shabkar's portrayal of Tibet, Shabkar depicts Buddhism—especially as materialized by Avalokiteśvara as the Tibetans' patron deity, a deity incarnated in the form of the Dalai Lamas—as the most significant coalescing force for Tibet. Unlike other authors who emphasize shared ethnic origins or Tibet's imperial period, Shabkar portrays Buddhism as the most significant marker of Tibet's identity.

## "Tibet" and "Tibetans"

"Tibet" is the English rendering of the Chinese name for Tibet (Tufan 吐蕃) from the *Old Tang Annals*.[9] The English word "Tibet" has a range of meanings. These meanings fall into two main categories, represented by the terms "political Tibet" and "cultural Tibet" or "ethnographic Tibet." The term "political Tibet" refers to the Tibet Autonomous Region (TAR) in the PRC. The term "cultural Tibet" or "ethnographic Tibet" refers to the culturally Tibetan regions located on the elevated geographical formation known as the Tibetan Plateau.[10]

The English word *Tibet* most often refers to the Tibetan word *bod* (pronounced *pö* in Lhasa dialect). *Bod* does not have a fixed referent in the Tibetan language; its usage is context dependent. In Tibet's earliest histories, *bod* most often referred to the region that is now known as the province of central Tibet (*dbus* or *dbus gtsang*).[11] Gradually, the term *bod* came to include other regions of the Tibetan plateau such as Ngari, Kham, and Amdo.[12] Gendun Chöpel, for instance, notes that Ngari was referred to as *bod* at one point.[13] In contemporary times, according to the Central Tibetan Administration, "Tibet" refers to the area encompassing the three provinces of central Tibet, Kham and Amdo.[14] Despite the historical contingency of the word *bod*, the term—along with the associated image of "land of snows"—nevertheless carries deep significance of denoting Tibet as a country, as is demonstrated by Gendun Chöpel's treatment of the term.[15]

Some scholars refer to this latter idea as "greater Tibet" (*bod chen po*, Ch. *daxizangqu*), a term which is not without controversy. The term "greater Tibet" has been criticized by the Tibetan government-in-exile as a deliberate misrepresentation by the People's Republic of China of the Fourteenth Dalai Lama's proposal to transform the culturally Tibetan areas of China into a "de-militarized Zone of Peace" as part of his Five-Point Peace Plan.[16] Nevertheless, the idea of a plateau-wide Tibet encompassing the TAR plus sections of the Chinese provinces of Qinghai, Sichuan, Gansu, and Yunnan is an ancient one that dates back to when Tibet's Yarlung dynasty conquered these regions in the seventh century.[17] After the fall of the Tibetan Empire, this idea has been revived and reinterpreted by various Tibetan thinkers for the last millennium. The first chorographical sources depicting the contemporary concept of Tibet's territory date to the eighteenth century.[18]

The term "great Tibet" (*bod chen po*), which is also translated as "greater Tibet," has historical precedent in documents such as the Chinese-Tibetan Treaty of 821–22, the writings of the Fifth Dalai Lama, and works by Jamgön Kongtrül and his contemporaries. However, in these historical texts, the meaning of the term "great Tibet" does not correspond to the modern concept of "greater Tibet." In the Chinese-Tibetan Treaty, for instance, the term "great" is used as an adjective for both Tibet and China while delineating each country's respective territories.[19] In the Fifth Dalai Lama's (1617–1682) decree appointing Sangyé Gyatso as regent, he describes "the kingdom of Great Tibet known as the three Skor, the four Ru and the six Sgang."[20] The Fifth Dalai Lama's concept of Great Tibet includes much of the territory delineated by the contemporary category of "greater Tibet" but does not include the Amdo region.[21] Shabkar's contemporary Jamgön Kongtrül (1813–1899) also uses the term "great Tibet" when he states that the activities of the treasure revealer Chokgyur Lingpa will pacify "all degeneration of the teachings and beings of greater Tibet."[22] He uses the term "great Tibet" in conjunction with what seems to be a variant spelling of the word for "district" (*bod chen po'i rdzongs*) or a possible misspelling of the word "realm" (*ljongs*).[23] From this quotation it is not clear what Kongtrül understands the territorial basis of "great Tibet" to be. Nevertheless, his usage of the term implies a pan-Tibetan connotation because his work is about sacred sites in the Kham region, which he understands to be part of Tibet. Chokgyur Lingpa (1829–1870) also uses the term "the realm of greater Tibet" (*bod chen po'i ljongs*).[24] It is equally not clear from the phrase's context what Lingpa takes to be greater Tibet's territorial basis although it is clear he considers Kham to be part of Tibet. Tenpo Nomönhen's (1789–1839) *Detailed Explanation of the World* contains a detailed discussion of the term "greater Tibet." In Nomönhen's discussion, the debate is not centered on the concept of a pan-plateau Tibet, but rather, whether or not central Tibet should be considered "little Tibet" and Kham should be considered "great Tibet."[25] A century later, Gendün Chopel continued Nomönhen's discussion by saying there was a point in history when *bod* referred to Ngari while "greater Tibet" referred to the rest of the country.[26]

Just as the English word "Tibet" has multiple referents in the Tibetan language, the English term "Tibetans" also lacks a fixed referent in Tibetan. The closest Tibetan language equivalent to the English "Tibetans" is *bod pa*. However, the usage of the term *bod pa* is highly dependent on context, and the term means different things to different people.[27] For instance, in the absence of another ethnic group, Tibetans from the eastern Tibetan provinces of Amdo and Kham will most often refer to themselves as *amdowa* or *khampa*, rather than as *bod pa*.[28] However, when Tibetans describe themselves in opposition to another ethnic group, such as the Han Chinese, the term *bod pa* becomes a "singular marking of identity" describing Tibetan people both within and outside of the PRC.[29] To complicate matters further, the term *bod pa* is also used by Tibetan refugees in India to describe ethnic Tibetans living in the PRC.[30]

Part of the confusion surrounding *bod pa* and *Tibetan* is that although these words can both refer to either an ethnic category or a national category, the two categories are often conflated. Sara Schneiderman has argued that "we must recognize the difference between 'Tibetan' as a dominant *national* identity which contains its own networks of ethnicity established through civilizing projects, and 'Tibetan' as a *peripheral* ethnic identity within other national contexts such as China, Nepal, and India."[31] This is because ethnicity itself is "a relational system that is fundamentally constituted within national frameworks."[32] In this book, I use the word "Tibetan" in the national sense, in order to mirror Shabkar's understanding of "people of Tibet" (*bod kyi mi*). I do not mean "national" in the sense of the nation-state, but in the sense that during this period, figures like Shabkar understood Tibet to be a civilizational center that actively sought to convert peoples of peripheral regions to Buddhism.[33]

## "Tibet" in Shabkar's Autobiography

Shabkar uses several terms that that can be rendered into English as "Tibet." These terms are *bod* and its variants: "the land of Tibet" (*bod yul*), "the realm of Tibet" (*bod khams*), and "the country of Tibet" (*bod kyi rgyal khams*). In Shabkar's autobiography and songs, "Tibet" is unambiguously a place name. This comes across, for instance, when Shabkar describes how Padmasambhava and Atiśa "came to Tibet" (bod du phebs).³⁴ Shabkar often uses the word *bod yul* interchangeably with *bod*. One example is when Shabkar describes how the Indian Buddhist master Atiśa and his spiritual sons came to "Tibet, Land of Snows" (bod yul gangs can ljongs).³⁵ Another example is when the Tiger Faced Ḍākinī tells Shabkar to "stay in Tibet" (bod yul du bzhugs) instead of going on pilgrimage to India.³⁶ The term *bod khams* also appears in Shabkar's autobiography and songs. For instance, Shabkar uses it when he prays at Tsipri for "auspiciousness to encompass the realm of Tibet" (bkra shis pas bod khams khyab gyur cig).³⁷ Another example occurs in a song that ends with a prayer for "May the auspiciousness of the sun / of joy shine on all in the realm of Tibet" (bod khams kun la bde skyid kyi / nyi ma 'char ba'i bkra shis shog).³⁸ Sometimes, Shabkar uses the phrase the "country of Tibet" (*bod gyi rgyal khams*), though he uses this term less often than "Tibet," "land of Tibet," or "realm of Tibet." Instances of this usage occur when he describes Avalokiteśvara as the patron deity of "the country of Tibet, Land of Snows" (bod kha ba can gyi rgyal khams),³⁹ or when he refers to himself as "the eloquent yogi Tsokdruk Rangdröl of the country of Tibet, Land of Snows" (bod yul kha ba can gyi rgyal khams kyi / rnal 'byor kha mkhas tshogs drug rang grol).⁴⁰

Most often, Shabkar uses the word for Tibet and its variants in conjunction with the concept of "snow" (*gangs* or *kha ba*) or "snow mountains" (*gangs ri*). Snow and mountains covered in snow are among the most ubiquitous geographical features of Tibet. In classical literature such as the *Book of Kadam* (*Bka' gdams glegs bam*), snow serves as a metonym for Tibet. An example of Shabkar's usage of the terms "Tibet" and "snow" in combination is "Tibet, Snow[land]" (bod gangs can) in a song lamenting the loss of his guru while at Takmo Dzong in Amdo.⁴¹ Sometimes, there is the sense that Tibet is enclosed within a ring of snow, as in the case of a song sung by Shabkar's disciple that compares Shabkar to Milarepa, who "roamed unbridled within the ring of snow, land of Tibet" (bod yul gangs kyi ra ba).⁴² Another example is found in the Panchen Lama's letter about Shabkar, in which he describes Tibet as "the realm enclosed by a fence of snow mountains" (gangs ri'i ra bas bskor ba'i zhing ljongs).⁴³ Within this ring of snow are "the people born within the land of Snows" (gangs ri'i ra bas yongs bskor ba'i / gangs can khrod du skyes pa'i mi).⁴⁴ On rare occasions, Shabkar evokes Tibet's high altitude — for example, in the phrase the "high realm of Tibet" (mngon mtho bod) — although the trope of snow is much more common.⁴⁵ The combination of such passages gives a strong sense of Tibet's territory being circumscribed within a ring of snow.

What is Tibet's territorial basis in Shabkar's autobiography? Shabkar describes traveling all over the Tibetan Plateau. However, he rarely states outright whether or not he considered these places to be part of Tibet. The place that is unambiguously the center of Tibet, according to Shabkar's portrayal, is central Tibet (*dbus gtsang*). In a song sung to express his desire to return to central Tibet after three years spent at Mount Lachi, Shabkar describes central Tibet as "the center of Tibet" (bod yul gyi dbus).[46] For much of Tibetan history and even in many contemporary contexts, the term *bod* has been most often used to refer to the province of central Tibet. Shabkar, however, does not use the word *bod* to refer to central Tibet, but rather, the terms "central Tibet" (*dbus gtsang*) or "the Center" (*dbus*).[47] Another region that Shabkar portrays as being unambiguously a part of Tibet is Amdo Province. Shabkar considers his home valley of Repgong located in Amdo Province to be part of Tibet. This is apparent when he requests that his spiritual role model Kelden Gyatso "lovingly protect the sentient beings within the realm of Tibet / Like a mother for her son; / and in particular, the disciples of Repgong who follow [you]."[48] Likewise, Shabkar's sense that his home valley is in Tibet is apparent when he sings, "I, [a] singer born in Tibet, Land of Snows" (gangs can bod du skyes pa'i glu ba nga'i).[49] Shabkar also portrays his main teacher, the Dharma King, as considering the Amdo region to be part of Tibet. Born in the district of Urgé in the Amdo region, the Dharma King describes himself as "I, old person born in Tibet, Land of Snows" (gangs can bod du skyes pa'i mi rgan nga).[50]

Aside from central Tibet and Amdo, it is ambiguous which other regions are part of Tibet. Shabkar seems to consider the three sacred mountains Kailash, Lachi, and Tsari to be part of Tibet, as he designates them respectively as being in the highlands, midlands, and lowlands (*stod bar smad*).[51] However, whether he means upper, middle, and lower *Tibet* is up to interpretation. In one instance, he seems to consider Lachi, located in southern Tibet bordering Nepal, as being unambiguously part of Tibet when he describes seeing the "Five Long Life Sisters, protectors of the realm of Tibet" (bod khams skyong ba'i tshe ring mched lnga) while meditating there.[52] However, after living in Lachi for three years, he writes of wanting to return to "Tibet, Land of Snows" (gangs can bod yul).[53] Mount Kailash is in the Ngari region of western Tibet. Shabkar describes attracting many disciples from the region with whom he keeps in touch after he returns to Amdo.[54] However, Shabkar does not directly comment on whether or not Mount Kailash is located within the confines of Tibet, Land of Snows. One would assume so, since it *is* after all a snow mountain within the ring of snow mountains that circumscribes Tibet. Shabkar is equally ambiguous with regards to the status of Tsari. On the one hand, he considers it to be one of the three major sacred mountains, along with Kailash and Lachi.[55] On the other hand, he portrays it as a border region where the Lhasa government offers sacrificial yaks as tribute to the "Loba people from the borderlands."[56]

Similarly, it is unclear whether Shabkar considers Kham to be part of Tibet. He describes the necessity of traveling through Kham in order to reach central Tibet.[57] He also describes having disciples from Kham.[58] However, unlike his detailed descriptions of the sacred sites of other regions of Tibet, he merely mentions Kham but does not describe it in any detail whatsoever. Although texts by the nineteenth-century Tibetan Buddhist luminaries Chokgyur Lingpa and Jamgön Kongtrül celebrate Kham's sacred sites, Shabkar seems to have considered Kham a place that one passed on the way to central Tibet, rather than a sacred destination in and of itself.

Shabkar does not use the common *chölkha sum* ("three regions" or *chol kha gsum*) model to organize Tibet, which contributes to the ambiguity surrounding his conception of Tibet's territorial basis. The framework of the *chölkha sum*, which dates to the Mongol period in the thirteenth to fourteenth centuries, divides the Tibetan plateau into three regions.[59] Exactly which three regions the *chölkha sum* is describing has evolved over time. Nevertheless, the convention of dividing Tibet into three regions became a common trope. In place of the *chölkha sum* model, Shabkar describes the different regions of Tibet using the word "districts" (*gzhung*).[60]

Shabkar overlays Indian Buddhist models for understanding the environment with indigenous Tibetan ones. The concept of the *maṇḍala* is one of the main Indian Buddhist models that Shabkar uses to organize Tibet's territory. In Vajrayana Buddhism, the *maṇḍala* is the divine palace of a main deity. The main deity sits in the center of the *maṇḍala*, surrounded by concentric circles of other deities. Using this model, Shabkar understands the center of Tibet to be the province of central Tibet (*dbus gtsang*).[61] He elevates central Tibet in this way, calling it "the pure realm of central Tibet."[62] With central Tibet serving as the center of Tibet, all the other landmarks are arranged around it, with those closer to the center being more significant. The *maṇḍala* is also a common model for organizing Buddhist polities throughout Asian history.[63]

The other model that Shabkar uses is the tripartite classification system of "upper, middle, and lower" (*stod bar smad*), which can also be rendered as "highlands, midlands, lowlands." This model is commonly found in indigenous Tibetan descriptions of territory. The referent of "upper, middle, and lower" shifts depending upon context. In the opening scene of Shabkar's autobiography, "upper" refers to Mount Machen, "middle" refers to Drakkar Treldzong, and "lower" refers to Tsonying Island in Qinghai Lake. In a song sung at Drakkar Treldzong, however, he categorizes central Tibet as the highlands, the lowlands as the Chinese emperor's palace, and midlands as his home valley of Repgong.⁶⁴ In this song, he also suggests that those born in these "upper, middle, and lowlands" are the "fortunate ones born in Tibet now." The shifting context of what is denoted by upper, middle, and lower makes it difficult to circumscribe regions with fixed borders upon the Tibetan plateau's territory, the way we do in the modern mapping system.

Although there is some ambiguity in Shabkar's portrayal of Tibet's external borders, he clearly conceives of Tibet as encompassing large regions of the Tibetan Plateau beyond the province of central Tibet. Shabkar's concept of Tibet includes central Tibet and Amdo and implicitly includes southern and western Tibet. Shabkar contributes to the history of the idea of Tibet by including the Amdo region as a part of Tibet. But his pan-plateau idea of Tibet drew from deep historical precedent. Shabkar's pan-plateau concept of Tibet continues a tradition, which began in the Later Transmission Period, of reviving the historical memory of the Tibetan Empire's territorial basis. In the twelfth century, the early treasure revealers sought to "recapture the lost might of the Tibetan empire" by revealing treasure objects that were believed to be hidden by the Indian tantric master Padmasambhava and his associates during the imperial period.⁶⁵ The early treasure revealers, alongside members of the Kadam sect, also propagated the myth of Avalokiteśvara as Tibet's destined deity. The concept of Tibet expressed in the *Clear Mirror of Royal Genealogies* by Sakyapa Sönam Gyeltsen (1312–1375) reflects the sense of collective identity (even the "proto-nationalism") that emerged in the Later Transmission Period. Gyaltsen's vision combines the myth of the Tibetans as Avalokiteśvara's chosen people and the memory of the territorial basis of the Tibetan Empire. In a scene from the text, Avalokiteśvara makes an oath to tame the beings within the territory of Tibet, Land of Snows, a territory that includes: (1) central Tibet (Wü and Tsang); (2) Ngari Korsum; and (3) Amdo, Khams, and the Three Ranges.⁶⁶ One of Shabkar's main spiritual predecessors from the Repgong Valley, Kelden Gyatso (1607–1677), echoes this idea of a plateau-wide Tibet in one of his songs, which names the: (1) "four horns" of Wü and Tsang; (2) Ngari Korsum; and (3) Dokham and the Three Ranges.⁶⁷

Shabkar's usage of the word "Tibet" (*bod*) and its variants such as "the land of Tibet" (*bod kyi yul*) to refer to an area extending beyond central Tibet is consistent with that of other geographically focused texts from nineteenth-century eastern Tibet. Such texts include Drakgön's *Oceanic Book*, Tenpo Nomönhen's *Detailed Explanation of the World*, and Chokgyur Lingpa's *A Brief Inventory of the Great Sites of Tibet*. The *Oceanic Book* uses the term "Tibet" (*bod*) and "the land of Tibet" (*bod yul*) to refer to a large geographical area that includes central Tibet, Kham, and Amdo.⁶⁸ Nomönhen's *Detailed Explanation of the World* includes Ngari, central Tibet, and the six ridges of Dokham in its concept of Tibet.[69] Chokgyur Lingpa considers Tibet to consist of Ngari, central Tibet, and Kham.[70]

## "Tibetans" and Tibetan Language in Shabkar's Autobiography

Shabkar uses several terms that may be glossed as "Tibetans" in English, but which carry subtle differences in their meaning. These terms include "disciples of Tibet" (*bod kyi gdul bya*), "persons of Tibet" (*bod kyi gang zag*), "transmigrators [of] Tibet" (*bod yul 'gro ba*), "sentient beings of Tibet" (*bod khams sems can* and *bod yul skye dgu*), "Tibetan subjects" (*bod 'bangs*), "people of Tibet" (*bod kyi mi*), "Tibetans" (*bod pa*), and "Tibetan lineage" or "Tibetan ethnicity" (*bod rigs*). In Shabkar's usage of these terms, all carry a pan-Tibetan connotation, with the exception of *bod pa*, which is used to denote both Tibetans in general and the inhabitants of central Tibet in particular. The wide range of words that Shabkar uses to describe Tibet's inhabitants is noteworthy because the vocabulary used by one of his main spiritual predecessors, Kelden Gyatso, to describe Tibet's inhabitants seems to be much more limited. Kelden Gyatso uses the terms "Tibetan subject-people" (*bod 'bangs mi*) and "Tibetan communities" (*bod lde*).[71]

The first four of these terms have Buddhist connotations. In Shabkar's dream vision of Avalokiteśvara in 1809, the deity addresses the "disciples of Tibet."[72] "Disciples" (*gdul bya*) is a term that is used to describe the students of a Buddhist teacher. The term "disciples" literally means "that which is to be tamed." It differs from the other term for "disciple" (*slob ma*) in that one can be a *slob ma* of a teacher for any subject matter, whereas *gdul bya* is a Buddhist term. The term "persons of Tibet" also has Buddhist connotations. It is a translation of the Sanskrit word *puruṣa*, which was transmitted to Tibet with the translation of Indian Buddhist scriptures.[73] The terms "the transmigrators [of] Tibet" and "the sentient beings of Tibet" are from the Buddhist tradition as well. Unlike the previous two terms, these two terms encompass both humans and nonhuman sentient beings. The term "sentient being" gestures to the Buddhist worldview that there are nonhuman beings who possess a consciousness. The word "transmigrators" describes the countless sentient beings who wander through cyclic existence (Skt. *saṃsāra*). Shabkar uses "the transmigrators [of] Tibet" in the context of describing the Ninth Dalai Lama as the "refuge and protector of all the transmigrators [of] Tibet" (*bod yul 'gro ba yongs kyi skyabs mgon*).[74] Shabkar uses "sentient beings of Tibet" in the context of describing the Indian tantric Buddhist master Padmasambhava's ability to dispel all of their obstacles as well as Atiśa's kindness in spreading Buddhism in Tibet.[75] The preponderance of Buddhist terms to describe the people and beings of Tibet emphasizes the centrality of Buddhism to Tibetans as understood by Shabkar.

The term "Tibetan subjects" evokes the plateau-wide Tibetan imperial period during the seventh through mid-ninth centuries. Shabkar uses "Tibetan subjects" rarely and only in the context of describing Tibet's imperial period. For example, he describes the seventh-century Tibetan king Songsten Gampo as addressing "my Tibetan subjects" (nga yi bod 'bangs rnams).[76] Shabkar's disciple Künzang Rangdröl also describes Padmasambhava as abandoning his "Tibetan lords and subjects" to tame the ogres.[77]

The terms "people of Tibet," "Tibetans," and "Tibetan lineage" or "Tibetan ethnicity" do not have a Buddhist connotation. The term "people of Tibet" has a pan-Tibetan connotation. The deity Avalokiteśvara uses this term to address Tibetans when he appears to Shabkar on Tsonying island.[78] In Shabkar's collected songs, he uses variations on this term, describing, for example, "each person of the Land of Snows" (kha ba can gyi mi re re) and "the faithful people of Tibet" (bod yul dad can mi rnams).[79] There is a dimension of shared genealogy to Shabkar's usage of the phrase "people of Tibet." In a passage that is present in the woodblock prints of the Shechen edition (2003) of Shabkar's *Collected Works,* but omitted from both the Qinghai edition (1985) and English translation (2001), Shabkar makes reference to the legend that "the people of Tibet" are descended from a monkey and a rock ogress.[80] It is clear from Shabkar's usage of "people of Tibet" and its variations that he distinguishes between Tibetans and non-Tibetans. For instance, he identifies the Tibetans as a group distinct from the Chinese, Mongols, and Indians. Examples of this include Shabkar's description of "Chinese, Tibetans, Mongols—the three" (rgya bod sog gsum) and the "people of India" (rgya gar gyi mi) in contrast to the "Tibetan ethnicity" (bod rigs).[81]

When distinguishing Tibetans from other groups, Shabkar sometimes uses the term *bod rigs*, which in modern Tibetan is rendered as the "Tibetan ethnicity." I argue that it is acceptable to translate this term as "Tibetan ethnicity" in Shabkar's context because his understanding of the term *rigs* is genealogical. Shabkar uses the term "Tibetan ethnicity" in the context of contrasting Indian family lineages from Tibetan ones. He explains how Indian people are born into "families of good lineage" because they are kind to their parents whereas Tibetans are not born into families of good lineage because they are not kind to their parents.[82] The usage of lineage in this context gives the sense of the word *rigs* having the connotation of genealogy or lineage. There is also a linguistic dimension to Shabkar's concept of *rigs*. For example, he describes a dream he had in which people from different nationalities speaking different languages ("mi rigs mi gcig pa skad rigs mi thun pa") were gathered together at Mount Lachi.[83] Thus, Shabkar's usage of the term *rigs* connotes the concept of family, lineage, and ethno-linguistic groups. For this context, I suggest "Tibetans" or "Tibetan ethnicity" as the translation of *bod rigs* because these phrases accord with the notion of Tibet as a civilizational center on par with China, India, and Mongolia.

Although there is a clear sense of a pan-Tibetan identity in Shabkar's usage of terms such as "the people of Tibet" or "the disciples of Tibet," Shabkar's usage of the word for "Tibetan" (*bod pa*) is more ambiguous. In some cases, the word *bod pa* is used in a pan-Tibetan sense—for example, to distinguish "great Tibetan translators" (bod pa lo tsa' ba) from Indian *paṇḍitas*.[84] However, when Shabkar uses the word "Tibetan songs" (*bod pa'i bzhas* and *bod glu*) in the context of a party in which both "Tibetan songs" and Mongolian songs (*sog glu*) are sung, it is not clear if these "Tibetan" songs denote songs from central Tibet or Tibetan songs in contradistinction to Mongolian ones.[85] Consistent with his usage of "central Tibet" (*dbus gtsang*) instead of "Tibet" (*bod*) to describe central Tibet, Shabkar does not refer to people from central Tibet as "Tibetans" (*bod pa*), but rather "person from Wü" (*dbus pa*) or "person from central Tibet" (*dbus gtsang pa*).[86] This is in contrast to the common usage of the term *bod pa* to refer to people from central Tibet.[87] Shabkar calls people from Kham as "Khampa" or "beings from Kham" (*mdo khams skye bo*).[88] For Shabkar, people from Amdo are "amdopa" (*a mdo pa*).[89] And he refers to people from Ngari as "the faithful disciples and patrons from the direction of Ngari" (*mnga' ris phyogs kyi dad can slob ma yon bdag rnams*).[90]

In terms of language, the word that Shabkar uses for the "Tibetan language" is *bod skad*. It is clear that Shabkar sees Tibetan is a distinct language. For example, Shabkar identifies the holy site of Tayenchi using both "Tibetan language" (*bod skad*) and "Mongolian language" (*sog skad*).[91] He also describes a high lama from the Amdo region discouraging him to go to Wutaishan in China because he does not know Chinese or Mongolian.[92] At the same time, Shabkar describes the regional variation in the spoken dialects of the Tibetan plateau. For example, he distinguishes between "the speech of central Tibet" (dbus gtsang phyogs kyi skad cha) and "the speech of Amdo" (a mdo'i skad).[93] Although he notes the differences between the Amdo dialect and the central Tibetan dialect, he does not record having difficulty communicating with central Tibetans, which is notable because the two dialects are almost mutually unintelligible. Shabkar's representation of the ability of Tibetans from different regions to communicate without obstacles is echoed in a modern setting by an ethnography by Robert Ekvall and James Downs on Tibetan pilgrimage. Ekvall and Downs attribute their informants' "need to project a picture of a totally homogenous Tibetan culture" to the plight of Tibetan refugees.[94] Similarly, for Shabkar, projecting the image of

Tibetans from different regions as having no problems communicating with one another would have fit into his great project of portraying the Tibetans as a single people.

Throughout my discussion of the terms "Tibet" and "Tibetans," I have noted the clear presence of a strong sense of pan-Tibetan identity. How is this pan-Tibetan identity reconciled with the strong sense of regionalism that also characterizes the communities of the Tibetan Plateau? For Shabkar, there is no contradiction between his local and pan-Tibetan identities; he occupies both identities simultaneously. Shabkar's local identity is defined by his home valley of Repgong and the greater Amdo region more generally. Shabkar frequently identifies himself as "the singer of Repgong" in his *Collected Songs*.[95] In his autobiography, Shabkar also refers to his homeland as Domé (*rang yul mdo smad*), which was used more frequently than Amdo to describe the region in the nineteenth century.[96] Nevertheless, in addition to a strong sense of local identity, Shabkar also embraces a pan-Tibetan identity by referring to himself as "the Singer of Tibet, Land of Snows"[97] as well as "the Yogi of Tibet, the Renunciant Tsokdruk Rangdröl."[98] Both local and pan-Tibetan identities are adopted without contradiction in his self-descriptions. What causes Shabkar to identify as "Tibetan" rather than being a "person from Repgong"? Tsering Shakya's observation that *bod pa* becomes a "singular marker of identity . . . only in opposition to 'the other'" is helpful for answering this question in certain contexts. For instance, Shabkar describes the Dalai Lama addressing him as "Amdo lama"[99] but a group of Chinese, Mongols, and Muslim Salars describing him as "Lama Shabkar of Tibet" (bod kyi bla ma zhabs dkar pa).[100] In the former case, the Dalai Lama emphasized Shabkar's regional identification while non-Tibetans emphasized Shabkar's Tibetan identification.

## The Idea of a Nation

The previous section explored how Shabkar depicts the idea of Tibet, Tibet's territory, Tibetans, and Tibetan language in his autobiography. Shabkar also portrays Tibet as having a long and illustrious Buddhist history, a distinct culture, and a shared myth of being Avalokiteśvara's chosen people.

In his autobiography, Shabkar portrays Tibet as a civilization with a Buddhist history stretching back to the Tibetan imperial period. He recalls, for example, King Songsten Gampo's role in establishing the Jokhang temple in Lhasa, which contains Tibet's first Buddhist statue; he quotes from the king as well.[101] He pays tribute to the dharma kings of the imperial period who sponsored translations of the Buddhist canon.[102] He also composes a trio of songs that pay tribute to three dharma kings of the imperial period: Lha

Totori Nyentsen, Songsten Gampo, and Trisong Détsen.[103] In addition to the dharma kings, Shabkar also recalls other key figures in the transmission of Buddhism to Tibet, such as the Indian Buddhist master Padmasambhava, who first tamed Tibet's indigenous deities and helped to establish Buddhism in Tibet in the eighth century.[104] While staying at the sacred site of Achung Namdzong, he reminds his audience of the story of the Three Wise Men of Tibet (*bod kyi mkhas pa mi gsum*) who had stayed there.[105] The Three Wise Men played a vital role in preserving and retransmitting Buddhist ordination vows after the fall of the Tibetan Empire. Elsewhere in his autobiography, Shabkar also frequently evokes the role Atiśa played in revitalizing Buddhist teachings in the tenth century.[106]

Shabkar also pays recurrent homage to key contributors to Tibetan Buddhist culture, such as the scholar-siddhas of India and Tibet and the great Tibetan translators.[107] One of Shabkar's songs in particular pays tribute to all the significant kings, translators or spiritual masters who were "very kind to the northern people of Tibet."[108] Altogether, Shabkar's recollection of key moments that defined Tibet as a Buddhist civilization gives a sense of Tibet's historical and temporal continuity. This history serves as the foundation for Shabkar's portrayal of Tibet's shared Buddhist heritage.

Shabkar depicts the inhabitants of the Tibetan Plateau as having a distinctive culture. While at Drakkar Treldzong in Amdo Province, Shabkar sings, "The people of Tibet, Land of Snows / hold celebrations with meat and alcohol in autumn."[109] Shabkar sings this song in order to encourage his audience not to partake in meat and alcohol, as this results in the accumulation of negative karma. He wants them to replace their cultural traditions with Buddhist ones. Song is another ubiquitous element of Tibetan culture that Shabkar portrays in his autobiography. This is most apparent in his description of his trip to Lhasa in which he and his companions sing songs to pass the time while traveling. This topic is discussed in detail in chapter 3.

The myth of Avalokiteśvara as the Tibetans' destined deity figures prominently in Shabkar's autobiography. Originally from India, Avalokiteśvara is the Buddhist bodhisattva of compassion. Between the tenth to thirteenth centuries, some Tibetan Buddhist leaders began to develop and propagate the idea that Avalokiteśvara was Tibet's patron deity. Shabkar revives this idea in his autobiography, frequently referring to Avalokiteśvara as "the deity of the snowland of Tibet" (*bod gang can lha gcig spyan ras gzigs*) and "Tibet's destined deity, the protector of the snow mountains, the Noble and Mighty Avalokiteśvara" (*bod kyi lha skal gangs ri'i mgon po 'phags pa spyan ras gzigs dbang phyug*).[110] There is a strain of the Avalokiteśvara myth developed during the Later Transmission Period that identifies Avalokiteśvara as the father of the Tibetan people who takes the form of a monkey. However, although Shabkar was aware of this myth and alludes to it, he does not dwell on Avalokiteśvara's genealogical links to the Tibetan people, but rather, on his role as a Buddhist deity. This is in keeping with the general direction of Shabkar portraying Buddhism—not ethnicity—as the most significant coalescing force for Tibetans in his autobiography.

This emphasis on the Buddhist dimension of the myth of Avalokiteśvara comes across in Shabkar's vision of the deity on Tsonying Island in Qinghai Lake in 1808. In the vision, Avalokiteśvara addresses Shabkar and Tibet's people as follows:

> I, the destined deity of Tibet, the mighty Avalokiteśvara
> always looks upon Tibet with compassion.
> You karmically fortunate beings of the central land of Tibet,
> all the people of Tibet, do as follows![111]

In the original Tibetan, each line of the stanza begins with the word "Tibet." The effect of this rhetorical device is that the word "Tibet" is emphasized. After this opening stanza, Avalokiteśvara proceeds to advise the "disciples of the realm of Tibet" (bod kyi gdul bya rnams) to behave ethically and engage in Buddhist practices that include reciting his six-syllable mantra. Shabkar's usage of "Tibet" in this passage suggests a pan-Tibetan identity where the people of Tibet are unified through their Buddhist practice and worship of their destined deity through the recitation of his mantra. The fact that Avalokiteśvara gives these instructions while in the province of Amdo gives the sense that Amdo is an essential part of Tibet. This is a particularly interesting fact because in traditional Buddhist histories prior to the eighteenth century, the Amdo region was clearly outside of the traditional designation of *bod*.[112] Throughout his autobiography, Shabkar continues to remind his audience of their special status as Avalokiteśvara's chosen people.

Shabkar's portrayal of Avalokiteśvara is intimately tied to the lineage of the Dalai Lamas. For instance, he describes the Fifth Dalai Lama as the "human emanation of Noble Avalokiteśvara, the protector of the snow mountains" (gangs ri'i mgon po 'phags pa spyan ras gzigs mi yi gar gyi rnam rol) and the Eleventh Dalai Lama as "the Destined Deity of the Beings of the Land of Snows, Emanation of Avalokiteśvara, Refuge Protector, the Dalai Lama Khédrup Gyatso" (gangs can 'gro ba'i lha skal phyag na padmo'i rnam 'phrul skyabs mgon rgyal ba mkhas grub rgya mtsho).[113] When lamenting the death of the Ninth Dalai Lama, he calls him the "the refuge protector of all the beings [of] Tibet, Land of Snows" (gangs can bod yul 'gro ba yongs kyi skyabs mgon).[114] Shabkar's portrayal of Tibet as being unified under the political rule of the Dalai Lamas as emanations of Avalokiteśvara is a highly

View from the shores of Tsonying Island in Qinghai Lake where Shabkar had his first vision of Avalokiteśvara. (Photograph by author)

idealized one. The actual political control that the Dalai Lama's government in central Tibet had on the eastern provinces of Kham and Amdo was always tenuous.[115] Nevertheless, such passages reveal that Shabkar conceived of the Dalai Lamas not just as the rulers of central Tibet, but also as the incarnation of Avalokiteśvara, who rules over all the regions of Tibet.

In addition to the Dalai Lama, Shabkar also makes reference to Demo Rinpoché, king of Tibet, who gave him an edict when he returned to Amdo.[116] The king's jurisdiction was limited to central Tibet. Nevertheless, when Shabkar appeals to the king, the Dalai Lama, and other religious leaders in central Tibet to issue laws banning the consumption of meat by monks, it is clear that central Tibet had its own laws and political system. Shabkar portrays eastern Tibet as lacking any centralized power, with lamas serving as mediators between the various political centers there. Shabkar also portrays the political systems of Tibetan communities as intertwined with the Qing dynasty, as we see the presence of the *ambans,* or officials appointed by Qing dynasty to supervise its protectorates, in his autobiography.[117] The point is that despite this relationship, Shabkar's autobiography gives an unambiguous sense of Tibet having its own political leaders and laws.

Here, I wish to return to the two non-state definitions of nation that I shared in the introduction. Grosby defines nation as "a territorial community of nativity" that "requires a relatively extensive, bounded territory or an image of such a territory, the existence of which usually involves the following: a self-designating name, a center (with institutions), a history that both asserts and is expressive of a temporal continuity, and a relatively uniform culture that is often based on a common language, religion, and law."[118] And Smith sees nation as "a named and self-defined human community whose members cultivate shared myths, memories, symbols, values, and traditions, resides in and identify with a historic homeland, create and disseminate a distinctive public culture, and observe shared customs and common laws."[119] Through our discussion of the elements that characterize Shabkar's portrayal of Tibet, we see that Shabkar portrays Tibet as having a self-designating name, a people, a historic homeland with a center, a common language, a shared myth of being Avalokiteśvara's chosen people, a history expressive of a temporal continuity, a common religion, a distinctive culture, and their own system of law. These elements, which make up Shabkar's notion of Tibet, are very much in line with both Grosby's and Smith's understanding of nation.

We could use these elements depicted in Shabkar's autobiography to argue that Tibet is a nation because it meets cultural definitions of nation, and end there. But I think the significance is more nuanced than this. First, holding Shabkar's portrayal of Tibet up against interpretative lenses such as the study of cultural nationalism demonstrates the significance of particular aspects of Shabkar's portrayal—such as vernacular literature, myth, and narrative mapping—in creating and sustaining a national consciousness. Prior to this study, Shabkar's descriptions of his travels across the Tibetan Plateau were taken at face value. They were understood exactly as Shabkar described them—as pilgrimage and as his method of spreading Buddhism across the Tibetan Plateau. However, reading Shabkar's narrative mapping of the Tibetan Plateau against studies of the chorographical literature of early modern England within the study of cultural nationalism reveals how the mapping of a territory can serve as an essential stage in acculturating a people to the idea of belonging to the imagined community of nation based on the mapped territory.[120] Studying Shabkar's autobiography through the lens of cultural nationalism highlights the role that literature and culture can play in the "perpetuation and reinforcement of Tibetan national consciousness," to borrow Lama Jabb's words.[121]

Second, it is important not to minimize the significance of the fact that Shabkar's portrayal of Tibet in the nineteenth century shares much in common with definitions of the nation within the study of cultural nationalism.

Since the incorporation of Tibetan regions into the PRC in 1959, Tibetans have been classified as an ethnic minority (Ch. *xiaoshu minzu*) within the Chinese nation-state. However, as Sara Schneiderman has demonstrated, "ethnicity codifies the relations of power between dominant groups at the centre and subjugated populations at the periphery initially constructed through civilizing projects."[122] Classifying Tibetans as an ethnic minority emphasizes their peripheral role in the Chinese nation-state. However, examining the notion of Tibet and Tibetans in Shabkar's autobiography demonstrates a different perspective from which to view Tibet: one in which Tibet is seen as the civilizing center exerting its power and influence on peripheral "ethnicities" such as the Mönpa and Loba peoples.[123] This perspective gives us a historically richer picture of the concept of "Tibet" and "Tibetans." In particular, it gives us a point of view where the Tibetans were on equal footing with other polities around them such as China, India, and Mongolia.

Finally, reading Shabkar's autobiography from the lens of cultural nationalism sheds light on the way in which articulating the *idea* of Tibet as a nation—even in the absence of a state—as being powerful. Adrian Hastings, a historian of nationalism, has argued that two of the key factors for the survival of a nation are the idea of a nation and the production of a vernacular literature.[124] Shabkar's autobiography expresses the idea of the nation in various ways: by naming it, mapping its territory, celebrating its vernacular literature, reiterating its history, reviving its main coalescing myths, and describing its shared religion and culture. Political scientists Jon Fox and Cynthia Miller-Idriss propose four ways in which nationhood is negotiated and reproduced from below by ordinary citizens: talking the nation, choosing the nation, performing the nation, and consuming the nation. Because this chapter focuses on the vocabulary that Shabkar used to discuss Tibet, in the context of this chapter, "talking the nation" is the most significant framework out of the four ways mentioned. Fox and Miller-Idriss define "talking the nation" as "talk[ing] about it" and making "discursive claims for, about and in the name of the nation."[125]

In his autobiography, Shabkar, as the Singer of Tibet, talks a lot about Tibet. He also portrays Tibet in a multidimensional and robust manner. Shabkar's autobiography is thus an important text for sustaining Tibetan national identity, with "national" here defined in terms of cultural nationalism: namely, as a "strong collective consciousness generated by a sense of nation embedded within a bewildering range of interconnected factors such as historical memories, cultural forces including literary production, territorial bonds, and the lived experience of the present."[126]

## Beyond the Framework of Nation: Considering Buddhist Frameworks

Thus far, this chapter has demonstrated how Shabkar gives a robust and multifaceted portrayal of Tibet in his autobiography and has highlighted the affinities between Shabkar's portrayal of Tibet and cultural definitions of nation from the Euro-American academy. Examining the concept of Tibet in Shabkar's autobiography from the perspective of cultural nationalism illuminates heretofore underappreciated elements of Shabkar's portrayal of Tibet. Still, there are limitations to viewing Shabkar's concept of Tibet through the framework of the nation—even a non-state-centric one. First, taking this line of inquiry too far could distort the author's intention and the original cultural context in which Shabkar's autobiography was read. It is clear that Shabkar composed his autobiography as spiritual advice to those on the Buddhist path and that he did not have a deliberate nationalistic agenda. Second, there are ways in which the concept of Tibet that Shabkar articulates lies beyond even cultural definitions of nation originating from the Euro-American academy. In particular, the majority of these modern definitions of nation fail to take into account the significance of religion as the fundamental coalescing force for nation in Shabkar's concept of Tibet.

For Shabkar, Buddhism is Tibet's greatest treasure. Throughout his autobiography, he compares the Buddha's teachings to the sun. The sun as metaphor for Buddhism is a common metaphor found throughout Tibetan Buddhist works. For example, for an audience of hundreds of disciples on the slopes of Anyé Machen, Shabkar begins a song with, "From the time of the dharma kings of the past up until now, / The sun that is the Protector—the Buddha's teachings—arose in Tibet."[127] Shabkar exhibits great pride that Buddhism is flourishing in Tibet. In his autobiography, he describes hearing about Buddhists living near Bodh Gayā in India who were impressed at how the Tibetans had preserved Buddhist teachings that had mostly disappeared in India. He notes how several of them visited him at Lachi and how some faithful Buddhists in India prostrated themselves towards Tibet.[128] Shabkar's great pride in Buddhism in Tibet is further reflected in how he frequently reminds his audience of Tibet's long Buddhist history. As portrayed by Shabkar, Buddhism—not ethnicity—is the main force that holds together the different communities of the Tibetan Plateau.

If cultural nationalism provides one useful lens for thinking about Tibet, several frameworks of community, identity, and belonging from Theravāda Buddhist societies provide lenses that may help us understand the religious aspect of Tibet as a Buddhist imagined community. These Theravāda Buddhist models may be closer analogies to Shabkar's idea of Tibet than that of the "nation." A famous example is Stanley Tambiah's notion of the "galactic polity." This idea is based on the *maṇḍala* model where the power center is surrounded by satellite sites that shift in terms of their relationship to the center and other centers.[129] Geoffrey Samuel has applied this framework to the Tibetan cultural world.[130] Another example is the concept of *sasana* found in the Buddhisms of Sri Lanka and Burma. *Sasana* has been defined various ways. In the context of Sri Lanka, Gananath Obeyeskere defines it as "a trans-local cultural consciousness" shared by the Buddhists there.[131] In the context of Burma, Alicia Turner defines it as "the life of the Buddha's teachings after he is gone; it is the condition of possibility for making merit and liberation."[132] Another concept of collective identity found in Theravāda societies is that of the "moral community," first identified by Stephen Berkwitz in the context of Sri Lanka. Berkwitz argues that "this identity as the collective beneficiaries of what the Buddha and others did before appears to trump other regional, caste, and family identities that could be expected to dominate in premodern Sri Lanka."[133]

Out of these three concepts, Shabkar's idea of Buddhist Tibet shares the closest affinities with the *sasana* and the "moral community." While Shabkar took great pride in the fact that Buddhism was flourishing in Tibet, he simultaneously felt great anxiety that the Buddhist teachings were in a state of degeneration there as well.[134] Shabkar's Tibet and the early-twentieth-century Burmese existed in different cultural milieus. However, both were concerned with the continuation of the life of the Buddha's teachings for future generations—the *sasana* in Theravāda Buddhist terminology. Moreover, these Buddhist knowledge and practices were fundamental to their identities as Tibetans and Burmese. Shabkar's portrayal of Buddhism in Tibet also resonates deeply with the idea of the "moral community." In particular, for Shabkar, one's identity as a Buddhist trumps other markers of identity such as one's family lineage, ethnicity, etc. Shabkar actively engages with a wide variety of communities from different ethnicities and religions. For example, he describes teaching Chinese, Mongols, and Salars.[135] In order to reach Mongol audiences when he does not speak Mongolian, he sings songs to them.[136] Thus, non-Tibetans and even non-Buddhists are welcomed into Shabkar's Buddhist imagined community. Perhaps the most notable example of Shabkar's attempts to incorporate non-Buddhist groups into his Buddhist imagined community occurs near the sacred mountain of Lachi where he preaches on karma to local Mönpa peoples and encourages them to pray to Avalokiteśvara using the six-syllable mantra.[137] From this incident, it is clear that although Avalokiteśvara is the Tibetan people's destined deity, other people are most welcome to pray to him. Shabkar's Buddhist imagined community is not predicated on ethnic lines.

Comparing Shabkar's concept of Tibet to that of *sasana* or "moral community" opens us up to alternative conceptions of identity, community, and territory that are rendered invisible by the contemporary framework of the "nation-state." As Gananath Obeyeskere has noted in the context of Sri Lanka, the word "nation" is an "alien word that has no parallel in the Sinhala lexicon" but belongs to the same polythetic class.[138] The case of precolonial Sri Lanka parallels Shabkar's case in that the word "nation" did not exist in Shabkar's lexicon. Instead, Buddhism was central to how Shabkar understood Tibet as an imagined community. Similarly, in her study of Burmese notions of collective belonging at the turn of the twentieth century, Alicia Turner "take[s] seriously the ways in which Buddhist discourse shaped a sense of collective belonging distinct from nation."[139] Likewise, in the case of trying to understand Shabkar's concept of Tibet, it is essential to consider the role that Buddhist discourse shaped a sense of collective belonging distinct from nation. *Sasana*, "moral community," and Shabkar's concept of Tibet show ways that humans have imagined collective belonging beyond the nation-state.

Thinking about Shabkar's portrayal of Tibet from the perspectives of *sasana* and "moral community" also helps to explain his amorphous portrayal of Tibet's borders. On the one hand, there is a clear sense that Tibet is a separate polity from China, India, and Nepal. This concept is made clear in examples from Shabkar's autobiography such as when he restores Tangtong Gyelpo's stupa according to the Panchen Lama's order in order to help prevent foreign invasions.[140] Moreover, in accordance with the framework of *maṇḍala* and galactic polity, borders are portrayed more as peripheral regions rather than as hard lines. Shabkar's most commonly used word for border is "peripheral regions" (*mtha' 'khob*), which is a region characterized by the absence of Buddhism.[141] The single instance in which Shabkar instead uses the word for "border" (*sa mtshams*) is when he refers to the border between Tibet and Nepal.[142] Moreover, between Tibet, the Qing dynasty, and Mongol regions, Shabkar does not portray borders as fixed entities. A good example is Qinghai Lake, which Shabkar describes as a "holy place of abundance where the essence of the land of Mongolia is gathered."[143] Simultaneously, Shabkar implies that the lake is part of Tibet's territory because it is the location where Avalokiteśvara appears to him in a vision, self-identifying as "Tibet's destined deity" and giving instructions to "the people of Tibet."[144] For Shabkar, the lake belongs to both the Tibetan and Mongolian Buddhist worlds; there is not the clear sense of demarcation that one finds in the modern nation-state system.

This amorphous sense of borders also helps us to understand a song that I alluded to earlier in the chapter, in which Shabkar says the inhabitants of central Tibet, the valley of Repgong, and the Chinese emperor's palace are fortunate to be born in the "highlands, midlands, and lowlands."[145] Shabkar conceives of Mongolia, Tibet, and the Qing dynasty through the lens of Buddhism. Eschewing the framework of the nation-state allows us to appreciate alternative conceptions of identity, community, and territory, in different times and places.

# 2

# Mapping Tibet's Buddhist Geography

One of the most remarkable aspects of Shabkar's autobiography is the role that territory plays in it. This role is apparent in the autobiography's chapter structure. Most Tibetan Buddhist life stories are organized according to the main deeds of its subject.[1] In particular, they usually follow some variation of the twelve deeds of the historical Buddha. The twelve deeds are the Buddha's descent from Tuṣita heaven, entrance into the womb of his mother, birth, youthful skill in sport and play, enjoying life with a harem, renunciation, austerities, going to the bodhi tree, subduing Māra, attaining complete enlightenment, turning the wheel of dharma, and passing into *parinirvāṇa*.[2] Tsangnyön Heruka's *The Life of Milarepa*, the main literary predecessor of Shabkar's autobiography, adopts this classic structure by organizing Milarepa's life according to twelve deeds. While the first four chapters of Shabkar's autobiography roughly mirror the standard structure of the typical Tibetan Buddhist life story, the remainder of the first volume is organized according to the various sacred sites that Shabkar visited and where he meditated. This structure both showcases Tibet's sacred territory at the chapter level and gives the impression that Tibet's sacred geography is inextricable from Shabkar's spiritual path.

In the nineteenth century, there were a variety of frameworks for understanding geography in the Tibetan cultural world. There were, for example, indigenous Tibetan frameworks for organizing terrain, such as that of the "highlands, midlands, and lowlands" (*stod smad bar gsum*). Indian Buddhist frameworks, such as the concept of the *maṇḍala* or the twenty-four sacred *pīṭhas*, were another widely available option. By this period, modern European models for organizing land in contiguous blocks of territory confined to a specific ethnostate had also made their way into the Tibetan cultural world.[3] Prominent examples include the world geographies created in the Tibetan language by the historian Sumpa Khenpo (1704–1788) and scholar Tenpo Nomönhen (1789–1839).[4] A visual example of European influence on Tibetan cartography can be found in the maps from the Wise Collection, commissioned by William Hay and drawn by an unknown Tibetan lama.[5]

Shabkar, however, did not adopt European frameworks, instead choosing to portray Tibetan space through Buddhist and indigenous Tibetan ones. This is fitting, given that Tibet's traditional cartography "was overwhelmingly religious" and conveyed a distinctively "Tibetan conception of space."[6] Specifically, Shabkar's conception of Tibet as a sacred Buddhist place is in accord with other portrayals of Tibet's geography in the nineteenth century, such as Jamyang Khyentsé Wangpo's *Guide to the Holy Places of Central Tibet* (*Dbus gtsang gi gnas rten rags rim gyi mtshan byang mdor bsdus*)[7] and Drakgön's *Oceanic Book*, and the unknown lama's paintings from the Wise Collection. This Tibetan conception of space uses Buddhism as its main way of thinking about space, rather than the ethnostate's framework of contiguous space. Thus, Shabkar's autobiography gives us a way to understand space that is an alternative to the modern Westphalian concept of the nation-state.

Within this context, Shabkar's autobiography makes two important contributions to the portrayal of Tibet as a Buddhist place. First, he combines a variety of genres with the genre of *namtar*, or Buddhist life story, in order to convey an indigenous concept of space where Tibet's landscape is portrayed as Buddhist, animate, multidimensional, and intimately linked to the spiritual practice of its inhabitants. These genres include pilgrimage guides (*gnas bshad* or *gnas yig*), gazetteers (*dkar chag*), praises of place (*gnas bstod*), literature about hidden lands (*sbas yul*), and *sūtra* literature. Shabkar's portrayal of an animate and multi-faceted landscape from the first-person perspective sets it apart from other geographical texts of Tibet, which generally merely name sites and mention key moments in their history. Linking these geographical genres with *namtar* makes the implicit argument that Tibet's sacred territory is an integral part of a Buddhist master's life. Second, Shabkar's portrayal of the Amdo region as a key part of Tibet's sacred territory represents an important contribution to the development of the idea of Tibet as including the eastern region of Amdo. The spatial aspect of Tibet that Shabkar articulates complements the rich set of terminology used to describe Tibet discussed in chapter 1.

## Shabkar's Buddhist Concept of Tibetan Space

Imbuing the landscape with sacred significance is an age-old function of Tibetan literature. The biographical literature on Milarepa, for instance, played a seminal role in developing the idea of Tibet as a sacred Buddhist land.[8] As Andrew Quintman remarks regarding an early version of the biography of Milarepa, "The description of Mi la ras pa's awakening has replaced the Buddha's own seat of enlightenment under the bodhi tree with the summit of high mountain glaciers; the fabled location of the Gangetic plain has been transformed into the snowy land, native metonym for Tibet itself."[9] The story of Milarepa's spiritual awakening in Tibet makes a powerful statement that enlightenment is possible there, and not only in the revered holy land of India. The most famous version of Milarepa's biography, Tsangnyön Heruka's *The Life of Milarepa*, placed Tibet on the Buddhist map, as immortalized by the famous scene of the Indian Buddhist saint Nāropā bowing towards Milarepa in Tibet.

The various versions of Milarepa's biography helped to shape the Tibetan landscape into a Buddhist one. Whereas the earlier biographies were vague about places, in that they "emphasize general setting (the mountains of Mang yul, or the forest of Sing ga la) over specific named meditation sites," later biographies named specific meditation sites and grouped them into categories such as the "outer, unknown inner, and secret fortresses."[10] Tsangnyön Heruka's *The Life of Milarepa* played a particularly important role in imbuing these sites with sacred significance through Milarepa's famous quotation: "If you meditate in these places, favorable conditions will gather in your solitude and you will receive blessings of the lineage."[11] Since the publication of this text in the fifteenth century, countless pilgrims and meditators continue to visit these sites to this very day, hoping to enhance their spiritual practice.

Still, in comparison to Shabkar's portrayal of Tibet's sacred territory, Tsangnyön Heruka's *The Life of Milarepa* portrayal falls flat. Heruka's text plays an important role in portraying Tibet's sacred geography by listing all the sites where Milarepa meditated. However, his portrayal of the places themselves is much more one-dimensional than Shabkar's. Shabkar, in contrast, portrays Tibet's Buddhist sites as animate and in a multifaceted way. Below, I discuss the multifaceted way in which Shabkar portrayed the Tibetan landscape.

## Indian Buddhist Frameworks

One of Shabkar's main strategies for conveying the Tibetan landscape as a Buddhist one is to overlay Indian Buddhist geographic models onto the Tibetan landscape. The practice of casting Tibetan geography as Buddhist dates to at least the twelfth century. Beginning in that period, Tibetan Buddhist lamas overlayed Indian Buddhist concepts such as the *maṇḍala*, or divine palace, over sacred mountains such as Tsari.[12] Overlaying Buddhist models such as the *maṇḍala* over sacred sites is a common practice found in Tibetan geographical literature such as pilgrimage guides and gazetteers.[13]

In his autobiography, Shabkar uses the Vajrāsana (*rdo rje gdan*) as a main geographical reference point. The Vajrāsana or Diamond Throne, located at Bodh Gayā in India, is the site of the historical Buddha's enlightenment. It is considered the center of the world in classical Indian Buddhist geography.

Shabkar situates "Tibet, the Land of Snows" "to the north of the Diamond Throne in India."[14] To give another example, Shabkar situates his home valley of Repgong to the north of the Diamond Throne in India, to the east of central Tibet, and to the south of Tsongkhé Kyéri mountain. In this latter example, Shabkar juxtaposes the Tibetan reference points with an Indian Buddhist one. This has the effect of melding together these systems in a seamless way, giving the impression that Buddhism and the Tibetan plateau are one. Shabkar's usage of the Vajrāsana as a reference point to situate Tibet is a common trope in Tibetan geographical literature. The *Oceanic Book* provides an example of this trope that is contemporaneous to Shabkar's autobiography.[15]

Shabkar also uses the Buddhist tantric model of the *maṇḍala* for understanding the Tibetan landscape. The *maṇḍala* is the divine palace of a deity. Shabkar uses this model to understand the holy sites of Mount Kailash and Lake Manasarovar. In praise of Mount Kailash and Lake Manasarovar, Shabkar sings:

> [The] palace of Cakrasaṃvara
> [The] abode of the five hundred arhats
> [The] pure land of the *ḍākas* and *ḍākinīs*
> [The] seat of siddhas of the past
> [The] center of Jambudvīpa continent
> [The] sacred site of Mount Kailash
> To circumambulate it once is good—
> [One] will purify the misdeeds of one lifetime.[16]

The "palace of Cakrasaṃvara" is a synonym for Mount Kailash. When Shabkar uses the word "palace," he is evoking the concept of Cakrasaṃvara's *maṇḍala*. Shabkar places Mount Kailash within the framework of the Indian Buddhist geographical frameworks of the continent of Jambudvīpa. Here, Shabkar is drawing from the tantric Buddhist model of understanding Mount Kailash that dates to the twelfth century.[17]

## Reading the Landscape

In addition to imposing Indian Buddhist frameworks onto the Tibetan landscape, Shabkar explains the significance of geographical features of the Tibetan landscape from a Buddhist lens. Tibetan pilgrimage guidebooks (*gnas bshad* or *gnas yig*) provide explanations of the Buddhist significance of the landscape. For example, the pilgrimage guide about Mount Kailash and Lake Manasarovar composed by the thirty-fourth patriarch of the Drigung Kagyü lineage in 1896 describes a meditation retreat site by Lake Manasarovar:

> The valley of the golden-surfaced Jambu river at the bathing entrance to the east of Lake Manasarovar—is a perfect practice site, which includes an upland area resembling an open lotus, a lowland area in the form of the protectors of the three classes, a mountain to the right like the eight auspicious symbols, a mountain to the left like the seven extraordinary treasures, an eight-spoked wheel in the sky and an eight-petaled lotus on the ground. In the future, at ceremonies to mark the invitation of statues of the Buddha, it will be a place where gods and goddesses take a bath.[18]

In this passage, the thirty-fourth patriarch identifies the site as conducive to meditation and explains its topography using Buddhist frameworks such as "an open lotus" and the "eight auspicious symbols." He describes the presence of beings unseen by ordinary beings, such as gods and goddesses who bathe in the waters.

In addition to the pilgrimage guide, another genre of Tibetan geographic literature, the "register" or "gazetteer" (*dkar chag*), plays a central role in explaining the Buddhist features of the landscape. For example, the gazetteer for Jamyang Khyentsé Wangpo's hermitage, Péma Shelpuk, claims that practitioners will experience tremendous accomplishments if they meditate and perform religious rituals at this site because it is the *maṇḍala* of *jinas*, or victors, and *ḍākinīs*, or female wisdom beings.[19]

Shabkar draws from both the pilgrimage guide and gazetteer genres in his portrayal of sacred sites in his autobiography. Below is an excerpt from Shabkar's autobiography, where he describes the sacred site of Drakkar of Loba near Chenza in Amdo:

> This place, viewed from the southern perspective, is like the color of crystal. And on top of a white mountain, there is a clean place [with] various trees like deity-trees, cedars, and so forth. Water and trees are assembled there, and one's mind is relaxed at this good mountain range. Through natural [means], this is a place with great blessings and the supreme gathering place of the *ḍākinīs* of the three places. It is particularly noble. Here, I stayed for a period of seven days, making a connection with the place. Because of this, I had a happy experience, a clear awareness, and generally, virtuous actions increased.[20]

As in the pilgrimage guide by the thirty-fourth patriarch, Shabkar describes the sacred site as being both conducive to meditation and a place where enlightened beings dwell. As in the gazetteer, he notes that this place is conducive to spiritual realization, because it is the gathering place of *ḍākinīs*.

In descriptions of other sites, the similarities between Shabkar's descriptions and those in the pilgrimage guide and gazetteer genres is even more apparent. Echoing the descriptions by the Drigung patriarch quoted above, Shabkar describes Ragya Monastery on the shores of the Machu River in Golok as being underneath an eight-spoked wheel and on top of an eight-petaled lotus.[21] Similarly, Shabkar describes a large rock in the vicinity of Trika as being a naturally manifesting form of the bodhisattva Maitreya.[22] By incorporating topographical interpretation from pilgrimage guides and gazetteers into his autobiography, Shabkar imbues the Tibetan landscape with Buddhist significance. Through this incorporation, he also makes the indirect argument that the sacred landscape is an inextricable part of one's spiritual journey.

## Kinesthetic Dimensions of Places and Pilgrimage

Shabkar gives readers a kinesthetic and spatial sense of Tibet's sacred places by describing his physical movement through them. Mount Kailash is one of the most important pilgrimage sites in the Himalayas for a variety of different religions. In the tantric Buddhist tradition, Mount Kailash is understood to be the *maṇḍala* of the deity Cakrasaṃvara.[23] In Tibetan literature, Mount Kailash is perhaps best remembered as one of the sites where Milarepa spent much time in meditative retreat. Milarepa's *Collected Songs* preserves many stories of Milarepa's experiences at this site, such as the oft-recounted story of Milarepa's magic battle with a Bönpo master at Mount Kailash.[24] Shabkar's autobiography also describes sacred sites and remembers the stories associated with them. In addition, Shabkar walks his audience through pilgrimage sites. For instance, in the excerpt below, he describes the circumambulation of Mount Kailash:

> During the waxing moon of the fifth month of the year called Wangchuk, [I] circumambulated the Snows in a clockwise [direction]. First, [I] went to Gyangdrak Monastery on the south face. [I] made offerings to the Snow [Mountain] and distributed tea and donations to the *sangha*. [I] met Serpuk Lama Rinpoché. [I] requested the transmission of the preliminary practices of Lord Drigungpa's Fivefold Mahāmudrā. [I] went to Nyenpo Ridzong of the western face. [I] met Chöku Rinpoché, made offerings to the Snow [Mountain], and distributed tea and donations to the *sangha*.[25]

In this quotation, Shabkar describes circumambulating the mountain, passing through each of its four gates on his pilgrimage around it.[26] He also describes the rituals and religious activities that he performed at each site. Thus, whereas it is common in the Tibetan Buddhist biographical tradition to describe the sacred sites of masters and even to tell stories associated with them, Shabkar takes things a step further by giving his audience a kinesthetic dimension of Tibet's sacred landscape.

In the above passage, Shabkar combines the genre of Tibetan Buddhist life writing, *namtar*, with the genre of pilgrimage guide discussed earlier in this chapter. Whereas Tibetan Buddhist life stories are meant to instill faith in the reader about its protagonist and to provide a paradigmatic model to emulate, pilgrimage guides generate faith in the reader about sacred sites and guide them through the significance of these sacred sites. By combining the two genres, Shabkar makes the implicit argument that interaction with Tibet's sacred sites is an essential part of a Tibetan Buddhist person's spiritual journey.

The first-person perspective that Shabkar uses to describe his pilgrimages to Tibet's sacred sites adds yet another dimension to the pilgrimage and gazetteer genres, which are typically written from a third-person perspective. The use of first person "brings the reader along," making such pilgrimages more relatable. Pilgrimage guides commonly use the third-person perspective to inform their audience of the benefits of circumambulating and performing religious rituals at the sacred site. For example, a pilgrimage guide to Anyé Machen informs its audience, "If having undertaken the circumambulation of these secondary places, one performs prostrations and circumambulations, one cannot conceive of the merit [which will be derived from them] for these are places where the Buddhas and Bodhisattvas reside in person."[27] Shabkar's first-person perspective adds an intimacy to pilgrimage literature that we do not find in the pilgrimage guide and gazetteer genres.

## Praises of Place

Another way that Shabkar conveys the sacrality of Tibet's geography is by singing praises of sacred sites. The genre of "praises of place" (*gnas bstod*) is part of a rich literary tradition in Tibet that dates back to figures such as Milarepa and Rangjung Dorjé.[28] Shabkar's praises of place all follow the same general format. He begins by praising attributes of his natural surroundings, including mountains, clouds, mists, climate, water, and vegetation. He then proceeds to mention previous masters who once practiced at the site and to describe unseen beings such as deities and *ḍākinīs* who inhabit it. He usually ends by describing how these sites are conducive to meditation. Because many of his praises of place are available in Matthieu Ricard's translation of the first volume of his autobiography, I will quote from a praise of place from the untranslated second volume. In the following excerpt, Shabkar praises his very own Trashikhyil Hermitage in the Repgong Valley:

> At the peak of the mountains behind [the hermitage]
> White clouds float like overflowing milk,
> The sun, moon, planets and stars appear in stages,
> Attached to the brilliant, white, mountain peaks,
> Silver mists coil around its waist.
> Leaves, flowers, and fruit
> Adorn the greenery and vegetation that flourish.
> Clean waters flow with sounds vociferous.
> Flowers beautify the soft meadows.
> Birds such as the divine bird,
> The cuckoo and nightingale sing.
> Wild animals roam carefree—
> Such as the deer, wild sheep, antelope.[29]

Shabkar's description of his natural surroundings give the reader a vivid image of his hermitage. He names the various aspects of surroundings that he sees—clouds, vegetation, and animals. He also deepens the reader's experience of them through the use of literary devices such as personification when he describes mist "coiling around [the mountain's] waist" and similes such as comparing floating white clouds to "overflowing milk." Shabkar's multi-sensory approach to praising place includes the aural aspect of song and the visual aspect of the descriptions. While the majority of Shabkar's praises of place are in verse, some of his praises are in prose as well.

The following is another description of his main hermitage Trashikhyil in Repgong, but in prose:

> After that, at the far shore beyond the bustle of the village, on the side of mountains of meadow and rock, at the border between farmers and nomads, the place where many scholar-adepts stay, [with] forests, blooming flowers and trees, surrounded by rainbow clouds and mist, the realm where gods and *ḍākinīs* gather, this holy valley foretold in the scriptures, the sacred abode, called Trashikhyil, at the vast peak at the top of a mountain, nearby the temple of the blissful one whose experience is happy and mind clear, at the retreat house called Ösel Nyiökhyil, I was maintaining the *samādhi* that is like a flowing river, my non-meditation [on] clear light. At this time, I was singing many songs of spiritual experience.[30]

Again, Shabkar gives a vivid visual description of the forests, flowers, trees, rainbows, clouds, and mist that mark his hermitage. Passages such as this give depth to the sacred sites that Shabkar describes throughout his autobiography. Heruka's *The Life of Milarepa* does not contain this degree of detail in its descriptions of places. Shabkar's praises of place also have an aesthetic dimension to them that reach the reader on yet another level. One of Shabkar's consistent concerns throughout his autobiography is to make his poetry and prose "pleasant" (*snyan po*) and "attractive" (*yid du 'ong ba*) to his audience. For Shabkar, doing so represents a skillful means for touching the reader in a way that inspires them to practice the Buddhist ideals he preaches. This mirrors the way in which the treasure revealer Terdak Lingpa's (1646–1714) works were believed to have a transformative effect on their audience by virtue of their beauty.[31] Thus, through his aesthetically pleasing prose, Shabkar seeks to inspire reverence towards Tibet's Buddhist landscape.

The visual, aural, and aesthetic dimensions of Shabkar's praises of place are not present in descriptions of sacred places found in several geographical texts contemporaneous to Shabkar. For example, in the *Oceanic Book*, Drakgön merely lists the sacred sites of the Amdo region.[32] There are some exceptions to this, such as in Drakgön's description of Tsonying Island. He describes Songsten Gampo's and Padmasambhava's prophecies about the island, its geographical features, the presence of sacred self-arisen images and footprints, and the pleasant sound of waves.[33] However, most of the time, his focus is on Géluk monasteries, the life stories of important masters associated with them, and their links to Mongol ruling families. Similarly, Tenpo Nomönhen, the author of the *Detailed Explanation of the World*, mentions many of the same sacred sites as Shabkar, including Anyé Machen, Qinghai Lake, and Mount Kailash. Although he gives details about each of them—mentioning, for example, some of Milarepa's stories at Mount Kailash or the Buddha's footprints on the four sides of the mountain—his descriptions are scant in comparison to Shabkar's aesthetic and multidimensional portrayal of the sites.[34] While other geographical sources name these sites, Shabkar gives his audience a deeper and more multifaceted impression of the sites.

Shabkar's praises of place borrow from other genres of Buddhist literature familiar to Shabkar's audience. The vivid descriptions of nature in Shabkar's praises of place are reminiscent of how Āryaśūra sets the scene through descriptions extolling the pleasant nature of the landscape in the *Jātakamālā*, for instance.[35] Shabkar's praises of place are also reminiscent of descriptions of the pure realms in the *sūtra* literature. The affinities between Shabkar's descriptions of places and those in the canonical literature help to reinforce the sacred nature of the Tibetan landscape that Shabkar describes.

Shabkar's praises of place may also have reminded his readers of descriptions of hidden lands (*sbas yul*) in Tibetan Buddhist literature.[36] While the meaning and significance of particular hidden lands depend on historical context, for Tibetan Buddhists, the term "hidden lands" generally connotes peaceful hidden locations that are imbued with spiritual power and represent sanctuaries where people could seek refuge in times of war and social disorder.[37] Hidden lands were predicted by Padmasambhava, an eighth-century figure remembered for his role in establishing Buddhism in Tibet, and continually revealed by treasure revealers. Below is an excerpt describing a hidden land:

> At the mountain's pinnacle, Gyelwa Gyatso (i.e. Avalokiteśvara),
> And all the roots and lineage lamas, buddhas, and bodhisattvas
> Abide like clouds gathered in the sky.
> At the mountain's waist, *yidam* deities gather
> Like a swirling snow blizzard,
> Surrounded by *ḍāka*, *ḍākinī*, and
> Activity protectors, gathered like star clusters in the sky,
> Impossible for the eyes to look at directly.
> The sounds of compassion, *kyu ru ru*, roars naturally,
> And waves of radiant nectar swirl, blazing with five-colored lights.
> In the upper valleys, where an excellent mist wafts,
> The medicinal plant Ludü Dorjé grows.
> The trees and forest are covered with the domed tent of a rainbow's light, and
> All the birds sing harmoniously, proclaiming the sounds of the dharma.[38]

This description is reminiscent of Shabkar's description of Trashikhyil Hermitage, cited at the beginning of this section. In this description, the author identifies the mountain, sky, clouds, light, trees, medicinal plants, and singing birds. In addition, he describes the enlightened beings such as *yidam* deities and *ḍākinīs*. This passage also contains multiple rhetorical devices such as personification (the mountain's "waist"), simile ("like a snow blizzard"), and onomatopoeia ("*kyu ru ru*"). The stylistic affinities between Shabkar's descriptions of sacred places such as Trashikhyil and these descriptions of hidden lands makes an implicit argument that these sacred places are like hidden lands as well. The fact that the hidden lands are associated with Padmasambhava and the treasure revealers makes this parallel particularly apt because of the centrality of Padmasambhava and the treasure tradition in Shabkar's concept of Tibet. Chapter 4 will explore Shabkar's revival and adaption of the Padmasambhava myth in detail.

Unlike the descriptions extolling nature in the *sūtra* literature, descriptions of the hidden lands have political dimensions to them. The Himalayan kingdom of Sikkim, which was incorporated into India in 1975, is portrayed in the *Chronicles of the Rulers of Sikkim* ('*Bras ljongs rgyal rabs*) as a hidden land.³⁹ During the political turbulence of central Tibet in the mid-seventeenth century, life became difficult for masters who were from sects other than the Géluk. In 1642, the Nyingma master Lhatsun Chenpo Namkha Jikmé (1597–1650) entered the hidden land of Sikkim through its northern gate. Along with two other Buddhist masters entering from the western and southern gates, they ordained the master who entered through the eastern gate as the first Buddhist king of Sikkim. In this way, the hidden land of Sikkim became the basis for a Buddhist state. For now, let us consider the political dimensions of this parallel between these hidden lands and some of Shabkar's descriptions of sacred sites on the Tibetan Plateau. If we were to follow this line of argument with regards to Shabkar's implicit comparison of some sacred sites to hidden lands, the "religious king" that rules over the sacred sites of Tibet would be Avalokiteśvara, incarnated as the Dalai Lamas. Furthermore, the hidden lands are associated with the propagation of Buddhism and territorial expansion.⁴⁰ In the case of Sikkim, the establishment of Sikkim as a Buddhist kingdom involved the conquest and conversion of the indigenous Lepcha peoples.⁴¹ Similar to this Shabkar portrays Tibet as a Buddhist civilization that propagates the religion to both its inhabitants and its neighbors. For instance, he portrays the conversion of the indigenous people at Tibet's periphery, such as the Mönpa, to Tibetan Buddhism.⁴²

## The Land Speaks: The Local Deities of Tibet

One of the main differences between Shabkar's depictions of sacred places and those found in nineteenth-century geographical texts is that Shabkar describes his interactions with the resident deities of the sacred sites. In interacting with these deities as one would usually interact with a person, Shabkar gives the impression that these sites are animate. Because one of the main functions of the *namtar* genre is to provide an exemplum for its audience to emulate, Shabkar's portrayal of his interactions with the resident deities of sacred sites suggests that Buddhists, too, should interact with the sites as they would a holy person.

When Shabkar first arrives at the sacred mountain Anyé Machen, he immediately sings a praise of the place and performs a juniper smoke offering to Machen Pomra, its resident deity.⁴³ According to Shabkar, Pomra seems to be pleased with this, and the local environment responds positively to Shabkar's friendly gesture; Shabkar describes the sun suddenly appearing through the clouds, a spontaneous shower of red flowers, and the sound of cracking ice, reminiscent of a thundering dragon. Shabkar responds by singing multiple songs in joy, praising the mountain. It seems the mountain's resident deity was pleased by these songs as well. The next day, at the break of dawn,

Shabkar describes having a dream of a messenger inviting him to Pomra's magnificent tent. In the tent, Pomra expresses his pleasure at how Shabkar has benefited Tibet's inhabitants with his songs. Machen Pomra even bestows the title of "Singer of the Land of Snows" upon Shabkar and promises to assist him with his spiritual activities. Shabkar's elaborate description of his interactions with Pomra from a first-person perspective differs significantly from the descriptions of local deities in pilgrimage guides. In a pilgrimage guide to Anyé Machen, the name of the resident deity Machen Pomra is mentioned alongside elaborate descriptions of the site as the *maṇḍala* of Cakrasaṃvara.[44] However, the descriptions are written from a third-person perspective, which gives them a detached and observational quality, in contrast to Shabkar's first-person interactions with Machen Pomra. Shabkar's description of the mountain's responses to his songs and offerings gives the impression that the mountain itself is animate, and not merely a site to be worshipped.

Another guardian deity of a sacred site with whom Shabkar describes interacting is Tsomen Gyelmo, the resident of Qinghai Lake. In 1806, Shabkar arrives at Tsonying Island, at the center of Qinghai Lake. As he does at other sacred sites, Shabkar sings a praise of place immediately upon arrival. In the same way that Machen Pomra was pleased with Shabkar's song, it seems that Tsomen Gyelmo was as well.[45] That evening, Shabkar describes seeing her in a dream where she asks one of her attendants to repeat Shabkar's song. Like many other local deities, Shabkar describes Gyelmo as continuing to be of service to him, including spontaneously blowing a piece of cloth toward him when he expresses the wish to have a piece of cloth to tend to his blistered feet.[46] A pilgrimage guide about Tsonying Island composed by Orgyen Samtenling in the sixteenth or seventeenth century describes the site as a pure land for enlightened beings. He describes the various deities that inhabit the island as well as the religious significance of topographical features such as pebbles with the self-arisen image of buddhas, that is, images that arise naturally without human intervention.[47] As is typical of the genre, it is written from the third-person perspective. In comparison to Shabkar's first-person description of his interactions with the resident deity of the island, the pilgrimage guide's description does not convey the sense that the island is animate. Likewise, Drakgön *Oceanic Book* has a section on Tsonying Island. He describes Songsten Gampo's and Padmasambhava's prophecies about the island, its geographical features, the presence of sacred self-arisen images and footprints, and the pleasant sound of waves.[48] However, there is no mention of Tsomen Gyelmo, let alone any interaction described between her and the author.

Further afield in southern Tibet, Shabkar describes meeting the Tséringma, or the "Five Long Life Sisters" (tshe ring mched lnga) at Mount Lachi.

They are indigenous deities whose role in Buddhism began when Milarepa first tamed them in the eleventh century. Shabkar calls the Tséringma "Tibet's protectors" (bod khams skyong ba).[49] In his autobiography, Shabkar claims that each time he did the *gaṇacakra* offering at Mount Lachi, rainbow-colored clouds would appear—a sign that Shabkar interpreted as the Tséringma being pleased. Shabkar's manner of interacting with the Tséringma is reminiscent of Milarepa's interactions with them as described in Tsangnyön Heruka's *Collected Songs of Milarepa*.[50] Such interactions with local deities, however, are not incorporated into Tsangnyön Heruka's *The Life of Milarepa*. Thus, it appears that Shabkar includes influences from the *Collected Songs* genre into his autobiography. More about this will be discussed in the next chapter on vernacular literature and the *namtar* genre.

## Amdo as a Part of Tibet's Territory

In contemporary times, the idea of Tibet's territory consisting of the three provinces of Kham, Amdo, and Wü-Tsang is "deeply embedded in the political culture of the Tibetan diaspora."[51] However, although the idea of Tibet encompassing the entire Tibetan plateau is an ancient one, the specific names of its provinces have varied over time. In the early modern period, the three provinces of Tibet were central Tibet, Upper Tö, and Lower Tö or central Tibet, Ngari and Dokham.[52] In particular, the notion of Amdo as a province in its own right and an integral part of Tibet is relatively modern. Prior to the late seventeenth century, histories of Buddhism in Tibet only included the Amdo region insofar as the information was relevant to central Tibet.[53] In this section, I demonstrate how Shabkar's autobiography made an important contribution to the idea of Amdo being an integral part of Tibet's sacred territory.

Tibet's Amdo Province is a region roughly the size of France that is situated in modern-day Qinghai, Gansu, Sichuan, and Yunnan provinces of the PRC. From the beginning of the Yuan dynasty (1279 CE) and well into the Qing dynasty (1644–1911 CE), this border area was the site of turbulent political struggles between the Tibetans, the Chinese, and the Mongols. Despite its pivotal role in the reintroduction of Buddhist ordination vows back into central Tibet in the tenth century, for most of its history, the Amdo region was largely viewed as a religio-cultural backwater by Lhasa and Beijing, the centers of Tibetan and Chinese political power. Amdo's southern neighbor, Kham Province, was also viewed as a borderland region by both Lhasa and Beijing and enjoyed a high degree of autonomy from these central powers for much of its history.[54]

Still, despite Lhasa's and Beijing's conception of these eastern Tibetan provinces as borderlands, in the words of Michael Aris, "Where the common notion of a frontier would lead one to expect a sense of marginality or alienation, so often one meets instead with a confident and ancient sense of centrality."[55] By the nineteenth century, the eastern Tibetan provinces of Amdo and Kham had become powerful religio-cultural centers in their own rights. Amdo was home to large monasteries such as Labrang and Kubum, which formed complex webs with both the Mongolian ruling families of eastern Tibet and the Geluk monasteries of Lhasa.[56] Kham was the center of a moment of tremendous religious flourishing centered on a group of Buddhist luminaries in and around the Dégé kingdom. The activities of these masters would have a profound influence on the direction of Tibetan Buddhism as a whole. A century later, Euro-American historians would characterize their activities as the "the nonsectarian movement."

Right at the moment when these eastern Tibetan provinces had reached the apex of their cultural and religious development, Lhasa and Beijing became interested in these regions as well. A central challenge faced by Asian polities in the nineteenth century was to transition into the nation-state model that was quickly becoming the international norm. Part and parcel of this process was staking claim to the territory of one's nation and establishing borders with one's neighbors. Both central Tibet and the Qing dynasty sought to claim the frontier regions at the edges of their empires and to establish well-defined borders.[57] Specifically, the Qing dynasty, threatened by the loss of its coastal territories to European imperial powers, felt an urgent need to secure its inland territories. Kham, which had been largely autonomous from both Tibet and China for centuries, was suddenly in peril, facing potential "divisions and annexation."[58]

It was within this context that we see a proliferation of literature from Amdo and Kham that mapped this region that had been previously remained vague in the Tibetan literary imagination. Prominent examples of these texts include Drakgön's *Oceanic Book*, Shabkar's autobiography, Chokgyur Lingpa's *A Brief Inventory of the Great Sites of Tibet*, and Jamgön Kongtrül's *Twenty-Five Great Sites of Khams*. Together, these texts place eastern Tibet on the map, contributing to the modern notion that "Tibet" is composed of the three provinces of Wü-Tsang, Kham, and Amdo. Collectively, these texts demonstrate that the nineteenth century was not moribund with regards to the concept of "greater Tibet," but rather, an important period for the development of the idea of Kham and Amdo being an integral part of Tibet. Moreover, it was this oft-overlooked region of the Tibetan Buddhist world that played an important role in the history of the idea of Tibet during a critical moment of transition in inner and east Asian history.

In particular, Jamgön Kongtrül's *Twenty-Five Great Sites of Khams* literally placed Kham on the map, so to speak, at a moment when the Kham region was about to suffer cartographic erasure due to internal instability as well as the struggle between Beijing and Lhasa over the region.[59] Alexander Gardner observes that, "without asserting either a nationalist project or drawing territorial borders" Jamgön Kongtrül's text "firmly establish[ed] the geographic territory of Khams."[60] Moreover, Kongtrül's narrative map represented "an example of a different sort of mapmaking, a native project that made use of indigenous means—conceptions of religious geographical networks, inter-sectarian alliance, and rituals of spatial representation—to establish its territorial identity."[61]

In the same way that Kongtrül's narrative map of sacred sites in Kham represented the first such map of its kind of the Kham region, Shabkar's narrative mapping of the Amdo region in his autobiography represented an important large-scale rethinking of the Amdo region and its significance in the Tibetan Buddhist world. The main difference between Shabkar and the authors from Kham is that Shabkar focused on Amdo while ignoring Kham, while the authors from Kham focused on Kham and ignored Amdo. Nonetheless, collectively, these authors from eastern Tibet were instrumental in putting eastern Tibet on the map in a way that earlier histories of Tibet did not.

Although Shabkar occasionally rehearses the trope of the Amdo region being barbaric and backward, on the whole, he portrays the Amdo region as being an integral part of Tibet in several ways. First, he reminds his audience of the vital role the Amdo region played in preserving and re-establishing Buddhism in central Tibet in the ninth and tenth centuries. When the King Lang Darma persecuted Buddhism in Tibet in the mid-ninth century, three monks known as the Three Wise Men fled central Tibet to Achung Namdzong in Amdo. Along with the help of two Chinese monks, the Three Wise Men ordained a young Tibetan man named Géwasel. In the late tenth century, a group of young men from central Tibet traveled to Amdo to receive ordination from Géwasel. The group of newly ordained monks then returned to central Tibet, thereby re-importing monastic ordination back into central Tibet. In this way, the region played a key role in the preservation and re-importation of Buddhism back into Tibet during the Later Transmission Period. Like other historical sources, Shabkar reminds his audience of the important role of Achung Namdzong in Tibetan Buddhist history.[62]

Second, many of the key moments where Shabkar expresses a pan-Tibetan identity occurs in the Amdo region. His first vision of Avalokiteśvara, for instance—in which Avalokiteśvara refers to himself as "Tibet's destined deity" (bod kyi lha skal) and gives instructions to "the people of Tibet" (bod khams mi rnams)—occurs on Tsonying island at the center of Qinghai Lake in Amdo Province.⁶³ Furthermore, Shabkar receives the epithet "Singer of Tibet, the Land of Snows" (gangs can bod kyi glu dbyangs mkhan) from the resident deity of the sacred mountain Anyé Machen, Machen Pomra. Alongside Qinghai Lake, Anyé Machen is one of the key sacred sites found in the Amdo region. In addition to these key moments in Shabkar's autobiography, he also mentions in passing that various places in Amdo are a part of Tibet. For example, he considers his home valley of Repgong to be part of Tibet, as well as his teacher's encampment at Urgé.⁶⁴ Finally, along with his identity as the Singer of Tibet, Shabkar equally asserts his Amdo origins as well. In a particularly memorable scene in his autobiography where he meets the Ninth Dalai Lama for the first time, he notes how the Dalai Lama and his entourage were amused by his Amdo dialect.⁶⁵

Still, the most significant way that Shabkar expresses the view that Amdo is part of Tibet's territory is through his autobiography's chapter structure. As mentioned in the introduction to this chapter, Shabkar adopts an uncommon chapter structure in his autobiography. While the first four chapters of his autobiography adhere to the conventional model of being organized according to the spiritual master's deeds, the rest of the first volume of his autobiography is organized according to the sacred sites that he visited. These sites include the Tayenchi cave at Tsézhung, Takmo Dzong, Tsonying Island, Mount Machen, Drakkar Treldzong, central Tibet, Tsari, Kailash, Nepal, Lachi, and the Amdo region. The chapter of Shabkar's *Collected Songs* roughly mirrors the chapter structure of his autobiography, thereby reinforcing it. The second volume of Shabkar's autobiography adopts a diary-like structure and takes place entirely in the Amdo region. When we combine the ten chapters in the first volume of his autobiography that take place in Amdo with the entire second volume, roughly two-thirds of Shabkar's autobiography takes place in Amdo. This is highly noteworthy. Shabkar, who styles himself as the Singer of Tibet and the reincarnation of Tibet's beloved poet-saint Milarepa, spends most of his life in the Amdo region. This makes a strong case for Amdo being an integral part of Tibet, as well as a region that has been important to Shabkar's spiritual path.

The implicit argument made through the chapter structure of Shabkar's autobiography—that the Amdo region is a part of the sacred territory of Tibet—is further buttressed by Shabkar's naming and descriptions of sacred sites in the Amdo region. The act of naming a place in itself is powerful. As Yi-fü Tuan once observed, the act of naming can represent the "creative power to call something into being, to render the invisible visible."⁶⁶ In addition to naming these sacred sites, Shabkar also describes them in detail. Many of the passages in the first part of this chapter that describe Tibet's sacred sites are taken from Shabkar's descriptions of sacred sites in Amdo.

By naming and recording all the sites of the Amdo region, Shabkar helps to place Amdo on the map, just as Jamgön Kongtrül does for Kham.

I counted a total of 327 sites mentioned in Shabkar's autobiography. I was able to find GIS coordinates for 175 of these sites.[67] In the case of a site being located within another site, such as Tsonying Island in Qinghai Lake, or the thirty-six temples of Trika being in the town of Trika, that is represented by a single point on the map. In instances where I could not find the exact GIS co-ordinates for a site, but it is known to exist near a GIS-identified location, I included the less well-known site within the one with known GIS coordinates. For example, Tsézhung Hermitage is included within the point for Chuzang Monastery. Appendix 1 contains a complete list of locations mentioned in Shabkar's autobiography—including those that I have not been able to identify. Most of the unidentified locations are in Amdo. The appendix also includes maps that show the scatter of the points that Shabkar mentions in his autobiography that I have identified, including close-ups of the sites mentioned in Amdo Province and those from western, central, and southern Tibet.

The scatter of points demonstrates the sacred sites named or described by Shabkar on the Tibetan Plateau in his autobiography. We see how these points span central and southern Tibet, western Tibet, Amdo Province, and parts of Nepal. The scatter gives an impression of how the Amdo region is connected to these other places because they are the sacred sites of Tibet.

Thus, the way in which Shabkar names and describes the sacred sites of Amdo in his autobiography, together with his chapter structure, makes the implicit argument that Amdo is an integral part of the Tibetan Buddhist world. This argument—made indirectly in Shabkar's autobiography and made in other texts as well—helped to acculturate Tibetan communities to the idea of Amdo as an essential part of the territory of the imagined community of Tibet. Like others who mapped eastern Tibet through narrative in the nineteenth century, such as Jamgön Kongtrül and Drakgön, Shabkar did not have a nationalistic agenda. His motives were purely religious. Nevertheless, as we will discover in the section below, mapping is a fundamental practice in the development of nations.

## Territory, Mapping, and the Visualization of a Nation

In this chapter, we have explored the spatial aspect of Shabkar's concept of Tibet on its own terms. This analysis has revealed that above all, for Shabkar, the most salient feature of Tibet's geography is that it is Buddhist. Shabkar describes Tibet's landscape as being full of Buddhist sacred sites that are linked together through pilgrimage networks. Shabkar's descriptions offer an alternative spatial logic for geographic cohesion other than the frameworks of contiguous space and ethnostate territory that dominates the nation-state model. Shabkar's Buddhist map of Tibet represents, to borrow Alexander Gardner's words, "a different sort of mapmaking." Describing Jamgön Kongtrül's maps, Gardner observes how he "made use of indigenous means—conceptions of religious geographical networks, inter-sectarian alliance, and rituals of spatial representation—to establish its territorial identity."[68] Shabkar, like Kongtrül, articulates an indigenous concept of Tibetan Buddhist space—one in which Tibet's Buddhist geography is animate, multidimensional, and an intimate part of a Tibetan Buddhist practitioner's spiritual practice.

Shabkar's narrative mapping of the Tibetan plateau in his autobiography serves another important purpose as well: it outlines the territorial basis for Tibet as an imagined Buddhist community. Anthony Smith once observed that "Whatever else it may be, nationalism always involves an assertion of, or struggle for, control of the land. A landless nation is a contradiction in terms."[69] The physical space of the ancestral homeland, he maintains, can "provide the emotional as well as physical security required by the citizens of a nation."[70] Viewed in this context, Shabkar and other nineteenth-century authors from eastern Tibet contributed to the modern idea of Tibet being composed of the three provinces of central Tibet, Amdo, and Kham. They collectively placed eastern Tibet on the map, so to speak. Although their motivations for describing the sacred sites on the Tibetan Plateau were religious, their narrative mapping of the Tibetan Plateau has deep significance for Tibetan nationalism because they articulate Tibet's territorial basis.

Mapping practices played a major role in the historical rise of the modern nation-state. In the mapping practices of early modern Europe, one of the most significant semiotic devices imposed by cartographers and chorographers upon European landscapes was the idea of the nation. In eighteenth-century Europe, for instance, the practice of mapping was crucial for the creation of the modern Westphalian notion of nation because it allowed for "the visualization of the nation as a people in a territory" before the actual rise of modern nation-states.[71] The act of mapping the landscape in these contexts played an essential role in the rise of the modern nation because the visualization of the nation as people in a territory "probably constitute[d] an essential stage of the process of acculturation of the individual in the formation of ... a national identity."[72] Mapping was not limited to cartography. In the context of early modern Spain, historical narratives mapped regions through their descriptions of the regions.[73] In this way, the practice of mapping—regardless of whether in cartographic or narrative form—is an important practice for establishing, remembering, and shaping the idea behind a nation's territory.

The example of mapping practices in early modern Europe and their contribution to the formation of national identities is a useful framework for thinking about the significance of Shabkar's extensive narrative mapping of the Tibetan Plateau in his autobiography. In his descriptions of his extended pilgrimages, Shabkar maps out large sections of the Tibetan Plateau. In particular, he maps the regions of Amdo, central Tibet, and Ngari in detail. Maps of central Tibet and Ngari were already well established by the nineteenth century. Shabkar's contribution was in incorporating the Amdo region into the concept of Tibet in a serious way.

Prior to the eighteenth century, the eastern regions of Amdo and Kham were only included in descriptions of Tibet in relation to central Tibet.[74] Just as Jamgön Kongtrül had created a narrative map of Kham, Shabkar did the same for Amdo. In writing about Kongtrül, Alexander Gardner notes that a map "might not hold back armies or administrators, but it would preserve a sense of place."[75] In the same way, Shabkar preserved the sense of Amdo as a Buddhist place—and as a place that was an essential part of Tibet as a whole.

In contemporary times, the territorial basis of the Tibetan nation as articulated by the CTA includes both Amdo and Kham.[76] Figures such as Shabkar and Kongtrül and their chorographical maps of Tibet were vital to the development of the spatial aspect of the history of the idea of Tibet. Shabkar's and Kongtrül's motives for mapping Amdo and Kham, respectively, were solely religious. But by including eastern Tibet as integral components of Tibet as a whole, Shabkar and Kongtrül played an essential role in the rise of the idea of Tibet encompassing the three provinces of central Tibet, Amdo, and Kham. Describing the sacred sites of Amdo and Kham in detail also assisted their audiences in visualizing these places. Because the visualization of the nation as people in a territory "probably constitute[d] an essential stage of the process of acculturation of the individual in the formation of . . . a national identity,"[77] one could argue that authors like Shabkar and Kongtrül contributed—albeit unintentionally—to the rise of the modern Tibetan nation in that they facilitated the visualization of the territorial basis of the modern Tibetan nation through their chorographical writings.

In addition to mapping out Tibet's territory in order to provide a geographical foundation for his imagined community of Tibet, Shabkar's autobiography plays an important role in territorializing historical and religious memories pertinent to Tibetan identity. That is to say that Shabkar imbued the land of Tibet with historical and religious meaning by imposing Indian Buddhist frameworks on it, interpreting geographical features as Buddhist symbols, singing praises of place, describing his pilgrimages at sacred sites, and describing his interactions with the local deities who inhabit the landscape. I concluded that these strategies in combination resulted in Shabkar conveying an indigenous notion of Tibetan space that is Buddhist, animate, multidimensional, and intimately linked to the spiritual practice of its inhabitants.

The significance of Shabkar imbuing the Tibetan landscape with sacred meaning shines forth when we view it from the lens of Anthony Smith's idea of the ethnoscape. According to Smith, the ancestral homeland of a people is often endowed "with the powerful collective emotions" of that people.[78] Human leaders and literary chronicles pass on the memory of important events that took place in the landscape, such as origin stories and key events that shaped the community. The land is also marked by the graves and tombs of forebearers, which give the living a sense of emotional continuity with their dead kin. All of this results in "the territorialization of memory" in which landscapes becomes "sites of memory."[79]

In the case of Shabkar, the land of Tibet is an ethnoscape endowed with powerful collective emotions as the ancestral homeland of the Tibetan people. This ethnoscape of Tibet has a strong religious dimension to it. Through his dual roles as the Singer of Tibet and Shabkar, Shabkar reminds his audience of the deep history and sacred significance of the geographical features and sacred monuments of the Tibetan Plateau. Like the chronicles and ballads that eulogized Tibet in the imperial period, Shabkar's autobiography celebrates Tibet's sacred landscape through song, poetry, and prose. Whereas in Smith's ethnoscape, the "terrain [is] invested with collective significance is felt to be integral to a particular historical culture community or *ethnie*, and the ethnic community is seen as an intrinsic part of that poetic landscape," for Shabkar, the terrain in invested with Buddhist significance, and the landscape becomes an integral part of Tibetans' spiritual practice.[80] Here, Shabkar is following in the footsteps of his spiritual and literary predecessors in the biographical tradition of Milarepa. The biographical tradition of Milarepa played a critical role in "actively landscaping the environment" of Tibet with "landscaping" defined as "the production and formulation of sacred space through a variety of means."[81] Shabkar just took things a step further than his spiritual predecessors in the amount of emphasis he placed on place in his autobiography.

Shabkar's portrayal of the Tibetan landscape as sacred is important for helping us to understand the deep ties between Tibetan national identity, Buddhism, and the historic homeland of Tibetans. Throughout the centuries, Tibetan Buddhist masters have endowed the Tibetan landscape with "special symbolic and mythic meaning," imbuing the landscape "with a sacred and extraordinary quality, generating powerful feelings of reverence and belonging."[82] This is in contrast to the modern Euro-American notions of state formation, which "[tend] to neglect the role of popular mobilization" and "[attach] no weight to the properties of territory and the role of ancestral homelands."[83] As we can see in Shabkar's portrayal, the Tibetan landscape is endowed with the history of Buddhist masters, the dharma kings of the imperial period, the mantra of Avalokiteśvara, and the presence of local deities. Moreover, Shabkar's portrayal of Tibetans is reminiscent of Anthony Smith's description of a "community of believers and a 'holy people' adhering to a single sacred lifestyle."[84] By describing the role that the Tibetan landscape played in his spiritual journey, recounting the sacred significance of various sites of Tibet, recalling his visions of Avalokiteśvara, and portraying Buddhism as the collective religion of the Tibetan people, Shabkar's autobiography and songs reinforce the idea of the inhabitants of Tibet forming a community of believers under the patronage of Avalokiteśvara.

In such a case, the political apparatus of centralized states—military force, bureaucracy, ethnographic controls—stand little chance in uprooting the powerful feelings of reverence and belonging generated by a territory endowed with the sacred and mythic significance of a people. Shabkar's portrayal of Tibet as a sacred place imbued with deep historical and religious significance helps us to understand the deep collective memories that continue to fuel vehement assertions of Tibetan nationalism in contemporary times.

# 3

# Vernacularizing the *Namtar* Genre

Shabkar's autobiography is one of the most celebrated examples of *namtar*, or "Buddhist life story," in Tibetan literature. The word *namtar* is a rendering of the Sanskrit term *vimokṣa*, which means "complete liberation." *Vimokṣa* refers to the ultimate goal for Buddhist practitioners: a state of complete liberation (Skt. *nirvāṇa*) from cyclic rebirth (Skt. *saṃsāra*).[1] In Sanskrit, *vimokṣa* refers to a state, not a literary genre. Indian Buddhist literature has a great variety of genres of life writing that may be translated as "life story," "biography," "autobiography," or "hagiography." There is, however, no direct equivalent to the *namtar* genre in Indian Buddhist literature. The *namtar* is a Tibetan Buddhist literary development inspired by existing Indian biographical genres. Indeed, as Andrew Quintman has observed, "it was largely in the form of *namtar* that Tibetan biographical writing developed and later flourished."[2] Thus, although inspired by early Indian Buddhist literary forms, the *namtar* is an indigenous form of Tibetan literature.

More specifically, Shabkar's autobiography belongs to the subgenre of *namtar* called *rangnam* or "Tibetan Buddhist autobiography." A *rangnam* is a Buddhist life story that one composes about oneself. The *rangnam* originated in the twelfth century, during the Later Dissemination Period, which followed a century of sociopolitical chaos. Also known as the "Tibetan renaissance," this period was characterized by the "radical overthrowing of the past and the construction of a new cultural identity that occurred with the introduction of Buddhism in Tibet."[3] Janet Gyatso attributes these two things as "the principal factor for the development and flourishing of autobiography" in Tibet.[4] Although Shabkar's autobiography is specifically a *rangnam*, it is more often described as a *namtar* by Tibetan Buddhists.

During Shabkar's time, in the nineteenth century, the *namtar* genre had reached the apex of its development in terms of its length and its subgenres, as well as the numbers of *namtar* being produced.[5] By the nineteenth century, a robust tradition of literary criticism surrounding the genre had developed as well. The leading *namtar* critics were elite Buddhist monks educated in the monastic college system. One of the most influential literary critics from the period was the Third Tukwan Lozang Chökyi Nyima (1737–1802) who, like Shabkar, was from the Amdo region. Maintaining that the form of the *namtar* needed to match the greatness of its subject, the Third Tukwan was critical of those who incorporated colloquial language and vernacular genres into the *namtar* of Buddhist masters. His preferred medium for *namtar* was ornate poetry, or *kāvya*.[6] Originating from India, *kāvya* was first made available to Tibetans through the translation of the Daṇḍin's *Kāvyādarśa* in the thirteenth century.[7] The language of *kāvya* eventually gained a central place in educated circles but remained incomprehensible to the ordinary populace. In addition to favoring ornate poetry as the medium of expression in *namtar*, the Third Tukwan opposed the practice of composing biographies in the "character [*dbyibs*] comparable to the Gésar epic."[8] He also objected to *namtar* being too long, arguing that including "songs, admonitory teachings, letters, and intermediate verse as well as a great deal of prose extolling the supreme master and criticizing others merely has the effect of producing a giant book."[9]

Shabkar's autobiography adopts *all* of the literary grievances that the Third Tukwan lists with regard to the *namtar*. At 1,540 folios spread across two volumes, Shabkar's autobiography is one of the longest examples of the genre. His autobiography contains songs, admonitions, spiritual advice, letters, and intermediate verses. Moreover, the text is not written in ornate *kāvya*, but rather in a simple idiom that is both aurally pleasing and easy for non-specialists to understand. As I will demonstrate below, Shabkar even incorporated elements from folk literature into his autobiography. Shabkar wanted to make his autobiography accessible to a broad audience. In doing so, he deliberately defied many of the conventions praised by the monastic literary critics of his day.

In this chapter, I demonstrate how Shabkar embraced the ethos of Tibetan vernacular literature in his autobiography by merging the *namtar* genre with elements of vernacular genres. I use the word "vernacular"—often interchangeably with "folk"—to describe a literature written in an idiom easily understood by the ordinary populace and that plays a role in upholding a nation's collective identity. By incorporating vernacular genres such as folk song and Tibetan opera, Shabkar imbued his autobiography with the rhythms and ethos of Tibetan vernacular literature. In this way, the form and rhythms of the text reflect the "heartbeat" of the Tibetan people, to borrow Pema Bhum's phrasing—just as the work as a whole implicitly argues for the presence of Tibet as a Buddhist imagined community.[10] In this way, the form of the Singer of Tibet's autobiography reflects the robust concept of Tibet that it portrays.

## Vernacular Literature and the Rise of Nation-States

Shabkar incorporated elements from Tibet's folk literatures into his autobiography in order to make his autobiography accessible to Tibet's ordinary populace. Adapting Buddhist stories to suit a local audience by incorporating indigenous literary elements is a practice that dates to at least the twelfth century in Tibet.[11] Like his spiritual predecessor the eleventh-century teacher Potowa, Shabkar's main intention in incorporating folk elements was to make Buddhist teachings appeal to Tibetans' aesthetic sensibilities. Nevertheless, because of Shabkar's elite status as a respected spiritual master, he elevated these vernacular literary traditions by incorporating elements from them into his autobiography. This elevation of vernacular traditions was significant for the development of a Tibetan national literature based on the vernacular, which in turn was significant for the rise of the modern Tibetan nation.

The vernacular literature of sixteenth-century England provides an analogy that is useful for understanding the significance of Shabkar's vernacularization of the *namtar* genre. Richard Helgerson has demonstrated how the poets of sixteenth-century England "opened a discursive space" in which they sought to articulate "the kingdom of our own language," which assisted the shift from a "dynastic conception of communal identity" to one based on "postdynastic nationalism."[12] In the case of Shabkar's autobiography, by promoting the use of the vernacular idiom in the elite genre of *namtar*, he is making the indirect argument that Tibetan folk genres should be taken seriously. By adopting elements of the vernacular in his work, he opens up the discursive space for the possibility of an elite literature that embraces the vernacular ethos. In turn, Shabkar's embrace of folk genres serves as an antecedent to the establishment of a nationalist modern Tibetan literature that would arise in the 1980s. While Shabkar did not embody the iconoclastic tendencies of "Tibet's first modernist," Gendün Chöpel, Shabkar's *namtar*—with its spirit of embracing a folk literary ethos—did represent an act of defiance against the sensibilities of elite monastic tastes. Although the notion of the modern Tibetan nation did not arise until the twentieth century, we can see in Shabkar's autobiography the beginnings of an elite literature based in a folk sensibility.

Returning to the analogy of sixteenth-century England, Shabkar's move to incorporate the folk idiom into the elite genre of *namtar* has a further significance as well. Commenting on sixteenth-century England, Andrew Hadfield has suggested that "Literature does not reflect debates about the nation and national identity: it invariably predicts and establishes them in periods before the creation of political institutions that have defined the contours of nations."[13] If we apply Hadfield's observation to Tibet and to the case of Shabkar's *namtar*, it follows that Shabkar's articulation of the imagined community of Tibet (which used an idiom rooted in Tibet's folk literature) would have played a role in predicting and establishing the *idea* of the Tibetan nation before the establishment of the political institutions that defined the nation. Although the historical-cultural context of sixteenth-century England is vastly different from that of nineteenth-century Tibet, comparing the two cases helps us to appreciate the prominent role that literature can play in forming an imagined community of the nation.

The presence of a vernacular literature also plays an important role in sustaining the nation. Historian Adrian Hastings has argued that the two most important factors for the survival of a nation are the idea of the nation and the presence of a vernacular literature.[14] The role of a vernacular literature is to create that very community in its readers by maintaining "the core identity of a nation through the exercise of collective memory."[15] He cites the example of the Jewish people who, "[w]hatever their spoken language," were "held together by the Hebrew Bible and related texts."[16] The example of the Jewish people is particularly salient in the case of contemporary Tibet because of the history of the Jewish people losing their ancestral homelands and existing in a diasporic state. The history of the Jewish people has similarities to the plight of the Tibetan people in the twentieth and twenty-first centuries.

## Shabkar's Songs and the Fabric of Tibetan Culture

As his epithet "Singer of Tibet" suggests, Shabkar was well-known for his ability to sing. In particular, Shabkar was known for composing and singing *gur* (*mgur*). Originally, the term *gur* was one of several ancient terms for "song" (the others being *mchid* and *glu*), dating to the imperial period of Tibet.[17] These songs were sung in the imperial court to recount royal genealogical histories, recount battle stories, and to express loyalty among court members. Beginning in the eleventh century, the term *gur* instead denoted songs sung by enlightened tantric figures. Although Shabkar's own *gur* retain associations with the ancient imperial genre, his songs belong to the latter category of *gur* and are best rendered into English as "songs of spiritual realization."

Songs of spiritual realization differ from other forms of Tibetan song because Buddhist tantric adepts compose and perform them extemporaneously to express their experience of spiritual awakening (Skt. *nirvāṇa*). The genre is inspired by the *dohā* genre sung by the ancient Indian *mahāsiddhas*, but is expressed in the idiom of Tibetan folk song.[18] Composed by tantric adepts

(Skt. *siddhas*) around 1000 CE in northeast India, the *dohā* are aphoristic rhyming couplets written in the Apabhraṃśa dialect that convey the spiritual realization of their authors and provide spiritual advice.[19] Tibetan translators re-importing Buddhism back into Tibet beginning in the late tenth century brought the first *dohā* to Tibet. It was under Milarepa, however, that the *dohās* "blossom[ed] into a truly Tibetan tradition."[20] In the same way that the *namtar* genre is an indigenous Tibetan genre that draws from Indian Buddhist biographical literature, the *gur* genre is an indigenous Tibetan genre inspired by Indian *dohā* but expressed in the idiom of Tibetan folk song.

Although Shabkar's songs belong to the *gur* genre because of their provenance and content, Shabkar consistently refers to them as *lu* (*glu*) in both his autobiography and *Collected Songs*. *Lu* can be rendered most accurately in English as "song." In contrast to *gur, lu* does not carry a religious connotation. Moreover, *lu* is deeply rooted in the popular, oral, and folk traditions of Tibet, in contrast to *kāvya*, which is generally associated with the learned Buddhist monastic tradition in Tibet. Although Shabkar claims not to have had any formal training in poetry and composition, some of his songs reveal his great skill at writing *kāvya*-style poetry.[21] One of the aspects of the *kāvya* tradition is the usage of extensive lists of poetic synonyms (*mngon brjod*) that aspiring poets must memorize beforehand. For example, synonyms for "sun" include "the friend of the lotus garden" (*pad gtshal gnyen*), "the lord [of the] seven horses" (*rta bdun bdag po*), and "the one who possesses the green horses" (*rta ljang can*). Synonyms for "sky" (*nam mkha'*) include "the path [of] no death" (*'chi med lam*) and "the path [of the] gods" (*lha lam*). In a passage from a song expressing grief over the death of the Arik Géshé, Shabkar laments:

> Pulled by the strength of green horses—previous aspiration prayers,
> In Tibet, [that is] as beautiful as the path of the gods,
> The thousand-ray web of enlightened activities—
> Lord Śākyamuni, the friend of the lotus garden—has departed.
> At the peak of the western earth grasper where the small fortuneless ones are,
> We call upon you.
> The moon rays that are so pleasing to the mind,
> Waver along with the night-lotus of [my] grieving heart.
> Although there is no firewood in my mind,
> The fire of sadness blazes greatly.
> And although there are no clouds in the sky of my eyes,
> A rain of tears falls violently.[22]

There are four poetic synonyms in this passage: "the one who possesses the green horses," "the path of the gods," "the friend of the lotus garden," and the "earth grasper" (*sa 'dzin*).[23] Despite claiming to know nothing about how to compose *kāvya*, Shabkar clearly possesses this ability. By deliberately aligning his songs with *lu* instead of *kāvya*, Shabkar is making a statement that his work is for ordinary Tibetans. Shabkar may also be adopting the word *lu* rather than the honorific term *gur* in order to express humility according to Tibetan cultural convention.

In keeping with the convention established by Tsangnyön Heruka of separating Milarepa's biography from his *Collected Songs*, Shabkar's autobiography and *Collected Songs* exist as separate texts. Nevertheless, his autobiography still includes some 600 songs, a point whose significance I will take up in the next section. At just under 1,200 songs, Shabkar's *Collected Songs* is one of the largest collections of songs of spiritual realization currently extant in Tibetan literature. It exceeds even the song collection we have for Milarepa, Tibet's most famous singer. Shabkar's *Collected Songs* contains songs that did not make it into his *namtar*. At three volumes and 1,769 folios, it is the next largest single section of his collected works aside from his *Emanated Scriptures* (*Sprul pa'i glegs bam*). His *Collected Songs* is organized according to the places where he meditated, roughly paralleling the structure of the first volume of his autobiography.

Shabkar had a strong sense that his song collection would benefit Tibetans specifically. When the deity Machen Pomra bestows the title of "Singer of Tibet" upon Shabkar, Pomra observes that Shabkar's *Collected Songs* will bring great benefit to the faithful in Tibet.[24] In the aspiration prayers at the end of the second volume of this *Collected Songs*, Shabkar tells us that he left a collection of his songs "in order to benefit future generations of Tibetan people."[25] In a passage that demonstrates Shabkar's eloquence and humor at its best, Shabkar remarks that the gods Indra and Brahmā atop Mount Meru, despite possessing the seven articles of royalty, are captivated by the *Collected Songs* that Shabkar has left in Tibet.[26] Finally, in a prayer of auspiciousness sung in the third volume of his *Collected Songs*, Shabkar sings, "Bestow [your] blessing so that the songs sung by me /—the unprecedented eloquent Singer of Tibet—will benefit Tibet."[27] There is a sense in this passage that in addition to benefitting people spiritually, as songs of spiritual realization are meant to do, Shabkar intended his *Collected Songs* to benefit the imagined community of Tibet as well.

At the same time, Shabkar did not conceive of his *Collected Songs* as benefiting Tibet exclusively. In keeping with the universal outlook of his impartial perspective, Shabkar also prays that wherever a volume of his *Collected Songs* resides it may bring auspiciousness, good harvests, and happiness to that place.²⁸ Elsewhere, he prays that his *Collected Songs* will bring happiness to all countries.²⁹ Most expansively of all, he prays that all who see, hear, copy, recite, memorize, or touch his songs attain both temporary happiness and the ultimate happiness of buddhahood.³⁰

It is of no small significance that songs are a central part of Shabkar's identity as Tibet's spokesperson. Songs, verse, and oral tradition such as proverbs permeate every aspect of Tibetan life. In traditional Tibet, there were love songs for courtship, harvesting songs for work in the fields, work songs for the laborers, songs for caravaneers as they loaded animals, as well as songs for drinking, social gatherings, and festivals.³¹ Each different type of song had a specific name for it, such as "celebration song" (*rten 'brel*) or "song of lament" (*smreng glu*).³² There was and also continues to be a rich folk tradition and cultural vocabulary of proverbs, oral banter, riddling, and call and response. Within the religious context, monks and nuns chant liturgies, and both monastics and lay people recited daily prayers. Religious practitioners are also only permitted to practice certain teachings after having received an oral transmission (*lung*) from a qualified lama.

Within this context, Shabkar's ability to compose and perform songs extemporaneously made him well-liked by his audience. This ability also gave him authority. This is because, in addition to having a rich tradition of written literature, Tibetan culture is one that highly values the spoken word. For instance, as Alexandru Anton-Luca observes, "The value of a spoken contract outweighs that of a written one even nowadays."³³ He states, "A leader's most appealing quality remains oratory ability, even at the expense of other, more practical skills. The smooth-talking icon (kha bde lce bde can— literally, "possessing a quick tongue and pleasant speech") pervades Tibetan society at every level." At one point in his *Collected Songs*, Shabkar describes himself as "I, [the] eloquent singer unprecedented in Tibet."³⁴ Shabkar's oral skills gave him authority in his society.

## Contrasting Shabkar's Autobiography with Milarepa's Life Story

Despite his claims of being unprecedented, Shabkar's oral skills surely were not unprecedented in Tibetan history. When Tibetan Buddhists hear the title the "Singer of Tibet," the figure that most likely comes to mind is the eleventh-century poet-saint Milarepa. By referring to himself as "Singer of Tibet," Shabkar is aligning himself with Tibetan history's most famous singer. This is fitting both because Shabkar and his disciples considered him to be a reincarnation of Milarepa, and because Shabkar spent his entire life emulating his spiritual predecessor. Shabkar also closely modeled many aspects of his autobiography after Tsangnyön Heruka's *The Life of Milarepa*, as discussed in the introduction to this text. However, the things that Shabkar chose to do differently from Milarepa are noteworthy. These differences become especially important within the context of Shabkar's role as the "Singer of Tibet."

One of Tsangnyön Heruka's great literary innovations in *The Life of Milarepa* is to separate the story of Milarepa's life from his songs. In doing so, he improves the formal aspects of the story; he tightens the narrative pace and so forth.[35] In contrast, Shabkar does not separate song and story in this way. His use of song in his *namtar* differs from Heruka's in four other important ways. First, in contrast to his main literary model, which incorporates some thirty songs, Shabkar's autobiography includes over six hundred. The song-to-prose ratio is much higher in Shabkar's autobiography, which gives the impression of the work being fully saturated with verse and song.

Second, whereas Heruka opts to use songs at strategic moments to enhance the dramatic narrative of the text, Shabkar peppers the narrative of his autobiography liberally with songs and verse. Songs and verse are absent in part one of *The Life of Milarepa*, describing Milarepa's "ordinary worldly deeds." Songs are only present in the second part of the text, which describes Milarepa's "deeds of supreme peace and transcendence." The presence or absence of songs is used to help accentuate the divide between Milarepa's mundane and awakened states. By contrast, in Shabkar's autobiography, songs are used indiscriminately and pervasively. Songs and verse are present in all chapters of the text, whether they are describing Shabkar in pre- or post-awakened states. The songs form an integral part of the overall structure of his autobiography.

Third, while songs and verse are used exclusively in religious contexts in *The Life of Milarepa*, in Shabkar's autobiography, they permeate both mundane and religious moments. In *The Life of Milarepa*, songs and verse are used *exclusively* in religious as opposed to mundane contexts. By religious contexts, I mean dialogues between master and disciple, songs of spiritual advice, or songs sung in the context of meditative practice. Moreover, in *The Life of Milarepa*, only spiritually awakened beings such as Marpa, Milarepa, and the *ḍākinīs* sing songs. Milarepa's unawakened relatives, such as his sister Peta or his aunt, never sing.[36] Even Milarepa himself only sings for the first time in chapter 7 after he has undergone a substantive period of meditative retreat. By contrast, in Shabkar's autobiography, songs are sung in a variety of contexts, both religious and mundane, and by a variety of individuals, enlightened and unenlightened. For example, in addition to songs of spiritual advice and song exchanges between master and disciple, songs are also used in Shabkar's autobiography to negotiate, to persuade others, and to say farewell.[37] While it is true that Shabkar infuses his mundane exchanges with Buddhist ideas, it is not customary for the subject of songs of spiritual realization to be so quotidian.[38] In this respect, Shabkar's versification of even mundane exchanges is reminiscent of the versified dialogues of Tibetan opera. Moreover, singers in Shabkar's autobiography include a variety of ordinary beings, including ordinary laymen, laywomen, flowers, and animals.

Fourth, whereas Heruka does not include song dialogue in Milarepa's autobiography, Shabkar does. For example, in *The Life of Milarepa*, Milarepa will sing to his aunt, sister, a hunter, and young maidens, but his interlocutors always reply in prose speech, not in verse or song.[39] Although in Milarepa's *Collected Songs*, there are episodes where Milarepa engages in songful exchange with his disciples, in the biography proper, there are no song or verse dialogues. This is highly significant because it suggests that although Milarepa and his disciples *did* engage in frequent song exchange, Heruka chose not to have that reflected in the *namtar*. Why? Possibly to keep the size of the text down and in order to maintain the story's tight narrative arc. It is also possible that he did not deem the inclusion of all the songs necessary in order to convey the main point of the biography.

Overall, Shabkar's liberal and pervasive use of song has the effect of saturating his autobiography with the impression of being full of songs. In turn, this mirrors the way in which song and verse are an important part of the fabric of traditional Tibetan culture. The significance of this is that Shabkar's *namtar* reflects the pervasiveness of song in Tibetan life. A song-filled autobiography is indeed fitting for the autobiography of Tibet's singer. Thus, in the same way that the content of Shabkar's autobiography demonstrates the presence of Tibet as an imagined community, the form of his autobiography reflects the rhythms of everyday life in traditional Tibet. Shabkar had a deep understanding of the cultural rhythms of his audience. Shabkar tells us he structured his autobiography in "alternating poetry and prose in order to be pleasing to their ears."[40] In this analysis, we see that it also had the effect of making the form of his autobiography reflect its content.

## Folk Song in Shabkar's Autobiography

Not only did Shabkar infuse his autobiography with song, but the majority of his songs bear the mark of Tibetan folk songs. This is not to say that Shabkar's songs of spiritual realization were not influenced by the *kāvya* tradition or that his songs did not have a high level of religious content in them. However, in the context of this book's argument, I will focus on the folk aspects of Shabkar's songs.

Döndrup Gyel distinguishes two main types of Tibetan songs: "folk songs" (*dmangs glu*) and "religious songs" (*chos glu*).[41] Folk songs from different regions differ in terms of poetic meter and are referred to using different terminology such as *gzhas* in central Tibet and *glu* in Amdo.[42] Within these genres of folk song are a variety of subgenres. In Shabkar's home region of Amdo for instance, subgenres include "question and answer songs" (*dri ba dris len*), "love songs" (*la ye*), and "songs of praise" (*bstod glu*).[43] Despite these differences, however, folk songs are distinguished from religious songs because they express aspects of everyday life and the emotions that accompany them. Folk songs may contain religious content, but their main aim is not to convey religious truths unlike in religious songs. Folk songs also share formal characteristics such as meter, parallelism, refrain, numerical sequences, and colloquial vocalizations.[44] Folk songs have been passed down orally from generation to generation since ancient times.[45] In contrast to folk songs that arose from the lives of Tibet's ordinary people, religious songs originated from the songs sung by religious masters in Tibet beginning with Padmasambhava's disciples in the eighth century and continued by the great masters of the Later Transmission Period beginning in the tenth century.[46]

Shabkar's songs belong to the lineage of Tibet's religious songs but embrace the idiom of folk songs. Shabkar's songs share similarities with folk song in terms of both content and form. First, with respect to the subject matter of Shabkar's songs: although many of the songs address religious topics, approximately a third of the songs encompass worldly matters such as saying farewell, offering a greeting, expressing grief, praising places, or celebrating a happy occasion.[47] Although these songs may contain religious themes or vocabulary, their main purpose is to enhance the narrative of Shabkar's life story rather than to communicate lofty religious truths or spiritual experiences. Many of these songs also correspond to subgenres of folk song typical of the Amdo region such as "celebration songs" (*rten 'brel*), "songs of lament" (*smreng glu*), and "farewell songs" (*bde mo*).[48] When we compare the songs in Shabkar's autobiography to the typical subject matter of *gur*, the subject matter of Shabkar's songs becomes particularly significant. In the *History and Features of Gur* (*Bod kyi mgur glu byung 'phel gyi lo rgyus dang khyad chos*), Döndrup Gyel identifies seven typical topics for songs of spiritual realization:

1. Meditating in the mountains, recalling the lama's kindness, and supplicating to him
2. Meditating upon the lama's oral instructions or upon the way in which spiritual experience and realization arises
3. Encouraging fortunate ones in the dharma
4. Giving advice to others and encouraging oneself

5. In response to requests from patrons and disciples, expounding dharma that is appropriate to each one of them

6. Exposing and critiquing monks who are not abiding by their ethical vows

7. Providing oral letters to one's lama and disciples[49]

Many of Shabkar's songs do fall under these subject headings. But his decision to also incorporate songs that treat more mundane topics typical of folk songs has the effect of Tibetanizing his *namtar*, making what is already a form of indigenous literature be even more in the idiom of its people.

The formal aspects of Shabkar's songs also bear the influence of Tibetan folk song. Shabkar's songs are written in a variety of meters. Two meters that he frequently uses are the meters of Amdo folk song 8 (1 + 2 + 2 + 3) and Lhasa folk song 6 (2 + 2 + 2).[50] Below is an example of such a song in the Lhasa folk song meter. The original flows with great ease and is easy for a general audience to understand.

> Having placed the holy Lama endowed with characteristics
> As an ornament atop my crown,
> The desire to go to Mount Machen
> Arises in Tsokdruk Rangdröl.
>
> The white snow mountain Machen,
> A stone hut big enough for just one,
> Together with Tsokdruk Rangdröl—
> The karmic conditions for gathering have arisen.
>
> Birds that trumpet beautiful sounds,
> Wild animals that are beautiful and pleasant,
> and Tsokdruk Rangdröl—
> The karmic conditions for friendship have arisen.
>
> The oral instructions given by the Lama,
> The provisions given by the patrons,
> This illusory body with no illnesses
> The karmic conditions for assembly have arisen.
>
> With no adverse conditions or obstacles,
> And completely favorable conditions,
> To practice according to the way of the holy Dharma,
> The karmic conditions for accomplishment have arisen.

> When favorable and good conditions arise,
> I stay happily alone.
> From the slopes of the utterly white snow mountains
> The desire to sing songs arises.
>
> From now on, [for] me and those like me
> Who practice Dharma in this way,
> If conducive conditions arise,
> Such a feeling will arise.[51]

In addition to adopting a meter typical of folk songs from Lhasa, this song also possesses recurrent refrain, nature imagery, and unpretentious vocabulary, which are characteristics of Tibetan folk song.

The following example is from an Amdo folk song that exhibits the qualities of simplicity, flow, natural imagery, parallelism, and refrain that we see in many of Shabkar's songs:

> Happy are rock and junipers together
> And even happier are the ferns of Ganden
> [We sing] this happy song again and again.
>
> Tea and milk together are happy
> And even happier is the yellow cow.
> [We sing] this happy song again and again.
>
> Father and uncle together are happy
> And so to people of the same age
> [We sing] this happy song again and again.[52]

Parallelism and refrain are an integral component of Tibetan folk song.[53] Many of Shabkar's songs share stylistic similarities with this one. In a farewell to his childhood friend Dorjé Tséten, Shabkar sings a touching song that strongly resembles aspects of the Amdo folk song quoted above. Each stanza begins with the parallel phrase "Born from . . ." and continues to compare Shabkar's relationship with this close friend to the relationships of animals in nature. The lines "I will be able to return soon—you'll see. / I pray that we will meet again" act as a refrain that is repeated after each stanza of the song. This makes the structure highly formulaic, as is typical of folk songs:[54]

> Born from the vulture, king of birds
> Two fledglings together since childhood

Now, here, it is time to spread our wings
Unattached to my nest
I will fly off to other places
You, for now [please] take care,
I will be able to return soon—let's see.
I pray that we will meet again.

Born from the wild yak,
Two calves together since childhood . . .

In the presence of the same Lama, [we] listened to the Dharma
Two friends together since childhood . . .

Numerical sequences are another common poetic figure in Tibetan folk song.[55] This is unsurprising because such sequences serve as a good memory aid, make the songs accessible, and make it easy for large gatherings to sing the songs together. The following song is sung by Shabkar in Amdo as he visits a series of villages. I have excerpted the first two stanzas, but the rest of the song basically continues this numbering motif, continuing on with what men and women "need":[56]

Supreme Lama who possesses blessings
Bless the body, speech, and mind of those assembled here
Listen to this song that says what
Chieftains, men, and women need:

One—to have good words
Two—to have good thoughts
Three—to speak with honesty
Four—to think carefully through things
Five—to be impartial
Six—to have few desires for himself
This is what chieftains need. . . .

Another aspect of Amdo folk song that Shabkar incorporates is the use of vocal interjections such as "O o," "Ah oo," "Kho re," "Heh heh," and "Ya yi ya yi." Shabkar's spiritual predecessor the Buddhist master Kelden Gyatso (1607–1677) also weaves such vocal interjections into his songs.[57] Shabkar's "The Song [called] Laughter of Mañjuśrī and Sarasvatī" is one song that includes such interjections:

O o! To the exquisite manifestation, [I] continuously
Ah oo! Pay homage through the power of the most affectionate devotion

Kho re! Lama Mañjuśrī, having laughed,
Heh Heh! Marvelous, how good, this essential point—yah!
Ya yi ya yi![58]

This song is particularly remarkable for its ability to effortlessly incorporate the most virtuosic of poetic devices from the *Kāvyādarśa* and include vocal interjections in the style of Amdo folk song, while maintaining a sense of ease, jest, and playful laughter.

In addition to songs that are in the style of folk song, Shabkar includes a handful of actual folk songs in his autobiography. For example, in the section of his autobiography describing his pilgrimage to central Tibet, he includes the folk songs sung by his travel companions, many of whom were not monks but ordinary merchants and pilgrims.[59] It is highly unconventional to include songs that do not contain any religious content in a *namtar*. And while, admittedly, he includes only a few such songs, the fact that he does so at all signals that the folk songs of the people were important enough to be included in the autobiography of a revered spiritual master. Their inclusion makes the indirect argument that Shabkar takes the folk traditions of his people seriously. By including these folk songs sung by ordinary folk, Shabkar demonstrates that he is truly "Tibet's Singer."

Shabkar's inclusion of both folk songs and folk-influenced songs in his autobiography is important for the imagined community of Tibet. A comparative case study from nineteenth-century Europe is useful for appreciating this point. Folk songs played an important role in the rise of nationalism in nineteenth-century Europe. In his studies of popular songs, Johannn Georg Herder (1744–1803) noticed how folk songs played an important role in "constituting national identities and securing the social cohesion of the people."[60] In contrast to other scholars, who focused on the study of "high" literature, Herder considered folk songs to be "national treasures" because they expressed the national character of the people.[61] Indeed, the folk songs and melodies sung widely during the revolutionary and Napoleonic periods served as the "unofficial national anthems in the first years of the nineteenth century" and became the basis of national anthems later on.[62]

Folk songs "can be considered as both a representation and a catalyst of the identity-forming processes,"[63] and indeed, the prevalence of the folk song style in Shabkar's autobiography infuses the work with a strong Tibetan identity. We should not take this point lightly in the context of the nineteenth-century Tibetan Buddhist world. The Bhutanese Legal Code of

1729, for instance, saw wandering orators as a potentially subversive threat due to the sense of proto-national identity that they spread.[64] In the same way that the nineteenth-century *volk* movement played an important role in the creation of national European literary canons that forms the basis for European national literatures in the eighteenth and nineteenth centuries, Shabkar's autobiography provided an antecedent for a national literature based in the vernacular in the twentieth century. Shabkar's incorporation of a vast number of songs that bear aspects of Tibetan folk songs into his autobiography is not merely a matter of literary style. Instead, this incorporation helped Shabkar, through his persona as the Singer of Tibet, to open up a discursive space for the articulation of Tibet as a modern nation.

The role of popular songs in sustaining the Tibetan national consciousness in contemporary times also helps us to appreciate the significance of Shabkar's employment of folk songs and elements from folk song into his autobiography. Lama Jabb has observed that "Tibetan popular music, like contemporary literature with which it is closely interlocked through lyric writing, is one of the artistic means through which Tibetans imagine themselves as a nation."[65] The folk songs of Shabkar's era are the rough equivalent of popular songs in the contemporary era. In the same way that modern Tibetan song writers and musicians—who serve as "the principal agents in the construction of a pan-Tibetan identity"—use a combination of melody and language to convey shared values, beliefs, and histories, the mode of folk song in Shabkar's autobiography creates a sense of pan-Tibetan identity.[66] Shabkar was not conscious or intentional in creating nationalistic sentiment, but the ubiquity and importance of song in Tibetan culture, combined with his Buddhist message and persona as Tibet's singer, gives a nationalistic dimension to his incorporation of folk styles into his autobiography.

The significance of folk song in the rise of nationalism also leads me to revisit one of the main components of Benedict Anderson's concept of the rise of imagined communities. According to Anderson, "the convergence of capitalism and print technology on the fatal diversity of human language created the possibility of a new form of imagined community, which in its basic morphology set the stage for the modern nation."[67] While Anderson makes a robust argument about the role that print-capitalism played in the rise of the modern nation in Europe and the Americas, the case of the "imagined nation" found in Shabkar's autobiography and in the use of popular songs to sustain the Tibetan national consciousness challenges the necessity of a print-capitalism culture for the rise of national identities in other contexts. It is true that Tibet had a robust printing culture in the nineteenth century, and Shabkar did have physical copies of his *namtar* printed. However, his main means of disseminating his message was oral. Shabkar traveled all over the

Tibetan plateau, singing his message. He self-reported meeting thousands of people while on pilgrimage, with his fame reaching even Bodh Gayā, India.[68] The majority of the population in early modern Tibet was illiterate. Their main form of literature was a rich tradition of orature, including folk songs, storytelling, bardic epics, and opera. Because Anderson's theory rests on certain assumptions about literature, the part of it that defines literature as based on print-capitalism does not apply to early modern Tibetan culture.

However, literature can play a role in the formation of national identity even when it is not in a written format. As Azar Gat has observed, "the emphasis on literacy has been largely misleading, because illiterate societies had their own potent means of wide-scale cultural transmission."[69] He cites dances, plays, games, festivals, and the oral epics of wandering bards as examples. Shabkar's *namtar* reminds us that literature can contribute to a sense of national identity even in oral forms.

## Shabkar's Links to the Founder of Tibetan Opera

Tibetan opera (*lhamo*) is an indigenous Tibetan dramatic art form that emerged shortly after the Later Dissemination Period of Buddhism into Tibet. Tibetan opera began when its founder, Tangtong Gyelpo (1361–1485), invented the genre as a way to teach Buddhist ideals to the ordinary populace while raising funds for his bridge-building projects in central Tibet.[70] Gyelpo drew on a foundation of Tibetan folk songs and dances that have pre-Buddhist roots.[71] His use of a popular art form to teach Buddhist ideals parallels Shabkar's efforts to incorporate aspects of folk literatures into his *namtar* in order to make his message accessible for a wide audience.

Shabkar shares reincarnational links with Tangtong Gyelpo through a complex network of Tibetan Buddhist deities and historical figures. The concept of *tulku*, or reincarnations of enlightened Buddhist figures, is unique to Tibetan Buddhism. Drawing from the Mahāyāna concept of the three bodies, the idea of the *tulku* emerged in thirteenth-century Tibet, with the Second Karmapa traditionally cited as being the first reincarnate lama. *Tulkus* are believed to be the reincarnations of famous Buddhist figures. Shabkar self-identified as both the reincarnation of the founder of Tibetan opera, Tangtong Gyelpo, and the bodhisattva of compassion, Avalokiteśvara.[72] Avalokiteśvara is also considered to be Tibet's patron deity and the father of the Tibetan people.[73] Tangtong Gyelpo was considered to be an emanation of Amitābha, Avalokiteśvara, and Padmasambhava.[74] Amitābha is the buddha who presides over the western paradise. Padmasambhava was the tantric Buddhist master who played an instrumental role in the transmission of Buddhism to Tibet in the eighth century CE. Amitābha, Avalokiteśvara, and Padmasambhava reinforce each other's roles in Tibetan Buddhist history: Avalokiteśvara and Padmasambhava are considered to be emanations of Amitābha, and their activities are revealed in epic literature beginning in the twelfth century.[75] Thus, all of these figures are interlinked with Shabkar and Tangtong Gyalpo through reincarnational networks.

Shabkar's position within the reincarnational networks of Tangtong Gyelpo, Avalokiteśvara, Padmasambhava, and the genealogical networks of Machen Pomra and other indigenous Tibetan deities grounds him deeply in Tibetan history, religion, literature, kinship networks, and territory. Moreover, his reincarnational relationship with Tangtong Gyelpo associates him indirectly with the tradition of Tibetan opera. His reincarnational links with Avalokiteśvara and Padmasambhava associate him with key moments in Tibetan Buddhist history and identity. His genealogical relationship to Machen Pomra links him to Tibet's landscape and kinship networks. This deep grounding in the history, religion, literature, territory, and kinship networks of Tibet is apt for an individual who self-identified as Tibet's singer.

In addition to being linked to Tangtong Gyelpo through reincarnation, Shabkar's autobiography also bears the influence of aspects of the genre of Tibetan opera invented by Tangtong Gyelpo. In particular, Shabkar's *namtar* shares the following characteristics with Tibetan opera: adopts the conceit of orality, uses songs in a pervasive manner, is a popular art form, is of long duration, incorporates vernacular dialogue, and capitalizes on a heightened emotional register. While these characteristics are not unique to Tibetan opera, the combined presence of them reflects the general ethos of the genre of Tibetan opera.

## The Conceit of Orality in Shabkar's Autobiography

One of the formal hallmarks of Tibetan opera is that the script consists of prose passages interspersed with songs and versified passages. The prose passages, which give background information and advance the plot, serve as the basic structural skeleton of the text, while the verse passages flesh out scenes. The recitation of the main text is also punctuated by episodes of song and dance.[76] Songs are also sung in a range of situations and by a wide variety of characters. In Shabkar's autobiography, as in Tibetan opera, songs are used pervasively and by many characters in different contexts. Shabkar's autobiography thus reflects the way that song and verse forms are deeply embedded in Tibetan culture and reflected in its folk literature. Both Shabkar's autobiography and the Lhamo genres reflect how song and dance are a fundamental part of everyday life in Tibetan culture.[77]

Although Tibet has a well-established tradition of the written word, orality and aurality were and continue to be a fundamental part of Tibetan culture. As discussed in the section on folk song, folk songs and oral traditions pervade every aspect of Tibetan culture. In addition to the robust tradition of Tibetan folk song, there is also a rich folk tradition and cultural vocabulary of proverbs, oral banter, riddling, and call and response. Additionally, eloquence is an important and respected character trait in Tibetan society.[78] The potency and primacy of the oral has its roots in the pre-literate and pre-Buddhist traditions of imperial Tibet, where its cultural, religious, and social structure were upheld through daily rituals and the oral recitation of origin myths, royal genealogies, historic myths, and "power-affirming tales" by national bards.[79] Thus, from the very beginning, the national culture of Tibet was deeply rooted in oral genres.

Tibetan opera belongs to Tibet's rich tradition of orature. The Lhamo tradition, despite having a written script, is primarily an oral theatrical art. Traditionally, many of its performers were illiterate and learned the text orally from their teachers.[80] And although there exists a written libretto for each opera (also coincidentally called a *namtar*), performers have considerable freedom with regard to how they perform certain sections of the opera.[81] This oral dimension of the folk literatures and arts that form the foundations of Tibetan culture are preserved in the form of an oral conceit in Shabkar's *namtar*. Despite being looked down upon by elite monastic critics, Shabkar's incorporation of elements of folk tradition—such as this oral conceit—help his autobiography resonate more profoundly with his early modern Tibetan audience.

While Shabkar dictated the first volume of his autobiography to his disciple Sangyé Rinchen, he wrote down the second volume of the text.[82] Nevertheless, both volumes are framed as if they were being recounted orally. In the introductory verses to both volumes of his autobiography, he tells his audience to "listen happily" to his story.[83] Throughout the autobiography, he maintains the oral conceit of "saying" or "telling" his life story.[84] Of course, many sections of his life story and all of his songs initially existed only in oral form, until he wrote them down. He allows the "oral residue" of his life story and songs to remain in their written version.[85]

Although Shabkar's oral conceits mirror the ethos of Tibetan opera, his main influence for his work's oral framing seems to have been his main literary predecessor: Tsangyön Heruka's *The Life of Milarepa*. Heruka's text is framed by three levels of oral conceit. At the first level, he frames the story with the same beginning used in Buddhist *sūtras*: "Thus did I hear."[86] This elevates Milarepa's status to that of a Buddha, and also implies that Milarepa's life story is orally transmitted dharma that the author heard directly from an authoritative source. Indeed, Heruka informs the reader that he is telling

Milarepa's life story "as it was recounted by an extraordinary master"[87] and that his work represents a record of "the Jetsün's words exactly as he spoke them."[88] This concept of an unbroken aural lineage was also central to how the Buddha's teaching derived their authority, and was central to the identity of the Kagyü (literally "oral transmission") sect to which both Heruka and Milarepa belonged.

The second level of oral conceit in Heruka's work is in the story's main narrative, where the narrator (Tsangnyön Heruka) tells the story of Rechungpa, which he heard from an enlightened master. The third level is a sub-narrative, where Rechungpa (Milarepa's disciple) asks his teacher Milarepa to tell his life story, and where Milarepa then tells his own life story. This oral framing of *The Life of Milarepa*, with its layered levels of oral conceit, makes it compatible with the primacy of the oral in traditional Tibetan culture. Although Shabkar's oral conceit is mostly modeled after Milarepa's, it also resonates with the oral ethos of Tibetan opera.

## Further Parallels with Tibetan Opera

Tibetan opera is a form of popular theater.[89] Unlike the traditions of Peking opera, classical Indian theater, or the Noh dramas of Japan, which were the dramatic arts enjoyed by the elites, Lhamo is linked to the tradition of popular song and dance and was performed during folk festivals in traditional Tibet.[90] The atmosphere of Lhamo performances was and continues to be informal and relaxed, with the audience coming and going at leisure, and children sometimes going on the "stage" to touch the actors.[91] Because the performances were designed for a broad audience, spectators from all walks of life were able to understand the character's identities through a combination of visual conventions and intuition.[92]

Similarly, Shabkar wrote his autobiography for individuals from all walks of life, ranging from ordinary Tibetans to the educated elite. In his own words, he sought to compose his autobiography in a style that would "please the ears of all—superior, inferior and middling [capacities]."[93] Tibetan Buddhist life stories, which were written for various reasons, were not always aimed at a wide audience. Sometimes, the target audience was elite and educated.[94] Shabkar's autobiography, however, embraces an inclusive attitude akin to the ethos of Tibetan folk genres such as Lhamo. These folk genres portray Buddhist truths in an accessible way to broad audiences. In this way, Shabkar's desire to broadcast his Buddhist message to the broad populace shares in the spirit of the Lhamo genre.

Tibetan opera is a genre of theatre that takes a long time to perform, rather than just a couple of hours, as for Euro-American opera or musicals.

Performed most typically during Tibetan festivals, at minimum, it lasts the entire day; sometimes, it can even last for three days or a week.[95] Shabkar's autobiography shares this characteristic of length with Tibetan opera. Although Shabkar's autobiography is not the longest example of the genre in Tibetan literature, it is certainly lengthy by the standards of Tibetan life writing. At just under 1,550 folios, it is five times the length of his main literary model *The Life of Milarepa* and ten times longer than his spiritual predecessor Kelden Gyatso's biography. One could even say that Shabkar's *namtar* is thus the epic or opera of *namtars*. Shabkar's decision to create such a long spiritual autobiography went against the aesthetics of literary critics such as the Third Tukwan in the nineteenth century. The Third Tukwan was critical of authors who produced a "giant book" that incorporated a variety of songs, letters, sermons, and so forth.[96] Shabkar's autobiography reflects the ethos of Tibetan folk literature, which tends to have no restrictions on its length.

A further similarity between Shabkar's autobiography and Tibetan opera is the incorporation of dialogue in the vernacular. In the Lhamo tradition, the show follows a formal script in literary Tibetan that is enlivened with inserted dialogue.[97] While the majority of the dialogue captured in Shabkar's autobiography follows the convention of classic Tibetan literature, there are a few points where he includes vernacular vocabulary and grammatical structures, especially elements from the Amdo dialect. For example, when Shabkar lies to his mother in order to secure her permission to leave, he says to her that he will return from Sokpo after gathering enough provisions to sustain his practice at Trashikhyil, the hermitage near to his home village. She replies, "If that is the case, that is all right," using a grammatical construction pervasive in the Amdo region (*de yin na chog gi*).[98] Another example occurs when a person asks Shabkar whether or not he knows how to build a meditation hut, and the questioner uses the question construction standard across Amdo dialects of (*e* + verb).[99] There are also many small phrases from the Amdo dialects that pepper the words of Amdo speakers in the text, including the word used to respect a brother or an older person (*a bo*);[100] the expression *gda' ye*, which translates to "is it there?";[101] and *dga' ldan po*,[102] which is an exclamation akin to "oh my goodness" that is used in some dialects of the Amdo region. According to the conventions of classical Tibetan literature, it is not acceptable to include vernacular language in the life story of a Tibetan Buddhist saint. As discussed above, the Third Tukwan, for example, opposed the use of colloquialisms in the *namtar* genre. Thus, in incorporating small amounts of Amdo dialect, Shabkar is pushing the boundaries of convention and implicitly arguing for the inclusion of the vernacular into "respected" forms of literature.

A heightened emotional register is one of the trademarks of Tibetan opera. One of Tangtong Gyelpo's main objectives in inventing the genre was to inspire the audience towards Buddhist values. One of the ways that this is done is through the skillful means (Skt. *upāya*) of a heightened emotional register that aims to generate an emotional response from the reader. "Skillful means" is a Mahāyāna Buddhist concept where the teacher may use whatever means necessary if it effectively conveys Buddhist truths to his audience. Indeed, ethnographic research has revealed that Tibetan audiences are not satisfied if they are not emotionally moved by a Lhamo performance.[103]

Reminiscent of Tibetan opera, Shabkar's autobiography exhibits a heightened emotional register, particularly in the very first sections of the text that describe his life before he reached enlightenment. One of the most dramatic scenes in the text occurs when he attempts to convince his mother to give him permission to renounce his householder's status to become a monk. The scene involves extended versified exchanges between Shabkar, his mother, and his sister.[104] To give an idea of the dramatic emotional register of the characters' speeches, I will quote a passage from the mother's speech:

> My dear son whom I have brought up since you were young,
> Having tossed out your mother and gone to some other place.
> [Even] a little *dri* that is an animal that does not separate from its mother,
> Son, you separate from your mother and run off to some place.
> Son, you are like the eyes on my forehead,
> If you go far away, I am like a blind person.
> Son, you are like the heart in my chest,
> If you go far away, I will be like dead.
> Son, you are like my limbs,
> If you go far away, I will be like a cripple.
> Thus, listen with your ear to mother
> You must stay where I can see you.[105]

Shabkar's mother pulls all the stops in terms of using emotions to convince her son to stay. Furthermore, the parallelism in her verses is reminiscent of that in Tibetan folk song and adds a further dimension of performativity to the passage. Shabkar could have described the entire incident in a couple of lines, but clearly chose to draw it out.

Shabkar's embellishments are especially apparent alongside other autobiographies, such as Jamgön Kongtrül's, where a truly dramatic or tragic event is reduced to a few lines of terse prose. In Jamgön Kongtrül's autobiography, for example, he describes a difficult period that his family underwent in his youth. Due to political conflict in the region, he notes: "All families, high and low, without regard for status, were brought to ruin, and even my old father was thrown into prison. The suffering went on and on. The general situation being so bad, with the heavy taxation and confiscation, my old mother said, "You needn't stay even one more day. You should leave in the face of such bad circumstances, and go to a monastery." She assured me that she would be able to get by somehow."[106] Like Milarepa's family, Jamgön Kongtrül's family had undergone tremendous suffering. However, in contrast to Shabkar's autobiography, Kongtrül does not attempt to maximize the dramatic effect of the incident in any way, but rather, describes it in a detached and matter-of-fact manner.

Still, I would be oversimplifying the matter if I traced the heightened emotional register of Shabkar's autobiography solely to the ethos of Tibetan opera. Shabkar's main literary model, *The Life of Milarepa,* is also famous for its use of a heightened emotional register. One of the most dramatic scenes in *The Life of Milarepa* is a scene where Milarepa's widowed and destitute mother discovers her drunk son:

> My mother was inside roasting barley and heard me. "What is this?" she wondered. "This voice sounds like my son's. But nowhere on earth is there anyone more miserable than me and my children, so how could he be singing?"
>
> Not believing what she heard, she came to look. She recognized me and, in her astonishment, cast away the tongs in her right hand and the barley whisk in her left, leaving the roasting barley to burn. Carrying a stick in her right hand and a handful of ashes in her left, she flew down the big steps, leapt over the small ones, and appeared outside. She threw the ashes in my face and struck me on the head several times with the stick, crying, "Father Mila Sherab Gyaltsen, a son such as this has been born to you! Your family line has been broken. Look upon the fate that has befallen us, mother and children." With this she fainted and fell to the ground.[107]

The scene continues with Milarepa's sister reprimanding her brother, the mother regaining consciousness, and Milarepa promising his mother to learn black magic to seek revenge upon his uncle and aunt. It is atypical for Tibetan Buddhist autobiographies to dwell on scenes that describe mundane aspects of a spiritual master's life in technicolor detail. The heightened emotional register in Shabkar's autobiography was influenced by *The Life of Milarepa* as well.

## Echoes of the Gésar Epic

The Gésar epic is often referred to as the longest epic in the world. Gésar is believed by Tibetans to have been a king of the eastern Tibetan polity of Ling in the eleventh century. The Gésar epic is chanted by bards.[108] The oral tradition of the Gésar bards emerged in eastern Tibet beginning in the eleventh century.[109] Although it would be anachronistic to call Gésar a nationalist figure because he was traditionally not thought to be the ruler of a centralized state, he has in contemporary times become a symbol of the Tibetan nationality.[110] The close link between the figure of the bard, oral history, and state power is an ancient theme in Tibetan literature and culture. Shabkar's autobiography does not make direct reference to the Gésar epic, but there are elements of the text and his persona as "Singer of Tibet" that reverberate with Tibet's longstanding bardic tradition. Before the arrival of Buddhism, bardic figures upheld Tibetan cultural, religious, and social structure through the oral recitation of origin myths, royal genealogies, historic myths, and "power-affirming tales" in the imperial court.[111]

Shabkar is loosely associated with the Gésar epic because he is thought to be an emanation of Avalokiteśvara and had a close relationship with Padmasambhava via dream-visions of the eighth century figure. Similarly, Gésar is considered to be an emanation of the three deities Mañjuśrī, Vajrapāṇi, Avalokiteśvara, as well as Padamasambhava's earthly representative.[112] Moreover, the Gésar tradition was believed to have been initiated by Avalokiteśvara in the twelfth century, when the bodhisattva witnessed the Tibetans in perpetual war.[113] In addition to these reincarnational associations, Shabkar also shares loose genealogical links to Gésar, through his descent from an ancestral deity who is part of Machen Pomra's retinue. Gésar is considered to be the son of the mountain god Gendzo and the female sky-goddess Manéné.[114] In indigenous Tibetan thought, Gendzo is believed to have a special relationship with Machen Pomra.

Most significantly, Shabkar shares with the Gésar bards the ability to recite songs and poems extemporaneously. The Gésar tradition began orally and was only written down in the fifteenth century.[115] The epic is a living one that revolves around the charisma of the visionary bards who continue to add new episodes. Their visions inspire oral verses, which are then subsequently written down. Like the bards, Shabkar is able to compose and perform songs extemporaneously through the power of his meditative realization. Both songs of spiritual realization and bardic verse tap into the primacy of the oral in Tibetan culture and the value placed on verse and song.

Although Shabkar's songs do not draw from the heroic songs (*dpa' glu*) of the Gésar epic in a concrete way as in the case of the treasure revealer Tarē Lhamo (1938–2002),[116] we cannot dismiss his autobiography's loose associations with the tradition as just reflecting a shared ethos. There are three pronounced similarities between Shabkar's autobiography and the Gésar epic. First, Shabkar's autobiography was meant for a popular audience, just as the

Gésar tradition was a form of popular literature that found its main audience in laypeople.[117] Samten Karmay places the milieu of Gésar among hunters, brigands, and traders "who read or told episodes that suited the actual conditions of their overnight stops in lonely places."[118] The songs within the epic share the names—*glu, gzhas,* and *mgur*—and characteristics of folk songs.[119] The recitation of Gésar was prohibited in monasteries and often viewed by elite monastic scholars with disdain as a form of popular religion.[120] As discussed earlier in this chapter, one of the leading literary critics of Tibetan Buddhist biography contemporaneous to Shabkar, the Third Tukwan, was opposed to merging aspects of popular literatures such as the Gésar epic with the *namtar* genre because he felt that such popular genres did not reflect the greatness of the *namtar*'s subject.

Second, the Gésar epic is thought to be one of the longest examples of epic literature in the world.[121] To this day, it is a living and growing text with new chapters being continually added. Its aesthetics of length is shared by Shabkar's autobiography, which is one of the longest examples of the genre of *namtar*.

Third, both the Gésar epic and Shabkar's autobiography share the literary format of prose narrative passages interspersed with songs. The Gésar epic consists of prose narrative passages that are punctuated by songs sung by various characters. These songs, like those from everyday Tibetan life, vary in their subject matter and are sung by different singers.[122] Likewise, Shabkar composed his autobiography in alternating prose and verse in order to make it appealing to a wide audience. This aspect of both Shabkar's autobiography and the Gésar epic reflect the way in which songs are a ubiquitous part of everyday life in Tibetan culture.

By alluding to aspects of the Gésar epic in his songs, Shabkar roots his songs in the sensibilities of the folk tradition and Tibet's ancient bardic tradition. Including aspects of these genres in his *namtar* causes the text to reflect the rhythm of Tibet's folk literature. This is befitting for the man who styled himself as the "Singer of Tibet." By incorporating vernacular genres in to his *namtar*, Shabkar opened up the discursive space for the possibility of an elite literature that embraces the vernacular ethos. In turn, this serves as one of the antecedents to the establishment of a nationalist modern Tibetan literature in the 1980s.

# 4

# Reviving and Adapting Two Foundational Myths

There is perhaps no deity more significant to the Tibetan people than Avalokiteśvara. Avalokiteśvara, or Chenrézik in Tibetan, is the Buddhist bodhisattva of compassion. Originally an Indian deity, Avalokiteśvara was first introduced into Tibet as part of the buddha Vairocana's retinue during the imperial period (mid-seventh through mid-ninth centuries). During this period, knowledge of the deity seems to have been limited to the Tibetan royal court, as there is no extant evidence of his widespread worship. From the eleventh through thirteenth centuries, figures such as the treasure revealers and members of the Kadam sect propagated the worship of Avalokiteśvara and his six-syllable mantra on a wide scale. By the twelfth century, Avalokiteśvara came to be known as Tibet's destined deity and the progenitor of the Tibetan people. The myth that the king Songsten Gampo from the imperial period was an incarnation of Avalokiteśvara also began during this period. Today, Avalokiteśvara is deeply embedded in the Tibetan national consciousness as Tibet's patron deity and the father of the Tibetan people, and as a deity who continues to be incarnated as Buddhist leaders such as the Dalai Lamas and Karmapas. Indeed, Avalokiteśvara is the deity with the most claimed incarnations in Tibetan history.[1]

Another important figure in Tibet's national imagination is Padmasambhava. According to the literature of the treasure tradition from the twelfth century onwards, Padmasambhava was an Indian tantric Buddhist master invited by the Tibetan king Trisong Détsen to tame Tibet's local deities after they prevented the Indian abbot Śāntarakṣita from teaching Buddhism in Tibet. The treasure literature portrays Padmasambhava as using magical powers to subdue the deities, thereby playing a fundamental role in the historical establishment of Buddhism in Tibet. Historical evidence, however, suggests that this famous legend of Padmasambhava was created after the eleventh century by the treasure tradition of the Nyingma sect. Some scholars even go as far as to doubt his historicity because he is absent from some key early sources of Tibet's imperial period. Nevertheless, despite the views of historians, the legend of Padmasambhava as one of the founding figures of Buddhism in Tibet remains firmly entrenched in the minds of Tibetan Buddhists today.

Both Avalokiteśvara and Padmasambhava figure prominently in Shabkar's autobiography. Shabkar engaged in spiritual practices associated with both figures, and describes both figures appearing to him repeatedly in dream visions to give spiritual instructions to him. Shabkar also claimed to be an incarnation of Avalokiteśvara and of Padmasambhava's disciple Drenpa Namkha.[2] Shabkar revives and adapts the myths of Avalokiteśvara from the *Maṇi Kabum*, the *Book of Kadam*, and the works of the Fifth Dalai Lama and incorporates them into his autobiography. And he also revives and adapts the myth of Padmasambhava from the treasure works of the early Tibetan renaissance period. In this chapter, we will explore how Shabkar revives and adapts myths about both figures.

Shabkar understood his engagement with both Avalokiteśvara and Padmasambhava within the religious context of the path to buddhahood. However, when we examine Shabkar's engagement with both figures from the lens of cultural nationalism, Shabkar's adaptation of these myths takes on an additional significance. According to Anthony Smith's ethnosymbolist theory of nationhood, myths of ethnic origin and election—that is, myths that describe the origin of a people and myths about a deity choosing a particular ethnic group—serve as a crucial building block for a nation.[3] Mythic specialists are influential figures who revive, adapt, and propagate these myths to ensure their perpetuation. Within this model, the myth of Avalokiteśvara qualifies as both a myth of ethnic origin and election because he is both Tibet's destined deity and the father of the Tibetan people. The myth of Padmasambhava is a myth of religious origin because Padmasambhava is remembered as having played a key role in establishing Buddhism in Tibet. Shabkar served as a mythic specialist: he revived, adapted, and propagated the myths of Avalokiteśvara and Padmasambhava, thus perpetuating two myths foundational to Tibetan national identity.

Through adopting the persona of the Singer of Tibet, Shabkar evokes not just the eleventh century poet-saint Milarepa, but also the bards of the imperial period. During pre-Buddhist times, these bards sustained the Tibetan Empire's cultural, religious, and social structure through daily rituals and the oral recitation of origin myths, royal genealogies, historic myths, and power-affirming tales.[4] The connection between Tibet's imperial bards and Shabkar's persona of the Singer of Tibet is reflected in how the term is translated in the English translation of the first volume of Shabkar's autobiography. The translation team has glossed "gangs can bod kyi glu dbyangs mkhan" as "the Bard of Tibet, Land of Snows."[5] By evoking the bards of the imperial period,

Shabkar unconsciously emphasizes his role as a mythic specialist. However, Shabkar's role differs from Smith's "mythic specialist" in a crucial way. Instead of emphasizing the ethnic election of the Tibetan people, he emphasizes the *Buddhist* aspect of the myths of Avalokiteśvara and Padmasambhava.

When Shabkar revives and adapts the myths of Avalokiteśvara and Padmasambhava, two figures foundational to Tibet as a Buddhist nation, he plays the role of Smith's mythological specialist. In this chapter, I demonstrate how Shabkar revives and adapts the myths of Avalokiteśvara and Padmasambhava from the early treasure texts, *Book of Kadam,* and works by the Fifth Dalai Lama to reinforce the idea of the Tibetan peoples' Buddhist destiny in general and their special status as Avalokiteśvara's chosen people in particular. In a departure from the texts of the Tibetan renaissance period, Shabkar does not dwell on Tibet's imperial past. Instead, he envisions Tibet as a Buddhist imagined community led by Avalokiteśvara (incarnated in the form of the Dalai Lamas) in which Buddhist historical-mythical figures continue to intervene. For Shabkar, the glue that holds the Tibetans together is not ethnic, but religious. Shabkar's adaptation of the myth is unmistakably forward-looking, and indeed, his vision of the Tibetan people's collective destiny presages the modern Tibetan nation-in-exile.

## The Myth of Avalokiteśvara as Tibet's Patron Deity

Traditional Tibetan Buddhist histories such as Sakyapa Sönam Gyeltsen's *The Clear Mirror of Royal Genealogies* present a story that continues to inform the Tibetan national imagination to this day, a story of Avalokiteśvara as Tibet's destined deity.[6] The story begins with a prophesy by the historical Buddha that Avalokiteśvara is the deity who is destined to tame the beings—local deities, people, and animals—of Tibet, the Land of Snows. After a blessing by the Buddha Amitābha and a solemn vow by Avalokiteśvara, Avalokiteśvara turns to witness the sufferings of the beings in Tibet. Moved by compassion for the beings he sees in Lhasa, which would become the capital city of Tibet, Avalokiteśvara sheds two tears. The tears manifest as the deities Bhrikuti and Tārā, who will later be reborn as a Nepalese princess and Chinese princess, respectively. Avalokiteśvara also blesses a monkey, who marries a rock-ogress to father the Tibetan people. The moment that Avalokiteśvara realizes the Tibetans are ripe for conversion to Buddhism, he radiates light rays from his eyes that result in the conception of the Nepalese and Chinese princesses who will come to Tibet to marry the king. From his mouth radiates the six-syllable mantra of Avalokiteśvara and from his heart emanates light rays that result in the birth of king Songsten Gampo. Buddhism was first imported into Tibet during the reign of Songsten Gampo. Traditional Tibetan histories present Avalokiteśvara's identity as the father of the Tibetan people, the destined deity of Tibet, and the emperor Songsten Gampo as a fait accompli. However, historical evidence tells a different version of the story.

According to extant art historical evidence, the figure Avalokiteśvara was first introduced to Tibet during the imperial period as part of the Maṇḍala of Eight Great Bodhisattvas. In this *maṇḍala*, the buddha Vairocana is the central deity and Avalokiteśvara is one of the accompanying bodhisattvas. The Maṇḍala of Eight Great Bodhisattvas was an important symbol of the Tibetan Empire,[7] with the emperor himself depicted as Mahāvairocana.[8] Images of Avalokiteśvara in cave shrines and paintings from Dunhuang caves suggest a flourishing Avalokiteśvara cult from the late eighth to early eleventh centuries. Based on this evidence, Michelle Wang suggests that the cult of Avalokiteśvara may not merely have been a product of the later transmission of Buddhism to Tibet in the eleventh century, but may instead have had earlier roots in this period.[9] Still, both Hugh Richardson and Matthew Kapstein doubt that the cult of Vairocana had reached Tibet by the seventh century.[10] Thus, we can conclude that Avalokiteśvara entered Tibet as part of Vairocana's pantheon, sometime in the eighth century.

Based on the scholarship currently available, Sam van Schaik argues that we cannot rule out the possibility of the popularization of the six-syllable mantra in the oral tradition before the eleventh century.[11] However, it is not until the tenth century that we have our first extant textual evidence of Avalokiteśvara's growing popularity in Tibet.[12] One of the most important early texts that promoted the legend of Avalokiteśvara as Tibet's destined deity was the *Maṇi Kabum*, a collection of treasure texts dated from the mid-twelfth to mid-thirteenth centuries.[13] It was also during this period that the myth of Avalokiteśvara became linked to the emperor Songsten Gampo. Brandon Dotson argues that the myth of Songsten Gampo dissolving into the Avalokiteśvara statue we find in the *The Clear Mirror of Royal Genealogies* results from a merging of two myths: (1) the myth of the Tibetan emperor as Vairocana from the imperial period and (2) the myth of Avalokiteśvara as Tibet's patron bodhisattva from the Later Transmission Period.[14] In this way, in the literature of the Later Transmission Period, the myth of Avalokiteśvara became inextricably linked with the Tibetan Empire. Indeed, Georges Dreyfus suggests that it was nostalgia for the Tibetan Empire in the eleventh century onwards that prompted Tibetans to try to "recapture the lost might of the Tibetan empire" through the imagination of a plateau-wide political community.[15] Anthony Smith has argued that myths of ethnic election typically emerge under conditions when a community is under threat, such as warfare or cultural pressure from a more powerful civilization.[16] The case of the emergence of the myth of Avalokiteśvara as Tibet's patron deity during the Later Transmission Period demonstrates that a community need not be under immediate threat for a myth of ethnic election to emerge; a state of political fragmentation that follows a period of unity can also produce circumstances conducive to the emergence of myths of ethnic election.

By the twelfth century, there was widespread promotion of the Avalokiteśvara cult in Tibet. Two of the most important groups who promoted the worship of Avalokiteśvara and the idea of the Tibetans as Avalokiteśvara's chosen people were the Nyingma treasure revealers and the Kadampas. Despite being born six centuries after both, Shabkar had links to both groups. The treasure revealers were adherents of the Nyingma or "ancient" school of Tibetan Buddhism. Shabkar is considered to be a nonsectarian master, but his main spiritual training was from the Dzokchen tradition of the Nyingma sect. His main practice was *Vajravārāhī and Hayagrīva: The Wish Fulfilling Jewel* (*Rta phag yid bzhin nor bu*), a text revealed by treasure revealer Künzang Déchen Gyelpo (b. 1736). Another important promoter of the worship of Avalokiteśvara was a Kashmiri princess whose Tibetan name was Gélongma Pelmo; she began a fasting practice associated with Avalokiteśvara that became widespread.[17] Shabkar and his spiritual community frequently engaged in this fasting practice.

Shabkar's portrayal of Avalokiteśvara bears the most influence from the early Nyingma treasure revealers and the Kadampas. The Nyingma school traces its roots to Padmasambhava. The Nyingma treasure tradition believes that during Padmasambhava's stay in Tibet, he and his associates concealed treasures in the form of texts, statues, and other items that would be revealed when Tibetans were karmically ready to practice them. Beginning in the eleventh century, treasure revealers would reveal these treasures, initiating a mechanism for introducing new "canonical" teachings into the Tibetan Buddhist canon. The early treasure revealers also played a central role in codifying the story of Tibet. The treasure texts created a sense of collective identity for Tibetans rooted in Buddhism and in recollections of the glory of the Tibetan Empire.[18] Perhaps Kapstein captures it best when he observes, "What these books achieve is to engender an understanding of Tibet and its place in the world, according to which the destiny of the Buddha's teaching and that of the Tibetan people themselves are inextricably linked."[19] Two treasure revealers in particular, Nyangrel Nyima Özer (1124/1135–1192/1204) and Guru Chöwang (1212–1270), were "together responsible for the kind of profound impact on the evolution of their nation's cultural, spiritual, and even civic identity that only the rarest of gifted saints—or bards—has ever achieved."[20] This "vision of a nation" would prove to be "stunningly prophetic," as it presaged the institution of the Ganden Potrang, the government established by the Fifth Dalai Lama, from the seventeenth to twentieth centuries.[21] One might say that six centuries later, Shabkar, a fellow adherent of the Nyingma school, would once again tap into the spiritual creativity of the Dzokchen tradition to articulate a grand vision of Tibet as a Buddhist imagined community in the nineteenth century.

In particular, Avalokiteśvara was central to the early treasure revealers' vision of Tibet. One of the most important texts that was fundamental to establishing the myth of Avalokiteśvara as the Tibetans' patron deity was the *Maṇi Kabum*. The *Maṇi Kabum* was a treasure text revealed by Nyangrel Nyima Özer and some two other treasure revealers between the mid-twelfth and mid-thirteenth centuries.[22] The *Maṇi Kambum* identifies Avalokiteśvara as the patron deity of Tibet and the seventh century Tibetan king Songsten Gampo as his embodiment. Most significantly, the text "develop[ed] a distinct view of Tibet, its history, and its place in the world," where the king's divinity and Avalokiteśvara's regard for Tibet are "grounded in the very nature of the world."[23] The *Maṇi Kabum* was one of the main influences on Shabkar's portrayal of Avalokiteśvara and his relationship to Tibet.

The other group that promoted the worship of Avalokiteśvara in the eleventh and twelfth century was the Kadampas. The Kadampas, or members of the Kadam sect, trace their lineage to the Indian master Atiśa, who was invited to Tibet to teach Buddhism in the eleventh century. The Kadampas eschewed elitism and promoted an egalitarian ideal, teaching Buddhism to the ordinary populace.[24] The worship of Avalokiteśvara was one of their main practices. The Kadampa tradition—both in terms of their doctrine and ethos—profoundly informed Shabkar's understanding of Buddhism and how he taught it. Shabkar was well-versed in the texts of the Kadampa. Not only did he refer to the Kadampa texts extensively in his *Collected Works*, but he also composed an *Emanated Scripture of the Kadampa* (*Bka' gdams sprul pa'i glegs bam*). The Kadampas played a historically important role in adapting the Indian Buddhist teachings to a Tibetan literary and cultural ethos.[25] Shabkar emulated their incorporation of the vernacular, their reliance on stories and sayings, and their adoption of a humble lifestyle.

One of the most important literary records of the Kadam sect's activities is the *Book of Kadam*, which advances the idea of Avalokiteśvara being Tibet's patron deity. The *Book of Kadam* had oral origins in the eleventh century and was written down in 1302.[26] The text records conversations between the Indian master Atiśa and his Tibetan disciple Dromtön. The former figure played an instrumental role in the revitalization of Buddhism in Tibet in the eleventh century, and the latter was seen as an incarnation of Avalokiteśvara himself. Both figures played an important role in spreading the Avalokiteśvara and Tārā cults in Tibet.[27] Like the *Maṇi Kambum*, the *Book of Kadam* also propagated the idea that some of the main kings of the Yarlung dynasty, such as Songsten Gampo, were incarnations of Avalokiteśvara. The *Book of Kadam*'s portrayal of Avalokiteśvara and his relationship to Tibet was one of Shabkar's main references for this topic.

As early as the twelfth century, different lineages began to lay claim to the idea that their masters were the reincarnation of Avalokiteśvara. An early example of this was the Kadam sect's claim that their founder Dromtön was an emanation of Avalokiteśvara.[28] The second Karmapa, Karma Pakshi, claimed that he was a manifestation of Avalokiteśvara.[29] Sachen Künga Nyingpo of the Sakya school, although less discussed, was also considered by some people to be a reincarnation of Avalokiteśvara.[30] The most famous of the Avalokiteśvara incarnations today is the lineage of the Dalai Lamas, although it is a relatively newer reincarnation lineage. In the late fifteenth century, the biographer of the First Dalai Lama (1391–1474) first advanced the idea that the Dalai Lama lineage was a manifestation of Avalokiteśvara.[31] A couple of centuries later, the Fifth Dalai Lama (1617–1682) himself played a pivotal role in linking his lineage with the myth of Avalokiteśvara and promoting it through various means.

## Shabkar's Portrayal of Avalokiteśvara

According to Shabkar's autobiography, in 1807, while meditating on compassion on the island in the middle of Qinghai Lake, Shabkar sees Avalokiteśvara for the first time. In the middle of the night, Avalokiteśvara appears to Shabkar in his meditation cave, emitting bright white colored light. His opening words to Shabkar are:

> I, mighty Avalokiteśvara, Tibet's destined deity,
> Always look upon Tibet with compassion.
> You, karmically endowed ones born in the central land of Tibet—
> People of Tibet should act in the following way.[32]

In this vision, Shabkar gives a clear indication that Tibetans share a collective identity as Avalokiteśvara's chosen people. Their identity is bound to Avalokiteśvara and grounded in the territory of Tibet. Shabkar's initial vision of Avalokiteśvara generates a series of songs that he sings to his disciples on Tsonying Island.[33] These songs mainly give spiritual instructions, such as encouraging his audience to recite Avalokiteśvara's six-syllable mantra.[34] However, these songs also reinforce the special relationship that the Tibetan people have with Avalokiteśvara. This relationship comes across in passages such as:

> Avalokiteśvara, destined deity of Tibet
> who looks upon Tibet with compassion.
> Bless [me] so that this song sung for the benefit of Tibet
> will bring benefit to Tibetans.³⁵

And:

> The deity, Great Compassion, Avalokiteśvara
> in general, looks upon all beings with compassion.
> Specifically, he looks upon Tibet with compassion.
> And even more specifically, he looks upon those assembled here with
>     compassion.³⁶

There is a clear sense in these passages that Avalokiteśvara pays special attention to the Tibetans as an imagined community. The territory of this imagined community is not limited to central Tibet but includes the Amdo region as well, because in this vision, Avalokiteśvara appears to Shabkar in the middle of Qinghai Lake in Amdo province.

Viewed through the lens of Anthony Smith's ethnosymbolist model of nationhood, the myth of the Tibetans as Avalokiteśvara's chosen people is a myth of ethnic election. Smith defines a myth of ethnic election as one which demonstrates how a people are "chosen by the deity for a special task or purpose."³⁷ Myths of ethnic election, along with myths of ethnic origin, are crucial components for creating a sense of national identity, which Smith defines as "the continuous reproduction and reinterpretation of the pattern of values, symbols, memories, myths, and traditions that compose the distinctive heritage of nations, and the identification of individuals within that pattern of heritage."³⁸ Such myths are propagated by specialists who cultivate "a heightened sense of collective distinctiveness and mission" for the ethnic community.³⁹ These specialists help to ensure the long-term survival of an ethnic group by reviving, adapting, and propagating the myths of ethnic origin and election. In the case of Tibet, Shabkar plays the role of the mythological specialist.

Of course, in discussing Shabkar and Tibet, we need to emphasize that the "nation" here is not referring to the nation-state but rather, to cultural definitions of nation discussed in chapter 1. It is also important to note that Shabkar was not intentionally trying to cultivate nationalistic sentiment in his audience. Nevertheless, the act of reviving, adapting, and propagating the myth of the Tibetans as Avalokiteśvara's chosen people has the effect of reinforcing the concept of a Tibetan people with a distinctive destiny. Whether or not one wants to call this a "national" identity or not, it is undeniable that this myth generates a "strong collective consciousness" of Tibetans as a distinct people under the patronage of Avalokiteśvara who are bonded through "shared values, beliefs, myths and symbols," to borrow Lama Jabb's words.[40] One may even characterize this collective consciousness as a "proto-national" identity, which Georges Dreyfus defines, in the context of early modern Tibet, as a sense of collective identity among Tibetans that is political but lacks a clear institutional component.[41] Another way to characterize this consciousness would be to say it inculcates a national identity, but not in the sense of the nation-state.

An important difference between Shabkar's use of the Avalokiteśvara myth and the concept of the myth of ethnic election is that in Shabkar's portrayal of Tibet, religion, rather than ethnicity, serves as the main coalescing force. This becomes especially clear when we examine the rest of Avalokiteśvara's speech to Shabkar in the above-mentioned vision. Initially, when Avalokiteśvara identifies himself as "Tibet's destined deity" who "always looks upon Tibet with compassion" and gives instructions to the people of Tibet, his words seem to indicate ethnic election. However, as he continues to speak, it becomes clear that the Tibetans are his chosen people not because of their ethnicity, but rather, because of their Buddhist faith. Following this opening passage, Avalokiteśvara continues to give specific spiritual instructions to monks, tantric practitioners, and householders. He concludes his advice with an exhortation:

> Act in this way, disciples of Tibet!
> In particular, all [of you], pray to me.
> The young and old, recite the six-syllable mantra.
> I myself am present before those with faith.
>
> I will lead all beings who have faith in me
> To the Land of Bliss . . .[42]

In this latter passage, it becomes clear that Avalokiteśvara's patronage is not granted exclusively to Tibetans, but instead, to all of those with faith in him. One might say that his chosen people are Buddhists in general and those with faith in him in particular. The Tibetans are "elected" by him, so to speak, because of they have faith in him and in Buddhism.

Shabkar's emphasis on religion rather than ethnicity is all the more apparent in his decision not to evoke the other side of the Avalokiteśvara myth—the side where Avalokiteśvara blesses a monkey-bodhisattva who mates with a rock ogress to create the Tibetan people. As discussed in chapter 1, Shabkar refers to the myth of the Tibetan people being descendants of the monkey and rock ogress.⁴³ However, instead of focusing on the genealogical commonalities between the Tibetan people, he chooses to focus on their shared Buddhist faith. This emphasis on Buddhism rather than ethnicity also comes across in Shabkar's songs that center Avalokiteśvara, sung on Tsonying Island. Although there are passages that emphasize Avalokiteśvara's role as Tibet's destined deity, the main focus is on Shabkar imparting spiritual instructions to his audience. His goal has nothing to do with engendering Tibetan national cohesion; instead, his goal is for his audience to attain spiritual goals such as rebirth in Amitābha's pure land or making their current human birth more meaningful.⁴⁴ This is consistent with how Shabkar teaches the Avalokiteśvara practice in his other works.⁴⁵

Shabkar's portrayal of the relationship between Avalokiteśvara, the six-syllable mantra, and Tibetans draws from the earliest examples of this idea from the *Maṇi Kabum* and the *Book of Kadam*, as well as from its seventeenth-century iteration by the Fifth Dalai Lama. By reviving and adapting the myth of Avalokiteśvara in this way, Shabkar is doing what Anthony Smith identifies as "reappropriation," or "reaching back into the ethnic past to obtain the authentic materials, and ethos for a distinct" nation.⁴⁶

Shabkar's portrayal of the relationship between Avalokiteśvara, the six-syllable mantra, and Tibetans draws from the earliest examples of this idea in the *Maṇi Kabum* and the *Book of Kadam*. Shabkar was deeply familiar with both, as he lists both texts as main influences behind his Collected Songs.⁴⁷ Both the *Maṇi Kabum* and the *Book of Kadam* are key texts in the development of the idea of Avalokiteśvara as Tibet's destined deity. The *Maṇi Kabum* advances "the belief that Avalokiteśvara was the patron deity of Tibet."⁴⁸ The *Book of Kadam* identifies Avalokiteśvara as "protector of the place called Tibet, the kingdom of Pu" (bod pu rgyal yul gyi mgon po) and "the protector of the snow mountains" (gangs ri'i mgon po), where the "snow mountains" serves as a synecdoche for Tibet.⁴⁹ Similarly, in Shabkar's first vision, Avalokiteśvara identifies himself as "Tibet's patron deity" (bod kyi lha skal). The *Book of Kadam* describes Tibetans as Avalokiteśvara's "disciples" (gdul bya).⁵⁰ In the first vision described above, Shabkar also describes Tibetans as Avalokiteśvara's "disciples." The idea that Tibetans should recite the six-syllable mantra is also found in both the *Maṇi Kambum* and the *Book of Kadam*.⁵¹ In the *Cycle of Precepts* section of the *Maṇi Kabum*, King Songsten Gampo, who is understood to be the embodiment of Avalokiteśvara, says,

> Men in the future: seek out Our Vast Noble Heart for your Lord! Recite the six-syllable mantra, "*Oṃ maṇi padme hūṃ*," as a refuge. Supplicate Avalokiteśvara!⁵²

In the *Book of Kadam*, Atiśa prophesizes a scene where Tibetans recite the six-syllable mantra as they pray to Avalokiteśvara.[53] In Shabkar's vision of Avalokiteśvara, the deity's main instruction to the Tibetans is to pray to him and recite the six-syllable mantra. Thus, Shabkar's portrayal of Avalokiteśvara is perfectly in line with the deity's portrayal in the *Maṇi Kambum* and *Book of Kadam*: namely, it shows that Avalokiteśvara is Tibet's patron deity and that Tibetans should engage in his veneration through practices such as reciting the six-syllable mantra.

Shabkar's second vision of Avalokiteśvara bears the mark of the *Book of Kadam*, and in particular, the practice of the Sixteen Spheres.[54] This vision occurs in 1840 while he is meditating at Machak Hermitage on the banks of the Machu River in Amdo Province. After Shabkar recites the required number of mantras, Avalokiteśvara appears to him in the form of Gyelwa Gyatso (*Rgyal ba rgya mtsho*; Skt. *Jinasāgara*) and bestows an empowerment on him. Shabkar describes the experience as follows:

> In the sky before me, within an expanse of rainbow light, were the Second Buddha Lord Atiśa and his spiritual sons. I supplicated with heartfelt faith. In an instant, the father and sons vanished into thusness, and then transformed into the *maṇḍala* of the Sixteen Spheres of the Great Compassionate One—the support and the supported. The Great Compassionate One, in the form of Gyelwa Gyatso, was clear and vivid, as if he were actually there. From his three places, white, red and dark blue nectar-light radiated in stages and simultaneously. [It] dissolved in my own three places—both in stages and simultaneously—and I attained the four empowerments of *samādhi*. And then, due to my faith and devotion, the Great Compassionate One's chest opened, and the Great Sage in the form of Namnang Gangchentso bestowed initiation as before. In the same way, the Great Sage's chest opened and the *dharmakāya* of the lama and buddha bestowed initiation. [The *dharmakāya*] opened its chest and [I] went inside. The *dharmakāya*-mind that is like the sky and my own mind—the two became one taste and inseparable, like sky mixing with sky. I rested naturally within that state.
>
> Then, arising from the state of *samādhi*, as before, I met Lord Atiśa and his spiritual sons. He said, "Fortunate noble son, through taming the outer and the inner secret mantra, beings will be benefited. I will always be inseparably united with you." Having said that, he went higher and higher, and, having gone to Joyous Heaven, disappeared from view. Then, afterwards, a feeling of continuous joy-bliss arose.[55]

The fact that Avalokiteśvara appears to Shabkar in the form of Gyelwa Gyatso is noteworthy because Atiśa identifies Tibet as Gyelwa Gyatso's realm in the

*Book of Kadam.*⁵⁶ The fact that Avalokiteśvara appears in the context of the practice of the Sixteen Spheres is significant because the Sixteen Spheres is the main meditative practice of the *Book of Kadam* that connects Avalokiteśvara to Tibet.⁵⁷ The Sixteen Spheres is a form of deity yoga that focuses on the "Sixteen Spheres," which are also known as the "Sixteen Drops." The Sixteen Spheres are:

1. The drop of the outer inconceivable array
2. The drop of this Endurance World
3. The drop of the realm of Tibet
4. The drop of one's abode and the drawn mandala
5. The drop of the Perfection of Wisdom Mother
6. The drop of her son, Buddha Śākyamuni
7. The drop of Great Compassion
8. The drop of Wisdom Tārā
9. The drop of her wrathful form
10. The drop of Acala, their immutable form
11. The drop of Atiśa
12. The drop of Dromtön Gyalwé Jungné
13. The drop of the vast practice
14. The drop of the profound view
15. The drop of the inspirational practice
16. The drop of great awakening⁵⁸

The practitioner begins by visualizing the widest frame of reference, "the drop of the outer inconceivable array," and proceeds to zoom in until they reach the level of their own body. Within their own body, they visualize "the drop of the Perfection of Wisdom Mother." Within her heart is Buddha Śākyamuni. The process continues until the focus is on a single drop.⁵⁹ Shabkar's description of his vision of Avalokiteśvara in the form of Gyelwa Gyatso unfolds in a pattern similar to the visualization sequence of the Sixteen Spheres, which involves a progressive "zooming in." Namely, Avalokiteśvara opens his chest, revealing Namnang Gangchentso within his chest, who in turn gives an initiation to Shabkar. Then, Namnang Gangchentso's chest opens, revealing the *dharmakāya* of the lama and the buddha, who bestows initiation. Then, the *dharmakāya* opens its chest and Shabkar dissolves himself in it. It is clear that Shabkar's vision of Avalokiteśvara here is influenced by the practice of the Sixteen Spheres from the *Book of Kadam*.

Although the *Maṇi Kabum* and *Book of Kadam* are important influences on Shabkar, his portrayal of Avalokiteśvara's relationship to Tibet also departs from these texts. One of the important ways in which Shabkar's portrayal of Avalokiteśvara differs from these two texts is with regard to Avalokiteśvara's relationship with the kings of Tibet's imperial period. Both the *Maṇi Kambum* and *Book of Kadam* identify several kings of the imperial period as being emanations of Avalokiteśvara. The *Maṇi Kambum* identifies king Songsten Gampo as an incarnation of Avalokiteśvara.[60] Songsten Gampo was the figure responsible for first importing Buddhism to Tibet in the mid-seventh century. The *Book of Kadam* also promotes the idea of Songsten Gampo as an incarnation of Avalokiteśvara, and identifies two other kings of the Yarlung dynasty, Nyatri Tsenpo and Lha Totori Nyentsen, as also being emanations of Avalokiteśvara.[61] In the *Book of Kadam*, Avalokiteśvara is not just embodied in a single king, but becomes inextricably intertwined with the glory of the Tibetan Empire that ruled inner Asia from the mid-seventh to the mid-ninth centuries.

Shabkar also considers Songsten Gampo, like the *Maṇi Kabum* and *Book of Kadampa*, as "the incarnation of the Great Compassionate One" (i.e., Avalokiteśvara).[62] He praises the legacy of the early Dharma kings, along with that of the translators and *paṇḍitas*, for bringing and establishing the Buddhist teachings in Tibet.[63] He even composes a series of three songs that pay tribute to the kings Lha Totori Nyentsen, Songsten Gampo, and Trisong Détsen from the imperial period.[64] However, these names are just mentioned at the beginning of the songs and he does not dwell on the glory of the imperial period in the way the *Book of Kadam* does. The Third Karmapa, Rangjung Dorje (1284–1339), was another figure who, like Shabkar, revived the myths of Avalokiteśvara and Padmasambhava.[65] The Third Karmapa, like many authors before him, also evoked the might of the Tibetan Empire. He did so by recounting visions that he had of the empire's great guardian deities.[66]

Whereas the early treasure revealers, the Kadam masters, and the Third Karmapa sought to resurrect the glory of Tibet's imperial period in their texts, Shabkar's vision of Tibet does not dwell on its imperial past. Instead, it looks forward to its future, envisioning Tibetans as a Buddhist people led by Avalokiteśvara incarnated in the form of the Dalai Lamas. In his autobiography, Shabkar refers to the Fifth Dalai Lama as the "human emanation of Noble Avalokiteśvara, the protector of the snow mountains" (gangs ri'i mgon po 'phags pa spyan ras gzigs mi yi gar gyi rnam rol) and the Ninth Dalai Lama as "Mighty Avalokiteśvara, Lungtok Gyatso" (spyan ras gzigs dbang lung rtogs rgya mtsho).[67] He states unambiguously that the leaders of Tibet are the Dalai Lama and the "King of Tibet" (bod kyi rgyal po), with the Dalai Lama being described as "the refuge protector of all Tibetans" (bod yul 'gro ba yongs kyi skyabs mgon).[68]

Shabkar's emphasis on the link between Avalokiteśvara and the lineage of the Dalai Lamas instead of the kings of the Yarlung dynasty owes much to the legacy of the Fifth Dalai Lama's (1617–1682) portrayal of Avalokiteśvara and his lineage. The Fifth Dalai Lama promoted the idea of his lineage as reincarnations of Avalokiteśvara through various means.

The first manner in which he promoted this idea was through biographical portrayals of the third and fourth Dalai Lamas where he emphasized their power and achievements in the secular sphere. In the biography of the third Dalai Lama, the Fifth Dalai Lama emphasized the achievements of Avalokiteśvara through his manifestations as members of Tibet's early imperial government.[69] In his biography of the fourth Dalai Lama, the Fifth Dalai Lama portrayed Tibet as being ruled by Avalokiteśvara in the form of the Dalai Lamas and China as being ruled by Mañjuśrī in the form of the Chinese emperors.[70] This portrayal emphasized the secular power of the Dalai Lamas. The second method the Dalai Lama used was artistic. He displayed murals of his incarnations stretching back to Avalokiteśvara in public viewing halls such as in the Potala's great assembly hall.[71] Such displays served as a means for "advertising" the idea that he and his reincarnation lineage were emanations of Avalokiteśvara.

The third method that the Fifth Dalai Lama used was ritual. After assuming the role of both secular and spiritual leader of Tibet in 1642, the Fifth Dalai Lama performed many Avalokiteśvara rituals in public and in the context of his travels to China.[72] In tantric Buddhism, the officiant of the rituals is identified with the deity itself, so this helped to solidify the Fifth Dalai Lama's identity as an incarnation of Avalokiteśvara. But perhaps the most important way that the Fifth Dalai Lama emphasized that he was an incarnation of Avalokiteśvara was by situating his Potala Palace on the site of an Avalokiteśvara temple that dates back to the time of Songsten Gampo.[73] The Potala Palace is named after the Pure Realm of Avalokiteśvara; placing it on the location of Songsten Gampo's ancient temple implies not only that the Dalai Lama is Avalokiteśvara, but also that the Dalai Lama has deep connections with the Yarlung dynasty from Tibet's imperial period. In addition to all of the above, the Fifth Dalai Lama restored sites associated with Songsten Gampo.[74]

Shabkar drew from portrayals of Avalokiteśvara from the *Maṇi Kambum* and *Book of Kadam,* melding these elements with the idea of the Dalai Lamas as emanations of Avalokiteśvara. However, unlike earlier authors who emphasized the continuity between Avalokiteśvara and Tibet's imperial period, Shabkar adapted the Avalokiteśvara myth to emphasize the Tibetan people's collective destiny under the deity's rule, through his incarnation in the form of the Dalai Lamas. Moreover, unlike earlier forms of the Avalokiteśvara myth that emphasize the deity's role as the father of the Tibetan people, Shabkar emphasizes Buddhism, not genealogical links, as the main coalescing force for Tibetans. Shabkar's revival and adaption of the Avalokiteśvara myth is reminiscent of the way in which modern Tibetan authors remember and reinscribe a Tibetan national consciousness by evoking a common sense of history, culture, territory, collective memories, shared values, and myths.[75] Although Shabkar's intentions were religious and he did not try to foster a national consciousness, Anthony Smith's ethnosymbolist lens demonstrates that Shabkar's revitalization and adaptation of the Avalokiteśvara myth had this effect nonetheless.

## The Myth of Padmasambhava

Padmasambhava is second to perhaps only Avalokiteśvara in influencing Tibet's Buddhist identity. Padmasambhava, in his main form, is instantly recognizable to Tibetan Buddhists with his lotus hat, distinctive ritual implements, and red robes. Although he is mostly associated with the Nyingma sect, he is venerated across sects as one of the figures responsible for establishing Buddhism in Tibet. According to the popular version of the Padmasambhava myth, Padmasambhava was a Buddhist tantric adept from what is now modern-day Pakistan. He was famed for his magical powers. In the mid-eighth century, Tibet's king Trisong Detsen invited the great Indian abbot Śāntarakṣita to transmit Buddhism to Tibet. However, after Śāntarakṣita experienced formidable resistance from both the Tibetan court and Tibet's local deities, Śāntarakṣita advised the emperor to invite Padmasambhava to subdue these autochthonous forces. In a series of sensational episodes, Padmasambhava subdued the opposing spirits of Tibet, creating the foundation upon which the king established Tibet's first monastery, Samyé. After hiding a series of treasures with his disciples for posterity, Padmasambhava departed to the mythical land of the Copper Colored Island.

As popular as this myth may be, Tibetan historians were aware of the discrepancies between the various textual sources about Padmsambhava.[76] Moreover, modern historians have yet to find eighth century sources that confirm the myth. Padmasambhava is also absent from significant early sources that detail Tibet's conversion to Buddhism, such as the *Edict* and *Authoritative Exposition of Samyé Monastery* (*Bsam yas bka' gtsigs*, *Bsam yas bka' mchid*), and plays only a tangential role in sources such as the earliest Dunhuang fragments of the *Testimony of Ba* (*Dba' bzhed*).[77] Even in the first complete narrative of the *Testament of Ba*, dating to sometime between the eleventh and thirteenth centuries, Padmasabhava does not accomplish many of the tasks he is famous for in the popular version of the myth.[78] The lack of extant historical sources contemporaneous with Padmasambhava has led some Euro-American scholars to question Padmasambhava's role in establishing Buddhism in Tibet, and even to question whether or not Padmasambhava was in fact a historical figure.

The first historical evidence we have of Padmasambhava is from a Dunhuang manuscript dating to the tenth century. Jacob Dalton indicates that there is evidence that the Padmasambhava legend initially flourished during the so-called "dark period" of Tibetan history, from roughly 842 CE to 978 CE.[79] Like the myth of Avalokiteśvara, the elaboration of the Padmasambhava myth took place during the fragmented socio-political context known as the Later Transmission Period from the tenth until twelfth centuries. And in another parallel to the Avalokiteśvara myth, the Nyingma treasure revealers were key players in forging the Padmasambhava myth as we know it. They likely took a myth local to southern Tibet and elaborated upon it.[80] As the myth developed over the centuries, Padmasambhava underwent a complete apotheosis, a transformation that culminated in the *Katang* treasure texts of the fourteenth century.[81] Subsequent authors from Tibet, Mongolia, and Bhutan would continue to revive and recast the Padmasambhava legend according to the shifting socio-political situations of their time.[82]

## Shabkar's Portrayal of Padmasambhava

Shabkar was one mythic specialist who revived and recast the Padmasambhava story according to the socio-political context of the nineteenth-century Tibetan Buddhist world. Just as he had a close association with Avalokiteśvara, Shabkar had an intimate connection to Padmasambhava as well. He describes himself as being the rebirth of both Padmasambhava's teacher Mañjuśrīmitra and Padmasambhava's disciple Drenpa Namkha.[83] In addition to this, Shabkar belonged to the Nyingma sect first founded by Padmasambhava and practiced rituals and meditation associated with Padmasambhava. In his autobiography, he describes his success at such practices resulting in Padmasambhava appearing to him in a vision in 1845. His multidimensional connection to Padmasambhava gives him authority when he revives and recasts Padmasambhava's mythic tradition.

Shabkar quotes from the *Chronicle of Péma* (*Padma bka'i thang*) and other later biographies of Padmasambhava in his *Collected Works*.[84] However, his portrayal of Padmasambhava in his autobiography owes the most to the earliest of Padmasambhava's biographies, Nyangrel's *Copper Island* (*Zangs gling ma*). *Chronicle of Péma* emphasizes Padmasambhava's cosmic quality, with the entire first volume devoted to describing Padmasambhava's life prior to coming to Tibet.[85] While *Copper Island* acknowledges Padmasambhava's transcendent aspects, it portrays a figure more grounded in Tibetan history and affairs. Unlike the *Chronicle of Péma,* which spends a mere five chapters describing Padmasambhava's activities in Tibet, *Copper Island* dedicates thirteen chapters to Padmasambhava giving advice to different groups of Tibetans (e.g., kings, ministers, yogis, men, women, sick people) as well as to Tibetans in general. In the *Chronicle of Péma,* Padmasambhava gives advice to Tibetans upon his departure but not in detail nor to the extent of *Copper Island.*

In his autobiography and other works, Shabkar portrays Padmasambhava as both a historical figure and a buddha who intervenes at a crucial point in Buddhist history in order to save the Buddhist teachings from degeneration by promoting an impartial approach to sectarian diversity. Thus, whereas Shabkar's portrayal of Avalokiteśvara is embedded in his political role as the patron deity of Tibetans as manifested in the form of the Dalai Lamas, Shabkar's depiction of Padmasambhava is more focused on Buddhism and his nonsectarian message. This depiction helps to emphasize the image of Tibet as a spiritual rather than a political community, an image that serves as an antecedent to the way that the Fourteenth Dalai Lama portrays the Tibetan nation in modern times. Shabkar's portrayal of Padmasambhava—including his emphasis on nonsectarianism and on the strong link between Padmasambhava and Avalokiteśvara—revives many elements of Padmasambhava's portrayals by the early treasure revealers.

Shabkar portrays Padmasambhava both as a historical figure who established Buddhism in Tibet and as a buddha. This portrayal of Padmasambhava's dual nature is consistent with the biographies of Padmasambhava from the Later Transmission Period onwards. On the one hand, Shabkar considers Padmasambhava to be a key historical figure who established Buddhism in Tibet. In *Elegant Sayings: The Self-Arising Sun* (*Legs bshad nyi ma rang shar*), Shabkar refutes the Third Tukwan Lozang Chökyi Nyima's claims in *The Cleansing Ketaka Jewel* (*Nor bu ke ta ka phyi dor*) based on the *Testament of Ba* that Padmasambhava did not play a major role in establishing Buddhism in Tibet.[86] On the other hand, Shabkar also portrays Padmasambhava as a buddha, such as when he says, "it is good to pray to Padmasambhava, the mind emanation of buddhas of the three times."[87]

Padmasambhava's main role, as portrayed in Shabkar's autobiography, is to prevent the degeneration of Buddhism by promoting inter-sectarian harmony. This role is revealed to Shabkar in a vision of Padmasambhava near the end of his life. In the vision, Padmasambhava reveals that he has appeared continually to Shabkar in disguised forms. Padmasambhava's intervention in Tibetan Buddhist affairs here is reminiscent of his intervention in *Copper Island,* discussed above. I will quote the exchange between Padmasambhava and Shabkar in full because it is so important for understanding this point:

One night, at dawn, [I] had the following vision: the appearance of Padmasambhava surrounded by an assembly of countless buddhas, bodhisattvas, and heroes of the ten directions. Having extensively offered both real and imagined offerings to them, with extreme respect, I joined my palms and said, "Although I supplicated to you since I was a little child, I had not seen a vision of your face until now. [Your] compassion is small."

Smiling, [Padmasambhava] said the following words: "Hark! Listen, son of noble family! As the auspicious connection for accomplishing the great objective of the teachings and beings, initially, at the Heart of the Lake, I appeared in the form of Tsongkhapa, blessed [your] mental continuum, and bestowed the *Lamrim*. Afterwards, when you were staying at Trashi Nyamgaling, the mountain hermitage on the banks of the Machu river, I appeared in the form of Lord Atiśa, opened the door of your mind, and bestowed the empowerment of the *Samādhi of Sixteen Spheres* and gave you the *Book of Kadam*. Now, having shown my actual face, I give you the teachings in actuality. Because of this, be glad! Generally, although all buddhas are "one taste" with the expanse of primordial wisdom, in particular, my three aspects are one with [their] mental continuum, just as you have previously known. In particular, you should understand the buddhas and bodhisattvas of the ten directions without exception to be emanations of your kind root lama. One's root lama is also the display of one's mind. From primordial times, the essence of the mind itself is also empty, uncompounded like the sky, and spontaneously established; it encompasses all that is animate and inanimate, and is the ground for the manifestation of *saṃsāra* and *nirvāṇa*. If one recognizes emptiness-clarity as the dharmakaya, one understands the depth of the Dharma."

And again [I] requested, "Now, I have thought of composing the *Emanated Scripture of Padmasambhava*, which is a conglomeration of all the essential points of generation, perfection and the great perfection—the heart nectar of you, Victorious Lord. Because of this, I supplicate for your blessings for the ability to compose in the way of your intended meaning." In response, he said, "O, the intended meaning of the ultimate secret mantra, the tantras, the essential points of the generation, perfection and great perfection are [in] the compositions of the lords of scholars—such as the emanation[s] of the Victors Longchenpa and Khyentsé. It is sufficient to practice that which was taught to you by your root lama. You do not need anything more. Because of this, in the future, in the degenerate age, according to the prophesy of the dream of King Kriki, the precious teachings of the Buddha will not be destroyed by outsiders and so forth. Rather, among themselves, Buddhists, having mutually quarreled regarding good and bad teachings, would have attachment and aversion, and fight. And, the teachings would be destroyed. Because of this, in the future, in the degenerate age, having placed [this] in the head of worldly practitioners, all sectarianism regarding Dharma will be pacified. It is good to compose the *Emanated Scriptures of Orgyen,* which benefits the teachings and beings—unprecedented elegant sayings that show pure perception and impartiality."[88]

The main point conveyed by this vision is nonsectarianism. Here, Padmasambhava intervenes at a key moment in this history of Buddhism with a reminder of King Kriki's prophecy that the deterioration of Buddhism will result from sectarian in-fighting. He intervenes at this moment in order to counteract the sectarianism present in Tibetan Buddhism in the nineteenth century. Padmasambhava's intervention serves to prolong the life of the Buddhist teachings on earth.

In the vision, Padmasambhava maintains that he had appeared to Shabkar before, but in the forms of Tsongkhapa (1357–1419) and Atiśa (982–1054). Padmasambhava is suggesting that he, Atiśa, and Tsongkhapa are ultimately the same figure. This claim is a controversial one. Whereas Padmasambhava is understood to be the founder of the Nyingma sect of Tibetan Buddhism, Atiśa's disciple Dromtön is seen as the founder of the Kadam sect and Tsongkhapa as the founder of the Géluk sect. While the Géluk sect emerged out of the Kadam sect, the Nyingma sect claims Padmasambhava as their founder. Shabkar is aware of the controversial nature of this claim, and supports it elsewhere in his *Collected Works* using quotations from the *Book of Kadam,* writings by the First Dalai Lama, and other sources.[89]

The issue of sectarianism threatens Tibet in two ways. First, if the demise of Buddhism is predicted to result from sectarian infighting, then the sectarianism present in nineteenth century Tibet would threaten the very religion that gives Tibet its unique identity as Avalokiteśvara's nation. Without Buddhism, Tibet loses its "heightened sense of collective distinctiveness and mission," to borrow Anthony Smith's words.[90] Second, inter-sectarian fighting would undermine the unity of Tibet as a whole. Already faced with formidable geographical barriers and oral linguistic diversity, sectarian in-fighting would be an additional force that could tear Tibet apart. This issue has become especially relevant in contemporary times, with the Tibetan nation-in-exile and with Buddhist masters from various sects promoting nonsectarianism. This second topic will be taken up in the epilogue.

Shabkar's portrayal of Padmasambhava in his autobiography revives three main elements of Padmasambhava's depiction by the early treasure revealers of the Later Transmission Period. First, Shabkar revives the relative arbitrariness of demarcations between different sects; during the Later

Transmission Period, the lines between sects were not as clear-cut as they generally were in the nineteenth century. For instance, the *Maṇi Kabum* contains a variety of practices and doctrinal systems, including the Nine Vehicles, Two Truths, Mahāmudrā, and Dzokchen.[91] These different systems are described as "magical fragments" of instruction, suited to each individual.[92] The *Maṇi Kabum* is Nyingma in origin and orientation, but also draws from the Avalokiteśvara traditions of the Sarma or "New" schools, particularly the early Kadampa.[93] Indeed, as discussed above, the *Book of Kadam* is one of the sources that Shabkar cites to defend his claim that Padmasambhava, Atiśa, and Tsongkhapa are ultimately the same figure. Thus, the impartial ethos of the *Maṇi Kabum* and early Kadam masters from the Tibetan renaissance period is picked up by and continued in Shabkar's portrayal of Padmasambhava in the nineteenth century.

Second, like the early treasure revealers, Shabkar promotes the myths of *both* Avalokiteśvara and Padmasambhava. In texts by the early treasure revealers, we see this promotion of both deities in the three chapters near the end of *Copper Island* (chaps. 37–39), which establish Avalokiteśvara's role in Tibetan history and teach his six-syllable mantra.[94] *Copper Island* is a biography of Padmasambhava, so the fact that it also discusses Avalokiteśvara's role in Tibet is significant. Like Shabkar, the early treasure revealers had regular visions of both figures and promoted myths and practices associated with them. Nyangrel, for instance, discovered sections of and promoted practices from the *Maṇi Kabum,* one of the main texts that established Avalokiteśvara as Tibet's patron deity during the Tibetan renaissance period. Nyangrel also authored the first full-length biography of Padmasambhava, playing an important role in the historical figure's apotheosis in the Tibetan imagination. Nyangrel's most "crucial innovation" for the worship of Avalokiteśvara in Tibet was to link it, through the treasure tradition, to Padmasambhava.[95] Similar to Nyangrel, Guru Chöwang also promoted practices associated with Avalokiteśvara, such as the recitation of the six-syllable mantra.[96] And like Nyangrel, he was involved in the apotheosis of Padmasambhava. Orgyen Lingpa (1323–1360), too, uncovered and promoted both the Avalokiteśvara and Padmasambhava legends.[97] He also played an important role in linking the two figures by coming up with the stipulation that a proper "authentic" treasure must contain the three elements of guru yoga, Dzokchen, and Avalokiteśvara.[98] Shabkar's involvement with both the myths of Avalokiteśvara and Padmasambhava draws from the ancient tradition of the early treasure revealers. Despite being six centuries apart, the characteristics they share are strong. To what extent this is due to their Nyingma affiliations is an interesting side point.

Third, in the biographical literature of Padmasambhava written by the early treasure revealers, Padmasambhava sometimes acts as a continuator or substitute for Avalokiteśvara's conversion activities in Tibet.[99] In *Copper Island*, for example, Padmasambhava promotes Avalokiteśvara's role as Tibet's destined deity, as well as the practices associated with him:

> Kings and disciples of future generations,
> Take the Great Compassionate One as your yidam.
> Recite the Six Syllables as the essence mantra.
> Be free from the fear of going to the lower realms.
>
> Avalokiteshvara is the destined deity of Tibet,
> So supplicate him with faith and devotions.
> You will receive blessings and attainments
> And be free from doubt and hesitation.
>
> To the knowledge of me, Padmakara,
> A teaching more profound and more swift
> Has never been taught by the buddhas of the three times.
>
> I, Padmasambhava, am now taking leave.
> Keep this in your hearts,
> Tibetan followers, kings, and disciples,
> Who are present now or will appear in the future.[100]

Padmasmabhava's words of advice echo the role that Avalokiteśvara plays in Shabkar's autobiography. In Shabkar's 1807 vision of Avalokiteśvara, Avalokiteśvara says the following:

> I, mighty Avalokiteśvara, principal deity of Tibet,
> Always watch over the world with eyes of compassion.
> You, fortunate one born in the central land, Tibet,
> And everyone who lives there should do this: . . .
>
> Please act accordingly, disciples of Tibet.
> In particular, everyone should pray to me;
> Young or old, they should recite the six-syllable mantra.
>
> I will always be present before those with faith . . .[101]

Still, Shabkar takes the idea of Padmasambhava as a substitute for Avalokiteśvara's activities even further than the early treasure revealers do.

In Shabkar's vision of Padmasambhava, he is portrayed as an autonomous figure surrounded by an assembly of buddhas, bodhisattvas, and heroes of the ten directions. This is in contrast to the way he appears in some of the earlier treasure literature. In Nyangrel's vision, for example, Amitābha is the central Buddha, with Avalokiteśvara to his right, and Padmasambhava and his consort seated on a lotus on Avalokiteśvara's left-hand side.[102] Shabkar's portrayal is significant because it shows Padmasambhava as a buddha in-and-of-himself rather than a supporting cast member, as in Nyangrel's portrayal. Shabkar's portrayal of Padmasambhava as the main figure can be seen as a continuation of the process of Padmasambhava's apotheosis that had begun in the treasure tradition of the eleventh century. In the eleventh century, the Nyingma treasure tradition began to portray Padmasambhava as a "second Buddha" as the main deity honored in rituals.[103] Read within the context of Padmasambhava's gradual apotheosis, Padmasmabhava becomes a true "second Buddha" in Shabkar's work, replacing Samantabhadra, who had been the main figure in the early Dzokchen tradition.[104]

Shabkar's portrayal of Padmasambhava differs significantly from the texts of the treasure tradition in one way: he deemphasizes the theme of subjugation so prevalent in the Padmasambhava myths and instead emphasizes the unity between Padmasambhava and the founders of other sects of Tibetan Buddhism. The hagiographies of Padmasambhava in the treasure tradition contain episode after episode of him subduing Tibet's resistant local deities and binding them under oath; these works show subjugation as a key aspect of Padmasambhava's activities in Tibet.[105] Indeed, one of Shabkar's predecessors—the Third Karmapa Rangjung Dorjé, with whom Shabkar shares many parallels—emphasizes Padmasambhava's role in subjugating and converting Tibet's local deities.[106] By contrast, Shabkar does not dwell on Padmasambhava's past deeds, but on his role as preserver of the Buddhist teachings in Tibet as Tibet moves into the future. This matches a key aspect of Shabkar's portrayal of Avalokiteśvara: he does not dwell on the imperial period, but instead looks forward toward Tibet's future as a Buddhist imagined community headed by Avalokiteśvara in the form of the Dalai Lamas.

# 5

# Imagining a Community Based on Buddhist Values and Practices

The landscape of the Tibetan plateau is stunning to behold. With vast skies, majestic mountains, and glistening turquoise lakes, the geography of this high-altitude terrain is one of the most unique in the world. The Tibetan Plateau is also one of the world's most unforgiving environments. The high altitude means that oxygen is scarce and temperatures chilling. One of the particular challenges of navigating the Tibetan Plateau is the presence of large mountain chains that dominate the landscape. The presence of large mountains creates obstacles for contact between communities that would otherwise be adjacent to one another. One of the effects of these geographic barriers is that it is difficult to unify the communities who live on the plateau. This difficulty is reflected in the diversity of dialects even within a single region of the Tibetan plateau; because communities are so isolated from one another, it is not uncommon that they develop linguistic differences despite being in neighboring valleys.

Still, even with Tibet's divisive geography, throughout its history, various coalescing forces have contributed to the unity of its communities. Sometimes, these forces were military or political. For instance, in the seventh century CE, the kings of the Yarlung dynasty united vast stretches of the Tibetan Plateau through military conquest. Likewise, the Mongol khans ruled over large swaths of Tibet and China from the late thirteenth through mid-fourteenth centuries. Other times, the coalescing forces were what we might term "soft" forces—cultural, religious, or literary. During the imperial period from the seventh through ninth centuries in Tibet, sacerdotal bards told and retold narratives of the Tibetan past, a practice that served as an important enactor of cultural memory at the royal court of the king. Beginning in the eleventh century, the Gésar bards roamed the Tibetan plateau telling tales of King Gésar to the ordinary populace. And during the same period, Buddhist teachers promoted pan-Tibetan Buddhist practices such as the worship of Avalokiteśvara. Finally, the institution of pilgrimage also played an important centripetal role in bringing communities from different regions of the Tibetan plateau together.

With the secular nation-state as the current international norm, it is easy to forget the crucial role that religion played in the formation of nations in premodern periods. For example, the Bible was the original model for the nation in the Christian world.[1] For some polities in Asia, including Cambodia, Burma, Sri Lanka, Thailand, and Tibet, Buddhism played a fundamental role in state formation.[2] In the case of Tibet, the system of government from the thirteenth century until the twentieth century—a system that emanated from the civilizational center of Lhasa, and in which political and spiritual spheres were interwoven—is best described as "the Tibetan Buddhist world."[3] The Tibetan Buddhist world did not have a central ruler, but rather, was ruled by different leaders in different regions. Nevertheless, the Tibetan Buddhist world was held together by "common overarching religiopolitical concepts, principles, and construct[s]."[4]

Rather than focusing on macro-level politics between polities within the Tibetan Buddhist world, this chapter engages in a micro-level examination of Shabkar's life writing, which I see as a literary source that can help us to understand Tibet's self-imagination in the early modern period. I am interested in the role that Buddhist concepts and practices played as coalescing forces for Tibet as an imagined community.

By promoting Buddhist values and practices through the persona of "White Feet," Shabkar entertains the discursive possibility that communities across the Tibetan plateau *can* and *should* be unified by shared Buddhist ideals and practices. Using Jon E. Fox's and Cynthia Miller-Idriss's theory of everyday nationalism, I demonstrate the significance of Shabkar's promotion of the worship of Avalokiteśvara, vegetarianism, pilgrimage, and nonsectarianism as forces of cohesion for Tibet as an imagined community. Here, Shabkar's conception of the relationship between identity, community, and territory lies beyond the idea of the nation-state. For Shabkar, Buddhism, rather than other aspects of nationhood, serves as the main coalescing force for the communities on the Tibetan Plateau. In previous chapters, I demonstrated how Buddhism is the most significant organizing concept for Tibet on semantic, spatial, literary, and mythic levels as portrayed by Shabkar in his autobiography and songs. In this chapter, I discuss the significance of Buddhist values and practices in Shabkar's portrayal of Tibet.

## "White Feet," Shabkar's Preferred Epithet

Of Shabkar's many epithets, "Shabkar" is the name that he wanted to be remembered by. This preference is apparent in the way in which he shifts from using a variety of epithets early in his life to using "Shabkar" most of the time after his early forties. Indeed, "Shabkar," in conjunction with his tantric initiation name of "Tsokdruk Rangdröl," is the name by which Tibetan Buddhist communities across the world remember him today.[5] However, there has been little analysis of the meaning and significance of his epithet. The name "Shabkar" reflects central aspects of Shabkar's life and oeuvre. In English, "Shabkar" is literally rendered as "White Foot" or "White Feet." In the exegesis of his own name, Shabkar explains that he is called "White Feet" because "wherever he sets foot, that land becomes white with virtue."[6] There are three dimensions to the name "White Feet": Buddhism, nonsectarianism, and pilgrimage. These three dimensions reflect three main aspects of Shabkar's legacy. These three dimensions also play a major role in holding together Tibet as imagined by Shabkar.

The earliest hint of this epithet is in Shabkar's *Collected Songs*, where a disciple addresses him as "you, with the white blossoming lotus feet."[7] This incident occurred sometime between the years 1806 and 1809, when he was meditating on Tsonying Island in Qinghai Lake. However, it was not until 1818, when Shabkar was en route to Kyidrong in southwestern Tibet, that the name "Shabkar" first appeared in his autobiography. At this point, Shabkar was thirty-seven years old and had spent the last decade on an extended pilgrimage stretching from Amdo to western Tibet. Traveling on foot, he had visited and meditated at great sacred sites such as Tsari and Kailash and gained a large following of disciples and patrons from all over the Tibetan Plateau. His fame would peak a couple of years later, when word of "the siddha Shabkar" would spread all the way to India.[8] Explaining his new identity to a group of curious passersby, Shabkar sings:

> Neither Nyingma nor Géluk,
> I am a yogin arising from their union
> In these parts, they call me Shabkar
> Unlike no other, but in harmony with all—how wondrous!⁹

The nonsectarian aspect of the name "Shabkar" comes through immediately in this stanza. In this scene, Shabkar's interlocutors are puzzled as to why he styles his hair in the coiled dreads of the tantric yogis while simultaneously wearing the robes of celibate monks. The former sartorial convention was standard for many members of the Nyingma sect, while the latter as the classic mode of dress for monastics associated with the Géluk sect. His name, "White Feet," like his mode of dress, did not indicate any particular sectarian affiliation. Both his name and clothing choices were aimed at destabilizing reified notions of sectarian affiliation in nineteenth-century Tibet. In the above stanza, Shabkar expresses a desire to be "in harmony with all" while preserving his unique identity. This is a classic expression of a nonsectarian attitude rooted in the Buddhist principles of "equanimity" (*btang snyoms*) and "unbiasedness" (*ris med*). Throughout his life, Shabkar embodied and zealously advocated the principle of unbiasedness.

The name "Shabkar" has a Buddhist dimension as well. This is apparent in Shabkar's explanation of his own name as symbolizing the way in which he brings virtue wherever he sets foot. In Tibetan Buddhism, the color white often represents virtue. "White [deeds]" (*rnam dkar*), for example, describe virtuous deeds. Throughout his autobiography, Shabkar documents in great detail how he encouraged Buddhist beliefs, values, and practices wherever he went. He notes how he gave spiritual advice and sang spiritual songs;[10] gave empowerments, transmissions, and teachings of Buddhist texts and practices;[11] built temples and meditative retreat huts in the wilderness;[12] meditated in the wilderness;[13] made house visits to villages;[14] and encouraged people to build Buddhist statues and to be generous towards the poor.[15] Shabkar also describes his important role in pacifying the frequent feuds that plagued communities in the Amdo region. Describing the effect of his religious activities in the Amdo in region in particular, Shabkar describes how "the entire region was rendered utterly white with dharma."[16] Here, the practice of Buddhism is associated with the practice of virtuous deeds that benefit others.

The "Feet" portion of the name "White Feet" serves as a metonym for pilgrimage. Pilgrimage is a religious practice at the very bedrock of Tibetan Buddhist cultures, and one which Shabkar practiced with great zeal. After he left his home village at the age of twenty, Shabkar spent the rest of his life as a wandering ascetic. He alternated meditative retreat with pilgrimage and teaching tours. Shabkar spent eighteen years on an extended pilgrimage throughout central, south, and western Tibet. After returning to his home province of Amdo, he spent the rest of his life alternating between meditative retreat, pilgrimage, and serving the communities of eastern Tibet. One of the most celebrated features of Shabkar's autobiography are the multiple pilgrimages that he documents.

Thus, the name "Shabkar" has three main connotations: Buddhism, nonsectarianism, and pilgrimage. Combined with his musical identity as the Singer of Tibet and as an emanation of Tibet's patron deity Avalokiteśvara, the persona of "White Feet" opens up the discursive possibility of the communities of the Tibetan Plateau being unified not by "hard" forces such as military might, but rather, by "soft" forces such as shared Buddhist ideals and practices. In the case of Shabkar's autobiography, such ideals include virtuous behavior and impartiality, and practices such as reflecting and meditating on the dharma, the worship of Avalokiteśvara, vegetarianism, and pilgrimage to sacred sites.

## Buddhist Ideals and Practices as Coalescing Force

In his autobiography, Shabkar portrays Buddhism as a centripetal force that has the potential to unify the diverse groups of the Tibetan Plateau by creating an imagined community based on shared values and practices. Shabkar spent his entire life promoting Buddhist values and practices "[w]herever [he] went in upper, middle and lower Tibet."[17] Shabkar's main aim in doing so was not to engender an imagined community. Rather, he understood his activities within the Buddhist framework of "turning minds towards the dharma" and "taming beings who have not been tamed by other buddhas."[18] Nevertheless, upon further analysis, Buddhist values and practices represent a powerful unifying force for the diverse communities of the Tibetan Plateau.

Shabkar's autobiography captures the cultural and linguistic diversity of the communities of the Tibetan plateau. As discussed in chapter 1, Shabkar describes the considerable differences between the oral languages of central Tibet and Amdo. Regarding the Amdo region in particular, he documents the various ethnic groups of the region, including the Tibetans, Mongols, Chinese, and Salars. These different ethnic groups speak different languages, and their speech is not always mutually intelligible. For instance, he notes the example of Mongolian ladies in the Lake Kokonor region who do not understand his words but are nevertheless moved by the melody of his songs.[19] Further afield, in the borderlands of the Tibetan Plateau, he also describes his interactions with non-Tibetan peoples such as the Mönpa.[20]

Conflict and violence were ongoing realities for the various communities of the Tibetan Plateau. This is apparent in Shabkar's detailed descriptions of the interaction between different communities living in the Amdo region. For example, Shabkar describes the Maṇi Tang temple in Gurong being burned down by armies of Chinese Salars who later rebuilt the temple at the urging of a Tibetan Buddhist lama.[21] Similarly, he documents the story of Alak Tendzin Nyima and others rebuilding a monastery in lower Gurong burned by Chinese soldiers.[22] Internecine feuds within Tibetan communities were also prevalent. Shabkar documents at least ten feuds between Tibetanized tribes and villages across both volumes of his autobiography. These feuds were not just petty battles but protracted conflicts that lasted many years and resulted in dozens of deaths at time.[23]

Shabkar portrays Buddhism as the force that can bring together these diverse and sometimes warring communities in a peaceful manner. Like many other high-profile Buddhist lamas, Shabkar was frequently called upon to mediate protracted conflicts in the region. In the mediation of these feuds, the Buddhist lama represented a neutral point of connection that helped the warring parties to come to a resolution. Shabkar also describes his sermons as having the ability to draw crowds from diverse ethnicities, sects of Buddhism, and even different religions. He preaches to groups including Buddhist, Bönpos, Muslim Salars, Tibetans, Chinese, Mongols, and the Mönpa peoples at the Himalayan borderlands.[24] For audience members with an inclination towards Buddhism, Shabkar describes being able to "to turn everyone's mind toward the dharma" through his sermons and empowerments.[25] As a result, they engage in various Buddhist practices suited to their abilities. Such practices range from completely renouncing worldly matters and going into retreat to vowing to stop killing animals and robbing others.[26] Shabkar also describes making meaningful connections with non-Buddhists in his sermons. After one of his sermons, he describes a group of Chinese, Mongolians, and Muslim Salars in the Amdo region observing, "The words of our Kachu Buddha and those of Lama Shabkar of Tibet are both the same."[27] In these examples, it is apparent that Shabkar includes non-Buddhists and non-Tibetans in his imagined community. This is in keeping with Shabkar's impartial outlook, which will be further elaborated upon later in this chapter.

In his autobiography, Shabkar describes how he inspires his followers to adopt Buddhist values and engage in Buddhist practices according to their relative levels of commitment and abilities. A frequent topic of his sermons for large audiences is the law of karma and how to incorporate this concept into their everyday lives. Shabkar describes several occasions where his followers abstain from negative deeds such as killing animals and human trafficking after hearing his songs or sermons.[28] He also frequently teaches his followers to pay homage to Avalokiteśvara and recite his six-syllable mantra. As discussed in chapter 4, the myth and worship of Avalokiteśvara was an important proto-national force for unifying communities in Tibet. Shabkar teaches more committed practitioners preliminary practices, training in *bodhicitta,* and more advanced tantric practices as well.[29] In addition to individual practices, Shabkar sometimes institutes group rituals. At Lachi, for example, he institutes community-wide annual rituals that involve elaborate processions, ritual music, and the circumambulation of holy sites.[30] Thus, by instilling a common repertoire of values and behaviors in the communities of the Tibetan plateau, Shabkar as "White Feet" opens up a discursive space for an imagined community of Tibet that is based on shared Buddhist ideals and practices.

Azar Gat has argued that religion was "the most powerful and all-pervasive mass medium of the premodern 'imagined community.'"[31] This is true for Shabkar's Buddhist imagined community of Tibet. Nevertheless, there are two important differences between Shabkar's Buddhist imagined community and forms of Buddhist nationalism we find in Asia today. The first is that Shabkar's Buddhist imagined community is inclusive of non-Tibetans.

That is, Tibetan ethnicity is *connected* to Buddhism but is *not coterminous* with Buddhism. This differs from cases such as the Buddhist nationalisms of Burma and Sri Lanka, where ethnicity is inseparable from religion.[32]

The second point is that Buddhism plays an ordering role rather than an instrumental one in unifying Shabkar's Tibet, which is to say, Buddhism is used as a guide for understanding and living in the world rather than a means for achieving a goal that has nothing to do with the religion's ideals. Buddhism plays an instrumental role in modern forms of Buddhist nationalism when it becomes "an adjunct to the nationalist project, no longer the project itself."[33] In the case of Burma, for example, prior to 1920, Buddhism was a unifying factor in Burmese society because Buddhists united over preserving the *sasana*, or life of the Buddhist teachings in the world.[34] However, after 1920, there was a "political and nationalist turn" where "Buddhism came to assume an instrumental rather than an ordering role for those who sought the political independence of the imagined nation."[35] In particular, "in the public discourse of nationalists and the governments that succeeded them, Buddhism became an essential element of national identity and a means of mobilization to national ends."[36] The role of Buddhism in Shabkar's Tibet is more similar to the ordering role of Buddhism in pre-1920s Burma than to the contemporary Buddhist nationalisms of Burma and Sri Lanka. For Shabkar, what mattered most was not so much Buddhist identity as the genuine practice and implementation of the Buddhist teachings.

## "Everyday Nationalism" and Religious Communities

In writing his autobiography, Shabkar was not primarily working to bring diverse communities together through his portrayal of Buddhism. Shabkar told his life story in order to provide a spiritual exemplum for his followers to emulate. Nevertheless, it is undeniable that shared Buddhist ideals and practices—which his autobiography promoted on a large scale—gave his readers something in common. At the very least, a shared Buddhist ethical code promoted harmony among communities of the Tibetan Plateau that had historically been fragmented by strong local powers.

In the context of fostering national unity, macro-level forces such as government, the military, institutions, or large-scale rituals such as parades may be the first to come to mind. However, there are also a host of soft forces that hold a nation together, such as language, a vernacular national literature, religion, and culture. In their theory of "everyday nationhood," Fox and Miller-Idriss argue that the nation is "not simply the product of macro-structural forces; it is simultaneously the practical accomplishment of ordinary people engaging in routine activities."[37] Proponents of this theory argue that

"Informal, symbolic practices undertaken in private may hold more meaning and engender greater feeling and attachment to the community than large-scale official displays."[38] In many cases, performers are not even consciously aware that their actions are engendering national unity.[39] Applying Fox and Miller-Idriss's theory of everyday nationhood to the portrayal of Buddhism in Shabkar's autobiography helps us appreciate the significance of Buddhism to Shabkar's conception of Tibet, a conception that I have termed a Buddhist imagined community.

Fox and Miller-Idriss propose four ways in which ordinary citizens negotiate and reproduce nationhood: talking the nation, choosing the nation, consuming the nation, and performing the nation. However, because Shabkar is building a community that does not map on exactly to the concept of the nation, I will adapt Fox and Miller-Idriss's object of study slightly. In analyzing Shabkar's autobiography, I use Fox and Miller-Idriss's model to understand how an imagined *religious* community could be engendered through talking choosing, consuming, and performing Buddhism. In promoting Buddhist ideals such as doing virtuous deeds and practices like the worship of Avalokiteśvara, Shabkar's main intention was to spread Buddhism. Although he was certainly influential—he self-reported teaching a total of 1,800 disciples[40]—his life and legacy never resulted in any kind of large-scale movement. My study focuses, however, on how Tibet was conceived in the early modern literary imagination—on Shabkar's act of imagining Tibet—rather than on the impact of that conception.

One of the Buddhist practices that Shabkar promoted in particular has deep significance for Tibetan national identity: the worship of Avalokiteśvara and the ritual and artistic engagement with his mantra. As demonstrated in chapter 1 and chapter 4, Avalokiteśvara is the patron deity of the Tibetan people. Two aspects of Fox and Miller-Idriss's theory—choosing and performing the nation—are particularly relevant for uncovering the significance of the worship of Avalokiteśvara as a unifying force for the communities of the Tibetan plateau. Fox and Miller-Idriss define "choosing the nation" as the way in which nationhood is "implicated in the choices people make."[41] When Shabkar's audience recites Avalokiteśvara's six-syllable mantra or etches his mantra on a rock, they are *choosing* to engage in the worship of Avalokiteśvara. Although their intention may not be to participate in an imagined community that is united in part through worship of Avalokiteśvara, they are in fact participating in it by dint of their actions. Thus, they may not be conscious or intentional about this participation, but the issue of Tibet as an imagined community is *implicated* in this choice.

There is also a dimension of performance to reciting the six-syllable mantra or etching Avalokiteśvara's mantra on a rock. Fox and Miller-Idriss define "performing the nation" as giving nationhood "symbolic meaning in the ritual performances of everyday (and not-so-everyday) life" and as the "choreographed exhibition and collective performance of national symbols."[42] When the people in Shabkar's autobiography recite Avalokiteśvara's mantra or etch it on rocks in the landscape, they are *performing* a symbol that represents the Buddhist imagined community of Tibet. Again, this performance may not be conscious, but collectively, the recitation and etching of the Avalokiteśvara mantra serve as a "choreographed exhibition and collective performance" of symbols that are important throughout the Tibetan Plateau. The six-syllable mantra—whether etched on the *maṇi* stones that dot the landscape or uttered from people's lips—is a ubiquitous and unifying presence on the Tibetan Plateau. Indeed, the mantra is the one thing that unites the plateau's diverse communities, regardless of dialect. Although it would be inaccurate to describe Shabkar's promotion of Avalokiteśvara as nationalistic in nature, it is undeniable that the worship of Avalokiteśvara and the recitation and usage of his mantra provide an important unifying force on the Tibetan Plateau.

## Pilgrimage

Pilgrimage is a core practice of Tibetan Buddhism and was a key aspect of both Shabkar's Buddhist practice and his identity as "White Feet." Before the introduction of Buddhism, Tibet had an indigenous practice of worshipping mountains deities. The Buddhist worship of and pilgrimage to sacred mountains in Tibet developed between the twelfth and fifteenth centuries CE.[43] The earliest extant textual evidence of Buddhist pilgrimage is from the thirteenth century.[44]

At the opening of this chapter, I discussed the many forces—geographical barriers, societal conflict, sectarian rivalry—that have continually threatened to pull apart the communities of the Tibetan plateau. Several Tibetologists have identified pilgrimage as one of the main centripetal forces that have prevented the populations of the Tibetan Plateau from radical separatism. Robert Ekvall and James Downs were among the first to consider this idea in a significant way. According to Ekvall and Downs, Buddhist pilgrimage—more than trade or other institutions—served to bring people and information from far reaching regions of the Tibetan plateau to the same place.[45] Moreover, "pilgrimage [to Lhasa, Tibet's civilizational center] acted to bring much of the population into a cultural network based on this single experience."[46] In a concrete enactment of Anderson's imagined community, the institution of pilgrimage served to bring together people who otherwise would not know each other.

In his autobiography, Shabkar portrays pilgrimage in a way that is in accord with Ekvall's and Downs's analysis. Shabkar documents himself traveling from Amdo to central Tibet, a journey of over 1,000 km that takes a minimum of three months; he traveled both on foot and with a caravan of horses, mules, yaks or camels.[47] Then, he proceeded to travel on foot to Mount Tsari in southeastern Tibet, Mount Lachi in southwestern Tibet, Kathmandu in Nepal, and Mount Kailash in western Tibet, another journey of well over a thousand miles. Shabkar's impulse to visit the sacred Buddhist sites of Tibet took him far away from his home valley of Repgong, to regions that spoke dialects that were unintelligible to him. Indeed, at one point, he describes the Dalai Lama and his entourage being amused by his own Amdo dialect.[48]

Shabkar also documents pilgrims from all over the Tibetan plateau undergoing similar journeys. At Mount Tsari, Shabkar describes people from places ranging from Kongpo to Kham gathering to embark on a circumambulation of the mountain that takes place only once every twelve years. He describes the pilgrims as developing deep bonds with each other, with many pilgrims assisting each other by carrying loads or providing support to ailing pilgrims on the arduous trek.[49] Camaraderie and mutual assistance also characterize Shabkar's portrayal of his pilgrimage caravan from Amdo to central Tibet. Traveling with a group of approximately fifty travelers and merchants from various locations, Shabkar describes the trip as a merry one full of song, mutual assistance, and moral behavior according to the rules of Buddhist ethics.[50] While on pilgrimage at the holy site of Lachi, Shabkar has a dream-vision that people of many different ethnic and linguistic groups, including Tibetans, Nepalese, Indians, and so forth, fill the great plain of Lachi.[51] In Shabkar's autobiography, he portrays pilgrimage as a spiritual practice that brings people together and that dissolves all sorts of conventional distinctions—social, ethnic, and sectarian. Shabkar's portrayal of pilgrimage is very much in accord with Ekvall's and Downs's description.

However, some of the research on pilgrimage in Tibet suggests that the practice does not always dissolve social divides, but that it can instead reinforce existent social divides and inequalities. In Katia Buffetrille's field study on the pilgrimage of Anyé Machen in Amdo, she notes that "during the pilgrimage there is not necessarily good fellowship, brotherhood and equality among all pilgrims."[52] Different groups on the pilgrimage do not mix with one another, and even within a single group, each family functions as an independent unit with the exception of mutual aid for difficult tasks. In Huber's study of the mountain cult of Tsari, he concludes that "while some Tibetan pilgrimages may offer the rare possibility of status increase [...], for the most part they serve as a ritual context in which existing social distinctions and hierarchies based on birth, wealth, gender, and so on, become explicit, are reproduced, and are reinforced."⁵³ Pilgrimage in the Tibetan context is a complex socio-religious practice. Nevertheless, Shabkar chooses to portray it as a strong centripetal force in Tibetan society.

The studies that contradict Shabkar's portrayal suggest that Shabkar's portrayal of pilgrimage may be idealized. Fox and Miller-Idriss's concept of "performing the nation" can help us appreciate the significance of Shabkar's idealized portrayal of pilgrimage. Fox and Miller-Idriss define "performing the nation" as "the production of national sensibilities through the ritual enactment of symbols."⁵⁴ It is during the ritual enactment of national symbols that "those in attendance are united in the transitory awareness of heightened national cohesion."⁵⁵ If we modify Fox and Miller-Idriss's concept slightly to make it about Shabkar's Buddhist imagined community rather than Tibetan nationalism, then within the context of "performing the imagined community," pilgrimage represents the production of a *Buddhist* sensibility through the ritual enactment of *Buddhist* values and practices. Shabkar notes how the pilgrims at Tsari assisted strangers by carrying loads or sharing food. These actions are an expression of Mahāyāna Buddhist ideals of generosity, compassion, and altruism. Shabkar also describes the group of pilgrims from Amdo to central Tibet as behaving morally according to Buddhist ethics during the duration of their pilgrimage. Again, this is an expression of the Mahāyāna Buddhist ideal of moral discipline, the second of the six perfections. Thus, in Shabkar's autobiography, pilgrimage acts as an observable manifestation of the Buddhist ideals and practices that unite his imagined Buddhist community of Tibet. The individuals in these pilgrimages enact transregional bonds that are constituted through their performance of Buddhist ideals and practices. Although Shabkar's motivations for portraying his pilgrimages were entirely religious, his portrayal nevertheless had implications for Tibet as a Buddhist imagined community.

Another way that the institution of pilgrimage engendered cultural unity among communities on the Tibetan plateau was by breaking down local understandings of space and imposing universal Buddhist ones. Both Katia Buffetrille and Toni Huber have observed the ways in which Buddhism subjugates Tibet's indigenous notions of space and time. Although local mountain cults follow an annual schedule based on the natural rhythms of the seasons, for instance, Buddhism imposes a "universal temporal context" that is "delinked from locality."⁵⁶ Shabkar's autobiography mentions the pilgrimage of Tsari, which takes place once every twelve years according to Tibetan Buddhism's twelve-year calendrical cycle.

Tibet also has a tradition of worshipping mountain gods that predates Buddhism. However, with the arrival of Buddhism, Buddhist spiritual leaders propagated narratives of how indigenous deities were "tamed" by

Buddhist masters such as Padmasambhava. Such narratives contributed to a shift in the jurisdiction of a deity's activities from mundane to universal concerns.[57] In indigenous Tibetan religion, only local populations would worship their local deity. However, once the deity was incorporated into the Buddhist pantheon, people from other locales sometimes worshipped the deity as well. A prime example from Shabkar's autobiography is the resident deity of Anyé Machen, Machen Pomra. Pomra is the local deity for the Golok region but also enjoys a pan-Tibetan authority as a deity who takes part in the Buddhist universe.

Thus, pilgrimage provides the ritual expression of Shabkar's idea of Tibet as a Buddhist imagined community. As we explored above, the practice of pilgrimage also constructs "a common order of time, space, and knowledge."[58] In this way, pilgrimages could act as a unifying force against the environmental, cultural, linguistic, and political barriers that acted as centrifugal forces in the region.

## Vegetarianism and Tibetan Buddhist Identity

One of the basic principles of Buddhism is non-harm (Skt. *ahiṃsā*). Because a meat-based diet involves killing animals, one might assume that Tibetan Buddhists are vegetarian. However, vegetarianism has never been a widespread practice in Tibet, in contrast to other Buddhist societies. One of the most commonly presented reasons for the dearth of vegetarians in Tibet in premodern times is that the harsh high-altitude climate made it particularly challenging to grow the variety of foods that are necessary for maintaining a healthy vegetarian diet. Thus, vegetarianism was not a sustainable option for the inhabitants of the Tibetan Plateau. Consequently, although Buddhism eventually came to influence every stratum of Tibetan culture since its introduction in the seventh century, diet was not one of those strata.

Still, despite the challenges of maintaining a vegetarian diet in premodern Tibet, since at least the twelfth century, vegetarianism was adopted by a small group of religious elites.[59] From the thirteenth through fifteenth centuries, Tibetan Buddhist monastics began to develop a sophisticated literature that debated whether or not the consumption of meat should be permitted in their communities.[60] These treatises were written by prominent figures across sectarian lines, indicating that the topic of vegetarianism was taken seriously by early modern Tibetan monastics across sects. The tradition of monastic vegetarianism continued to be a topic of debate among religious elites from the sixteenth through the eighteenth centuries.

A pivotal moment for the history of vegetarianism in Tibet came in the eighteenth century with the figure Jikmé Lingpa. Jikmé Lingpa is best known as a luminary of the Nyingma sect of Tibetan Buddhism who revealed a series of treasure texts called the *Longchen Nyingtik*, which means the "Heart Essence of Longchenpa." Another important legacy of Jikmé Lingpa is the way in which he introduced innovative arguments for the adoption of vegetarianism. Prior to Lingpa, the conversation about vegetarianism in Tibet was aimed at a monastic audience and was devoted to examining the permissibility of meat consumption for monks who had taken religious vows. Classic examples include Sakya Paṇḍita's *Clearly Differentiating the Three Vows* or Khedrup Jé Gelek Pelzang's *Concise Presentation of the Three Vows*.[61] However, Lingpa shifted his style from the philosophical and legalistic style of his predecessors to one that aimed to create an emotional, empathetic response in the reader.[62] The latter style is more akin to the ethos of Tibetan folk literature, which appeals to the sensibilities of the ordinary Tibetan populace. Jikmé Lingpa was from the Kham region of eastern Tibet, directly to the south of Shabkar. Due to the influence of Lingpa and other masters in the Kham region, the Kham region developed a flourishing vegetarian culture in the nineteenth century.[63]

Shabkar continued in the footsteps of Jikmé Lingpa, continuing to craft arguments that aimed to evoke his audience's emotions to inspire them to abstain from eating meat. Shabkar was one of the most important vegetarian thinkers in Tibetan history. In addition to promoting vegetarianism through songs and sermons, he also composed entire works devoted to the topic. His major writings on vegetarianism include his autobiography, collected songs, *Nectar of Immortality* (*Legs bshad bdud rtsi'i chu rgyun*), the *Wondrous Emanated Scripture* (*Rmad byung sprul pa'i glegs bam*), *Emanated Scripture of Compassion* (*Snying rje sprul pa'i glegs bam*), *Dharma Discourse: the Beneficial Sun* (*Chos bshad gzhan phan nyi ma*), and sections of the *Amazing Emanated Scripture* (*Ya mtshan sprul pa'i glegs bam*). Without counting the autobiography, songs, or shorter passages in his collected works that address vegetarianism, these works provide some 220 folios devoted to the sustained treatment of vegetarianism. This makes Shabkar's texts on vegetarianism one of the most sustained treatments of the topic in Tibetan literature. Within the context of the argument of this book, Shabkar's usage of heightened emotional appeals, genres, and styles rooted in Tibetan culture is especially significant. By drawing on Tibetan culture in his promotion of vegetarianism, Shabkar contributes to the creation of an imagined community of vegetarians on the Tibetan Plateau that cuts across class, region, and socio-economic identity.

In promoting vegetarianism, Shabkar was working against the status quo of Tibetan culture. And overall, vegetarianism never became widespread in Amdo during Shabkar's lifetime. He observes that 300 out of his 1,800 disciples became vegetarian.[64] Even among many Tibetan communities today, meat eating is the norm. Nevertheless, I argue that Shabkar's linkage of vegetarianism to Tibetan and Buddhist identity is significant because it represents the act of *imagining* a community that expresses religious identity through dietary choices. This moment of Shabkar's imagining is an important moment in the history of the idea of Tibet because it opens up the *possibility* of a community united by a shared diet.

## Shabkar's Arguments for Vegetarianism

Shabkar's staunch commitment to vegetarianism is immortalized in a scene from his autobiography, at one of the holiest sites in Tibet, where he vows to never eat meat again. At the age of twenty-nine, while on a pilgrimage to Lhasa, Shabkar witnessed hundreds of carcasses of slaughtered goats and sheep stacked along the route for sale by butchers. Shabkar recounts, "Feeling unbearable compassion for all the animals in the world who are killed for food, I went back before the Jowo Rinpoché, prostrated myself, and made this vow: 'From today on, I give up the negative act that is eating the flesh of beings, each one of whom was once my parent.'"[65] In this scene, Shabkar is motivated to abstain from consuming meat for the rest of his life due to compassion for the dead animals. The cultivation of compassion is one of the main reasons why Shabkar argues that Buddhists should abstain from meat. The reasoning is as follows: If a Buddhist craves meat, the fulfillment of that craving would involve the killing of a sentient being who is believed to have been one's parents in a previous life. The act of killing associated with the consumption of meat prevents one from generating genuine compassion. Without generating compassion, it is not possible for the practitioner to develop the mind of awakening, or *bodhicitta*.[66] Without *bodhicitta*, it is not possible to attain enlightenment.

In addition to the cultivation of compassion, Shabkar offers a host of other reasons why Buddhists should adopt a vegetarian diet. These include avoiding rebirth in the hells and cultivating positive states of mind, as well as economic and health benefits.[67] However, one of the arguments that sets Shabkar apart from most writers on vegetarianism is the way in which he links vegetarianism to Buddhist and Tibetan identity. An example of this is found in a song that he sings while confronted with the scene of the stacked carcasses of slaughtered animals described above. He sings:

> In the degenerate age, the Buddha's teachings have deteriorated.
> Outsiders have no need to come to Tibet:
> slaughterers have covered the iron mountain of monasteries and temples

that surround us with crimson flesh and blood;
buddhas and bodhisattvas have left for other pure realms.⁶⁸

In this stanza, Shabkar conceives of Tibet's worthiness as being intimately tied to the presence of Buddhism. He laments that those from beyond the plateau "have no need to come to Tibet" because the ubiquity of meat-eating, especially in the monasteries, is a sign that "the Buddha's teachings have deteriorated" and that "buddhas and bodhisattvas have left for other pure realms." Later in the same song, Shabkar sings that those who kill and witness such killing of sentient beings who "were once their mothers" are no better than ogres and should go to the land of ogres southwest of Oḍḍiyāna. By presenting the idea that Tibet's worthiness is due to the presence of Buddhism and saying that Buddhists who kill or allow the killing of animals for meat should go to the land of the ogres, Shabkar establishes a strong link between Buddhism, vegetarianism, and Tibetan identity. The link between Buddhism, vegetarianism, and Tibetan identity is also apparent in Shabkar's statement that "[s]inful butchers render Tibet red." Throughout his life, Shabkar—whose preferred epithet means "White Feet"—sought to make Tibet "white" with virtue. The killing of animals for meat has the opposite effect, rendering Tibet "red" with the blood of murdered animals.

In another passage from the same poem, Shabkar further develops the idea of the relationship between the rejection of meat eating as an essential part of Buddhist identity. In this passage, he directs his criticisms to the monks who are the upholders of the Buddhist doctrine in Tibet. He sings:

> These days, in the monasteries and temples that surround us,
> sinful slaughterers hang *tangkas* of meat,
> display offerings of lungs, hearts, and entrails,
> and explicate their worth—who displays such things?
> Amidst heaps of flesh and bones from beings who were once our mothers,
> the monks, wielding knives, stuff their gaping mouths.
> Alas! If Buddhists dare do this to beings,
> let's not speak of non-Buddhists!⁶⁹

Here, Shabkar links vegetarianism with Buddhist identity. He expresses horror that those who profess themselves to be Buddhist endorse the killing of animals for meat. Shabkar uses the dramatic metaphor of people hanging *tangkas* of meat in their monasteries and temples to give dramatic gravity to his point. In the same song, Shabkar takes this link between Buddhist identity and eating meat even further when he tries to shame those who are guilty. He sings:

> All those high and low who witness these sinners
> slaughtering the flesh of their own parents gulp their saliva.
> They show the fault of lacking loving-kindness and compassion.[70]

He says that the Buddhist Tibetans of Lhasa who witness the slaughter and sale of hundreds of livestock daily "gulp their saliva" due to shame at the fact that they "show the fault of lacking loving-kindness and compassion."

While in central Tibet, Shabkar also lobbies its political and religious leaders to implement laws that prohibit the killing of animals. In a song composed extemporaneously upon witnessing monks carrying meat that they bought within the confines of Drépung Monastery in Lhasa, Shabkar makes the following plea to all religious and political leaders in Tibet's capital city, including the Dalai Lama:

> In order not to take the lives of our parents,
> I beg you to teach Dharma and establish laws
> that encourage all monks to rely on the three whites and sweets,
> and prohibit killing by male and female butchers.
> Please consider this fervent cry for mercy![71]

In Shabkar's request that religious and political leaders implement dharmic laws (*chos khrims*) prohibiting the killing of animals, vegetarianism shifts from being an individual moral choice to a society-wide value undergirded by legislation. Thus, under this proposed legislation, vegetarianism would not just be a moral choice based on Buddhist values but would also be reinforced by the state. In Shabkar's *Emanated Scripture of Compassion*, he goes even further than this, evoking decrees by the dharma kings of the Tibetan imperial period that monks should sustain themselves on tea, molasses, grains, and dairy products.[72] The fact that Shabkar appeals to the Dalai Lama himself in the stanza above also has significance. For Shabkar and his audience, the Dalai Lama is understood to be an incarnation of Tibet's patron deity Avalokiteśvara and the leader of the Tibetan people. When Shabkar asks the Dalai Lama to implement laws requiring vegetarianism, the implication is that vegetarianism should become one of the shared values of the "imagined community" of Tibet. In this way, Shabkar's request for legally requiring monks and nuns to be vegetarian and for butchers not to kill in Tibet's capital contributes to the construction of an imagined community defined by the Buddhist values of not killing and non-harm. For Shabkar, vegetarianism should not just be the diet of a monastery or town, but rather, the diet of the Buddhist imagined community of Tibet.

In addition to promoting abstinence from killing animals for meat as part of Buddhist practice "in Upper, Middle, and Lower Tibet," Shabkar takes his message to the borderlands of the Tibetan plateau.[73] For instance, in Nepal, Shabkar describes convincing the Magar and Yalong peoples to take up vows to stop hunting.[74] In the Dingri area, he convinces the wealthy not to slaughter as many sheep.[75] He even inspires some non-Buddhist Nepali merchants to substitute offerings to their gods that do not involve animal sacrifice.[76] All of these communities live on the peripheries of the Tibetan Buddhist cultural world. Their actions—in either reducing the number of animals they kill or abstaining from killing entirely—will mark them as Buddhist. Along with Shabkar's promotion of the worship of Avalokiteśvara in this region, Buddhist-inspired practices unite, on a symbolic level, the disparate communities on the Tibetan plateau. This is an example of non-Tibetan communities on the peripheries of the Tibetan cultural world that are viewed as "barbarian" by Tibetans being assimilated into the Tibetan Buddhist world.[77]

## Vegetarianism and Everyday Nationalism

Fox and Miller-Idriss's idea of "consuming the nation" is helpful for understanding the significance of Shabkar linking vegetarianism to Tibetan and Buddhist identity. Fox and Miller-Idriss define "consuming the nation" as the way in which ordinary people act as "creative producers [of the nation] through everyday acts of consumption."[78] The act of consuming commodified aspects of the nation such as nationalist literature, media, music, and food serves to "constitute national sensibilities, embody national pride, negotiate national meanings" and so forth.[79] It would be anachronistic and inaccurate to describe Shabkar's promotion of vegetarianism as a way of buttressing Tibetan national identity. However, and so once again, we must modify the object of this theory. Shabkar's motivations for promoting vegetarianism were entirely religious, and the imagined community that he portrayed was a religious—not nationalistic—one.

David Stroup's study of the identity maintenance of Hui Muslims in the People's Republic of China is a helpful analogy for understanding the significance of Shabkar's promotion of vegetarianism in Tibet. Hui Muslims, one of the fifty-five ethnic minorities (Ch. *xiaoshu minzu*) in the PRC, are ethnically Han and religiously Muslim. They are a religious minority that live scattered throughout the PRC. Unlike the Uighers, the Hui do not have the desire to establish a nation-state. Nevertheless, the Hui mark and maintain their identity as a nationality through citizenship, faith, marriage, dietary habits, rituals, and dress. One of the ways that the Hui mark their religious identity is through the observation of *qingzhen,* or halal, dietary codes. For the Hui, buying and eating *qingzhen* "is not just an act of religious observation but a means of ethnic differentiation."[80] This is an excellent case of an imagined community that is not a nation-state but maintains its distinct identity through everyday practices such as diet.

In a similar vein, Shabkar links vegetarianism to Buddhist identity and portrays it as an ideal behavior that should be adopted in the everyday lives of his audience. Recall from our earlier discussion that prior to figures such as Jikmé Lingpa and Shabkar, the target audience for texts on vegetarianism was the monastic elite. However, Shabkar sought to promote vegetarianism beyond the monastery to the ordinary populace. This is evidenced by the way in which Shabkar gave examples in his sermons that the average farmer or herder in his audience could relate to.

For example, in his discussion of the precept of "not taking life," Shabkar places the act of killing within the context of the livelihood of herders by informing herders that there is no difference between selling livestock to a butcher for profit and killing the animals oneself.[81] He discourages herders from selling large numbers of livestock for profit,[82] and he encourages those who can to abstain from selling livestock at all and to sustain themselves by selling the wool of their livestock.[83] Shabkar also criticizes the custom of serving meat to monks who come to visit householders. He highlights the hypocrisy of this practice, pointing out that serving meat to a lama does not make the killing of the animal morally acceptable in the first place.[84] Shabkar also advises his audience not to exploit animals in the course of their everyday lives as herders and farmers. He lists the many ways that humans exploit animals: placing horses in stirrups and harnesses and whipping them as if their buttocks were a drum; selling *dzo,* yaks, and donkeys for profit; throwing stones at dogs; and so forth.[85] He also gives more specific examples, such as of people who abandon old dogs after they have committed a life of service to their family,[86] or "demon women" who do not feed these dogs, in effect starving them to death.[87] The key point here is that Shabkar's discussion of abstinence from meat and the mistreatment of animals lies not within abstract Buddhist philosophical concepts or monastic regulations, but rather, is embedded within the context of the everyday lives of lay Tibetans.

The decision for a Tibetan farmer or herder to treat their livestock humanely and not to kill or trade them for meat would represent a conscious choice to *consume* in a Buddhist manner. Whether or not they were conscious of choosing this Buddhist identity or not, the practice of vegetarianism or the humane treatment of animals would constitute a marker of their differentiation from other religious and ethnic groups in the area.

It is also obvious that Shabkar sought to reach a lay audience through his writings and sermons on vegetarianism, because he eschews the philosophical and legalistic style of the monastic elite in favor of a style that aims to create an emotional, empathetic response in the reader. The latter style is more akin to the ethos of Tibetan folk literature such as Tibetan opera, discussed in the vernacular literature chapter. An example of this can be found in the following passage, which discourages Shabkar's audience from consuming meat:

> The parent-beings—sheep, yak, *dri*—are transported from afar, and they suffer from hunger and thirst during the journey. They meet the sinful butcher, who kills them by either chopping off their head, gagging them, plunging a sharp knife to pierce their heart through the side ribs, cleaving their chest, or inserting a hand into the cavity and severing the major artery. At the time of being murdered, the goat or sheep—whoever it is—writhes in terror. They cry out and their four legs tremble. They stare piercingly at the face of the butcher. Some sheep's eyes pool with tears. Shouldn't this be cause for compassion? Seeing or hearing this, one needn't be a lama or monk. Young or old, compassionate ones would shed tears. Reflecting on this, how could you eat the flesh of your parents? When their life force is severed, an intolerable and inconceivable pain arises. Not immediately dead, their body trembles. Let's not talk about being beheaded, being suffocated by having our mouth and nose gagged, or being killed by having a hand thrust into our chest cavity, severing our major artery—if we squeeze our flesh with two of our nails, we can't tolerate the pain . . . If your own old mother were slaughtered and her meat sold, would compassion arise in you? In the same way, in previous lives, the yaks, sheep, etc. were also your parents. If they were killed, for whom would compassion not arise?[88]

The graphic imagery, visualization techniques, and skilled rhetoric would have spoken to the heightened emotional register favored by traditional Tibetan audiences. As noted in chapter 3's discussion of Tibetan opera, an intense appeal to the emotions is used as a "skillful means" to move the audience towards moral behavior. Ethnographic research indicates that audiences indeed expect to be moved by the performance and are disappointed if they are not.[89] This is not to say that Buddhist texts do not also have a robust tradition of appealing to emotions—they certainly do, as we can see in cases such as the *Laṇkāvatāra Sūtra*. However, the point I am trying to make here is that this appeal to the emotions fits into the general ethos of indigenous Tibetan folk literatures, which in turn contributes to creating a sense of community in Tibet as an imagined Buddhist community.

By promoting vegetarianism and the humane treatment of animals to ordinary Tibetans, Shabkar is not just promoting a Buddhist practice, but also opening up the discursive possibility for a vegetarian diet to serve as a force of cohesion for Tibet as an imagined community. Shabkar's imagined community of vegetarians acts as antecedent to contemporary examples where vegetarianism is an important marker of Tibetan identity, such as the Larung Gar monastery and the Lhakar movement. Larung Gar Monastery is home to some of the most vocal contemporary promoters of vegetarianism in Tibetan Buddhism and the Lhakar movement is a grassroots movement that "resist[s] against Chinese commercial marginalization" and serves as a "crusade of creative expression and celebration of Tibetan values."[90] Shabkar, along with other promoters of vegetarianism in eastern Tibet in the nineteenth century,[91] was paving the way for the possibility of vegetarianism becoming the diet of the Tibetan nation.

## Non-Sectarianism

Although Tibet is a majority Buddhist culture, there are strong sectarian divisions within Tibetan Buddhism. As a prominent Tibetologist once observed, "The roots of eclecticism and tolerance are sunk as deep into the soil of Tibetan traditions as those of sectarianism and bigotry."[92] Before the systematization of Buddhist doctrine in the fourteenth century, it was common for Buddhist masters to study with teachers from other sects and lineages. Famous examples of masters who did this include the third Karmapa Rangjung Dorjé (1284–1339), Longchenpa (1308–1363), and Tsongkhapa (1357–1419). However, with the increasing solidification of lineages and their associated institutions, the Buddhist scene became increasingly fractured in the fifteenth century.[93] Sometimes, the conflicts were purely polemical, focusing on issues such as scriptural authority.[94] Other times, the sectarian divisions would interlink with political conflict, resulting in irreparable schisms and even outright violence.[95] It was not uncommon for divisions over doctrinal matters to arise within sects or even within a single monastery, such as when Jetsünpa tried to displace the textbooks of Lodrö Rinchen Sengé at Sera Jé Monastery.[96]

Thus, although Buddhism has the potential to act as coalescing force in Tibet, internal divisions within the Buddhist community have historically threatened this unity. Indeed, internal schisms continue to be a reality to this day in Tibetan Buddhist communities, with prominent examples of protracted conflicts within both the Dalai Lama's and Karmapa's lineages. However, a tendency toward inter-sectarian openness and cross-fertilization coexisted with this tendency toward internal division. The nonsectarianism of nineteenth-century eastern Tibet is the most famous example of this second tendency.[97] There were also figures from earlier eras who embraced inter-sectarian openness, such as Shākya Chokden, Gö Lotsāwa, and the seventh Karmapa.[98]

The pernicious threat of sectarian division undermining Tibet's national unity is not lost upon contemporary Tibetan Buddhist leaders. Especially with the precarious situation of the contemporary Tibetan government in exile being stateless, this is no minor issue. Several Tibetan Buddhist leaders with an international profile have been known to promote inter-sectarian and interfaith harmony, a subject that will be taken up in the epilogue. Indeed, nonsectarianism (*ris med*) was adopted in the Central Tibetan Administration's charter on an institutional level.

Shabkar was one of the most important proponents of nonsectarianism in Tibetan Buddhist history.[99] Shabkar promoted nonsectarianism as a result of his understanding of the enlightenment experience and the ecumenical sociopolitical context of nineteenth-century Amdo. He did not promote nonsectarianism in order to engender Tibetan national unity. Nevertheless, Shabkar's promotion of nonsectarianism is significant within the context of his conception of Tibet as an imagined Buddhist community. Therefore, in this section, I will discuss this aspect of Shabkar's oeuvre.

Shabkar's nonsectarian attitude was shaped both by the sociopolitical context of nineteenth century eastern Tibet and by his own spiritual insights into Buddhism. Shabkar's home province of Amdo had a longstanding history of religious and ethnic diversity. By Shabkar's time in the nineteenth century, communities representing all major sects of Tibetan Buddhism—Nyingma, Sakya, Kagyü, Géluk, Jonang—as well as the Bön religion were flourishing in Amdo.[100] Some of these sects, such as the Jonang sect, had taken refuge in the Amdo region after fleeing sectarian persecution in central Tibet. Important religio-cultural centers of trade in the Amdo region, such as Labrang, were exposed to Muslim, Daoist, Confucian, and Christian religious communities as well.[101] While the region was certainly not without its share of both political and religious conflict,[102] as a whole, "religious diversity was relatively tolerated, or ignored," especially in contrast with the fierce sectarian rivalries of central Tibet."[103] Indeed, part of the reason why the region could support such a diversity of religions and sects was due to its relative independence from both Lhasa and Beijing.[104]

Shabkar received his formative education in Amdo province, a region with a long and rich history of inter-sectarian cooperation, especially between the Nyingma and Géluk sects. In both the Labrang region and Repgong Valley, Géluk monk-scholars and *ngakpa*, or non-celibate tantric practitioners belonging to the Nyingma sect, lived in close proximity to one another where "inter-religious tolerance and dialogue were the norm."¹⁰⁵ As early as the eighteenth century, the various abbots of Labrang Monastery "worked to bridge rather than widen the gap between Gélukpa, Nyingma and other Buddhist and non-Buddhist groups."¹⁰⁶ For example, the Fourth Jamyang Zhépa (1856–1916) pursued a variety of ecumenical activities, including instituting an order of *ngakpas,* within his Géluk-associated monastery who studied a "hybridized" curriculum of both *ngakpa* and Géluk elements.¹⁰⁷ Although such actions were not without their critics, they did give Labrang Monastery a reputation for religious pluralism. And the embrace of sectarian difference contributed to the stability of the region.¹⁰⁸

The region also had a strong legacy of masters with nonsectarian attitudes. In Shabkar's home valley of Repgong, one such nonsectarian figure was Kelden Gyatso (1607–1677). Gyatso was an important Géluk master who retired to the mountains to emulate the life of the Kagyü master Milarepa.¹⁰⁹ Shabkar sang Kelden Gyatso's songs, saw him in a dream-vision, and considered him as a role model. Another contemporary of Kelden Gyatso who belonged to the Géluk sect but embraced ecumenical sensibilities was Denma Tsültrim Gyatso (1578–1663/5). Denma was the son of a Nyingma master who was trained at a prominent Géluk monastery but embraced Kagyü practices at important Kagyü sacred sites.¹¹⁰ Shabkar described many of his own teachers from the Amdo region as being nonsectarian. One of his first teachers, Jamyang Gyatso Rinpoché, is described by Shabkar as being "well-versed in the Old and New Schools."¹¹¹ In his teens, Shabkar studied with Ngakwang Trashi Rinpoché, who "mastered the teachings in a nonsectarian manner."¹¹² The teacher who bestowed Shabkar's monastic ordination vows, Arik Géshé, was said to have faith in the teachings of non-Buddhist minorities such as the Bönpos, the Salars, and so forth, and in turn, these communities came to listen to his teachings as well.¹¹³ Shabkar's root guru, Chögyel Ngakgi Wangpo, came from a Mongolian family associated with the Géluk sect, but was simultaneously a lineage holder of the Nyingma *Longchen Nyingtik* teachings.¹¹⁴ He was described by Shabkar as teaching "both Nyingma and Sarma" teachings, and he instructed Shabkar to train in seeing all teachings and individuals with pure perception.¹¹⁵ Hence, from a young age, Shabkar lived in a religio-cultural environment where he had many models of nonsectarian attitudes to emulate.

Shabkar's own spiritual insights into Buddhism were his other source of nonsectarian thought. Shabkar's understanding of nonsectarianism was deeply tied to his meditative experiences. The relationship between such experiences and Shabkar's understanding of nonsectarianism corroborates Marc-Henri Deroche's work on the term "impartial" (*ris med*) and its variants, which demonstrates that the term was used in a soteriological context in Great Perfection literature from the Nyingma sect.[116] Shabkar describes the experience of spiritual awakening (Skt. *nirvāṇa*) as "like the sun rising in a cloudless sky, [the] wisdom that arises from meditation comes forth without fixed direction, [and] from that, [the meditator] comes to know all Dharma impartially, Nyingma [and] Sarma."[117] Thus, from the perspective of an enlightened individual, the wisdom of the awakened mind transcends the concept of "sect." In turn, the various tenet systems represent different ways of describing the same thing. In one of his songs, Shabkar maintains that the three main tenet systems in Tibet—Madhyamaka, Dzokchen, and Mahāmudrā—are three distinct descriptions of the enlightened state or the mind "free from extremes":

> Like the sky free from extremes, however you observe it,
> one's mind is free from extremes, going towards the center.
> As there is nothing greater than this,
> it is called great Madhyamaka, free from extremes.
>
> In the unimpeded vast expanse of the mind itself: emptiness-clarity,
> are all the phenomena of *saṃsāra* and *nirvāṇa* without remainder
> As they have all entered utter perfection, and there is nothing greater than this,
> It is called the Dzokchen.
>
> The emptiness-clarity of mind itself, like the seal of the king,
> seals everything in *saṃsāra* and *nirvāṇa* without exceptions.
> As there is no seal greater than this,
> It is called the Mahāmudrā.[118]

In turn, Shabkar sees the various Buddhist tenet systems of the different sects—Madhyamaka, Dzokchen, Mahāmudrā, Zhijé, and Chö—as different and valid paths to buddhahood.[119] The various tenet systems are present in order to appeal to different types of beings. Shabkar explains this idea using the Mahāyāna notion of skillful means (Skt. *upāya*): the teachings of the buddhas exist in an infinite variety of forms, because different audiences have different needs, likes, and propensities.[120] Shabkar explains that just as different types of food are appropriate for people of different ages, different teachings are best suited for different groups.[121] Consequently, although different Buddhist teachings may seem contradictory on the surface, in an ultimate sense, they are not—they are simply meant for different audiences.[122] The teachings from the various sects that branched off from the Buddha's historical teachings are essentially the same, because they "arose solely from the teachings of the Buddha, like two butter lamps proliferating from one."[123] Shabkar argues that the more diverse the teachings, the more types of people they will benefit.[124] He emphasizes that in prayers for the "flourishing and increase" of Buddhist teachings, the "increase" aspect is as important as the "flourish" aspect.[125]

Following this line of logic, Shabkar maintains that a variety of teachers in different forms are necessary to cater to the diversity of the audience. Shabkar describes various enlightened beings in the forms of buddhas, bodhisattvas, and spiritual teachers who, through their omniscience, "emanate in a body appropriate for the beings to be tamed."[126] Their compassion is described as being "impartial" or "non-referential" in that it is utterly unbiased with regards to whom it tames.[127] Shabkar describes buddhas manifesting in an astonishing variety of forms, ranging from spiritual teachers, bodhisattvas, and *pratyekabuddhas* to various beings in the six realms such as Brahmā, Indra, kings, queens, ministers, lamas, monks, women, the mentally and physically disabled, beggars, hunters, and fishermen.[128] He even considers particular inanimate objects to be emanations of the buddhas: Shabkar lists holy sites such as Bodh Gayā in India, Swayambunath in Nepal, and Wutaishan in China as examples of the "body" of the Buddha.[129] Shabkar believes that holy beings who have passed beyond cyclic existence manifest as relics, flower showers, rainbows, rocks, trees, and the four elements.[130] Shabkar even sees Buddhas as manifesting aurally in the form of "inanimate sound": natural dharma teachings arising from the sky, the sound of the five elements, drums, and so forth.[131] Another form of aural emanation is "awareness-speech," which includes treatises; oral instructions; signs or symbols; poetry; songs; the sounds of gods, nags, and yakshas; and even "nonsensical chatter."[132] Because enlightened beings manifest in an infinite variety of forms, Shabkar notes that it is often difficult to ascertain the true identity of an entity. As a result, Shabkar advises his audience to "perceive them all as buddhas" and "feel particular respect for them."[133]

Perhaps the boldest part of Shabkar's extrapolation of this argument is how he maintains that *both* Buddhist and non-Buddhist religions are the skillful means of the Buddha. In a sermon advocating for nonsectarianism preached to an assembly of Buddhists, Bönpos, *ngakpas*, Chinese, Tibetans, and Mongols, Shabkar advises his audience not to slander other religions, but rather, to practice faith, devotion and pure perception towards them.[134] In this sermon, he gives the example of the Buddha taking rebirth as the son of the eight-legged king in order to preach the scriptures of non-Buddhists. To support his points, he also cites a passage from the *Tantra of the Enlightenment of Mahāvairocana* that reads "My teachings have two aspects: the lower vehicle of the heretics, and the supreme vehicle of the buddhas." In other words, Buddhist teachings can appear in non-Buddhist forms. Because the Buddhist teachings manifest in different forms, it is difficult to judge the true status of a doctrine. Therefore, Shabkar advises Buddhist practitioners to never slander the teachings of any religion.[135] Shabkar's promotion of nonsectarianism helped to maintain the unity of his imagined community of Tibet.

# Epilogue

## THE DEEP HISTORICAL AND RELIGIOUS ROOTS OF TIBETAN NATIONAL IDENTITY

Some of the most influential theorists of nation and nationalism in the past few decades, such as Eric Hobsbawm, Ernest Gellner, and Benedict Anderson, have focused on the nation-states that have arisen as a result of modernization.[1] From this theoretical perspective, the French Revolution, the rise of industrialization, the emergence of print capitalism, and state-run institutions formed some of the necessary preconditions for the rise of the modern nation-state. However, other theorists, such as Anthony Smith, have criticized this point of view as being "materialistic" and "overly deterministic" in neglecting the premodern roots of the modern nation-state.[2] In her study of how the national cultures of Europe were shaped between 1600 and 1815, Lotte Jensen remarked that "premodern developments are not just introductory to the 'real thing' that occurred in the nineteenth century, but integral, vital parts of a larger picture."[3]

If we define modernity in Euro-American terms, namely the "colonial, capitalist, Western" modernity that emerged in the nineteenth-century Europe and became the dominant form globally,[4] then Tibet's modern period would begin in 1959 with the incursion of the People's Republic of China into Tibet and the Fourteenth Dalai Lama's flight and exile into India. Indeed, 1959 is a common threshold for understanding the division between "modern" and "premodern" Tibet. However, as historical research has shown, Tibet's transition to modernity was not so stark, with the process beginning in the early twentieth century. The Tibetan government under the thirteenth Dalai Lama, for example, took many initiatives to modernize Tibet, such as modernizing its army, introducing paper currency, postage stamps, and sending Tibetan students to England to receive a Western education.[5] These attempts, however, were thwarted by Tibet's conservative monks.[6] The Fourteenth Dalai Lama furthered the modernization efforts of the thirteenth by reforming the taxation system and the relationship between peasants and large private estates.[7] Gendün Chöpel, the monk sometimes called "Tibet's first modernist," also attempted to harmonize Buddhist points of view with evidence from modern science around this period.[8] And Chöpel's encounter with modern European science was in fact not Tibet's first, but rather part of a process that was begun in the early eighteenth century.[9]

In his critique of the theories of nationalism that regard nations and nationalism as a distinctly modern phenomenon, Anthony Smith argues that in order to fully understand the modern nation, we need to examine its history in the *longue durée* rather than limit our understanding to the modern period.[10] Only by considering the myths, memories, traditions, and symbols that form the heritage of nations can we understand what gives nationalism its power.[11] Throughout Tibetan history, many authors have revived and adapted the myths, memories, traditions, and symbols that give Tibet its distinctive identity. The Avalokiteśvara myth is one such example. Another example is the idea of a plateau-wide Tibet—an idea that was not a product of modern times but rather was a concept with deep premodern roots. Moving from a trope of stark rupture to one of continuity helps us to understand the powerful affective dimensions of Tibetan nationalism.

The notion of a stark rupture between "premodern" and "modern" periods in Tibet has had crucial implications for Tibetan communities both within and outside of the PRC. For instance, the Chinese state has used this idea to advance the notion that Tibet was a "backwards" (Ch. *luohou*) civilization prior to the 1950s. This notion has served to justify the Chinese state's "civilizing" projects on the Tibetan plateau and to emphasize the kindness of the state's "gift of development" to Tibetans.[12] On a more global level, the notion of a premodern versus a modern Tibet has also contributed to Euro-American fantasies about Tibet as a pristine paradise.[13]

By demonstrating continuities between Tibet's past and present, this study urges us towards thinking beyond stark binaries. This study follows in the footsteps of Lama Jabb's analysis of modern Tibetan literature, which demonstrates significant continuities between modern and premodern periods in Tibetan literature and culture. In order to appreciate the rich cultural history in which Tibetans continue to imagine themselves and their relationship to the rest of the world, it is necessary to consider *both* the ruptures and continuities throughout Tibetan history. In this chapter, I use the term "early modern" rather than "premodern" to describe the historical milieu of Shabkar and other nineteenth-century figures. The main reason for this is because the term "early modern" connotes continuity with the modern period whereas the terms "modern" and "premodern" convey the sense of a binary. Although Sheldon Pollack defines "early modern" as the period between 1500–1800 in India and Tibet,[14] Janet Gyatso offers a more expansive definition, namely, as the period "roughly correspond[ing] to the development of Tibetan self-consciousness of its political and cultural position vis-à-vis other powers in the region."¹⁵ I adopt Gyatso's definition because its description fits well with Shabkar's cultural context.

This book has demonstrated how Shabkar presents a concept of Tibet as a Buddhist imagined community. His multidimensional portrayal of Tibet encompasses geographical, linguistic, historical, literary, mythical, religious, and cultural dimensions. He conceives of Tibet as including people from different regions unified by their bond as Avalokiteśvara's chosen people. While Shabkar's concept of Tibet fits many cultural definitions of nation, this concept of territory, community, and belonging lies outside of the Westphalian state-centric framework for nationhood. Because Shabkar's concept of Tibet as a Buddhist imagined community serves as an antecedent to some forms of contemporary Tibetan nationalism, his work challenges the notion of stark rupture between early modern and modern concepts of Tibet.

This epilogue traces the links between the work of Shabkar (and other early modern leaders) and three key components of contemporary Tibetan identity and nationalism: the importance of nonsectarianism within Tibetan Buddhism, Buddhism as the bedrock of national identity, and a vegetarian diet as a marker of national identity.

## Antecedents to the Nonsectarianism of Contemporary Tibetan Leaders

Nonsectarianism is one of the hallmarks of contemporary Tibetan Buddhism, especially as espoused by many high-profile Tibetan Buddhist leaders with international influence. Prominent examples of such figures include the Fourteenth Dalai Lama, Dilgo Khyentsé Rinpoché, Dezhung Rinpoché, Chogyam Trungpa, Situ Ripoche, and the Karmapa. The most prominent of these is the Fourteenth Dalai Lama, who takes his nonsectarianism approach a step further by engaging in interfaith dialogue with high-profile leaders from other faiths such as Thomas Merton, Desmond Tutu, and Zalman Schacter-Shalomi.¹⁶ In addition to building constructive relationships with other faiths, the Dalai Lama has also encouraged surviving Tibetan Buddhist masters to adopt a collaborative approach in preserving Tibetan Buddhism.¹⁷ Under his influence, a nonsectarian attitude is also embedded into the governmental structures of the Central Tibetan Administration. Article 17 of the Charter of the Tibetans-in-Exile maintains the CTA's commitment to disseminating Buddhism with a nonsectarian orientation.¹⁸ The Tibetan Assembly is also required to include elected members from each of Tibet's main sectarian denominations: Nyingma, Kagyü, Sakya, Géluk, and Yungdrung Bön.¹⁹

Still, this commitment to nonsectarianism by both Tibetan Buddhist leaders and the Tibetan government in exile was not always the norm in Tibetan Buddhist history. As the prominent Tibetologist Gene Smith once remarked, "The roots of eclecticism and tolerance are sunk as deep into the soil of Tibetan traditions as those of sectarianism and bigotry."[20] Why have many modern Tibetan Buddhist leaders embraced a nonsectarian attitude? As with all important questions, the reasons are complex. At the most basic level, nonsectarianism is an expression of some of the fundamental values of Mahāyāna Buddhism, including impartiality. There are many examples of Tibetan Buddhist masters throughout history who embraced a nonsectarian approach. At the same time, however, the reasons for espousing nonsectarian attitudes have political implications as well. With the loss of its ancestral territories, one of the Central Tibetan Administration's main concerns is how to sustain national unity. Constant fighting amongst the various sects of Tibetan Buddhism would undermine not just Tibetan unity but Tibetan Buddhism as well. Thus, in the contemporary context, the promotion of nonsectarianism is not just a matter of maintaining religious ideals; rather, the very survival of both Tibetan Buddhism and the Tibetan nation depends on it.

The Dalai Lama's nonsectarian attitude is the result of many influences. However, in this section, I will focus on the antecedents that are related to Shabkar. The Dalai Lama has praised Shabkar for "the absolute purity of his approach to his lama and his personal practice, which freed him from the snare of sectarianism."[21] His nonsectarian stance is influenced by several of Shabkar's spiritual heirs as well: Japa Dongak Gyatso (1824–1902), the Third Dodrupchen Jigmé Tenpé Nyima (1865–1926), and Dongak Chökyi Gyatso (1903–1957).

Shabkar's disciple Japa Dongak Gyatso was from the Golok region of Amdo Province. Despite being a reincarnate lama belonging to the Géluk sect, Japa taught at the Nyingma-affiliated Dodrup Monastery.[22] The type of Nyingma-Géluk cross-fertilization was typical of the Amdo region in the eighteenth and nineteenth centuries.[23] Japa was a disciple of both Shabkar and Patrul Rinpoché (1808–1887). Patrul Rinpoché was an important representative of the nonsectarian "movement" from Kham Province. Thus, by studying with main figures from both the nonsectarian traditions of Amdo and Kham, Japa united these approaches. In turn, he united these two streams of nineteenth century nonsectarianism and passed them on to his disciple, the Third Dodrupchen Jigmé Tenpé Nyima. Japa is also believed to have subsequently reincarnated as Dongak Chökyi Gyatso, and to have carried on this nonsectarian work as Dongak.

The Third Dodrupchen Jigmé Tenpé Nyima was born into an elite Nyingma family in Golok. Jigmé Tenpé Nyima was the disciple of one master, the philosopher Mipam (1846–1912), who represented the Kham nonsectarian tradition, and another master, Japa Dongak Gyatso, who represented the Amdo nonsectarian traditions. However, unlike his teacher Mipam, Nyima was "inclusive" and "irenic" in his treatment of the ideas of other sects.[24] This type of open-minded attitude towards sectarian difference—especially between the Géluk and Nyingma—reflects the legacy of many nonsectarian teachers he studied with, including Japa Dongak Gyatso. Notably, his teachings have directly informed the Fourteenth Dalai Lama's nonsectarian views.[25]

Like his two spiritual predecessors, Dongak Chökyi Gyatso was also born in the Golok region of Amdo. Recognized as the reincarnation of Japa Dongak Gyatso at age fifteen, he was enthroned at Pel Nyenmo Monastery and received full ordination at age eighteen.[26] Like Shabkar, Japa Dongak, and Jigmé Tenpé Nyima before him, he studied with both Nyingma and Géluk masters.[27] Dongak Chökyi Gyatso inherited the nonsectarian orientation of his spiritual predecessors. He composed *A Jeweled Mirror of Pure Appearances* (*Dag snang nor bu'i me long*) in order to "dispel the darkness of sectarian division" that weakens the Buddhist teachings.[28] He also hoped that his text would help others to "avoid abandoning the Dharma."[29] Statements such as these could have been taken directly out of Shabkar's *Collected Works*.

Still, the most significant contribution of this text and *The Offering Clouds of the Nectar of the Path of Reasoning* (*Rigs lam bdud rtsi'i mchod sprin*) was not so much in his nonsectarian attitude as in his approach to doctrinal differences between Nyingma and Géluk sects. He argued that although the doctrines appear to differ, they "share a common viewpoint."[30] His innovation was that he combined elements of Géluk and Nyingma doctrine in a syncretic manner,[31] which was an unprecedented move.[32] In his syncretism, he was reacting against both conservative stances within the Géluk sect and exclusivist strands of Nyingma thought. He created a syncretic form of Nyingma-Géluk philosophy in a couple of works.[33] This is vital because although previous figures like Jigmé Tenpé Nyima, Japa Dongak, and Shabkar adopted inclusivist attitudes towards sectarian difference, they kept the Nyingma and Géluk doctrinal systems separate. Dongak Chökyi Gyatso's innovations are also significant in light of the fact that they ignore and in effect annul Mipam's philosophical innovations by turning to pre-Mipam interpretations of Dzokchen.[34] He seems to have been pushing back against Mipam's move to further differentiate the doctrinal system of Nyingma philosophy from other sects, especially the Géluk.[35] With Mipam being the *premiere* figure in Nyingma thought since Longchenpa in the fourteenth century, Dongak's move was both bold and controversial.

Despite his innovations, Dongak Chökyi Gyatso's texts do not seem to have made an impact beyond his local community in Golok and Amdo. Adam Pearcey attributes the influence of Dongak Chökyi Gyatso's texts to Shabkar's legacy in the region.[36] I would also add that Amdo, and especially the Labrang and Golok regions, had a strong history of Nyingma and Géluk cooperation, making Gyatso's work possible. Nevertheless, the incursion of the PRC's People's Liberation Army onto the Tibetan plateau soon after his death would extinguish any attention to his texts. With the Dalai Lama and tens of thousands of Tibetans fleeing over the Himalayas into exile in India in 1959, the emphasis for the Tibetan community was to focus on "preservation and restoration," resulting in the persistence of sectarian differentiation rather than syncretism.[37] However, this was not the end of the story for Dongak Chökyi Gyatso's ideas. His contributions to nonsectarian thought would find a greater audience through the attention given to his ideas by the Fourteenth Dalai Lama in the twentieth and twenty-first centuries.[38]

## Contemporary Leaders Who Link Buddhism to Tibetan Identity

Contemporary Tibetan nationalism exists in diverse forms. For Tibetans living outside of the PRC, on one end of the spectrum is the Tibetan independence movement, which advocates for a separate Tibetan nation-state. A prominent example of this orientation is the Tibetan Youth Congress (TYC), a Tibetan NGO that self-describes as a "national movement" devoted to "the restoration of complete independence for the whole of Tibet."[39] On the other end of the spectrum is the Dalai Lama's Middle Way approach, currently adopted by the Central Tibetan Administration, which does not seek a separate nation-state, but rather "genuine autonomy for all Tibetan people under a single administration."[40] For Tibetans living within the PRC, there are also a variety of expressions of nationalism. There is the "hard nationalism" of Tibetans who self-immolated beginning in 2009 in order to protest Chinese state suppression of elements of Tibetan culture that are key to their national and cultural identity, such as language and Buddhism.[41] There is also the "soft nationalism" of the Tibetan Buddhist encampments in the PRC, which maintain Tibetan Buddhism, language, and culture while cooperating with the restrictions of the Chinese state.[42] Another variety of Tibetan nationalism within the PRC grounds Tibetan identity not in Buddhism but in a newly constructed secular Tibetan identity.[43]

The versions of Tibetan nationalism that are most explicitly intertwined with Buddhism are the ones that most closely resemble the framework of the "Tibetan Buddhist world." [44] This type of nationalism is espoused by several prominent lamas with international followings, from both within the PRC and the Tibetan diaspora: the Fourteenth Dalai Lama, the Seventeenth Karmapa, and several of the leaders of the Larung Gar Buddhist Academy.

The Fourteenth Dalai Lama (b. 1935) is the most famous Tibetan Buddhist leader today. For the Dalai Lama, Tibetan identity is inextricably linked to Buddhist values.[45] In a speech to a group of Tibetans in New York in 1999, he urges, "We must not lose the feeling that we are Tibetans. In whatever society we find ourselves, we must not forget. Most importantly, it is necessary to be a good person."[46] Here, the Dalai Lama is implying that being a "good person" is a fundamental part of Tibetan identity. For his audience, "good person" is a reference to the Buddhist observance of moral discipline in which one engages in actions that benefit others and abstain from actions that harms others. The way in which the Dalai Lama links Buddhist and Tibetan identity differs from other forms of Buddhist nationalism, such as those prevalent in Sri Lanka and Myanmar, where one's ethnicity makes one *necessarily* Buddhist. By contrast, the Dalai Lama maintains that one is Buddhist only if one practices the values and practices of Buddhists. He criticizes Tibetans who say they are Buddhist because their parents were Buddhist, arguing that it is necessary to understand the fundamental principles of Buddhism and to know *why* one is Buddhist.[47] Thus, according to the Dalai Lama, although Buddhism is something fundamental to Tibetan identity, the relationship between Buddhism and Tibetan national identity is not something that can be taken for granted, but rather, something that Tibetans need to continuously strive at.

Although some analysts have tended to view the Dalai Lama's promotion of Buddhist-based values as a political strategy,[48] here I will consider this issue from a historical and religious studies perspective. In particular, the Dalai Lama's promotion of Buddhism and its relationship to Tibetan national identity can be seen as the continuation of a way of understanding the relationship between Buddhism and Tibetan identity with deep historical roots.

The Seventeenth Karmapa is another prominent Tibetan Buddhist leader who is considered by many to be the Dalai Lama's future successor as Tibet's spiritual head. Like the Dalai Lama, the Karmapa presents Tibetan identity as being inextricable from Buddhism. In his 2017 speech to Sarah College in India, he observes, "Tibetans are a bit different from other people. They have a close connection to their customs and traditional ways of doing things, which are in turn deeply related to the philosophy and practice of Buddhism. If we were to eliminate them all, we would be left without our precious jewel, our beautiful ornament, bereft of something we could show to others."[49] Like the Dalai Lama, the Karmapa maintains that Buddhism is inextricably linked to Tibetan identity, and that the Tibetan peoples' greatest asset is their Buddhist character. The Karmapa's statement echoes the Dalai

Lama's speech when he says, "Our greatest treasure is being a good person."[50] Reminiscent of the way in which early modern Tibetan Buddhist texts like Shabkar's autobiography refer to Avalokiteśvara (the bodhisattva of compassion) as the patron deity of the Tibetan people, the Karmapa evoked the myth of Avalokiteśvara as the Tibetan peoples' destined deity in a dharma teaching to a group of Tibetan disciples at Gyütö Monastery in 2002. After introducing Avalokiteśvara as the essence of all the buddhas' compassion and Tibet's patron deity, the Karmapa proceeded to discuss the deity's importance in Tibetan history.[51] He stated, "Avalokiteśvara is very important. In the example of Tibet, he has incarnated as the dharma kings, many different lamas from all lineages, and in particular, in contemporary times, as the Fourteenth Dalai Lama and many such enlightened beings. We Tibetans and the realm of Tibet have received his blessings a lot. He is the father of the Tibetan people."[52] By evoking the myth of Avalokiteśvara, the Karmapa gives an ontological backing to the Tibetan peoples' relationship with Buddhism. This resonates with the long tradition of linking Avalokiteśvara to Tibet's identity and fate that we can see in Shabkar's work. In turn, this can be traced to ideas from the *Maṇi Kabum,* the mid-twelfth to mid-thirteenth century text that provides the textual basis for how Avalokiteśvara, a Buddhist deity of Indian origin, would eventually become Tibet's destined deity after the eleventh century.

It is noteworthy, however, that the Karmapa does not evoke Avalokiteśvara to stir up nationalist sentiment. Instead, he does so in order to encourage Tibetans to practice and embody qualities cherished in the Buddhist tradition. At the end of the dharma teaching, he emphasizes that the point of practicing the Avalokiteśvara *sadhana* and reciting the six-syllable mantra is to pacify one's own negative emotions and lead others onto a pure path.[53] Echoing the Dalai Lama's spiritual advice to Tibetans, he emphasizes that practicing Buddhism in an authentic way would be the "best offering to the buddhas."[54] The emphasis on the importance of Buddhism being embodied in people's minds is also apparent in his 2017 speech to members of Sarah College, where he states that "a mind imbued with Dharma and a stable sincerity are essential" for the future. Finally, in line with how he does not evoke Avalokiteśvara to make a nationalistic claim, he also does not confine Buddhism to belonging to a particular people. He stated to a group of eight-thousand Tibetans attending the Dalai Lama's Kalacakra empowerment in Bodh Gayā that the dharma, with its values of non-violence and altruism, is a "common treasure for all the world to use and enjoy."[55] For both the Karmapa and the Dalai Lama, it is the *attitude* and *practices* that make one Buddhist, not the label of being Buddhist.

Both the Dalai Lama and the Karmapa are examples of Tibetan Buddhist leaders in exile. Khenpo Jigmé Phuntsok (1933–2004) and Khenpo Tsultrim Lodrö (b. 1962) are both important leaders from the Larung Gar Buddhist Academy in Sichuan Province of the PRC who promote the idea of Buddhism and Tibetan identity as being intertwined.

Khenpo Jigmé Phuntsok was one of the most important figures in the revitalization of Tibetan Buddhism within the PRC in the aftermath of the Cultural Revolution, post-1980s. Although his influence was mostly limited to the PRC, he offers us a perspective onto how one of the most influential Tibetan Buddhist leaders in the PRC conceived of the relationship between Buddhism and Tibetan national identity in contemporary times. Like the Dalai Lama and the Karmapa, Khenpo Jigmé Phuntsok "links culture and ethics to his construction of Tibetan identity."[56] In particular, he depicts Tibetans as "pious people who for several thousands of years have intrinsically remained noble in demeanor—imbued with bravery, fortitude, kindness, and candor."[57] Echoing both the Dalai Lama and the Karmapa, in Khenpo Jigmé Phuntsok's *Heart Advice*, "the principle of compassion is depicted as integral to the fabric of Tibetan culture."[58] Thus, for Khenpo Jigmé Phuntsok, Buddhist values such as compassion, kindness, moral conduct (i.e., being "noble in demeanor") and mental fortitude are essential parts of the Tibetan nationality's identity. Similar to the Dalai Lama, Khenpo Jigmé Phuntsok defines Buddhism not as a reified label, but in terms of a cluster of mental qualities. Still, because these are cultural and ethical values, these "principal markers of 'Tibetaness'" can be easily lost due to assimilation.[59]

In Khenpo Jigmé Phuntsok's writings, there is an overwhelming sense that Tibetan language, culture, and knowledge traditions are under threat from both hegemonic Han Chinese discourse and "new ways of thinking."[60] Like the Dalai Lama and Karmapa, he advocates for the necessity of cultural survival, calling for "the preservation of Tibetan language (*skad yig*), erudition (*rig gzhung*) and customs (*yul srol*), likening esteem for these to the 'life force' (*srog*) of a people, without which they are no longer a discrete nationality (*mi rigs*)."[61] Although he does not mention Buddhism explicitly, his discussion of "Values for Our Tibetan People in the 21st century" contains key Buddhist components. He lists four main values. Two of these values—to always endeavor to have a good attitude, and to be genuinely honest without pretext—are implicitly Buddhist. And a third—to have conviction in the sublime dharma, including conviction in present and future lives, in karma, and in the buddhas—is explicitly Buddhist.[62] Hence, it is clear that for Khenpo Jigmé Phuntsok, the values that constitute the "life force" of the Tibetan people include Buddhist principles.

Khenpo Tsultrim Lodrö is one of Khenpo Jigmé Phuntsok's main successors. He is highly influential within the PRC, with disciples from both

Tibetan and Han backgrounds. He has also done some teaching tours abroad as well. For Khenpo Tsultrim Lodrö, Buddhism is the essence of Tibetan identity and culture. During his sermons to followers near Lake Kokonor, he said, "What is Tibetan culture? Fundamentally, Tibetan culture (*bod gyi rig gnas*) is about 'not harming other beings,' which is both our culture as well as our religious belief.... The slaughtering of animals for the sake of our own life goes against both our culture and our religion in the same way."[63] Stated just as unequivocally at Pelyül Monastery in Golok, he argues, "the most urgent thing for us is to protect our culture including *chos* (Buddhism) and language.... Tibetan world view (*lta ba*) indeed is a Buddhist world view, if we stick to this world view, we will have a better life in this world and good one in the next life."[64] For Khenpo Tsultrim Lodrö, Buddhism is inseparable from Tibetan culture.

What unifies the approaches of the Dalai Lama, Karmapa, Khenpo Jigmé Phuntsok and Khenpo Tsultrim Lodrö is the promotion of Buddhist-inspired values to serve as a cultural glue that holds together the Tibetan people via their national identity. In a context where one's nation has lost its historical territories, the promotion of the nation's common values and practices serves as the glue that sustains the idea of a nation. Although the linkage between Buddhism and Tibetan identity is not as clearly articulated in Shabkar's works as it is in those of contemporary Tibetan Buddhist masters, we nevertheless see evidence of this idea in Shabkar's autobiography. Thus, Shabkar's usage of shared beliefs and practices to reinforce the imagined community of Tibet serves as an antecedent to the way in which contemporary Tibetan Buddhist leaders use Buddhism as one of the ways of holding the imagined community of contemporary Tibet together, despite Tibetan populations being scattered all over the world.

## Two Contemporary Leaders' Promotion of Vegetarianism as Core to Tibetan Identity

Related to Buddhism as a coalescing force is the way in which vegetarianism and the ethical treatment of animals are becoming practices that mark national identity in Tibetan communities across the world. The vegetarian, anti-slaughter, and fur renunciation movements are a series of distinct but interrelated movements all originating from the religious leaders of the Larung Buddhist Academy in Serta County at the border between Qinghai and Sichuan Provinces in the PRC. These movements trace their roots to Khenpo Jigmé Phuntsok and his cultural revitalization movements in eastern Tibet, which occurred after the Chinese state's Opening Up and Reform policies (Ch. *gaige kaifang*) in the 1980s. So far, the primary way in which these movements have been examined have been within the context of the central government's Great Western Development (Ch. *xibu da kaifa*) to accelerate development of regions in western China and the religious leaders of Larung Buddhist Academy's response to it. However, comparing these movements to Shabkar's promotion of vegetarianism illuminates different aspects of this phenomenon as well.

Beginning in the 2000s, the central government initiated the Great Western Development to accelerate development of regions in western China. This is because the largely rural areas of western China lagged behind the economic development of coastal areas and large cities. The central government proceeded to engage in a "civilizing mission" on the Tibetan plateau that introduced "neoliberal ideology embodied in post-Mao state-sponsored initiatives to promote market capitalism" to a Tibetan society that was portrayed as "backward" by the state media.[65] However, the state's initiatives to promote market capitalism occurred too rapidly, resulting in "corrosive effects" on Tibetan societies.[66] In response to this situation, Khenpo Jigmé Phuntsok published *Heart Advice to Tibetans for the 21st Century* in 1995. In contrast to state ideologies that portray Buddhism and Tibetan culture as being "backward" in comparison to neoliberal measures of economic progress, Khenpo Jigmé Phuntsok "redefines the very language of progress (*yar rgyas*) to promote a Tibetan vision of modernity in explicitly Buddhist terms."[67] It is within this context of efforts to preserve Tibetan Buddhist culture in the face of state-sponsored development initiatives that the vegetarian movement and related movements emerged.

The vegetarian and anti-slaughter movements began in 2000 when Khenpo Jigmé Phuntsok made a speech to thousands to stop selling yaks and sheep for slaughter.[68] His speech was in reaction to witnessing a great surge of animals killed for slaughter as a result of state-sponsored economic developments, and to seeing the mistreatment of these animals before they were slaughtered. While this exhortation to abandon killing was rooted in belief in the laws of karma and the classic Mahāyāna Buddhist virtue of compassion for sentient beings, there was also an "anti-assimilationist bent" to it; that is, an element of "resist[ing] the project of commodification, particularly the integration of local goods into a wider Chinese economy."[69] In other words, while this exhortation was informed by religious values, it was also informed by a sense of needing to protect Buddhist values and Tibetan identity in the face of the increased integration of Tibetan societies into the dominant hegemonic Han culture of the PRC. Khenpo Jigmé Phuntsok's concept of Tibetan identity is inextricable from Buddhist values.[70]

The issue of Tibetan identity and its relationship to the vegetarian diet also figures significantly in one of Khenpo Jigmé Phuntsok's main successors at

Larung Gar, Khenpo Tsultrim Lodrö. Like Khenpo Jigmé Phuntsok, Khenpo Tsultrim Lodrö articulates a concept of development that is deeply informed by Buddhist ethics. He argues, for example, that "Buddhism is the only asset that Tibetan people have now. If they give up this tradition, then they will become 'backward' not only economically, but also culturally."[71] Khenpo Tsultrim Lodrö's promotion of vegetarianism is informed by a combination of Buddhist values, modern scientific studies, and issues surrounding Tibetan identity.[72] With regard to the point about identity, he is mainly concerned with the preservation of their culture and the image of Tibetans in relation to the other cultural groups. For Khenpo Tsultrim Lodrö, Tibetan identity, vegetarianism, and a commitment to anti-slaughter are interlinked. In a sermon near Qinghai Lake, he says, "What is Tibetan culture? Fundamentally, Tibetan culture (*bod gyi rig gnas*) is about 'not harming other beings,' which is both our culture as well as our religious belief.... The slaughtering of animals for the sake of our own life goes against both our culture and our religion in the same way."[73]

Khenpo Tsultrim Lodrö is also concerned with issues of how Tibetans are perceived by others. For example, with regard to the long-standing Tibetan cultural norm of wearing furs to display wealth, he expressed concern that if the international community were to see Tibetans wearing fur, they would perceive Tibetans as being "cruel, malicious, disgusting and ignorant."[74] In the case of promoting a vegetarian diet, he urges Tibetans not to assimilate into certain practices of the Han Chinese, such as consuming banquet dishes that involve cruelty towards animals.[75] Thus, while Khenpo Tsultrim Lodrö's promotion of a vegetarian diet is rooted in Buddhist ethics and informed by modern scientific studies on human health, the preservation of Tibetan identity and culture through the adoption of a vegetarian diet is also an important dimension. In that way, for Khenpo Tsultrim Lodrö, one might say that a vegetarian diet is the ideal diet for the Tibetan nationality (*mi rigs*, Ch. *minzu*).

When Khenpo Tsultrim Lodrö says that "the slaughtering of animals for the sake of our own life goes against both our culture and our religion in the same way,"[76] his words represent, in Fox and Miller Idriss' terms, "discursive claims for, about and in the name of the nation."[77] Talking about the nation on a regular basis becomes a means of creating the "micro-settings for the invocation and reproduction of nationhood in everyday life."[78] In this way, especially with the lack of an internationally recognized nation-state in the Tibetan exile situation, "talking the nation"—by making claims about its dietary practices—represents a way in which nationhood can be "meaningfully embodied, expressed and sometimes performed in the routine contexts of everyday life."[79]

Although Khenpo Jigmé Phuntsok and Khenpo Tsultrim Lodrö come from a different historical context from Shabkar, all three figures share the notion that the worthiness of Tibetan identity is rooted in Buddhist values. While Khenpo Jigmé Phuntsok and Khenpo Tsultrim Lodrö's promotion of vegetarianism and related causes is rooted in Buddhist values of compassion and non-harm, they also link these values to Tibetan identity. This linkage of vegetarianism and the protection of animals to Tibetan and Buddhist identity is found in Shabkar's promotion of these issues. Thus, Shabkar serves as an antecedent of these contemporary movements, despite not being a direct influence on the Serta *khenpos*' promotion of vegetarianism. Some have argued that vegetarianism in Tibetan Buddhist communities is due to the influence of Chinese Buddhism. That may certainly be the case—but the influence is likely not entirely from Chinese Buddhism, since the precedent was there in Shabkar's time. The cultural building blocks for the idea of the link between vegetarianism and Tibetan and Buddhist identity were present from before.

In addition to Khenpo Jigmé Phuntsok and Khenpo Tsultrim Lodrö, there are other groups of Tibetans for whom a vegetarian diet is linked to the maintenance of their cultural identity. Some educated Tibetans in the PRC for example, such as those working in government work offices, choose to abstain from meat as a way of expressing their cultural identity.[80] Similarly, in the Lhakar or "White Wednesday" movement, some Tibetans choose to adopt a vegetarian diet each Wednesday as a way of expressing their Tibetan identity; other methods of expressing their cultural identity include adopting Tibetan dress, speaking Tibetan language, and so forth.[81]

## The Framework of the Countermodern

This book has demonstrated how Buddhism and Tibetan identity are inextricably linked in the autobiography of an early modern Tibetan author. For Shabkar, Buddhism was not something that could be divorced from the rest of life, but instead was a framework for understanding the world and the main coalescing force for the communities of the Tibetan plateau. Indeed, as one historian has observed, "At the height of the opposition to Chinese rule, the Tibetans were mobilised not in the name of their nation but in the defence of their faith. The 'other' was identified as *Tendra*, 'enemy of the faith', and the resistance fighters were *Tenzhung mang mi*, 'defenders of the faith.'"[82] As demonstrated in chapter 1, Shabkar's concept of Tibet as a Buddhist imagined community has strong parallels to the concept of *sasana* and moral community from early modern Theravāda Buddhist societies.

The inextricability between Buddhism and Tibetan identity in the early modern period helps to explain how despite the strong forces of globalization and modernization, Buddhism remains a vibrant presence in Tibetan culture and politics. In the context of the diaspora, the Central Tibetan Administration—despite being more secular than its theocratic predecessor the Ganden Potrang—still bears Buddhist elements such as its usage of the state oracle.[83] In the international Tibet movement, ideas of human international law, human rights, democracy are being expressed by Tibetans through Tibetan Buddhist idioms such as an emphasis on nonviolent protest.[84] Even within the context of the PRC, with strong state pressure for Tibetans to assimilate to Han Chinese culture, we see the flourishing of Tibetan Buddhism in Buddhist encampments such as in the case of the Larung Gar Buddhist academy. The leaders of the Larung Gar Buddhist academy understand Buddhism as an essential element of the Tibetan nationality.

The perdurance of Buddhism in Tibetan culture and political life calls for us to reconsider the role of religion in Tibetan nationalism. While in contemporary times, there has been certainly a shift to a more secular Tibetan identity as epitomized in Tsering Shakya's memorable phrase "from the faith to the flag,"[85] Buddhism still appears in all but the most radical secular iterations of Tibetan nationalism. This is apparent, for example, in the case of the hundreds of Tibetans who have self-immolated as an act of protest in the PRC since 2009. While the self-immolators cited different reasons for why they decided to self-immolate, these acts were mainly ethno-nationalistic in nature and meant to express the self-immolators' opposition to "Tibetan culture and identity as being on the verge of being destroyed by the modernist state project."[86] In addition to this political dimension, Tibetans also framed the actions of self-immolators from a religious dimension as well. Many Tibetans understood the self-immolations "not only as acts of sacrifice but as acts with religious meaning, as in the tradition of offering one's body for the benefit of others."[87] This latter reason refers to the concept of the bodhisattva in Mahāyāna Buddhism whose spiritual practice involves working for the altruistic benefit of others.[88]

Thus, when the Chinese government suppresses Buddhism in Tibetan cultural areas, it is not just Buddhism they are suppressing, but a key part of Tibetan culture and identity with roots dating to the Later Transmission Period beginning in the tenth century. As one analyst has observed, "the suppression of religion has alienated the Tibetan people from their Chinese rulers."[89] Anthony Smith has argued that "it is impossible to grasp the meanings of nations and nationalism without an understanding of the links between religious motifs and rituals and later ethnic and national myths, memories, and symbols."[90] When the central government suppresses Buddhism, Tibetan language, and the Dalai Lama, they are suppressing the main symbols of Tibetan religiosity and identity. The religious roots of Tibetan nationalism are deep and go back centuries.

Understanding the deep historical origins of the link between Buddhism and Tibetan national identity can give us a new perspective on the spiritual activities of contemporary Tibetan Buddhist leaders who promote the link between Buddhism and Tibetan identity. On the one hand, these initiatives need to be understood within the context of the precarious political context in which the Tibetan nation finds itself in the twentieth and twenty-first centuries. On the other hand, these initiatives also represent a continuation of age-old ways of being on the Tibetan plateau. In other words, this intertwining of Buddhist and Tibetan identity is not a modern phenomenon, but rather, has deep historical roots. This reframing allows us to see continuities between the contemporary Tibetan Buddhist leaders' attempts to preserve Buddhism as an essential part of Tibetan national identity, the early-twentieth century attempts by the Ganden Phodrang government to create a modern nation-state that was simultaneously Buddhist,[91] and the legacy of the intertwined nature of the religious and secular of the "Tibetan Buddhist world" from the thirteenth through twentieth centuries.

In the past decade, there has been a robust debate about what "Buddhist modernity" means within discussions of alternative modernities. The idea of "alternative modernities" was first bought forth by Dilip Goankar to challenge the notion of a monolithic "modernity" couched in Euro-American terms.[92] Goanker's work built upon earlier contributions by scholars such as Sudipta Kaviraj who questioned the uncritical imposition of the concept of "modernity" onto non-European historical cases.[93] In Buddhist studies, the consensus is that there isn't a monolithic "Buddhist modernity" but rather, "many different 'Buddhisms'" that arose from different variants of modernity.[94] Within this debate, Matthew King has most recently advanced the idea of a "hybrid, countermodern" Buddhism that is distinct from the well-studied Buddhist modernisms of Japan, Myanmar, and Sri Lanka. The example that King explores is the countermodern vision of the Mongol polymath Zawa Damdin in the early twentieth century. Damdin was aware of the modern discourses present during his time but chose to talk past them, formulating his own Buddhist countermodernity that existed in "a third register beyond the Qing and the national subject."[95]

The way that Tibetan Buddhist leaders such as the Dalai Lama and Khenpo Jigmé Phuntsok try to maintain the link between Buddhism and Tibetan national identity is reminiscent of how the Damdin chose to talk past discourses of secular nationhood in the early twentieth century. The way in which contemporary Tibetan Buddhist leaders link Buddhism with Tibetan national identity, casting the Tibetan people in a way that garners international support for the Tibetan national cause, can certainly be seen as a strategy of survival. However, we can also consider the contemporary Tibetan

Buddhist leaders' impulse to link Tibetan national identity with Buddhism as a "countermodern" impulse. These leaders are drawing from a deeply rooted cultural sense of what ties their people together that is apparent in texts such as Shabkar's autobiography. The way in which they portray Tibetan national identity as being inseparable from Buddhism flies in the face of notions of secular nationhood and points to a third register beyond the dichotomy of the secular and religious, the nation and the nation-state, modern and premodern. Looking at the situation from this perspective gives more agency to the leaders themselves; they are not merely reacting to a situation, but rather, are trying to redefine their nation's future on their own terms. They are, to borrow Holly Gayley's words regarding Khenpo Jigmé Phuntsok, articulating "a Tibetan vision of modernity in explicitly Buddhist terms."[96]

In his book on Zawa Damdin, King challenges scholars of cultural history of Inner Asia to "better attend to such neglected but widespread 'countermodern' Buddhist formations across late- and post-imperial and colonial Asia."[97] He argues that such "countermodern" Buddhist formations are "made invisible in the rationalist creation of national peoples, territories, histories, and religions (which, it seems to me, is really what we mean by Buddhist modernism)."[98] Along the same lines, I argue that reevaluating the initiatives of these Tibetan Buddhist leaders within the framework of the countermodern helps us move beyond seeing Tibetan modernity as the result of either European and Chinese forces. Such a reevaluation attributes a strong sense of agency to the Tibetan Buddhist leaders themselves.

I see Charlene Makley's example of "counterdevelopment" on the part of Tibetan communities in Shabkar's hometown of the Repgong Valley in Qinghai Province in the PRC as aligning with King's notion of the "countermodern." These examples of Tibetan counterdevelopment are situated within state-led development initiatives that are framed in the stark dichotomies associated with the discourse of modernity: modern versus traditional, developed versus backwards, rational versus superstitious, scientific versus religious. Central to these Tibetan counterdevelopment initiatives is that they draw from "a variety of much older notions of landscape, jurisdiction, and sovereign fortune to envision hybrid, yet specifically Tibetan modernities."[99] The main similarity between the Tibetan Buddhist leaders trying to maintain the relationship between Buddhism and Tibetan national identity and the initiatives of the villagers of the Repgong Valley is the impulse to define Tibetan modernity on their own terms. Thus, the lens of the countermodern allows us to glimpse other modes of community, identity, and belonging beyond the Westphalian notion of nation-state that originated in Europe and the Americas.

# APPENDIX: LOCATIONS MENTIONED IN SHABKAR'S AUTOBIOGRAPHY

The following tables list all the sites that are mentioned in both volumes of Shabkar's autobiography in Wylie transcription and THL phonetics. In some instances, when a site has a well-established name, I use that instead of THL phonetics (e.g., Rongwo Monastery or Zhopong village). The tables also indicate if a site has been identified in the maps within this book. The first volume of Shabkar's autobiography is available in English translation.[1] The appendix of my dissertation shows the context in which the places of the second volume are situated.[2]

Locations in Amdo Province

| Wylie | Phonetics | Identified |
| --- | --- | --- |
| a 'gang rta mgrin | Agang Tamdrin | No |
| a 'byung | Ajung | No |
| a bar the'u | Abar Teu | No |
| a chung gnam rdzong | Achung Namdzong | Yes |
| a dar chags ka'i thang | Adar Chakké Tang | No |
| a myes ge tho | Anyé Géto | No |
| a myes ja sgron gyi sgrub gnas | hermitages of Anyé Jadrön | No |
| a rig | Arik | Yes |
| bal | Bel | No |
| bal mdo | Beldo | No |
| ban le | Benlé | No |
| ban rgyag | Bengyak | No |
| ban shul | Benshul | Yes |
| bde chen dgon pa | Dechen Gönpa | Yes |
| bdud shul | Düshül | No |
| bkra shis 'khyil | Trashikhyil | Yes |
| bkra shis g.yang chags spangs lug brag | Trashi Yangchak Pangluk Drak | No |
| bkra shis nyams dga' at go'u | Trashi Nyamga at Gou | No |

*(continues)*

## Locations in Amdo Province (*continued*)

| Wylie | Phonetics | Identified |
|---|---|---|
| bkra shis nyams dga' of go'u sde'i phu | caves at Trashi Nyamga at Gou | No |
| bkra tsha | Tratsa | No |
| bla brang bkra shis 'khyil ba'i dgon | Labrang Trashikhyil | Yes |
| bod bya tshang | Böja Tsang | Yes |
| bon rgya | Bön gya | Yes |
| brag dkar | Drakkar | No |
| brag dkar at rgan rgya | Drakkar at Gengya | Yes |
| brag dkar me long | Drakkar Mélong | No |
| brag dkar sprel rdzong | Drakkar Treldzong | Yes |
| brjid par gyi nags khrod | Jipargyi Naktrö | No |
| brong lung | Dronglung | Yes |
| bya khyung dgon pa | Jakhyung Gönpa | Yes |
| byams pa 'bum gling | Jampa Bumling | Yes |
| chu bzang | Chuzang | Yes |
| co ne | Choné | Yes |
| dgon phug | Gönpuk | No |
| dgu rong | Gurong | Yes |
| dgu rong ma ni thang gi lha khang | Gurong | Yes |
| dgur steng | Gurteng | No |
| dmag gsar | Maksar | No |
| dme shul | Meshül | Yes |
| do rgya | Dogya | Yes |
| do sho | Dosho | No |
| dpal mchog | Pelchok | No |
| dpyi ba | Chiba | No |
| dung dkar | Dungkar | No |
| dwang rgya | Danggya | No |
| g.yer gshong | Yershong | No |
| g.yu rngogs | Yungok | No |
| gad mgo su'i thugs rje chen po rang byon | Self-arising image at Gégosü Tukjé Chenpo | No |
| gcan za | Chenza | Yes |
| gle ba | Léba | No |
| gling rgya'i sde pa gsum | Linggyé Dépa Sum | No |
| gnyan rgya | Nyengya | Yes |
| gnyan thog | Nyenthok | Yes |
| go'u sde | Goudé | No |
| gra tsha'i phyag rdor skor | Dratsé Chakdor Kor | No |
| khri ka | Trika | Yes |

(*continues*)

## Locations in Amdo Province (*continued*)

| Wylie | Phonetics | Identified |
|---|---|---|
| khri ka's 36 monasteries | Trika's 36 monasteries | Yes |
| khri kha'i jo bo'i lha khang | Trikhé Jowö Lhakhang | Yes |
| khri kha'i sde gzhung gi dgon pa | Trika Dezhunggi Gonpa | Yes |
| gser khang | Serkhang | No |
| gser lag dgon | Serlak Gön | Yes |
| gshong mo che | Shongmoché | No |
| gtsang dgon | Tsang Gön | Yes |
| gzhi gsar sde ba | Zhisar Dewa | No |
| ha tho'i la | Hathöla | No |
| hor | Hor | Yes |
| hor pa shi | Horpashi | No |
| hor sde gnyis | Hordényi | No |
| hris nag | Hrinak | No |
| jam smad pa sde bdun | Jamépa Dédun | No |
| jam smad pa sde pa bcu | Jamépa Dépa Chu | Yes |
| ke'u chu | Keuchu | No |
| kha kya ban shul | Khakya Benshül | No |
| khe tsho'i rab kha | Khétsö Rapkha | Yes |
| khen rgya | Khengya | Yes |
| kho nag | Khonak | No |
| khrom lha | Tromlha | No |
| khyams ru rkang rtsa | Khyamru Kangtsa | Yes |
| khyams tshang | Khyamtsang | No |
| khyung dgon | Khyung Gön | Yes |
| klu chu thang | Luchu Tang | No |
| ku pa | Kupa | No |
| la mo bde chen dgon | Lamo Dechen Gön | Yes |
| la rnga | Langa | Yes |
| lam bde mo bcos | Lam Démo Chö | No |
| lam dkar po | Lam Karpo | No |
| lha chen dpal 'bar of zhong shan | Lachen Pelbar of Zhongshan | No |
| lha chung | Lhachung | Yes |
| lha gnyan rgod rtse'i ri | Mount Lhanyen Götsé | Yes |
| lha lung | Lhalung | No |
| lha zhis | Lhazhi | Yes |
| lo ba'i brag dkar | Lobé Drakkar | No |
| lo rdo rje brag's holy object | Lo Drojé Drak's holy object | No |
| lo rgya dun bde mchog rang byon | Lo Gyadün Déchok Rangjön | No |
| lto tshang | Totsang | No |
| lug ra pad dkar chos gling | Lukra Pékar Chöling | Yes |

(*continues*)

## Locations in Amdo Province (*continued*)

| Wylie | Phonetics | Identified |
|---|---|---|
| ma ni lha khang | Mani Lhakhang | No |
| ma phyag dgon | Machak Gön | No |
| mang ra | Mangra | Yes |
| mar nang tsho lnga | Marnang Tsonga | No |
| mchod rten dkar po | Chörten Karpo | No |
| mchod rten rnam dag chen mo | Chörten Namtak Chenmo | No |
| mdo pa | Dopa | No |
| mgo log | Golok | Yes |
| skal ldan rgya mtsho's meditation sites | Kelden Gyatso's meditation sites | No |
| mgar rtse | Gartsé | Yes |
| mgon shul | Gönshül | Yes |
| mkhar gong | Khargong | No |
| monastery of lama rgya lu hu thog | Monastery of Lama Gyalu Hutok | No |
| mtshar lung | Tsarlung | No |
| mtsho sngon po and mtsho snying | Tsongönpo and Tsonying | Yes |
| na mo wan | Namowen | No |
| ngang rong | Ngangrong | Yes |
| nu rong | Nurong | No |
| nya lung | Nyalung | Yes |
| nyi ma lung gi dgon | Nyimalunggi Gön | Yes |
| padma rdzong | Péma Dzong | No |
| rang ngan | Rangngan | No |
| rdis tsha | Ditsa | Yes |
| rdo bis dgon | Dobi Gön | Yes |
| rdo ring | Doring | No |
| rdzong dkar | Dzongkar | Yes |
| rdzong dmar | Dzongmar | No |
| rdzong dmar grub gnas | Dzongmar Drupné | No |
| rdzong sngon | Dzong Ngön | Yes |
| reb gong grub pa thob pa'i gnas chen brgyad | The Eight Sites of the Meditators of Repgong | No |
| reb gong | Repgong | Yes |
| rgan rgya | Gengya | Yes |
| rgya khres tsi bzhi po | Gyatré Tsi Zhipo | Yes |
| rgya phyogs | China | No |
| ri bo rma chen | Mount Machen | Yes |
| ri snying po | Ri Nyingpo | No |
| rkang tsha | Kangtsa | Yes |
| rkang tsha 'khyams | Kangtsa Khyam | Yes |

(*continues*)

## Locations in Amdo Province (*continued*)

| Wylie | Phonetics | Identified |
|---|---|---|
| rma chu'i tshur kha | banks of Machu River | Yes |
| rma pha ri | Mapari | No |
| rnga mong thang | Ngamong Tang | No |
| rong po'i dgon chen | Rongwo Monastery | Yes |
| rong po'i sde bdun | Seven villages of Rongwo | Yes |
| rtag mo rdzong | Takmo Dzong | No |
| rtse gzhung | Tsézhung | Yes |
| rwa rgya'i dgon | Ragya Gön | Yes |
| sa bzang | Sazang | Yes |
| sa dkar shar jo khang | Sakarshar Jokhang | Yes |
| sbra na khag gsum | Bana Khaksum | No |
| sbub chol | Bupchöl | No |
| se cang | Séchang | No |
| sgo me | Gomé | Yes |
| sha brang | Shadrang | No |
| shar rdzong | Shardzong | No |
| shar tshang | Shartshang | No |
| shel dgon | Shel Gön | Yes |
| shel rdi | Sheldi | No |
| shing dkar | Shingkar | No |
| shug 'dus grub gnas | Shukdü Drupné | Yes |
| ska phug tsho | Kapuktso | Yes |
| sku 'bum | Kubum | Yes |
| skya ring mchod rten | Kyaring Chörten | Yes |
| snang ra | Nangra | Yes |
| snang ra'i gser khang gi ten gyi gtso bo | Serkhanggi Tengyi Tsowo of Nangra | Yes |
| so nag | Sonak | No |
| sog po | Sokpo | Yes |
| spre'u mdo'i dgon | Treudo Gön | No |
| sprul lce | Trülché | No |
| spyang lung | Changlung | No |
| spyi pa | Chipa | No |
| srin mo | Sinmo | Yes |
| stod kyi bkra shis dge 'phel | Upper Trashi Gépel | No |
| su rug | Suruk | No |
| tan tig and yang tig | Tentik and Yangtik | Yes |
| tho no ji | Tonoji | No |
| tho rgya | Togya | No |
| tsong kha'i skyes ri | Tsongkha's birth mountain | Yes |

(*continues*)

## Locations in Amdo Province (*continued*)

| Wylie | Phonetics | Identified |
|---|---|---|
| Urge | Urgé | Yes |
| valley below hang nga ri rgan | valley below Hangnga Rigen | No |
| stong skor | Tongkor | Yes |
| wo' bu | Wobu | No |
| yang dgon | Yang Gön | No |
| yar nang 'dam bu brag dkar | Yarnang Dambu Drakkar | No |
| zho 'dzom la kha | Zhodzom Lakha | No |
| zho 'ong | Zhopong | Yes |
| zi ling | Ziling | Yes |

## Locations Enroute between Amdo Province and Central Tibet

| Wylie | Phonetics | Identified |
|---|---|---|
| bri chu | Drichu | Yes |
| byang lam ring mo | Janglam Ringmo | No |
| mtsho mo ra | Tsomora | No |
| nags chu kha pa | Nakchu Khapa | Yes |
| rdza zor ba | Dzazorwa | No |

## Locations in Central Tibet (Wü-Tsang)

| Wylie | Phonetics | Identified |
|---|---|---|
| bka' brgyad | Kagyé | No |
| bkra shis lhun po | Trashi Lhünpo | Yes |
| bo dong bkra shis sgang khro phu'i byams chen | Bodong Trashi Gangtropü Jamchen | Yes |
| brag dmar g.ya' ma lung gi dben gnas | Hermitage of Drakmar Yamalung | Yes |
| brag lha klu phug | Drak Lhalupuk | Yes |
| brag yer pa | Drak Yerpa | Yes |
| bras spung | Drépung | Yes |
| bsam yas | Samyé | Yes |
| bsam yas mchims phu | Samyé Chimpu | Yes |
| byams pa gling gi mchod rten chen po | Chörten Chenpo of Jampa Ling | No |
| byang gi lha rtse | Janggi Lhatsé | No |
| chos lung | Chölung | No |
| dga' ldan | Ganden | Yes |
| dga' ldan phun tshogs gling | Ganden Püntsok Ling | Yes |
| dga' ldan rab brtan dgon pa | Ganden Rabten Gönpa | No |
| dwags la sgam po | Dakla Gampo | Yes |
| dwags po bshad sgrub gling | Dakpo Shédrup Ling | Yes |
| e rig pa'i 'byung gnas | Érikpé Jungné | No |
| g.yu khang | Yukhang | No |
| gdan sa mthil | Densatil | Yes |
| gling gsum: tshe smon gling, bstan rgyas gling, kun bde gling | Tsémönling, Tengyéling, Kündéling | Yes |
| gtsang po | Tsangpo River | Yes |
| gu ru byang ma | Guru Jangma | No |
| gzhis ka rtse | Zhikatsé | Yes |
| jo bo | Jowo | Yes |
| klung dkar dgon | Lungkar Gön | Yes |
| lcags po ri | Chakpori | Yes |
| lha sa | Lhasa | Yes |
| mchod rten bkra shis sgo mang at gcung gi ri bo che | Chörten Trashi Gomang at Chunggi Riwoché | Yes |
| mkhar rdo | Khardo | Yes |
| mkhar rdo bsam gtan gling | Khardo Samten Ling | Yes |
| ne'u ring dgon | Neuring Gön | No |
| ngor dgon | Ngor Gön | Yes |
| nya mo | Nyamo | Yes |

*(continues)*

## Locations in Central Tibet (Wü-Tsang) (*continued*)

| Wylie | Phonetics | Identified |
|---|---|---|
| po ta la | Potala | Yes |
| rdo rje brag dgon | Dorjédrak Gön | Yes |
| rgyang gi yon po lung | Gyanggi Yönpolung | No |
| rgyud stod smad | Lower Gyütö | Yes |
| ri sna dgon | Rina Gön | Yes |
| rme ru gzhi sde | Méru Zhidé | No |
| rong chung | Rongchung | No |
| rong mchad dkar chos sde | Rongchékar Chödé | No |
| rtse thang | Tsetang | Yes |
| rtswa chang dga' | Tsachangga | No |
| rwa sgreng | Radreng | Yes |
| sa skya'i chos sde | Sakya Chödé | Yes |
| se ra | Sera | Yes |
| shar dwags po bkra shis rnam rgyal | Shar Dakpo Trashi Namgyel | Yes |
| shel brag slob dpon gsung 'byon | Sheldrak Loppön Sungjön | No |
| sman dgon | Mengön | No |
| smin grol gling | Mindrölling | Yes |
| snye mo | Nyémo | Yes |
| thar pa gling rin chen sdings | Tarpa Ling Rinchen Ding | Yes |
| tsha rong | Tsarong | No |
| zab mo ri | Zabmori | No |
| zangs ri mkhar dmar | Zangri Kharmar | Yes |
| zangs ri sde pa | Zangri Dépa | Yes |
| zwa lung | Zhalung | No |

## Locations near Mount Kailash

| Wylie | Phonetics | Identified |
|---|---|---|
| bar kha rta zam | Barkha Tazam | Yes |
| bka' 'gyur lha khang of bshad 'phel gling | Kagyur Lhakhang of Shépelling | Yes |
| bon mo phug gi dgon pa | Bönmo Pukgi Gönpa | No |
| bon ri dgon | Bönri Gön | Yes |
| bre ta pu ri | Pretapuri | No |
| bri thim phug | Dritim Puk | Yes |
| dga' chos dgon | Gachö Gön | No |
| gang zag pa | Gangzakpa | No |
| gangs dkar gyi rgyal bo te se | Mount Kailash | Yes |
| gli mi | Limi | Yes |
| gnyal la phyug po'i skor | Nyella Chukpö Kor | No |
| gnyan po ri rdzong | Nyenpori Dzong | Yes |
| go pa rin chen gyi skor | Gopa Rinchengyi Kor | No |
| gro shod | Droshö | No |
| gser gyi bya skyibs dgon | Sergyi Jakyip Gön | Yes |
| khyung lung dgon | Khyunglung Gön | Yes |
| ma pham g.yu mtsho | Laka Manasarovar | Yes |
| ma pham g.yu mtsho'i khrus sgo lho | Mapam Yutsö Trügolho | Yes |
| rdo chu'i dgon pa | Dochu Gön | Yes |
| rdzong mdo | Dzongdo | No |
| rdzu 'phrul phug | Dzuntrül Puk | Yes |
| rgyangs grags dgon | Gyangdrak Gön | Yes |
| rtse brgyad dgon | Tségyé Gön | Yes |
| ser ra lung dgon | Seralung Gön | Yes |
| spu hrengs | Puhreng | Yes |
| spu hrengs bshad 'phel gling | Shépelling of Puhreng | Yes |

## Locations near Mount Lachi

| Wylie | Phonetics | Identified |
|---|---|---|
| ba' ro | Baro | Yes |
| bdud 'dul phug | Düdül Puk | Yes |
| be rtse 'dod yon rdzong | Bétsé Döyön Dzong | No |
| brag dmar mchong lung | Drakmar Chonglung | No |
| bsam gling of rtsib ri | Samling of Tsibri | Yes |
| chu dbar dgon | Chuwar Gön | Yes |
| ding ri glang bskor | Dingri Langkor | Yes |
| ding ri sgang dkar | Dingri Gangkar | Yes |
| du lung | Dulung | Yes |
| gnya' nang grod pa phug | Nyanang Dröpa Puk | No |
| gnya' nang tshong 'dus | Nyanang Market | Yes |
| grub thob gtsang smyon pa'i sgrub gnas | Tsangnyön's meditation sites | No |
| la phyi | Lachi | Yes |
| las shing sgrol ma gsung 'byon | Léshing Drölma Sungjön | No |
| lung | Lung | No |
| mtsho gsham dgon pa | Tsosham Gönpa | No |
| o zangs dgon | Ozang Gön | No |
| phel rgyas gling gi dgon pa | Pelkyé Ling Gönpa | No |
| shel phug chu shing rdzong | Shelpuk Chushing Dzong | Yes |
| skyid phug nyi ma rdzong | Kyipuk Nyima Dzong | No |
| spo mtho nam mkha' rdzong | Poto Namkha Dzong | No |
| spo sde rdzong | Podé Dzong | No |
| zur tsho | Zurtso | No |

## Locations near Mount Tsari

| Wylie | Phonetics | Identified |
|---|---|---|
| byar gsang sngags chos gling | Char Sangngak Chöling | Yes |
| chos rgyal lha rgya ri'i 'brog ru yod sa | Chögyel Lhagyari's pastures | No |
| chos zam | Chözam | Yes |
| cig char sgrub sde | Chikchar Drupdé | Yes |
| gong mo la | Gongmola | No |
| o rgyan sgrub phug | Orgyen Druppuk | Yes |
| phag mo'i lha khang | Pakmö Lhakhang | Yes |
| rdo mtshan tshul pa | Dotsen rest house | Yes |
| rdo rje rwa ba | Dorjé Rawa | Yes |
| tswa ri | Mount Tsari | Yes |
| yang dgon | Yang Gön | Yes |

## Locations in Southwestern Tibet and Nepal

| Wylie | Phonetics | Identified |
|---|---|---|
| brtsigs pa'i mgon gnang | Tsikpé Gönnang | Yes |
| bya mang po | Ja Mangpo | No |
| bya rung kha shor | Bodhnath | Yes |
| chu mig brgya rta | Muktinath | Yes |
| dben gnas brag dkar rta so | Drakkar Taso | Yes |
| glo man thang | Lo Manthang | Yes |
| gro thang | Drotang | No |
| gung thang | Gungtang | Yes |
| jo bo wa ti bzang po | Jowo Wati Zangpo | Yes |
| ka thog rig 'dzin chen po'i gser gdung | Katok Rigdzin Chenpo's Reliquary | Yes |
| mnga' ris rdzong dkar | Ngari Dzongkar | No |
| mnga' ris rdzong | Ngari Dzong | Yes |
| 'od gsal phug | Ösel Puk | Yes |
| phags pa shing kun | Svayambunath | Yes |
| ra la za 'og phug | Rala Za Ok Puk | Yes |
| rag ma byang chub rdzong | Rakma Jangchup Dzong | Yes |
| ri bo dpal 'bar | Ribo Pembar | Yes |
| rkang tshugs phug | Kangtsuk Puk | Yes |
| rkyang phan nam mkha' rdzong | Kyangpan Namkha Dzong | No |
| rnam rgyal lha rtse | Namgyel Lhatsé | No |
| skya rnga rtsa | Kyangatsa | Yes |
| skyid grong bsam gtan gling | Kyidrong Samten Ling | Yes |
| skyid sgrong | Kyidrong | Yes |

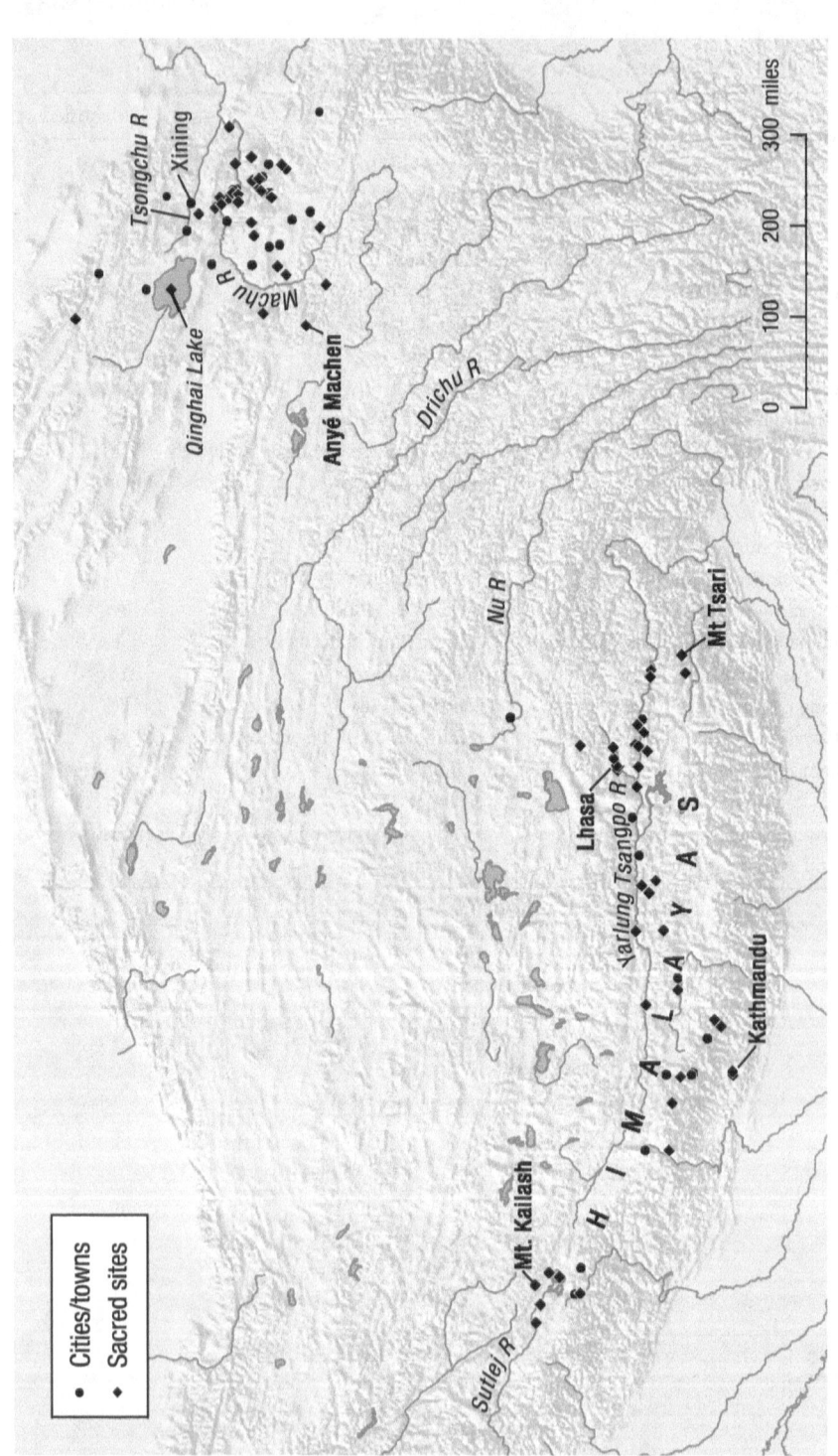

Identified locations that Shabkar mentions visiting in his autobiography. (Map by Nat Case, INCase LLC)

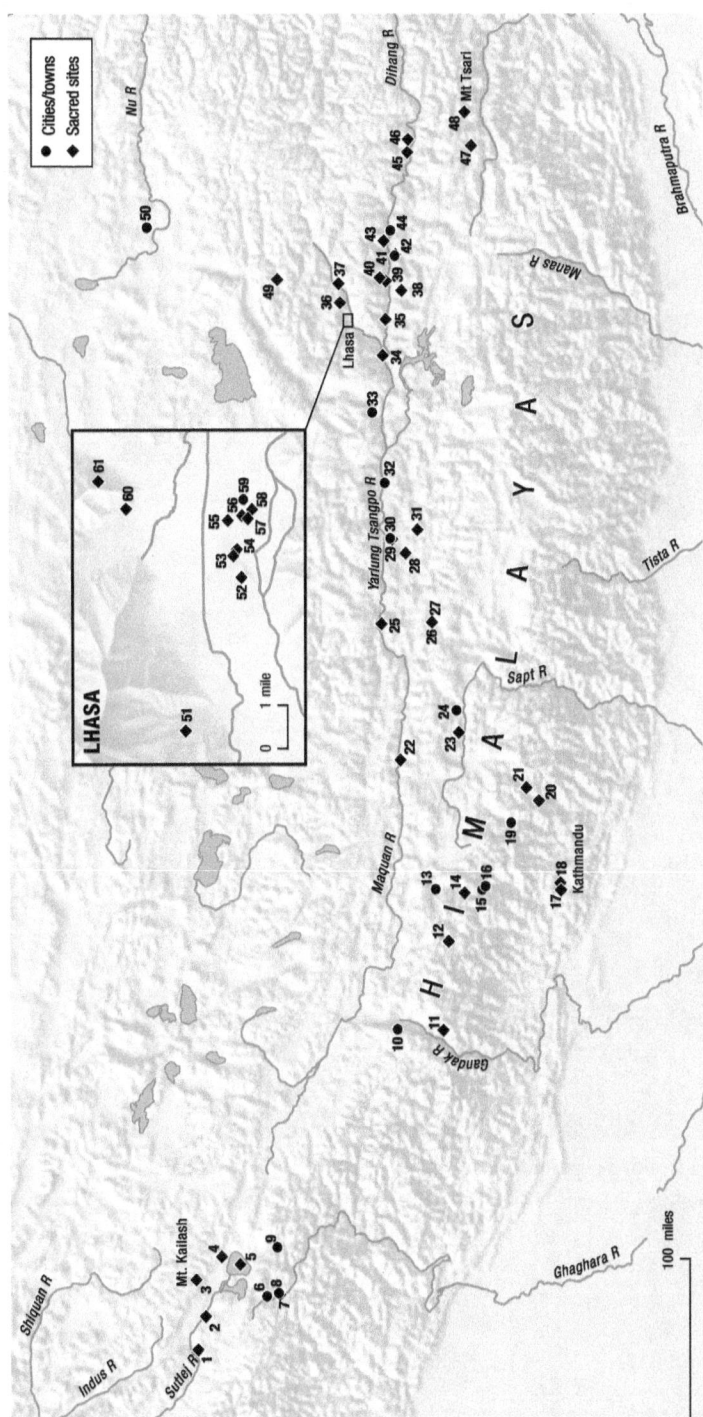

Identified locations that Shabkar visited in western, central, and southern Tibet, with a Lhasa inset. (Map by Nat Case, INCase LLC)

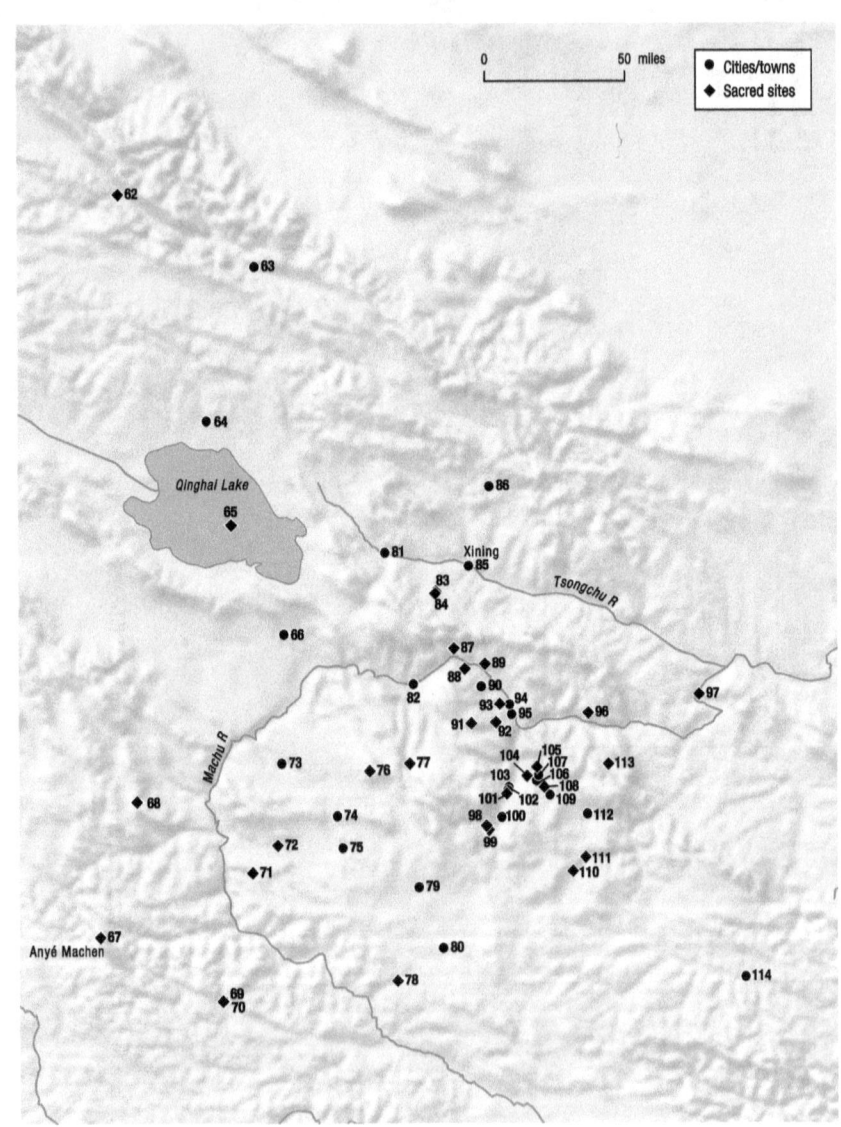

Identified locations that Shabkar visited in Amdo Province.
(Map by Nat Case, INCase LLC)

# APPENDIX 165

KEY to maps 2 and 3

1. Khyunglung Gön
2. Dochu Gön
3. Mount Kailash
4. Bönri Gön
5. Lake Manasarovar
6. Ngari
7. Puhreng Shépelling
8. Puhreng
9. Limi
10. Lo Mentang
11. Muktinath
12. Gungtang
13. Kyidrong County
14. Drakkar Taso
15. Mangyul
16. Kyidrong Town
17. Swayambhunath
18. Boudhanath
19. Nyanang
20. Mount Lachi
21. Chuwar Gön
22. Chunggi Riboché
23. Samling of Tsipri
24. Dingri
25. Ganden Püntsokling
26. Sakya Chödé
27. Bodong Trashi Gangtropü Jamchen
28. Ngor Gön
29. Trashilhunpo
30. Zhikatsé
31. Tarpaling Rinchending
32. Nyamo
33. Nyémo
34. Rina Gön
35. Dorjé Drak Gön
36. Yerpa
37. Ganden
38. Mindröl Ling
39. Samyé
40. Chimpu
41. Tsetang
42. Lungkar Gön
43. Densatil
44. Zangri
45. Daklha Gampo
46. Ganden Rapten Gönpa
47. Sangngak Chöling of Char
48. Mount Tsari
49. Radreng
50. Nakchu
51. Drepung
52. Kundéling
53. Chakpori
54. Potala
55. Gyütö
56. Tsémönling
57. Tenkyélling
58. Jokhang Temple
59. Lhasa
60. Sera Gön
61. Khardo
62. Dronglung
63. Arik
64. Kangtsa
65. Qinghai Lake
66. Gomé
67. Mount Machen
68. Drakkar Treldzong
69. Ragya Gön
70. Golok
71. Serlak Gön
72. Tsang Gön
73. Mangra
74. Böngya
75. Hor
76. Lukra Pékar Chöling
77. Benshül
78. Urgé
79. Méshul
80. Sokpo
81. Tongkor
82. Trika
83. Tsongkha Mountain
84. Kubum
85. Xining
86. Chuzang
87. Ditsa Gön
88. Achung Namdzong
89. Jakhyung Gön
90. Dogya
91. Ngangrong Trashi Chöpelling
92. Lamo Dechen Gön
93. Kyaring Chörten
94. Chenza
95. Nangra
96. Tentik and Yangtik
97. Jampa Bumling
98. Dechen Gönpa
99. Dzongngön Gön
100. Gönshül
101. Rongwo Gön
102. Rebgong
103. Nyentok
104. Sakar Shar Jokhang
105. Shelgön
106. Zhopong
107. Nyengya
108. Trashikhyil
109. Gartsé
110. Nyimalunggi Gön
111. Labrang Gön
112. Gengya
113. Dobi Gön
114. Choné

# NOTES

## Introduction

1. These names in Tibetan Wylie transliteration are: *Gangs can bod kyi glu dbyangs mkhan, Tshogs drug rang grol, Zhabs dkar pa*. In particular, the epithet "Self-Liberation of the Six Senses" alludes to the Buddhist tantric idea of "self-liberation" (*rang grol*), which is also translated as "natural-liberation," in which the six senses are not liberated by another, but are "self-liberated."
2. Brag dgon pa, *Mdo smad chos 'byung*, 340. Although this text is frequently referred to colloquially as the *Religious History of Amdo* (*Mdo smad chos 'byung*), its full title is *The Oceanic Book, the Elucidation of how the Buddhist Teachings Spread in the Valleys of the Mdo smad Country* (*Yul mdo smad kyi ljongs su thub bstan rin po che ji ltar dar ba'i tshul gsal bar brjod pa deb ther rgya mtsho*) composed between the 1830s to 1865 by Brag dgon zhabs drung dkon mchog bstan pa rab rgyas (1800/1–1869) (Tuttle, "Challenging Central Tibet's Dominance of History," 136–37). Hereafter, I will refer to this work as *Oceanic Book*.
3. Lopez, *Forest of Faded Wisdom*, 43–45.
4. Lce nag tshang hum chen and Ye shes 'od zer sgrol ma, *Reb kong sngags mang gi lo rgyus phyogs bsgrigs*, 160–62.
5. 'Brug thar dang sangs rgyas tshe ring, *Mdo smad rma khug tsha 'gram yul gru'i lo rgyus deb ther chen mo*, 547–48.
6. Don grub rgyal, *Bod kyi mgur glu*, 486–88.
7. "mi dkar po zhig byung ste bos nas song bas / gur dkar po brgya phrag du ma phub pa'i dbus na / shin tu mdzes shing yid du 'ong ba'i gur chen po zhig phub yod pa'i nang du song ba'i tshe / rab tu mtho ba'i khri chen po zhig gi steng na rgyal po chen po zhig bzhugs / mdun gyi g.yas phyogs su khri zhig yod pa'i khar nga sdod ces zer der bsdad pa'i tshe / rgyal po de yar la bzhengs nas dri ma med pa'i kha btags ring po zhig dang / rab tu mdzes pa'i zhwa zhig gnang nas / khyed kyis deng sang dam pa gong ma'i rnam thar bskyangs te dam pa'i chos kyi mgur dbyangs len pa ngo mtshar che / khyed kyi mtshan la gangs can bod kyi glu dbyangs mkhan zhes gsol ba yin / mgur 'bum bod la 'jog pa ru bzhag pa bka' drin che / ma 'ongs pa na dad can gyi gdul bya rnams la phan thogs rgya chen po 'ongs / da dung sgrub pa snying por mdzod la sgrub 'bras kyis bstan 'gro yongs la gang phan mdzod / de'i zhor la rgyal ba'i gsung rab kyi dgongs don glu ru longs dang khyed kyis phyin chad chos ldan gyi bya ba gang bsgrub dus bdag gis grogs byed par khas blangs pa yin gsungs pa'i sngang ba shar" (Zhabs dkar, *Snyigs dus*, 1: 276.1–6; Shabkar, *Life of Shabkar*, 162).
8. For example, see Zhabs dkar, *Bya btang*, 3:58.1–2, 85.6, 137.6.
9. "bod kyi tshogs drug rang grol" (Zhabs dkar, *Bya btang*, 3:155.4).
10. Jacoby, *Love and Liberation*, 105.
11. Karmay, "The Cult of Mountain Deities and its Political Significance," 436, 440–41.

12. Ibid., 432.
13. Jabb, *Oral and Literary Continuities in Modern Tibetan Literature*, 35–36.
14. This idea was first discussed by Ariane Macdonald. Geoffrey Samuel has a general overview of it in *Civilized Shamans*, 186–89. Barbara Gerke (2007) has a detailed analysis of *bla* rituals in the Himalayas.
15. Karmay, "The Cult of Mountain Deities and its Political Significance," 441.
16. Zhabs dkar, *Snyigs dus*, 1:25; Shabkar, *Life of Shabkar*, 15.
17. "sngon med bod kyi glu pa kha bde nga'i / glu dbyangs bod la phan par byin gyis rlobs" (Zhabs dkar, *Bya btang*, 3:752.4).
18. For Shabkar self-identifying as an incarnation of Avalokiteśvara, see Zhabs dkar, *Snyigs dus*, 1:826.4–6; Shabkar, *Life of Shabkar*, 471. For Shabkar's visions of Avalokiteśvara, see chapter 4.
19. Gamble, *Reincarnation in Tibetan Buddhism*, 229, 242–43, 248; Rang byung rdo rje, *Thams cad*, 383, 399, 403–11.
20. Sujata, *Tibetan Songs of Realization*, 419–21.
21. Skal ldan rgya mtsho, *Grub chen*, 27.
22. Skal ldan rgya mtsho, *Grub chen*, 35–36, 46, 52.
23. Zhabs dkar, *Snyigs dus*, 2:275.4, 340.1–2.
24. Zhabs dkar, *Snyigs dus*, 1:205.5–6.6; Shabkar, *Life of Shabkar*, 123.
25. "bod kyi yul 'phags pa thugs rje chen po'i gdul bya'i zhing du gyur ba" (Wylie, "The Geography of Tibet According to the 'Dzam-gling-rgyas-bshad," 2, 55). The full title of Tenpo's text is *The Clear Mirror which Illuminates the Vessel and its Contents and Explains Fully the Great World* ('*Dzam gling chen po rgyas bshad snod bcud kun gsal me long zhes bya ba*) (Wylie, "The Geography of Tibet According to the 'Dzam-gling-rgyas-bshad," viii). Lobsang Yongdan has a dissertation on this text (Cambridge, 2014). Hereafter, Lama Tenpo's text will be referred to by the abbreviated title, *Detailed Explanation of the World*.
26. "spyan ras gzigs kyi 'dul zhing kha ba can gyi rgyal khams" (Brag dgon pa, *Mdo smad chos 'byung*, 1).
27. Sheldon Pollock, for example, has identified the period between 1500 and 1800 CE as constituting the early modern period in India and Tibet. He adopts this "threshold" of time mainly for the sake of synchronicity with the early modern period in Europe ("Introduction," 3–4).
28. Gyatso, *Being Human in a Buddhist World*, 409, n.1.
29. Mills, "Chapter 16 Who Belongs to Tibet?" 408.
30. Mills, "Chapter 16 Who Belongs to Tibet?" 414. The full title of Jamgön Kongtrül's *Twenty-Five Sites of Khams* is *A Short, Brief Clarification of the List of the Twenty-Five Great Sites of Khams Together with their Auxiliaries* (*Mdo khams gnas chen nyer lnga yan lag dang bcas pa'i mdo byang gi gsal byed zin thung nyung ngu*) (Gardner, "The Twenty-five Great Sites of Khams," 271). Hereafter, I will refer to this work as *Twenty-Five Sites of Khams*.
31. Central Tibetan Administration, "Tibet at a Glance."
32. Mills, "Chapter 16 Who Belongs to Tibet?" 398; Richardson, *Tibet and its History*, 1–2; Goldstein, "Introduction," 4; van Schaick, *Tibet*, xv.

33. Van Schaik, *Tibet,* xv; Mills, "Chapter 16 Who Belongs to Tibet?" 398–403.
34. Central Tibetan Administration, "Middle Way Approach."
35. Mills, "Chapter 16 Who Belongs to Tibet?" 398.
36. See Davidson, *Tibetan Renaissance.*
37. Dreyfus, "Proto-Nationalism in Tibet," 207.
38. Mills, chap. 16, "Who Belongs to Tibet?" 403–4.
39. Mills, chap. 16, "Who Belongs to Tibet?" 403. For English translations of the text see Sørenson (1994) and Sakyapa (1996).
40. Kapstein, *The Tibetans,* 136–37.
41. Ishihama, "On the Dissemination of the Belief in the Dalai Lama as a Manifestation of the Bodhisattva Avalokiteśvara," 53–54.
42. Mills, "Chapter 16 Who Belongs to Tibet?" 406.
43. Central Tibetan Administration, "Tibet at a Glance."
44. Shakya, *Dragon in the Land of Snows,* 387.
45. Mills, "Chapter 16 Who Belongs to Tibet?" 405. Yang, "Tracing the *Chol kha gsum.*"
46. Mills, "Chapter 16 Who Belongs to Tibet?" 408.
47. Kang and Sutton, *Contesting the Yellow Dragon,* 81–83; Nietupski, "Understanding Sovereignty in Amdo"; Nietupski, "Nationalism in Labrang, Amdo"; Samuel, *Civilized Shamans,* 64–98; Tuttle, "Challenging Central Tibet's Dominance of History," 141; Tsomu, *Rise of Gonpo Namgyel in Kham,* 1–56; van Spengen and Jabb, *Studies in the History of Eastern Tibet.*
48. The full title of Chokgyur Lingpa's text is *Bod kyi gnas chen rnams kyi mdo byang dkar chags o rgyan gyi mkhas pa padma 'byung gnas kyis bkod pa* (Gardner, "The Twenty-five Great Sites of Khams," 272). Hereafter, Lingpa's work will be referred to as *A Brief Inventory of the Great Sites of Tibet.*
49. Warren Smith's *Tibetan Nation* is the most comprehensive study to date of Tibetan nationalism.
50. Smith, *Cultural Foundations of Nations,* 13.
51. Brook et al., *Sacred Mandates,* 19.
52. Smith, *Cultural Foundations of Nations,* 19.
53. Grosby, *Nationalism,* 23.
54. Examples of some of the most influential studies of nations and nationalism include Hobsbawm, *Nations and Nationalism Since 1780;* Gellner, *Nations and Nationalism;* and Anderson, *Imagined Communities.* Examples of the study of cultural nationalism include Leerssen, *National Thought in Europe* and Jensen, *Roots of Nationalism.*
55. Leerssen, *National Thought in Europe,* 2.
56. Jabb, *Oral and Literary Continuities in Modern Tibetan Literature,* 236.
57. Smith, *Cultural Foundations of Nations,* 11.
58. Ramble, "Tibetan Pride of Place," 383; Shakya, "Wither the Tsampa Eaters?" 10.
59. Smith, *The Cultural Foundations of Nations,* 8.
60. Azar Gat, *Nations,* 11.
61. Anderson, *Imagined Communities,* 46.
62. Anderson, *Imagined Communities,* 46.
63. Chatterjee, *Nation and its Fragments,* 5.

64. Brook et al., *Sacred Mandates*, 14–15.
65. Brook et al., *Sacred Mandates*, 100.
66. Smith, *Cultural Foundations of Nations*, 40.
67. Smith, *Cultural Foundations of Nations*, 40.
68. Jabb, *Oral and Literary Continuities in Modern Tibetan Literature*, 237.
69. Jabb, *Oral and Literary Continuities in Modern Tibetan Literature*, 29–30, 33.
70. Brag dgon pa, *Mdo smad chos 'byung*, 340; 'Brug thar dang sangs rgyas tshe ring, *Mdo smad rma khug tsha 'gram yul gru'i lo rgyus deb ther chen mo*, 547–48; Lce nag tshang hum chen and ye shes 'od zer sgrol ma, *Reb kong sngags mang gi lo rgyus*, 160–62; Gling rgya ba bla ma tshe ring, *Reb gong gser mo ljongs kyi chos srid byung ba brjod pa 'dod 'byung gter gyi bum bzang*, 121.
71. The first volume of Shabkar's *namtar* is available in translation. See Shabkar, *The Life of Shabkar*.
72. "gangs can ljongs kyi phyi rabs gang zag la / phan pa'i 'jog pa byed rgyu gzhan ma mchis" (Zhabs dkar, *bya btang*, 4:604.4).
73. Zhabs dkar *Snyigs dus*, 1:14.4–5; Shabkar, *Life of Shabkar*, 5.
74. Zhabs dkar, *Snyigs dus* 1:967.5-6; Shabkar, *Life of Shabkar*, 545.
75. Zhabs dkar, *Snyigs dus* 2:20.4.
76. Zhabs dkar, *Snyigs dus* 1: 248.6; Shabkar, *Life of Shabkar*, 146.
77. Zhabs dkar, *Snyigs dus*, 2:200.1–5.
78. Zhabs dkar, *Snyigs dus*, 2:402.3.
79. Zhabs dkar, *Snyigs dus*, 2:437.2–38.1.
80. Zhabs dkar, *Snyigs dus*, 2:614.1–3.
81. Zhabs dkar, *Snyigs dus*, 1:251.6; Shabkar, *Life of Shabkar*, 148. I would like to express my gratitude to Yongdzin Lama Nyima for pointing this out to me.
82. Gyatso, *Being Human in a Buddhist World*, 45.
83. Lopez, *Gendun Chopel*, 245.
84. Quintman, "Mi la ras pa's Many Lives," 186.
85. Quintman, "Toward a Geographic Biography."
86. Heruka, *The Life of Milarepa*, 94.
87. Wintle, "Emergent Nationalism in European Maps of the Eighteenth Century," 272.
88. For an early modern case study, see Hadfield, "Vanishing Primordialism," 47–66; for a premodern example see Hastings, *The Construction of Nationhood*.
89. Smith, *Myth and Memories of the Nation*, 129.
90. Smith, *The Cultural Foundations of Nations*, 8.

## 1. "Tibet" and "Tibetans" in Shabkar's Autobiography

1. Zhabs dkar, *Snyigs dus*, 1:29.2; Shabkar, *Life of Shabkar*, 17.
2. Zhabs dkar, *Snyigs dus*, 1:33.1; Shabkar, *Life of Shabkar*, 18.
3. Zhabs dkar, *Snyigs dus*, 1:57.2; Shabkar, *Life of Shabkar*, 33.
4. Zhabs dkar, *Snyigs dus*, 1: 72.3–4; Shabkar, *Life of Shabkar*, 44.
5. For some examples, see Zhabs dkar, *Bya btang*, 3:137.6, 141.3, 158.1.
6. Zhabs dkar, *Bya btang*, 3:155.4, 752.4.

7. Zhabs dkar, *Bya btang*, 3:729.6.
8. Zhabs dkar, *Snyigs dus*, 1:623.4; Shabkar, *Life of Shabkar*, 359.
9. Sperling, "Les noms du Tibet: Géographie et identité," 27–28.
10. Mills, "Chapter 16 Who Belongs to Tibet?" 398; Richardson, *Tibet and its History*, 1–2; Goldstein, "Introduction," 4; van Schaick, *Tibet*, xv.
11. Tuttle, "Challenging Central Tibet's Dominance of History," 155.
12. Tuttle, "Challenging Central Tibet's Dominance of History," 142.
13. Dge 'dun chos 'phel, *Deb ther dkar po*, 9.
14. Central Tibetan Administration, "Tibet at a Glance."
15. "rang re'i yul 'di la ches snga mo zhig nas / rang skad du bod kyi yul zhes bya bar grags" (Dge 'dun chos 'phel, *Deb ther dkar po*, 5).
16. Central Tibetan Administration, "Middle Way Approach."
17. Sperling, "Tubote, Tibet, and the Power of Naming."
18. Tuttle, "Challenging Central Tibet's Dominance of History," 135.
19. Richardson translates these terms as follows: "the country of Great China" (*rgya chen po'i yul*) and "the country of Great Tibet" (*bod chen po'i yul*) (Richardson, "The Sino-Tibetan Treaty Inscription of A.D. 821–23 at Lhasa," 150, 153).
20. "skor gsum ru bzhi sgang drug ces bod chen po'i rgyal khams" (Richardson, "The Fifth Dalai Lama's Decree Appointing Sangs-rgyas rgya-mtsho as Regent," 330, 332).
21. Tuttle, "Challenging Central Tibet's Dominance of History," 139 n. 10.
22. Gardner, "The Twenty-five Great Sites of Khams," 218.
23. 'Jam mgon kong sprul, *Mdo khams gnas chen nyer lnga*, 143.2.
24. Gardner, "The Twenty-five Great Sites of Khams," 266.
25. Wylie, "The Geography of Tibet According to the 'Dzam-gling-rgyas-bshad," 65–66.
26. Dge 'dun chos 'phel, *Deb ther dkar po*, 9.
27. Gerke, *Long Lives and Untimely Deaths*, 318.
28. Dreyfus, "Proto-Nationalism in Tibet," 210.
29. Shakya, "Wither the Tsampa Eaters?" 9.
30. Shakya, "Wither the Tsampa Eaters?" 9.
31. Schneiderman, "Barbarians at the Border and Civilising Projects," 2.
32. Schneiderman, "Barbarians at the Border and Civilising Projects," 6.
33. Schneiderman, "Barbarians at the Border and Civilising Projects," 19–22; Huber, *The Cult of Pure Crystal Mountain*, 177–95.
34. Zhabs dkar, *Snyigs dus*, 2:8.2–3.
35. Zhabs dkar, *Snyigs dus*, 2:57.2.
36. Zhabs dkar, *Snyigs dus*, 1:689.2–4; Shabkar, *Life of Shabkar*, 398.
37. Zhabs dkar, *Snyigs dus*, 1: 776.4–5; Shabkar, *Life of Shabkar*, 449.
38. Zhabs dkar, *Snyigs dus*, 2:267.1.
39. Zhabs dkar, *Snyigs dus*, 1:618.4; Shabkar, *Life of Shabkar*, 357.
40. Zhabs dkar, *Bya btang*, 3:161.1.
41. Zhabs dkar, *Snyigs dus*, 1:146.4; Shabkar, *Life of Shabkar*, 90.
42. Zhabs dkar, *Snyigs dus*, 1:496.1; Shabkar, *Life of Shabkar*, 291.
43. Zhabs dkar, *Snyigs dus*, 1:802.5; Shabkar, *Life of Shabkar*, 461.
44. Zhabs dkar, *Bya btang*, 3:755.5–56.1.

45. Zhabs dkar, *Snyigs dus*, 1:325.2; Shabkar, *Life of Shabkar*, 188.
46. Zhabs dkar, *Snyigs dus*, 1:753.1; Shabkar, *Life of Shabkar*, 434.
47. Zhabs dkar, *Snyigs dus*, 2:45.2, 131.4.
48. Zhabs dkar, *Snyigs dus*, 1:231.3; Shabkar, *Life of Shabkar*, 137.
49. Zhabs dkar, *Bya btang*, 4: 392.3.
50. Zhabs dkar, *Snyigs dus*, 1:201.1; Shabkar, *Life of Shabkar*, 120.
51. The "upper, middle, and lower" categorization is not obvious in the English translation of Shabkar's autobiography. Moreover, in the Shechen edition, "upper" is misspelled as "*bstod*" instead of "*stod*," which the Qinghai edition corrects. The Qinghai's editorial correction is consistent with the way in which Shabkar describes Kailash as being in "upper" Tibet (*stod*), Lachi in "middle" Tibet (*bar*) and Tsari in "lower" Tibet (*smad*). Zhabs dkar, *Snyigs dus* 2003, 1:465.6; Zhabs dkar, *Snyigs dus* 1985, 1:533; Shabkar, *Life of Shabkar*, 275. Zhabs dkar, *Snyigs dus*, 1:683.3; Shabkar, *Life of Shabkar*, 395. Zhabs dkar, *Snyigs dus*, 1:416.1; Shabkar, *Life of Shabkar*, 243.
52. Zhabs dkar, *Snyigs dus*, 1:688.4–689.1; Shabkar, *Life of Shabkar*, 398.
53. Zhabs dkar, *Snyigs dus*, 1:752.2; Shabkar, *Life of Shabkar*, 433.
54. Zhabs dkar, *Snyigs dus*, 1:575.1–79.6; Shabkar, *Life of Shabkar*, 331–33; Zhabs dkar, *Snyigs dus*, 2:267.2–68.2.
55. Zhabs dkar, *Snyigs dus*, 1:421.2; Shabkar, *Life of Shabkar*, 245.
56. "mtha' 'khob glo ba" (Zhabs dkar, *Snyigs dus*, 1:417.6. Shabkar, *Life of Shabkar*, 243).
57. Zhabs dkar, *Snyigs dus*, 2:63.5, 301.3.
58. Zhabs dkar, *Snyigs dus*, 1:421.5, 323.4; Shabkar, *Life of Shabkar*, 245, 187. Zhabs dkar, *Snyigs dus*, 2:510.6–11.1.
59. Eveline Yang challenges that idea, arguing it is a term that is "better understood as part of an aggrandized remembering of Sa skya history rather than a geo-administrative term with concrete administrative applications during its time" (Yang, "Tracing the *Chol kha gsum*," 551).
60. "bod yul gyi gzhung thams cad la ltad mo lta bzhin 'ong ba" (Zhabs dkar, *Snyigs dus*, 1:233.6). The word *gzhung* has various meanings, including "government," "public," "*śāstra*," "main text," "lengthwise," "center," and "disposition." As none of these definitions fit Shabkar's usage, I have glossed *gzhung* as "district" in accordance with the Ricard translation of Shabkar's autobiography (Shabkar, *Life of Shabkar*, 138; *Bod rgya tshig mdzod chen mo*, 2426).
61. "bod yul gyi dbus" (Zhabs dkar, *Snyigs dus*, 1:753.1; Shabkar, *Life of Shabkar*, 434).
62. Zhabs dkar, *Snyigs dus*, 2:87.5.
63. Tambiah, "The Galactic Polity in Southeast Asia."
64. Zhabs dkar, *Snyigs dus*, 1:322.1–23.3; Shabkar, *Life of Shabkar*, 186.
65. Dreyfus, "Proto-Nationalism in Tibet," 207.
66. Sakyapa, *The Clear Mirror*, 63–64.
67. The terminology that Kelden Gyatso uses is "dbus gtsang rus bzhi," "mnga' ris skor gsum," and "mdo khams sgang gsum" (Sujata, *Tibetan Songs of Realization*, 10–11). Gray Tuttle has created a map depicting Kalden Gyatso's description, which is in accord with the *Oceanic Book* (Tuttle, "Challenging Central Tibet's Dominance of History," 140).

68. Tuttle, "Challenging Central Tibet's Dominance of History," 142.
69. Wylie, "The Geography of Tibet According to the 'Dzam-gling-rgyas-bshad," 56.
70. Gardner, "The Twenty-five Great Sites of Khams," 188.
71. Sujata, *Tibetan Songs of Realization*, 2, 4. This conclusion is based on the limited number of poems available in English translation in Sujata's monograph and translation of a portion of Kalden Gyatso's *Collected Songs* (Sujata, *Journey to Distant Groves*). A thorough analysis of Kalden Gyatso's entire song collection is necessary to make a definitive conclusion.
72. Zhabs dkar, *Snyigs dus*, 1:206.5; Shabkar, *Life of Shabkar*, 123.
73. Zhabs dkar, *Bya btang*, 4:604.4.
74. Zhabs dkar, *Snyigs dus*, 1:474.4; Shabkar, *Life of Shabkar*, 279.
75. Zhabs dkar, *Bya btang*, 4:263.3, 268.1.
76. Zhabs dkar, *Snyigs dus*, 1:387.4; Shabkar, *Life of Shabkar*, 224.
77. Zhabs dkar, *Snyigs dus*, 1:823.2; Shabkar, *Life of Shabkar*, 469.
78. Zhabs dkar, *Snyigs dus*, 1:206; Shabkar, *The Life of Shabkar*, 123.
79. Zhabs dkar, *Bya btang*, 4:224.3, 3:583.3.
80. "nags kyi spre'u ma yin srin mo'ang min / de gnyis mthun las byung ba'i phrug gu yin / ming la gangs can bod kyi mi rnams zer / gang dang mi 'dra kun dang mthun pa mtshar" (Zhabs dkar, *Snyigs dus* 2003, 1:623.2–3). This stanza is omitted from the longer poem in both the Qinghai edition of Shabkar's autobiography (Zhabs dkar, *Snyigs dus* 1985, 1:707) and the English translation of it (Shabkar, *Life of Shabkar*, 359). This leads me to hypothesize that at least parts of the English translation were done from the Qinghai edition of Shabkar's autobiography. It is not clear if this passage was omitted from the Qinghai edition deliberately or not. It is possible that it was omitted due to censorship.
81. Zhabs dkar, *Snyigs dus* 1:272.2; Shabkar, *Life of Shabkar*, 159. Zhabs dkar, *Snyigs dus*, 2:105.5, 94.1.
82. Zhabs dkar, *Snyigs dus*, 2:94.1–2.
83. Zhabs dkar, *Snyigs dus* 1:689.5–6; Shabkar, *Life of Shabkar*, 398.
84. Zhabs dkar, *Snyigs dus*, 2:117.4.
85. Zhabs dkar, *Snyigs dus* 1:255.2–3; Shabkar, *Life of Shabkar*, 149.
86. Zhabs dkar, *Snyigs dus*, 2:64.1. Zhabs dkar, *Snyigs dus* 1:916.2–18.5; Shabkar, *Life of Shabkar*, 516.
87. Langelaar, "Chasing the Colours of the Rainbow," 330.
88. Zhabs dkar, *Snyigs dus*, 1:748.1; Shabkar, *Life of Shabkar*, 432. Zhabs dkar, *Snyigs dus*, 2:130.3, 131.3.
89. Zhabs dkar, *Snyigs dus*, 1:943.4–45.5; Shabkar, *Life of Shabkar*, 529–30. The other four references occur on Zhabs dkar, *Snyigs dus*, 1:404.4, 389.1, 482.1, 842.2; Shabkar, *Life of Shabkar*, 233, 225, 283, and 479.
90. Zhabs dkar, *Snyigs dus*, 2:267.2.
91. Zhabs dkar, *Snyigs dus*, 1:79.4; Shabkar, *Life of Shabkar*, 49.
92. Zhabs dkar, *Snyigs dus*, 1:930.4; Shabkar, *Life of Shabkar*, 523.
93. Zhabs dkar, *Snyigs dus*, 2:133.6. Zhabs dkar, *Snyigs dus*, 1:388.6–89.1; Shabkar, *Life of Shabkar*, 225.

94. Ekvall and Downs, *Tibetan Pilgrimage*, 147.
95. For some examples, see Zhabs dkar, *Bya btang*, 3:137.6, 141.3, 158.1.
96. Zhabs dkar, *Snyigs dus*, 1:849.6; Shabkar, *Life of Shabkar*, 485.
97. "gangs can bod yul glu pa ngas" Zhabs dkar, *Snyigs dus*, 1:431.3; Shabkar, *Life of Shabkar*, 250.
98. "bod kyi rnal 'byor pa / bya btang tshogs drug rang grol ngas" (Zhabs dkar, *Snyigs dus*, 1:404.5–6; Shabkar, *Life of Shabkar*, 233).
99. Zhabs dkar, *Snyigs dus*, 1:388.5; Shabkar, *Life of Shabkar*, 225.
100. Zhabs dkar, *Snyigs dus*, 1:884.5; Shabkar, *Life of Shabkar*, 502.
101. Zhabs dkar, *Snyigs dus*, 1:387; Shabkar, *Life of Shabkar*, 224.
102. Zhabs dkar, *Snyigs dus*, 2:38.4.
103. Zhabs dkar, *Bya btang*, 3:584.1, 587.6, 591.6.
104. Zhabs dkar, *Snyigs dus*, 2:8.2, 117.2.
105. Zhabs dkar, *Snyigs dus*, 2:136.6–37.1.
106. Zhabs dkar, *Snyigs dus*, 2:8.3.
107. Zhabs dkar, *Snyigs dus*, 2:38.4–39.2; 117.4.
108. Zhabs dkar, *Bya btang*, 3:122.3.
109. "gangs can bod kyi mi rnams kyis / ston dus sha chang ston mo byed" (Zhabs dkar, *Snyigs dus*, 1:337.4; Shabkar, *Life of Shabkar*, 195).
110. Zhabs dkar, *Snyigs dus*, 2:275.4, 340.1–2.
111. "bod kyi lha skal spyan ras gzigs dbang ngas / bod la rtag tu thugs rje'i spyan gyis gzigs / bod yul dbus skyes las 'phro can khyod dang / bod khams mi rnams kun gyis 'di ltar gyis" (Zhabs dkar, *Snyigs dus* 1: 206.1–2; Shabkar, *Life of Shabkar*, 123).
112. Tuttle, "Challenging Central Tibet's Dominance of History," 135, 139.
113. Zhabs dkar, *Snyigs dus* 1:808.3; Zhabs dkar, *Snyigs dus*, 2: 399.6.
114. Zhabs dkar, *Snyigs dus*, 1:474.4; Shabkar, *Life of Shabkar*, 279.
115. Samuel, *Civilized Shamans*, 64–98; Tuttle, "Challenging Central Tibet's Dominance of History," 141; Tsomo, *Rise of Gonpo Namgyel in Kham*, 1–56; Nietupski, "Understanding Sovereignty in Amdo"; Nietupski, "Nationalism in Labrang, Amdo."
116. "bod kyi rgyal po de mo rin po che" (Zhabs dkar, *Snyigs dus* 1:397.4, 841.4; Shabkar, *Life of Shabkar*, 230, 479).
117. Zhabs dkar, *Snyigs dus*, 1:741.4–43.3; Shabkar, *Life of Shabkar*, 429. Zhabs dkar, *Snyigs dus*, 1:856.5; Shabkar, *Life of Shabkar*, 488.
118. Grosby, *Nationalism*, 23.
119. Smith, *Cultural Foundations of Nations*, 19.
120. Wintle, "Emergent Nationalism in European Maps of the Eighteenth Century," 272.
121. Jabb, *Oral and Literary Continuities in Modern Tibetan Literature*, 236.
122. Schneiderman, "Barbarians at the Border and Civilising Projects," 2.
123. Schneiderman, "Barbarians at the Border and Civilising Projects," 19–22.
124. Hastings, *The Construction of Nationhood*, 198.
125. Fox and Miller-Idriss, "Everyday Nationhood," 538.
126. Jabb, *Oral and Literary Continuities in Modern Tibetan Literature*, 2.
127. "sgnon chos rgyal dus nas da lta'i bar/ mgon thub bstan nyi ma bod la shar" (Zhabs dkar, *Snyigs dus*, 2:91).

128. Zhabs dkar, *Snyigs dus*, 1:750.1–51.2; Shabkar, *Life of Shabkar*, 433.
129. Tambiah, "The Galactic Polity in Southeast Asia."
130. Samuel, *Civilized Shamans*, 61–63.
131. Obeyesekere, "Buddhism, Ethnicity and Identity," 216. Elsewhere, Obeyeskere distinguished between two notions of *sasana*. The first is doctrinal and "refers to the universal Buddhist community or church that transcends ethnic and other boundaries" and the second is found in post-canonical historical texts, which he defines as "the Buddhist "church" that is particularized in the physical bounds of the land consecrated by the Buddha—in the present instance, Sri Lanka" ("Buddhism, Nationhood, and Cultural Identity," 239).
132. Turner, *Saving Buddhism*, 1.
133. Berkwitz, "History and Gratitude in Theravāda Buddhism," 599.
134. Zhabs dkar, *Snyigs dus*, 2:91.4.
135. Zhabs dkar, *Snyigs dus*, 1:884.4; Shabkar, *Life of Shabkar*, 501.
136. Zhabs dkar, *Snyigs dus*, 1:264.5–6; Shabkar, *Life of Shabkar*, 155–56.
137. Zhabs dkar, *Snyigs dus*, 1:751.3–52.1; Shabkar, *Life of Shabkar*, 433.
138. Obeyeskere, "Buddhism, Ethnicity and Identity," 207.
139. Turner, *Saving Buddhism*, 3.
140. Zhabs dkar, *Snyigs dus*, 1:802.6; Shabkar, *Life of Shabkar*, 461.
141. Zhabs dkar, *Snyigs dus*, 1:417.6; Shabkar, *Life of Shabkar*, 243.
142. Zhabs dkar, *Snyigs dus*, 1: 638.6–39.1; Shabkar, *Life of Shabkar*, 366. Zhabs dkar, *Snyigs dus*, 2:396.1.
143. "gnas phun sum tshogs pa sogs po'i yul gyi bcud 'dus pa" (Zhabs dkar, *Snyigs dus*, 1:9.4; Shabkar, *Life of Shabkar*, 4).
144. Zhabs dkar, *Snyigs dus*, 1:206.1–2; Shabkar, *Life of Shabkar*, 123.
145. Zhabs dkar, *Snyigs dus*, 1:322.1–23.3; Shabkar, *Life of Shabkar*, 186.

## 2. Mapping Tibet's Buddhist Geography

1. Roesler, "Operas, Novels, and Religious Instructions," 120–23.
2. Quintman, "Translator's Introduction," xxix; Dargyay, "The Twelve Deeds of the Buddha," 3–12.
3. Tuttle, "Challenging Central Tibet's Dominance of History," 128, 163.
4. Tuttle, "Challenging Central Tibet's Dominance of History," 163. There are two dissertations on Tenpo Nomönhen's text: Yongdan's "Geographical Conceptualizations in a Nineteenth-Century Tibetan Text" and Wylie's "The Geography of Tibet According to the 'Dzam-gling-rgyas-bshad."
5. Lange, *An Atlas of the Himalayas by a 19th Century Tibetan Lama*.
6. Schwartzberg, "Maps of Greater Tibet," 671, 673; Lange, *An Atlas of the Himalayas by a 19th Century Tibetan Lama*, 344.
7. Full title is *Dbus gtsang gi gnas rten rags rim gyi mtshan byang mdor bsdus dad pa'i sa bon zhes bya ba* (Ferrari, *Mk'yen brtse's Guide to the Holy Places of Central Tibet*); Akester, *Jamyang Khyentsé Wangpo's Guide to Central Tibet*. Hereafter, the text is referred to as the *Guide to the Holy Places of Central Tibet*.

8. Quintman, "Toward a Geographic Biography."
9. Quintman, "Mi la ras pa's Many Lives," 186.
10. Quintman, "Toward a Geographic Biography," 374, 383.
11. Heruka, *Life of Milarepa*, 170.
12. Huber, *The Cult of Pure Crystal Mountain*, 25–26.
13. Gardner, "The Twenty-five Great Sites of Khams," 193.
14. Zhabs dkar, *Snyigs dus*, 2:37.1–2.
15. Brag dgon pa, *Mdo smad chos 'byung*, 1.
16. "'khor lo sdom pa'i pho brang / dgra bcom lnga brgya'i bzhugs gnas / dpa' bo mkha' 'gro'i zhing khams / grub thob gong ma'i gdan sa / 'dzam gling sa yi lte ba / gnas chen gangs dkar ti ser / bskor ba lan cig byas rung / tshe gcig sdig pa dag yong" (Zhabs dkar, *Snyigs dus*, 1:539.2–3; Shabkar, *Life of Shabkar*, 314).
17. Huber, *The Cult of Pure Crystal Mountain*, 25–26.
18. Huber and Rigdzin, "A Tibetan Guide for Pilgrimage of Ti-se (Mount Kailash) and mTsho Ma-pham (Lake Manasarovar)," 11–12, 39–40.
19. Gardner, "The Twenty-five Great Sites of Khams," 13, n. 30.
20. "de nas gnas chen lo ba'i brag dkar du song / gnas de ni kha lhor blta ba / mdog shel ltar dkar ba ri mtho la sa gtsang ba / lha shing shug pa sogs shing sna tshogs skyes pa chu shing 'dzom pa yid mthun bag phebs ri brgyud bzang zhing byin ldan gnas gsum mkha' 'gro rang bzhin gyi 'du ba'i gnas mchog khyad par can zhig gda' / der zhag po bdun gyi bar du gnas 'brel bzhag pas / nyams dga' rig pa dwangs pa spyir dge sbyor 'phel zhing" (Zhabs dkar, *Snyigs dus*, 2:160.6–61.3).
21. Zhabs dkar, *Snyigs dus*, 2: 214.2–3.
22. Zhabs dkar, *Snyigs dus*, 2:134.4–5.
23. Huber and Rigdzin, "A Tibetan Guide for Pilgrimage of Ti-se (Mount Kailash) and mTsho Ma-pham (Lake Manasarovar)," 15.
24. Chang, *Hundred Thousand Songs of Milarepa*, 215–24.
25. "de nas dbang phyug gi lo'i snron zla'i yar tshes la gangs la g.yas bskor byas te / thog mar lho ngos kyi rgyangs grags dgon du song / gangs mchod phul 'gyed mang ja btang / gser phug bla ma rin po cher mjal / rgyal ba 'bri khung pa'i lnga ldan khrid kyi sngon 'gro'i lung zhus / nub ngos kyi gnyan po ri rdzong du song / chos sku rin po cher mjal gangs mchod phul 'gyed mang ja btang" (Zhabs dkar, *Snyigs dus*, 1:546.2–3; Shabkar, *Life of Shabkar*, 317).
26. Zhabs dkar, *Snyigs dus*, 1: 546.2–48.1; Shabkar, *Life of Shabkar*, 317–18.
27. Buffetrille, "The Great Pilgrimage of A-mnyes rma-chen," 94.
28. Gamble, *Reincarnation in Tibetan Buddhism*; Chang, *Hundred Thousand Songs of Milarepa*.
29. "rgyab ri mthon po'i steng phyogs na / sprin dkar 'o ma 'phyar bzhin lding / nyi zla gza' skar rim bzhin 'char / ri rtse rab dkar gangs ri chags / na bun dngul mdog sked la 'khril / lo ma me tog 'bras bu yis / brgyan pa'i sngo ljang rtsi shing rgyas / chu gtsang lhung sgra sgrogs bzhin 'bab / spang zhongs bde 'jam me tog bkra / bzugs mdzes sbrang mas glu dbyangs len / lha bya khyu byug 'jol mo sogs / bya rnams snyan pa'i skad 'byin 'phya / sha ba rna ba rgo ba sogs / ri dwags du ma bag phebs rgyu" (Zhabs dkar, *Snyigs dus*, 2:540.2–5).

30. "yang de'i rjes su 'du 'dzi grong gi pha rol / g.ya' dang spang gi 'dab rol / rong dang 'brog pa'i so mtshams / mkhas grub mang po'i bzhugs gnas / nags tshal me tog rgyas shing 'ja' sprin na bun 'khor ba / lha dang D'akki 'du zhing dam pa'i lung gis zin pa'i gnas chen bkra shis 'khyil ba zhes ri bo mtho la yangs pa'i rtse mo / nyams dga'i rig pa drangs pa'i bde ba can gyi lha khang gi nye 'dab mtshams khang 'od gsal nyi 'od 'khyil ba na bdag gi sgom med 'od gsal chu bo rgyun gyi ting nge 'dzin skyong zhing / nyams mgur mang po len bzhin gnas pa'i skabs shig" (Zhabs dkar, *Snyigs dus*, 2:16.2–5).
31. Townsend, *A Buddhist Sensibility*, 11–12.
32. Brag dgon pa, *Mdo smad chos 'byung*, 22–26, 165, 341.
33. Brag dgon pa, *Mdo smad chos 'byung*, 26.
34. Wylie, "The Geography of Tibet According to the 'Dzam-gling-rgyas-bshad," 110, 117.
35. Thanks to Nancy Lin for pointing out the similarities between Shabkar's praises of places and descriptions of place in the *Jātakamālā* and *sūtra* literature at the AAR THRG panel on "Interspecies Relations on the Tibetan Plateau" in December 2020. There are several translations of the *Jātakamālā* available, such as Haksar, *Jatakamala*; Khoroche: *Once the Buddha was a Monkey*, and Meiland, *Garland of the Buddha's Past Lives*. For a translation of the Longer Sukhāvatīvyūha Sūtra, see Gomez, *The Land of Bliss*.
36. Thanks to Amelia Hall for pointing this out to me at the AAR THRG panel on "Interspecies Relations on the Tibetan Plateau" in December 2020.
37. Samuel, "Hidden Lands of Tibet in Myth and History," 51.
38. Hazelton, "Bdud 'joms gling pa's Hidden Sacred Land of Padma bkod," 344.
39. Samuel, "Hidden Lands of Tibet in Myth and History," 67.
40. Hall, "How is this Sacred Place Arrayed?" 312.
41. Samuel, "Hidden Lands of Tibet in Myth and History," 68.
42. Zhabs dkar, *Snyigs dus*, 1:751.4–52.2; Shabkar, *Life of Shabkar*, 433.
43. Shabkar, *Life of Shabkar*, 160; Zhabs dkar, *Snyigs dus*, 1:272.5–274.1.
44. Buffetrille, "The Great Pilgrimage of A-mnyes rma-chen," 90–91.
45. Shabkar, *Life of Shabkar*, 111; Zhabs dkar, *Snyigs dus*, 1:183.2–6.
46. Shabkar, *Life of Shabkar*, 155; Zhabs dkar, *Snyigs dus*, 1:262.6.
47. Buffetrille, "The Blue Lake of A-mdo and Its Island," 11.
48. Brag dgon pa, *Mdo smad chos 'byung*, 26.
49. Shabkar, *Life of Shabkar*, 398; Zhabs dkar, *Snyigs dus*, 1:688.5.
50. Chang, *Hundred Thousand Songs of Milarepa*, 296–332.
51. Shakya, *The Dragon in the Land of Snows*, 387.
52. Mills, "Chapter 16 Who Belongs to Tibet?" 405.
53. Tuttle, "Challenging Central Tibet's Dominance of History," 153, 162.
54. Samuel, *Civilized Shamans*, 64–98; Tuttle, "Challenging Central Tibet's Dominance of History," 141; Tsomo, *Rise of Gonpo Namgyel in Kham*, 1–56; Nietupski, "Understanding Sovereignty in Amdo"; Nietupski, "Nationalism in Labrang, Amdo."
55. Aris, "Tibetan Borderlands," 13.
56. Nietupski, *Labrang Monastery*; Sullivan, *Building a Religious Empire*.

57. Gardner, "The Twenty-five Great Sites of Khams," 152, 145–47; Gros, ed., *Frontier Tibet*, 143–49.
58. Gardner, "The Twenty-five Great Sites of Khams," viii.
59. Gardner, "The Twenty-five Great Sites of Khams," viii.
60. Gardner, "The Twenty-five Great Sites of Khams," xii–xiii.
61. Gardner, "The Twenty-five Great Sites of Khams," xiii.
62. Zhabs dkar, *Snyigs dus*, 2:136.6–139.3.
63. Zhabs dkar, *Snyigs dus*, 1:206.1–2; Shabkar, *Life of Shabkar*, 123.
64. Shabkar, *Life of Shabkar*, 137, 120; Zhabs dkar, *Snyigs dus*, 1: 231.3, 201.1.
65. Shabkar, *Life of Shabkar*, 225; Zhabs dkar, *Snyigs dus*, 1: 388.6–89.1.
66. Tuan, "Language and the Making of Place," 688.
67. I relied on the following sources to locate the points: Google Maps; the maps in the Tibetan and Himalayan Library, Treasury of Lives, and Buddhist Digital Resource Center websites; Karl Ryavec's *A Historical Atlas of Tibet*; and Tsering Wangyel Shawa's *Tibet: Township Map & Place Name Index*. Another source that is useful for giving an idea of the locations that Shabkar mentions are the series of maps at the end of the Ricard translation of the first volume of Shabkar's autobiography. Sites on Ricard's maps do not indicate GIS coordinates.
68. Gardner, "The Twenty-five Great Sites of Khams," xiii.
69. Smith, *Myth and Memories of the Nation*, 149.
70. Ibid.
71. Wintle, "Emergent Nationalism in European Maps of the Eighteenth Century," 284.
72. Jacob, *The Sovereign Map*, 57, 240.
73. Padrón, *The Spacious Word*, 21.
74. Tuttle, "Challenging Central Tibet's Dominance of History," 153.
75. Gardner, "The Twenty-five Great Sites of Khams," 154.
76. Central Tibetan Administration, "Tibet at a Glance." The idea of Tibet consisting of Amdo, Kham, and central Tibet is relatively modern. In premodern times, the Tibetan civilization was organized according to the geographic organizational principle of the *chölka sum*, that is, central Tibet, Upper Tö, and Lower Tö (*dbus gtsang, mdo stod,* and *mdo smad*) (Mills, "Chapter 16 Who Belongs to Tibet?" 405). For more on *chölka sum* see Yang, "Tracing the *Chol kha gsum*."
77. Jacob, *Sovereign Map*, 57, 240.
78. Smith, *Myth and Memories of the Nation*, 150.
79. Smith, *Myth and Memories of the Nation*, 152.
80. Smith, *Myth and Memories of the Nation*, 150.
81. Quintman, "Toward a Geographic Biography," 370, 384, 385.
82. Smith, *Myth and Memories of the Nation*, 152.
83. Smith, *Myth and Memories of the Nation*, 149.
84. Smith, *Myth and Memories of the Nation*, 153.

## 3. Vernacularizing the *Namtar* Genre

1. Quintman, *Yogin and the Madman*, 7.
2. Quintman, *Yogin and the Madman*, 7.

NOTES TO PAGES 63-69    179

3. Gyatso, *Apparitions of the Self*, 119.
4. Gyatso, *Apparitions of the Self*, 119.
5. Schaeffer, "Tibetan Biography," 268, 270.
6. Schaeffer, "Tibetan Biography," 282.
7. The *Kāvyādarśa* (*The Mirror of Poetry*) was written by Daṇḍin in the seventh to eighth century (Eppling, "A Calculus of Creative Expression," 3). It was translated into Tibetan in the thirteenth century by Shongtong Dorjé Gyaltsen (Reb gong ba dge 'dun rab bsal, *Bod kyi rtsom rig*, 170).
8. Schaeffer, "Tibetan Biography," 286, 284.
9. Schaeffer, "Tibetan Biography," 284–85, 287.
10. Bhum, "Heartbeat of a New Generation," 112–34.
11. Roesler, "Not a Mere Imitation," 156–57.
12. Helgerson, *Forms of Nationhood*, 2.
13. Hadfield, "Vanishing Primordialism," 54.
14. Hastings, *Construction of Nationhood*, 198.
15. Hastings, *Construction of Nationhood*, 31.
16. Hastings, *Construction of Nationhood*, 31.
17. Reb gong ba dge 'dun rab bsal, *Bod kyi rtsom rig*, 45; Jackson, "'Poetry' in Tibet," 369, 372.
18. Per K. Sørenson describes Milarepa's songs of spiritual realization as "folk-inspired religious poetry" and that his "poems are essentially folk songs" (*Divinity Secularized*, 14); Roger Jackson, on the other hand, observes, "In Tibet, the dohās inspired the development of the most personal and spiritually profound of poetic forms, the 'song of experience' (*nyams mgur*)" (*Tantric Treasures*, 42).
19. Jackson, *Tantric Treasures*, 9. There is some disagreement regarding the dating of the *dohās*. Kurtis Schaeffer, for example, dates them to "as early as the seventh century CE" (Schaffer, *Dreaming the Great Brahmin*, 5).
20. Schaeffer, *Dreaming the Great Brahmin*, 68.
21. Zhabs dkar, *Snyigs dus*, 1: 218.1–2; Shabkar, *Life of Shabkar*, 130.
22. "sngon smon lam rta ljang stobs kyis drangs / bod gangs can lha yi lam la mdzes / phrin las kyi 'od stong dra ba can / rje thub bstan pad tshal gnyen gcig nub / phran skal med nub kyi sa 'dzin rster / mgon nyin byed khyod kyis bor ba'i mod / yid dga' ba nyams pa'i zla zer dang / sems gdungs pa'i ku mud mnyam du g.yos / bdag yid la bud shing med na yang / sdug bsngal gyi me chen rab tu sbar / gdong mig gi mkha' la sprin med kyang / mchi ma yi char rgyun drag tu babs" (Zhabs dkar, *Snyigs dus*, 1: 146.3–5; Shabkar, *Life of Shabkar*, 90).
23. I would like to thank Yongdzin Lama Nyima for showing me the *kāvya* elements in Shabkar's songs.
24. Zhabs dkar, *Snyigs dus*, 1: 276.4–5; Shabkar, *Life of Shabkar*, 162.
25. "gangs can ljongs kyi phyi rab gang zag la / phan pa' 'jog pa byed rgyu gzhan ma mchis" (Zhabs dkar, *Bya btang*, 4:604.4).
26. Zhabs dkar, *Bya btang*, 4:383.3–4.
27. "sngon med bod kyi glu pa kha bde nga'i / glu dbyangs bod la phan par byin gyis rlobs" (Zhabs dkar, *Bya btang*, 3: 752.4).
28. Zhabs dkar, *Bya btang*, 4:391.5–392.1; 605.4–5.

29. Zhabs dkar, *Bya btang*, 4:382..3–4.
30. Zhabs dkar, *Bya btang*, 4:392.1–2; 605.4–5.
31. Tucci, "Tibetan Folk Songs from Gyantse and Western Tibet," 14; Anton-Luca, "Glu and La ye in A mdo," 178; Dewang, *Musical Tradition of the Tibetan People*, 207–9, 339, 343, 347.
32. Anton-Luca, "Glu and La ye in A mdo," 188.
33. Anton-Luca, "Glu and La ye in A mdo," 174–75.
34. "sngon med bod kyi glu pa kha bde nga'i" (Zhabs dkar, *bya btang*, 3:752.4).
35. Quintman, "Mi la ras pa's Many Lives," 215.
36. In Milarepa's *Collected Songs*, spiritually unawakened individuals sing, such as in the case of Rechungma in her initial approach to Milarepa, but it does not occur in the *namtar* proper.
37. Pang, "Dissipating Boundaries," 95.
38. Compare for example to the subject matter of Kelden Gyatso's songs (Sujata, *Tibetan Songs of Realization*, 86).
39. See for example Milarepa (in Tsangnyön Heruka, *The Life of Milarepa*) singing to aunt (126), to sister (143), to hunter (151), young maidens (153). They reply in prose.
40. Zhabs dkar, *Snyigs dus*, 1: 22.6–23.1; Shabkar, *Life of Shabkar*, 10.
41. Don grub rgyal, *Bod kyi mgur glu*, 334. Roger Jackson also provides an overview of *glu* in "'Poetry' in Tibet."
42. Don grub rgyal, *Bod kyi mgur glu*, 334–37. Victoria Sujata has compiled a robust bibliography of literature on *gzhas* from central, western, and eastern Tibet (Sujata, *Tibetan Songs of Realization*, 122, n.27–29).
43. Anton-Luca, "Glu and La ye in A mdo," 187–88.
44. Sujata, *Tibetan Songs of Realization*, 112–38, 185–246.
45. Dewang, *Musical Tradition of the Tibetan People*, 207.
46. Don grub rgyal, *Bod kyi mgur glu*, 337–38. Döndrup Gyel bases his definition of religious songs on Shabkar's introduction to his own *Collected Songs* (Zhabs dkar, *Bya btang*, 3:7.5–9.2).
47. For a chart summarizing the content of the songs of Shabkar's autobiography see Pang, "Dissipating Boundaries," 94–99. For examples of: a farewell song (Zhabs dkar, *Snyigs dus*, 1: 66.1–6; Shabkar, *Life of Shabkar*, 41); a song of lament (Zhabs dkar, *Snyigs dus*, 1:348.1–49.1; Shabkar, *Life of Shabkar*, 201–2); a song of greeting (Zhabs dkar, *Snyigs dus*, 1:226.5–6; Shabkar, *Life of Shabkar*, 135); a playful conversation song (Zhabs dkar, *Snyigs dus*, 1:277.4–5; Shabkar, *Life of Shabkar*, 162); a celebration song during new year (Zhabs dkar, *Snyigs dus*, 2: 342.4–43.2); praise of place (Zhabs dkar, *Snyigs dus*, 2:335.6–37.3).
48. Anton-Luca, "Glu and La ye in A mdo," 187–88.
49. Don grub rgyal, *Bod kyi mgur glu*, 489.
50. Sujata, *Tibetan Songs of Realization*, 122–23, 130.
51. "mtshan ldan bla ma dam pa / spyi bo'i rgyan du bzung nas / tshogs drug rang grol rma chen / ri la 'gro 'dod skyes byung / gangs dkar rma chen ri bos / rang shong rdo yi khang pa / tshogs drug rang grol lhan cig / 'dzoms pa'i rten 'brel 'grig byung / skad snyan sgrogs pa'i bya dang / lus mdzes yid 'ong ri dwags/ rnams dang tshogs

drug rang grol / 'grogs pa'i rten 'brel 'grig byung / bla mas gnang ba'i gdams ngag / yon bdag rnams kyi phul zas / na tsha med pa'i sgyu lus / 'tshogs pa'i rten 'brel 'grig byung / 'gal rkyen bar chad med par / mthun rkyen tshang ba'i sgo nas / dam pa'i lha chos tshul bzhin / sgrub pa'i rten 'brel 'grig byung / mthun rkyen legs po 'grig tshe / nyams dga' gcig pur 'dug dus / rab dkar gangs ri'i mgul nas / rgyangs glu len 'dod skyes byung / phyin chad bdag dang bdag 'dra'i / chos byed rnams la 'di 'dra'i / rten 'brel legs par 'grig na / snyam pa zhig kyang skyes byung" (Zhabs dkar, *Snyigs dus* (2003) 1: 273.3–74.1; Zhabs dkar, *Snyigs dus* (1985), 1:319–20; Shabkar, *Life of Shabkar*, 160). The version of the poem in the Zhechen woodblock edition (2003) contains a few typographic errors that were corrected in the Qinghai edition (1985). I base this translation on the edited Qinghai edition.

52. Rta mgrin srungs, *A mdo'i dmangs glu gces bsdus*, 20.
53. Sujata, *Tibetan Songs of Realization*, 217–23.
54. "bya rgyal rgod las skyes pa yi / chung nas 'grogs pa'i rgod phrug gnyis / da lta 'dab gshog rgyas dus 'dir /nga ni tshang la mi chags par / yul phyogs gzhan du 'phur nas 'gro / khyod ni da lta bde bar bzhugs / myur du nga phyir 'ong thub ltos / slar yang mjal ba'i smon lam 'tshal // bre ser 'brong las skyes pa yi / chung nas 'grogs pa'i 'brong phrug gnyis . . . bla ma gcig drung chos nyan pa'i / chung nas 'grogs pa'i grogs po gnyis." (Zhabs dkar, *Snyigs dus*, 1: 66.1–6; Shabkar, *Life of Shabkar*, 41).
55. Sujata, *Tibetan Songs of Realization*, 226–28.
56. "bla ma dkon mchog byin rlabs can / 'dir 'tshogs sgo gsum byin gyis rlobs / dpon po pho skyes bud med la / dgos pa'i glu dbyangs len gyis nyon / kha yi smra ba bzang dang gcig / khog gi bsam pa yags dang gnyis / gtam rnams drang por smrad dang gsum / bsam mno legs par gtong dang bzhi / nye ring mi byed pa dang lnga / rang 'dod chung dang drug po 'di / dpon po rnams la dgos pa yin" (Zhabs dkar, *Snyigs dus*, 1: 920.1–6; Shabkar, *Life of Shabkar*, 518).
57. Sujata, *Tibetan Songs of Realization*, 228–45.
58. "'o 'o phul byung sprul skur rgyan du / a'u dung dung gdungs shugs gus 'dud / kho re bla ma 'jam dbyangs bzhad nas / he he ya mtshan gang bzang gnad ya / ya yi ya yi" (Zhabs dkar, *Snyigs dus*, 1:294.2–95.5; Shabkar, *Life of Shabkar*, 171).
59. Zhabs dkar, *Snyigs dus*, 1:383.3–85.4; Shabkar, *Life of Shabkar*, 222–23.
60. Verheijen, "Singing the Nation," 314.
61. Verheijen, "Singing the Nation," 314.
62. Verheijen, "Singing the Nation," 314.
63. Verheijen, "Singing the Nation," 323.
64. Dreyfus, "Tibetan Religious Nationalism," 214.
65. Jabb, *Oral and Literary Continuities in Modern Tibetan Literature*, 29–30.
66. Jabb, *Oral and Literary Continuities in Modern Tibetan Literature*, 33.
67. Anderson, *Imagined Communities*, 58.
68. Zhabs dkar, *Snyigs dus*, 1:750.1–51.2; Shabkar, *Life of Shabkar*, 433.
69. Gat, *Nations*, 12.
70. Henrion-Dourcy, *Le théâtre "ache lhamo,"* 76.
71. Dorjee et al., "Lhamo: Folk Opera of Tibet," 14.
72. Zhabs dkar, *Snyigs dus*, 1: 826.4–6; Shabkar, *Life of Shabkar*, 471.

73. Kapstein, *Tibetan Assimilation of Buddhism*, 149.
74. Henrion-Dourcy, *Le théâtre "ache lhamo,"* 59–60.
75. Kapstein, *Tibetan Assimilation of Buddhism*, 155.
76. Henrion-Dourcy, *Le théâtre "ache lhamo,"* 525.
77. Henrion-Dourcy, *Le théâtre "ache lhamo,"* 211–14.
78. Henrion-Dourcy, *Le théâtre "ache lhamo,"* 220.
79. Sørenson, "Introduction," 1–2.
80. Henrion-Dourcy, *Le théâtre "ache lhamo,"* 231.
81. Henrion-Dourcy, *Le théâtre "ache lhamo,"* 526.
82. Zhabs dkar, *Snyigs dus* 1:967.5–6; Shabkar, *Life of Shabkar*, 545. Zhabs dkar, *Snyigs dus* 2:20.4–5.
83. Zhabs dkar, *Snyigs dus*, 1:9.1–9.3; Shabkar, *Life of Shabkar*, 4; Zhabs dkar, *Snyigs dus*, 2:9.4–5.
84. Zhabs dkar, *Snyigs dus*, 1:22.6; Shabkar, *Life of Shabkar*, 10; Zhabs dkar, *Snyigs dus*, 2:21.1.
85. Jabb, *Oral and Literary Continuities in Modern Tibetan Literature*, 17. Here, Jabb quoting a term coined by Walter Ong "to denote the enduring features of orality in the literature world following the introduction of writing."
86. Tsangnyön Heruka, *The Life of Milarepa*, 11.
87. Tsangnyön Heruka, *The Life of Milarepa*, 234.
88. Tsangnyön Heruka, *The Life of Milarepa*, 171.
89. Henrion-Dourcy, *Le théâtre "ache lhamo,"* 190.
90. Henrion-Dourcy, *Le théâtre "ache lhamo,"* 190, 211, 526.
91. Henrion-Dourcy, *Le théâtre "ache lhamo,"* 426.
92. Henrion-Dourcy, *Le théâtre "ache lhamo,"* 426, 526.
93. Zhabs dkar, *Snyigs dus*, 1: 22.6–23.1; Shabkar, *Life of Shabkar*, 10.
94. Schaeffer, "Tibetan Biography: Growth and Criticism," 287.
95. Henrion-Dourcy, *Le théâtre "ache lhamo,"* 417.
96. Schaeffer, "Tibetan Biography: Growth and Criticism," 284–85.
97. Henrion-Dourcy, *Le théâtre "ache lhamo,"* 277.
98. Zhabs dkar, *Snyigs dus*, 1:65.4; Shabkar, *Life of Shabkar*, 41.
99. Zhabs dkar, *Snyigs dus*, 1:137.3; Shabkar, *Life of Shabkar*, 84.
100. Zhabs dkar, *Snyigs dus*, 1:284.5; Shabkar, *Life of Shabkar*, 166.
101. Zhabs dkar, *Snyigs dus*, 1:137.2; Shabkar, *Life of Shabkar*, 84.
102. Zhabs dkar, *Snyigs dus*, 1:175.1; Shabkar, *Life of Shabkar*, 106.
103. Henrion-Dourcy, *Le théâtre "ache lhamo,"* 274.
104. See Ricard et al.'s translation for the full scene (Shabkar, *Life of Shabkar*, 40–41).
105. "ma ngas chung nas bskyangs pa'i snying gi bu / a ma bskyur nas yul phyogs gang du 'gro / dud 'gro'i be'u yin yang mar mi 'bral / bu khyod ma dang 'bral bar ga la phod / bu khyod ma nga'i dpral ba'i mig dang 'dra / thag ring song na ma nga long dang 'dra / bu khyod ma nga'i khog pa'i snying dang 'dra / thag ring song na ma nga shi dang 'dra / bu khyod ma nga'i yan lag rnams dang 'dra / thag ring song na ma nga zha dang 'dra / de phyir ma nga'i rna bas thos dang /mig gis mthongs zhig nas cis kyang sdod" (Zhabs dkar, *Snyigs dus*, 1:63.5–64.1; Shabkar, *Life of Shabkar*, 40).

106. Kongtrül, *Autobiography of Jamgön Kongtrül*, 14.
107. Heruka, *Life of Milarepa*, 27–28.
108. Yang, "The Forms of Chanting Gesar and the Bon Religion in Tibet," 434.
109. This is a contested issue. While some scholars place its origins as an oral literature in the eleventh century, it is widely believed that the written form dates to around the fifteenth century (Karmay, "Gesar," 465).
110. Samuel, "The Gesar Epic of East Tibet," 184, 187.
111. Sørenson, "Introduction," 1–2.
112. Samuel, "The Epic and Nationalism in Tibet," 185.
113. Kornman and Chonam, *Epic of Gesar of Ling*, xxviii–xxix.
114. Samuel, "The Epic and Nationalism in Tibet," 185.
115. Karmay, "Gesar: The Epic Tradition of the Tibetan People," 465.
116. Gayley, *Love Letters from Golok*, 182–86.
117. Karmay, "Gesar: The Epic Tradition of the Tibetan People," 466.
118. Karmay, "Gesar," 466.
119. Hellfer, "Tibetan Culture in South Asia," 710–11.
120. Karmay "Gesar," 466; Schaeffer, "Tibetan Biography: Growth and Criticism," 284.
121. Karmay, "Gesar," 465.
122. Samuel, "The Gesar Epic of East Tibet," 363.

## 4. Reviving and Adapting Two Foundational Myths

1. Gamble, *Reincarnation in Tibetan Buddhism*, 68.
2. Zhabs dkar, *Snyigs dus*, 1:826.4–6; Shabkar, *Life of Shabkar*, 471.
3. Smith, *The Cultural Foundations of Nations*, 11.
4. Sørenson, "Introduction," 1–2.
5. Shabkar, *Life of Shabkar*, 162; Zhabs dkar, *Snyigs dus*, 1:276.4.
6. Sakyapa, *The Clear Mirror of Royal Genealogies*, 52–96.
7. Wang, *Maṇḍala of Eight Great Bodhisattvas*, 5.
8. Richardson, "The Cult of Vairocana in Early Tibet"; Heller, "Early Ninth Century Images of Vairochana from Eastern Tibet"; Heller, "Buddhist images and rock inscriptions from Eastern Tibet, Part IV."
9. Wang, *Maṇḍala of Eight Great Bodhisattvas*, 139, 141–42.
10. Richardson, "The Cult of Vairocana in Early Tibet," 272; Kapstein, *Tibetan Assimilation*, 54.
11. van Schaik, "The Tibetan Avalokiteśvara Cult in the Tenth Century," 67.
12. van Schaik, "The Tibetan Avalokiteśvara Cult in the Tenth Century," 66.
13. Kapstein, *Tibetan Assimilation of Buddhism*, 145.
14. Dotson, "Chapter 3: The Emanated Emperor and His Cosmopolitan Contradictions," 74.
15. Dreyfus, "Proto-Nationalism in Tibet," 207.
16. Smith, *Myth and Memories of the Nation*, 84.
17. Vargas-O'Brian, "The Life of dGe slong ma dPal mo," 157–85.
18. Dreyfus, "Proto-Nationalism in Tibet," 207–8.

19. Kapstein, *Tibetan Assimilation of Buddhism*, 33.
20. Phillips, "Consummation and Compassion in Medieval Tibet," 36; Hirshberg, "Nyangrel Nyima Wozer"; Leschly, "Guru Chowang."
21. Phillips, "Consummation and Compassion in Medieval Tibet," 35–36.
22. Kapstein, *Tibetan Assimilation of Buddhism*, 145.
23. Kapstein, *The Tibetan Assimilation of Buddhism*, 147.
24. Davidson, *Tibetan Renaissance*, 251–54.
25. Roesler, "Not a Mere Imitation," 156–57.
26. Jinpa, "Introduction," 21–28.
27. Jinpa, "Introduction," 2.
28. Van der Kuijp, "The Dalai Lamas and the Origins of Reincarnate Lamas," 342.
29. Gamble, *Reincarnation in Tibetan Buddhism*, 69.
30. Van der Kuijp, "The Dalai Lamas and the Origins of Reincarnate Lamas," 339.
31. Ishihama, "On the Dissemination of the Belief in the Dalai Lama as a Manifestation of the Bodhisattva Avalokiteśvara," 45.
32. See chapter 1, n.111 (Zhabs dkar, *Snyigs dus*, 1:206; Shabkar, *Life of Shabkar*, 123).
33. Zhabs dkar, *Bya btang*, 3:429–577.
34. Zhabs dkar, *Bya btang*, 3:431.3–4, 432.6–33.1, 433.5–6; Zhabs dkar, *Bya btang*, 4:207.6–8.1, 229.2, 232.1, 246.4.
35. "bod yul gyi lha skal spyan ras gzigs / bod rnams la thugs rje spyan gyis gzigs / bod phyogs la phan pa'i glu zhig len / bod mi la phan par byin gyis rlobs" (Zhabs dkar, *Bya btang*, 3:431.6).
36. "lha thugs rje chen po spyan ras gzigs / sphyir 'gro ba yongs la thugs rje gzigs / khyed par du bod la thugs rje gzigs / sgos 'dir 'tshogs rnams la thugs rje gzigs" (Zhabs dkar, *Bya btang*, 3:453.1).
37. Smith, *The Cultural Foundations of Nations*, 40.
38. Smith, *The Cultural Foundations of Nations*, 19.
39. Smith, *Myth and Memories of the Nation*, 129.
40. Jabb, *Oral and Literary Continuities in Modern Tibetan Literature*, 2, 33.
41. Dreyfus, "Proto-Nationalism in Tibet," 207.
42. "de ltar mdzod cig bod kyi gdul bya rnams / khyad par kun gyis nga la gsol ba thob / che chung med par yi ge drug ma thon / dad pa can gyi mdun na nga nyid bzhugs / sngon chad nga la dad chad skye bo kun / bde ba chan gyi zhing du nga yis drangs" (Zhabs dkar, *Snyigs dus*, 1:206.5–6.6; Shabkar, *Life of Shabkar*, 123).
43. Zhabs dkar, *Snyigs dus*, 1:623.2–3.
44. Zhabs dkar, *Bya btang*, 3:436.6–37.1; Zhabs dkar, *Bya btang*, 3:432.6–33.1.
45. Zhabs dkar, *Ngo mtshar*, 153–57.
46. Smith, *Myth and Memories of the Nation*, 12.
47. Zhabs dkar, *Snyigs dus*, 1:248.2–4; Shabkar, *Life of Shabkar*, 146.
48. Kapstein, *The Tibetan Assimilation of Buddhism*, 147.
49. Jo bo rje dpal ldan a ti sha, *Brom ston rgyal ba' 'byung gnas*, 160, 162; Jinpa, "Introduction," 19.
50. Jo bo rje dpal ldan a ti sha, *Brom ston rgyal ba'i 'byung gnas*, 167.
51. Kapstein, *The Tibetan Assimilation of Buddhism*, 151.

## NOTES TO PAGES 96–100

52. Phillips, Bradford Lyman, "Consummation and Compassion in Medieval Tibet," 203.
53. Jo bo rje dpal ldan a ti sha, *Brom ston rgyal ba'i 'byung gnas kyi skyes rabs bka' gdams bu chos*, 487.
54. Ehrhard, "The Transmission of the Thig-le bcu-drug and the bka' gdams glegs bam."
55. "nyams snang la mdun gyi nam mkhar 'ja' 'od kyis gang ba'i klong na sangs rgyas gnyis pa jo bo yab sras rnams bzhugs pa la bdag gi snying nas dad pas gsol ba btab pas / jo bo yab sras rnams skad cig de nyid la mi snang bar gnas 'gyur nas / thugs rje chen po thig le bcu drug gi rten dang brten pa'i dkyil 'khor du gyur / mngon sum khra lam me bzhugs pa'i thugs rje chen po rgyal ba rgya mtsho'i gnas gsum las bdud rtsi'i 'od zer dkar dmar mthing gsum rim pa bzhin dang cig char du 'phros / rang gi gnas gsum du rim dang cig char du thim pas ting nge 'dzin gyi dbang bzhi thob / de nas yang mos gus byas pas thugs rje chen po'i thugs ka'i sgo phyes / thub pa chen po rnam snang gangs can mtshos sngar ltar dbang bskur /de bzhin du thub pa'i thugs ka nas bzung bla ma sangs rgyas chos kyi sku'i thugs ka'i bar gyi sgo phyes nas dbang bskur / de'i thugs ka'i sgo phyes nas nang du song bas thugs chos sku nam mkha' lta bu dang rang sems gnyis / nam mkha' la nam mkha' 'dres pa bzhin dbyer med ro cig tu gyur pa'i ngang la rang bzhin shugs kyis gnas pa byung / de nas ting nge 'dzin de las langs pa dang jo bo yab sras rnams sngar ltar mjal ba'i snang ba byung / zhal nas skal ldan rigs kyi bu phyi 'dul ba nang gsang sngags gyis dang bstan 'gro la phan thogs nga dang dus nam yang 'du 'bral med pa yod zhes je mtho je mthor gyur nas yar dga' ldan du gshegs nas mi snang bar gyur / de nas bzung ste sems la dga' bde rgyun mi 'chad pa zhig byung" (Zhabs dkar, *Snyigs dus*, 2:176.3–177.5).
56. Jo bo rje dpal ldan a ti sha, *Brom ston rgyal ba'i 'byung gnas kyi skyes rabs bka' gdams bu chos*, 489.
57. Jinpa, "Introduction," 13–14; Jo bo rje dpal ldan a ti sha, *Brom ston rgyal ba'i 'byung gnas kyi skyes rabs bka' gdams bu chos*, 489.
58. Jinpa, "Introduction," 14.
59. Jinpa, "Introduction," 15.
60. Kapstein, *The Tibetan Assimilation of Buddhism*, 147.
61. Jo bo rje dpal ldan a ti sha, *Brom ston rgyal ba'i 'byung gnas kyi skyes rabs bka' gdams bu chos*, 154, 160, 485–87, 491.
62. Zhabs dkar, *Snyigs dus*, 1:248.3–4; Shabkar Tsogdruk Rangdrol, *The Life of Shabkar*, 146.
63. Zhabs dkar, *Snyigs dus*, 2:38.1.
64. Zhabs dkar, *Bya btang*, 3:412.2, 584.1, 587.6, 591.6.
65. Gamble, *Reincarnation in Tibetan Buddhism*, 86.
66. Gamble, *Reincarnation in Tibetan Buddhism*, 111–12.
67. Zhabs dkar, *Snyigs dus*, 1:808.3, 474.4; Shabkar, *Life of Shabkar*, 463, 279..
68. Zhabs dkar, *Snyigs dus*, 1:841.4, 474.4. Shabkar, *Life of Shabkar*, 479, 279..
69. Ishihama, "On the Dissemination of the Belief in the Dalai Lama as a Manifestation of the Bodhisattva Avalokiteśvara," 45.
70. Ishihama, "On the Dissemination of the Belief in the Dalai Lama as a Manifestation of the Bodhisattva Avalokiteśvara," 46–47.

71. Ishihama, "On the Dissemination of the Belief in the Dalai Lama as a Manifestation of the Bodhisattva Avalokiteśvara," 48–49.
72. Ishihama, "On the Dissemination of the Belief in the Dalai Lama as a Manifestation of the Bodhisattva Avalokiteśvara," 49, 53.
73. Ishihama, "On the Dissemination of the Belief in the Dalai Lama as a Manifestation of the Bodhisattva Avalokiteśvara," 53–54.
74. Ishihama, "On the Dissemination of the Belief in the Dalai Lama as a Manifestation of the Bodhisattva Avalokiteśvara," 54.
75. Jabb, *Oral and Literary Continuities in Modern Tibetan Literature*, 33.
76. Gentry, "Historicism, Philology, and State-Building in 17th Century Tibet," 223–27.
77. Hirschberg, *Remembering the Lotus-Born*, 9–14.
78. Hirshberg, *Remembering the Lotus Born*, 11–14.
79. Dalton "The Early Development of the Padmasambhava Legend in Tibet," 759.
80. Doney, "Padmasambhava in Tibetan Buddhism," 1197, 1210.
81. Blondeau, "Padmasambhava et Avalokiteśvara," 81.
82. Samuel and Oliphant, *Padmasambhava*.
83. Zhabs dkar, *Snyigs dus*, 1:826.4–6; Shabkar, *Life of Shabkar*, 471.
84. Zhabs dkar, *O rgyan*, 398.1; Zhabs dkar, *Legs bshad nyi ma rang shar*, 331.5.
85. Douglas and Bays, *The Life and Liberation of Padmasambhava, Padma bka'i thang*.
86. Zhabs dkar, *Legs bshad nyi ma rang shar*, 337.
87. Zhabs dkar, *Chos bshad gzhan phan nyi ma*, 223.5.
88. "nub cig gi tho rengs nyams snang la / o rgyan gyi gu ru padma 'byung gnas la [364] 'khor phyogs bcu'i sangs rgyas dang byang chub sems dpa' bgrangs las 'das pa'i tshogs kyis bskor ba'i zhal gzigs pa'i snang shar / de dag rnams la dngos su 'byor ba dang yid kyis sprul pa'i mchod pa rgya chen po phul nas rab tu gus pas thal mo sbyar te / bdag gis chung nas bzung ste dus da bar du gsol ba btabs kyang lha zhal da bar du mi gzigs pa thugs rje re chung zhus pas / zhal 'dzum pa dang bcas te dgyes bzhin bka' bstal ba / kye rigs kyi bu nyon cig / ngas sngon khyod kyi bstan 'gro'i don chen 'grub pa'i rten 'brel du / thog mar mtsho snying nas rje rin po che'i rnam par bstan nas rgyud byin gyis brlabs te lam rim gnang / de'i rjes su rma 'gram ri khrod bkra shis nyams dga' gling na 'dug dus jo bo rje'i rnam par bstan nas / thugs ka'i sgo phyes thig le bcu drug gi ting nge 'dzin gyi dbang bskur bka' gdams glegs bam gnang / da ni zhal dngos su bstan nas chos dngos su gnang ba yin pas dga' bar mdzod cig / spyir rgyal ba thams cad ye shes kyi klong du ro gcig cing / sgos su nged rnam pa gsum thugs rgyud gcig tshul khyod kyis sngar shes pa de ka ltar yin la / khyad par phyogs bcu'i rgyal ba sras dang bcas pa ma lus [365] pa rang gi drin can rtsa ba'i bla ma'i rnam 'phrul du go dgos shing / rtsa ba'i bla ma yang rang gi sems kyi rnam rol / sems nyid kyi ngo bo yang gdod nas stong pa nam mkha' bzhin 'dus ma byas shing lhun gyis grub pa / brtan g.yo kun la khyab pa / 'khor 'das kyi 'char gzhir gyur pa stong gsal chos sku ru ngo shes chos kyi gting go ba yin gsungs // yang zhus pa / nga ni rgyal dbang khyed kyi thugs bcud bskyed rdzogs rdzogs pa chen po'i gnang thams cad 'dus pa'i pad 'byung sprul pa'i glegs bam zhes bya ba zhig brtsams na snyams pa / khyed kyi dgongs don ji lta ba bzhin rtsom nus par byin gyis brlab tu gsol zhes zhus pas / khong gi zhal nas / 'o gsang sngags kyi mthar

thug rgyud kyi dgongs don bskyed rdzogs rdzogs pa chen po'i gnad rnams / rgyal ba'i rnam 'phrul klong chen rab 'byams dang mkhyen rtse sogs mkhas pa'i dbang po rnams kyis brtsams pa dang / khyed kyi rtsa ba'i bla mas gsungs pa rnams nyams su longs na de kas chog par 'dug / de'i lhag cig mi dgos / de bas ma 'ongs snyigs ma'i dus su rgyal po kri kri'i rmi lam gyi lung bstan ltar/ sangs rgyas kyi bstan pa rin po che 'di phyi rol [366] pa sogs kyis mi 'jig par / nang pa'i chos pa nang phan tshun gyis chos kyi bzang ngan brtsad nas chags sdang 'thab rtsod byas bstan pa 'jig par gsungs pas / de'i phyir ma 'ongs pa'i dus su chos pa 'jig rten pa su zhig gi mgo thog tu bzhag kyang / chos kyi phyogs ris kun zhi nas dag snang phyogs med du 'char ba'i sngar med pa'i legs bshad / bstan 'gro yongs la phan pa'i o rgyan sprul pa'i glegs bam zhes bya ba zhig rtsom dang bzang zhes" (Zhabs dkar, *Snyigs dus* 2: 363.6–366.3).
89. Zhabs dkar, *O rgyan*, 441.1–43.1.
90. Smith, *Myth and Memories of the Nation*, 129.
91. Kapstein, *The Tibetan Assimilation of Buddhism*, 153.
92. Kapstein, *The Tibetan Assimilation of Buddhism*, 153.
93. Kapstein, *The Tibetan Assimilation of Buddhism*, 155.
94. Kunsang, *The Lotus-Born*, 189.
95. Phillips, "Consummation and Compassion in Medieval Tibet," 144.
96. Phillips, "Consummation and Compassion in Medieval Tibet," 22, 24, 35.
97. Leschly, "Orgyen Lingpa."
98. Leschly, "Guru Chowang."
99. Blondeau, "Padmasambhava et Avalokiteśvara," 77.
100. Kunsang, *The Lotus-Born*, 197.
101. "bod kyi lha skal spyan ras gzigs dbang ngas / bod la rtag tu thugs rje'i spyan gyis gzigs / bod yul dbus skyes las 'phro can khyod dang / bod khams mi rnams kun gyis 'di ltar gyis / . . . de ltar mdzod cig bod kyi gdul bya rnams / khyad par kun gyis nga la gsol ba thob / che chung med par yi ge drug ma thon/ dad pa can gyi mdun na nga nyid bzhugs" (Zhabs dkar, *Snyigs dus*, 1:206; Shabkar, *Life of Shabkar*, 123).
102. Phillips, "Consummation and Compassion in Medieval Tibet," 142–44.
103. Blondeau, "Padmasambhava et Avalokiteśvara," 81.
104. Blondeau, "Padmasambhava et Avalokiteśvara," 80; Phillips, "Consummation and Compassion in Medieval Tibet," 385–86.
105. Kunsang, *The Lotus Born*, 62–74; Douglas and Bays, *Life and Liberation of Padmasambhava*, 370–90.
106. Gamble, *Reincarnation in Tibetan Buddhism*, 116–17.

## 5. Imagining a Community Based on Buddhist Values and Practices

1. Hastings, *The Construction of Nationhood*, 3–4.
2. Gyallay-Pap, "Reconstructing the Cambodian Polity"; Brook et al., *Sacred Mandates*; Raghavan, *Buddhist Monks and the Politics of Lanka's Civil War*; Walton, *Buddhism, Politics and Political Thought in Myanmar*; Keyes, *Thailand*.
3. Brook et al., *Sacred Mandates*, 90.
4. Brook et al., *Sacred Mandates*, 100.

5. Hum chen & Ye shes 'od zer sgrol ma, *Reb kong sngags mang*, 159; 'Brug thar dang sangs rgyas tshe ring, *Mdo smad rma khug tsha 'gram yul*, 547–48.
6. Zhab dkar, *Snyigs dus*, 1:750.3–4.
7. Zhab dkar, *Bya btang*, 3:729.6.
8. Zhab dkar, *Snyigs dus*, 1:750.1–51.2.
9. "rnying ma ma yin dge lugs pa yang min / de gnyis mthun las byung ba'i rnal 'byor yin / ming la phyogs 'dir zhab dkar bla ma zer / gang dang mi 'dra kun dang mthun pa mtshar" (Zhab dkar, *Snyigs dus*, 1:623.4; Shabkar, *Life of Shabkar*, 359).
10. Zhab dkar, *Snyigs dus*, 2:72.
11. Zhab dkar, *Snyigs dus*, 2:77.6–78.1. "Empowerments" (*dbang*) are initiation rituals in the Vajrayana Buddhist tradition, "Transmissions" (*lung*) involve the teacher reading the entire text aloud to his or her disciple. One must receive the empowerment, transmission, and instructions associated with a practice before they are authorized to engage in a practice in Vajrayana Buddhism.
12. Zhab dkar, *Snyigs dus*, 2:239.3, 357.
13. Zhab dkar, *Snyigs dus*, 2:134.
14. Zhab dkar, *Snyigs dus*, 2:154.
15. Zhab dkar, *Snyigs dus*, 2:133, 152, 154, 158.
16. Zhab dkar, *Snyigs dus*, 1:943.3–4; Shabkar, *Life of Shabkar*, 529.
17. Zhabs dkar, *Snyigs dus* 1:960.1; Shabkar, *Life of Shabkar*, 541.
18. Zhabs dkar, *Snyigs dus* 1:930.5; Shabkar, *Life of Shabkar*, 523.
19. Zhabs dkar, *Snyigs dus* 1:264.5–6; Shabkar, *Life of Shabkar*, 156.
20. Zhabs dkar, *Snyigs dus* 1:734.4; Shabkar, *Life of Shabkar*, 425.
21. Zhab dkar, *Snyigs dus*, 1:919.1; Shabkar, *Life of Shabkar*, 518.
22. Zhab dkar, *Snyigs dus*, 1:949.6; Shabkar, *Life of Shabkar*, 532.
23. In the first volume, Shabkar writes of feuds in lower Repgong, between the three villages of Lingya and seven villages of lower Jam, an eighteen-year feud between Dobi and Secang, between the Banak Khaksum and Hor tribes in the ethnically Mongolian area, between Repgong and the Banak Khaksum, and between the tribes of Adar Chakka and Shézhin at Mapari (Zhab dkar, *Snyigs dus*, 1:358.6, 866.3, 884.1, 892.1, 908.5, 921.3). In the second volume, Shabkar documents feuds between Hor and Sog, between the Nyentok and Kyi clans, between his home village of Zhopong and Peudo, and between Rongwo Monastery and Labrang Monastery (2:238.6, 240.1–2, 359.3–5, 359.2–3).
24. Zhab dkar, *Snyigs dus*, 1:734.4–5, 884.4–5; Shabkar, *Life of Shabkar*, 425, 501–2. Zhab dkar, *Snyigs dus*, 2:105.5, 112.1.
25. "thams cad kyi blo kha chos la 'gyur" (Zhabs dkar, *Snyigs dus* 1: 872.5; Shabkar, *Life of Shabkar*, 496).
26. Zhabs dkar, *Snyigs dus* 1: 364.2–65.2; Shabkar, *Life of Shabkar*, 210–11.
27. "nged tso'i ka cu'i sangs rgyas gsung dang bod kyi bla ma zhabs dkar pa'i gnyis gcig red zer skad" (Zhabs dkar, *Snyigs dus* 1: 884.4–5; Shabkar, *Life of Shabkar*, 501).
28. Zhabs dkar, *Snyigs dus* 1:676.6–77.4, 772.6–73.2, 780.3–5; Shabkar, *Life of Shabkar*, 387, 447, 450.

29. Zhab dkar, *Snyigs dus*, 1:961.2; Shabkar, *Life of Shabkar*, 542.
30. Zhab dkar, *Snyigs dus*, 1:737.2–38.3; Shabkar, *Life of Shabkar*, 427.
31. Gat, *Nations*, 11.
32. Lehr, *Militant Buddhism*, 115, 157.
33. Turner, *Saving Buddhism*, 139.
34. Turner, *Saving Buddhism*, 1.
35. Turner, *Saving Buddhism*, 140.
36. Turner, *Saving Buddhism*, 139.
37. Fox and Miller-Idriss, "Everyday Nationhood," 537.
38. Stroup, *Pure and True*, 13.
39. Stroup, *Pure and True*, 113.
40. Shabkar, *Life of Shabkar*, 542; Zhab dkar, *Snyigs dus*, 1:961.2.
41. Fox and Miller-Idriss, "Everyday Nationhood," 542.
42. Fox and Miller-Idriss, "Everyday Nationhood," 545.
43. Huber, *Cult of Pure Crystal Mountain*, 25.
44. Buffetrille "Reflections on Pilgrimages to Sacred Mountains, Lakes and Caves," 19.
45. Ekvall and Downs, *Tibetan Pilgrimage*, 147, 149.
46. Ekvall and Downs, *Tibetan Pilgrimage*, 151.
47. Ryavec, *Historical Atlas of Tibet*, 18–19.
48. Zhabs dkar, *Snyigs dus*, 1:388.6–89.1; Shabkar, *Life of Shabkar*, 225.
49. Zhab dkar, *Snyigs dus*, 1:420.2–6; Shabkar, *Life of Shabkar*, 245.
50. Zhab dkar, *Snyigs dus*, 1:372–86; Shabkar, *Life of Shabkar*, 215–23.
51. Zhab dkar, *Snyigs dus*, 1:689.5–6; Shabkar, *Life of Shabkar*, 398.
52. Buffetrille, "The Great Pilgrimage of A-myes rma-chen," 88.
53. Huber, *Pure Crystal Mountain*, 18.
54. Fox and Miller-Idriss, "Everyday Nationhood," 538.
55. Fox and Miller-Idriss, "Everyday Nationhood," 545.
56. Huber, *Pure Crystal Mountain*, 33.
57. Buffetrille, "Reflections on Pilgrimages to Sacred Mountains, Lakes and Caves," 23.
58. Kapstein, "A Pilgrimage of Rebirth Reborn," 117.
59. Barstow, *Food of Sinful Demons*, 31–33.
60. Barstow, *Food of Sinful Demons*, 33–34.
61. Barstow, *Food of Sinful Demons*, 46, 57.
62. Barstow, "Buddhism Between Abstinence and Indulgence," 36.
63. Barstow, *Food of Sinful Demons*, 37–40.
64. Shabkar, *Life of Shabkar*, 542; Zhab dkar, *Snyigs dus*, 1:96.
65. "de ltar 'jig rten khams na gsod pa rnams la snying rje shas mi bzod pa zhig skyes nas slar jo bo'i mdun du song / phyag 'tshal nas / phyin chad sdig zas pha ma'i sha mi za ba'i dam bca' phul ba" (Shabkar, *Life of Shabkar*, 232; Zhab dkar, *Snyigs dus*, 1:401.6–2.1).
66. Zhab dkar, *Snyigs dus*, 2:488.1–88.4.
67. Pang, "Songs against Meat by Shabkar."
68. "snyigs dus sangs rgyas bstan pa nyams re dma' / phyi rol pa yang bod la yong ma

dgos / dgon pa'i ljags ri lha khang khor yug kun / shan pas sha dang khrag gis dmar por btang / sangs rgyas byang sems zhing gzhan gshegs pa'i mod" (Zhabs dkar, *Bya btang*, 5:236.6–37.2).

69. "deng sang lha khang khor yug sde dgon na / sdig can shan pas sha yi thang kha bshams / glo snying nang khrol mchod rdzas gcal du bkram / rin thang rten bshad byed 'di su yis bstan / ma gyur 'gro ba'i sha rus spungs dkyil du / btsun pas gri 'phyar kha gdangs za la chas / kye hud nang pas 'gro la 'di phod dam / phyi rol pa yis phod pa smos ci dgos" (Zhabs dkar, *Bya btang*, 5:237.6–38.2).
70. "sdig can shan pas bsad pa'i pha ma'i sha / mthong na mchog dman kun gyis mchil ma mid / byams dang snying rje med pa'i rang mtshang ston" (Zhabs dkar, *Bya btang*, 5:237.2–3).
71. "pha ma'i srog la 'tshe ba med slad du / dge 'dun yong kyis dkar gsum mngar gsum sten / shan pa pho mor srog gcod mi rung zhes / chos gsungs khrims kyang zhog ces thal mo sbyar / sha tsha'i nga ro che na bzod par gsol" (Zhabs dkar, *Bya btang*, 5:240.4–5).
72. Zhabs dkar, *Snying rje sprul pa'i glegs bam*, 424.2–25.3.
73. Zhabs dkar, *Snyigs dus* 1: 960.1; Shabkar, *Life of Shabkar*, 541.
74. Zhabs dkar, *Snyigs dus* 1: 747.5; Shabkar, *Life of Shabkar*, 432. The Magar are an ethnolinguistic group in Nepal (Shabkar, *Life of Shabkar*, 342, n.4).
75. Zhabs dkar, *Snyigs dus* 1: 774.1–3; Shabkar, *Life of Shabkar*, 447.
76. Zhabs dkar, *Snyigs dus* 1: 772.6–73.2; Shabkar, *Life of Shabkar*, 447.
77. Huber, *Cult of Pure Crystal Mountain*, 179–82.
78. Fox and Miller-Idriss, "Everyday Nationhood," 550.
79. Fox and Miller-Idriss, "Everyday Nationhood," 551.
80. Stroup, *Pure and True*, 98.
81. Zhabs dkar, *Chos bshad gzhan phan nyi ma*, 71.5.
82. Zhabs dkar, *Chos bshad gzhan phan nyi ma*, 69.6.
83. Zhabs dkar, *Chos bshad gzhan phan nyi ma*, 72.3.
84. Zhabs dkar, *Chos bshad gzhan phan nyi ma*, 81.4.
85. Zhabs dkar, *Chos bshad gzhan phan nyi ma*, 101.5.
86. Zhabs dkar, *Chos bshad gzhan phan nyi ma*, 92.1.
87. Zhabs dkar, *Chos bshad gzhan phan nyi ma*, 92.5.
88. "pha ma ra lug 'bri g.yag la sogs sems can las ngan pa mang po yul thag ring po nas ded 'ong dus ltogs skom ngal bas sdug bsngal myang / shan pa'i sgo drung du slebs nas / sdig can shan pa mig dmar gyi lag tu sprad nas mgo bcad de gsod pa'm / yang na kha bsum / yang na rtsib logs nas snying la gri phra mo'm / 'bug rnon po rgyag / yang na brang gshags nas khog tu lag pa btang te srog rtsa dmar po bcad nas gsod pa'i dus skabs rnams su / ra lug gang yin yang dngangs shing skrag nas 'then bskor byas / skad 'don sug bzhi 'dar / bshan pa'i gdong la mig hrig hrig blta / lug 'ga' re mig mthar chu 'khyil mchi ma khril ler gtong / snying rje rgyu de na yod mod / de mthong zhing thos na bla ma dge 'dun pa zhig mi dgos / rgan rgon gzhon nu snying rje can gyi mig nas mchi ma 'chor / de tsho bsam na sha zos pa pha ma gnyis kyi sha zos pa las thu / srog dbugs gcod dus bzod blags med pa'i na tsha sdug bsngal bsam gyis mi khyab pa myong / ja theb re la 'chi rgyu med / lus po shig shig yom yom 'gul /

'o skol rnams kyi mgo gcod pa dang / kha sna bsum pa'm / yang na khog tu lag pa btang nas srog rtsa 'then pa phar zhog / rang gi sha sen mo gnyis kyi bar du 'tshir dang / de tsam gyi sdug bsngal mi bzod na / pha ma ra lug rnams kyi de bas brgya stong 'gyur gyi sdug bsngal myangs nas shi ba yin pas / de ltar rang lus la dpe blangs bsam mno zhib tu btang na byang chub sems dpa' rnams snying rlung ldangs na / 'o skol rnams la snying med na ma gtogs yod na snying rje zhig skye dgos te / dper na tshe 'di'i rang gi ma rgan gzhan gyis bsad nas sha btsos drangs na ma de la snying rje skye'm mi skye / dpe de bzhin du ra lug g.yag gsum gang yin yang rang gi tshe sngon ma'i ma drin can yin pas / gzhan gyis bsad nas byin kyang snying rje zhig ci la mi skye / gal te snying rje mi skye rung / 'dod sred cig skyes nas za mkhan rnams las kyi srin po bas snying rje chung zhing / khra dang spyang ki bas sha dad chen ba yin te" (Zhabs dkar, *Snying rje sprul pa'i glegs bam*, 411.6–13.5).

89. Henrion-Dourcy, *Le théâtre "ache lhamo,"* 274.
90. Barstow, "Monastic Meat"; Tibet in Review, "Lhakar Wednesday Movement"; Buffetrille, "Self-Immolation in Tibet," 3.
91. Barstow, *Food of Sinful Demons*, 37–40.
92. Smith, "Jam mgon Kong sprul and the Nonsectarian Movement," 237.
93. Smith, "Jam mgon Kong sprul and the Nonsectarian Movement," 241.
94. Komarovski, *Visions of Unity*, 19; Cabezón and Dargyay, *Freedom from Extremes*, 11–33.
95. Smith, "Jam mgon Kong sprul and the Nonsectarian Movement," 242.
96. Ary, *Authorized Lives*, 78–93.
97. Mathes and Coura, *Nonsectarian (ris med) in 19th-and 20th-Century Eastern Tibet*.
98. Komarovski, *Visions of Unity*, 21.
99. Pang, "The *Rimé* Activities of Shabkar Tsokdruk Rangdrol (1781–1851)."
100. Nietupski, *Labrang Monastery*, 16.
101. Nietupski, *Labrang Monastery*, 16.
102. Dhondup, "Reb kong," 33–59.
103. Nietupski, *Labrang Monastery*, 15.
104. Mathes, "Introduction," 2.
105. Nietupski, *Labrang Monastery*, 31.
106. Nietupski, *Labrang Monastery*, 32.
107. Nietupski, *Labrang Monastery*, 33.
108. Nietupski, *Labrang Monastery*, 36, 17.
109. Sujata, *Tibetan Songs of Realization*.
110. Sullivan, "The first generation of dGe lugs evangelists in Amdo."
111. Zhab dkar, *Snyigs dus*, 1:39.1–2; Shabkar, *Life of Shabkar*, 21.
112. Zhab dkar, *Snyigs dus*, 1:52.6; Shabkar, *Life of Shabkar*, 32.
113. Zhabs dkar, *Chos bshad gzhan phan nor bu*, 530.4.
114. Shabkar, *Life of Shabkar*, 569.
115. Zhab dkar, *Snyigs dus*, 1:75.5, 155.6; Shabkar, *Life of Shabkar*, 46, 97.
116. Deroche, Marc-Henri. "On Being 'Impartial' (ris med)," 143. For use of the term "phyogs ris med pa" and its variants in Shabkar, see Pang, "*Rimé* Revisited."
117. "sprin med nam mkha' la nyi ma shar ba bzhin sgom byung gi shes rab phyogs med

du rdol nas / gsar snying ris med kyi chos thams cad la mkhas par gyur te" (Zhab dkar, *Snyigs dus*, 2:280.2-3).
118. "nam mkha' mtha' med bzhin du rang sems la / gang nas bltas kyang mtha' med dbus su song / 'di las chen po gzhan na ma mchis pas / mtha' bral dbu ma chen mo zhes kyang zer / sems nyid stong gsal zang thal klong yangs su / 'khor 'das chos rnams gcig kyang ma lus pa / yong rdzogs chud cing 'di las rgya chen po / gzhan na med pas rdzogs pa chen po zer / sems nyid stong gsal rgyal po'i phyag lta bus / 'khor 'das yongs la rgya yis ma thebs med / phyag rgya zhig la 'di las chen po zhig / gzhan na med pas phyag rgya chen po zer" (Zhabs dkar, *Bya btang*, 5:63.2-5).
119. Zhabs dkar, *Bya btang*, 3:610-11.
120. Zhabs dkar, *Legs bshad kun bzang*, 127.5.
121. Zhabs dkar, *Legs bshad kun bzang* 127.5; Zhabs dkar, *Chos bshad gzhan phan nor bu*, 532.2, 526.4, 527.1.
122. Zhabs dkar, *Legs bshad kun bzang*, 82.5, 129.1.
123. Zhabs dkar, *O rgyan*, 417.
124. Zhabs dkar, *Chos bshad gzhan phan nor bu*, 527.1.
125. Zhabs dkar, *Chos bshad gzhan phan nor bu*, 527.3.
126. Zhab dkar, *Snyigs dus*, 2:35.5-36.2.
127. Zhabs dkar, *Legs bshad kun bzang*, 104.6, 105.4.
128. Zhabs dkar, *Legs bshad kun bzang*, 17.2, 244.5, 102.4.
129. Zhabs dkar, *Legs bshad kun bzang*, 38.1, 101.2.
130. Zhabs dkar, *Legs bshad kun bzang*, 101.6.
131. Zhabs dkar, *Legs bshad kun bzang*, 103.1.
132. Zhabs dkar, *Legs bshad kun bzang*, 103.3.
133. Zhabs dkar, *Chos bshad gzhan phan nor bu*, 51.5.
134. "'o bdag cag gi ston pa thabs mkhas la thugs rje che ba de nyid kyis mkha' mnyam gyi sems can thams cad mngon mtho lha mi'i go 'phang dang / mthar thug nges legs thar pa dang thams cad mkhyen pa sangs rgyas kyi go 'phang thob par bya ba'i phyir / gang 'dul gyi sku'i bkod pa cir yang bstan nas gang 'tshams kyi chos ston pa yin te / rnam snang mngon byang las / nga yi bstan pa rnam gnyis te / dman pa mu stegs theg pa dang / mchog gyur sangs rgyas theg pa'o / zhes gsungs / sngon sangs rgyas kyi rang gi bstan pa'i che ba 'byin phyir / rgyal po rkang pa brgyad pa'i sras su sku'i skyes ba bzhes pa'i tshul bstan nas / mu stegs pa'i gzhung lugs thams cad gsungs pa yin skad / des na dad gus dag snang byed pa ma gtogs smad cing spangs mi rung ste" (Zhab dkar, *Snyigs dus*, 2:105.5-6.3).
135. Zhabs dkar, *Legs bshad*, 13.4; Zhab dkar, *Snyigs dus*, 2:108.2-4.

## Epilogue

1. Hobsbawm, *Nations and Nationalism Since 1780*; Gellner, *Nations and Nationalism*; Anderson, *Imagined Communities*.
2. Smith, *Myth and Memories of the Nation*, 7.
3. Jensen, *The Roots of Nationalism*, 14.
4. Pollack, "Introduction," 3.

5. Goldstein, *A History of Modern Tibet*, 78; Shakabpa, *Tibet: A Political History*, 249–50; Bstan-'dzin rgya mtsho, *Freedom in Exile*, 33.
6. Goldstein, *A History of Modern Tibet*, 89–138.
7. Bstan-'dzin rgya mtsho, *My Land and My People*, 43–46.
8. Sheehy, "The Offering of Mount Meru," 336.
9. Sheehy, "The Offering of Mount Meru," 327.
10. Smith, *The Cultural Foundations of Nations*, 11.
11. Smith, *The Cultural Foundations of Nations*, 9.
12. Yeh, *Taming Tibet*.
13. Lopez, *Prisoners of Shangri-La*.
14. Pollack, *Forms of Knowledge in Early Modern Asia*.
15. Gyatso, *Being Human in a Buddhist World*, 409, n.1.
16. See Park, *Thomas Merton's Encounter with Buddhism and Beyond*; Kamenetz, *The Jew in the Lotus*; Dalai Lama and Desmond Tutu, *The Book of Joy*.
17. Knauft, "Tibetan Buddhist Leadership," 174.
18. Tibetan Parliament-in-Exile. *Charter of the Tibetans-in-Exile*, Article 17 "Education and Culture," no. 11, p. 4.
19. Tibetan Parliament-in-Exile. *Charter of the Tibetans-in-Exile*, Article 37, no. 37 "Composition of the Tibetan Assembly," p. 9.
20. Smith, "Jam mgon Kong sprul and the Nonsectarian Movement," 237.
21. Shabkar, *Life of Shabkar*, vii.
22. Pearcey, "Japa Dongak Gyatso"; Pearcey, "A Greater Perfection?" 45.
23. Mathes and Coura, eds, *Nonsectarian (ris med) in 19th- and 20th-Century Eastern Tibet*.
24. Pearcey, "A Greater Perfection?" 133–34.
25. Bstan-'dzin rgya mtsho, *Kindness, Clarity and Insight*, 206–24.
26. Pearcey. "Dongak Chokyi Gyatso."
27. Pearcey. "Dongak Chokyi Gyatso."
28. Pearcey, "A Greater Perfection?" 183–84. The full title of the work is *A Jeweled Mirror of Pure Appearances: Establishing the Unity of the Views of the Old and New Translation Schools of the Secret Mantrayāna* (gsang sngags gsar rnying gi lta bag cig tu sgrub pa dag snang nor bu'i me long). It is translated in B. Allan Wallace's *Open Mind* (2018).
29. Pearcey, "A Greater Perfection?" 185.
30. Pearcey, "A Greater Perfection?" 183–84. The full title of this text is *The Offering Clouds of the Nectar of the Path of Reasoning: Establishing the Unity of the Intention of the Scholars of the Old and New Translation Schools* (Gsar rnying mkhas pa'i dgongs bzhed gcig tu sgrub pa rigs lam bdud rtsi'i mchod sprin).
31. Pearcey, "A Greater Perfection?" 168.
32. Pearcey, "A Greater Perfection?" 183.
33. Pearcey, "A Greater Perfection?" 168–69.
34. Pearcey, "A Greater Perfection?" 193.
35. Pearcey, "A Greater Perfection?" 201.
36. Pearcey, "A Greater Perfection?" 194.

37. Pearcey, "A Greater Perfection?" 205.
38. Pearcey, "A Greater Perfection?" 206.
39. Tibetan Youth Congress Central Executive Committee, "About TYC."
40. Central Tibetan Administration, "Middle Way Approach: Frequently Asked Questions."
41. Terrone, "10. Nationalism Matters," 297–301.
42. Terrone, "10. Nationalism Matters," 291–96.
43. Hartley, "'Inventing Modernity' in Amdo," 8–9; Gaerrang, "Development as Entangled Knot," 945.
44. The Tibetan Buddhist World is Tibet's unique model of international law from the thirteenth through the early twentieth century. This concept was first introduced in the introduction chapter of this book (Brook et al., *Sacred Mandates*, 14–15).
45. Bstan 'dzin rgya mtsho, *Srid zhi'i*, 3:534.
46. Bstan 'dzin rgya mtsho, *Srid zhi'i*, 3:594.
47. Bstan 'dzin rgya mtsho, *Srid zhi'i*, 3:535, 512, 212.
48. Knauft, "Tibetan Buddhist Leadership," 185–87.
49. Tsurphu, "The Gyalwang Karmapa Rings an Alarm."
50. Bstan 'dzin rgya mtsho, *Srid zhi'i*, vol. 3, 594.
51. O rgyan 'phrin las rdo rje, "Phags pa," 2:2.
52. O rgyan 'phrin las rdo rje, "Phags pa," 2:10–11.
53. O rgyan 'phrin las rdo rje, "Phags pa," 2:12.
54. O rgyan 'phrin las rdo rje, "Phags pa," 2:12.
55. Tsurphu Labrang, "Addressing 8,000 Newly-Arrived Tibetans in Bodhgaya."
56. Gayley, "The Ethics of Cultural Survival," 442.
57. Gayley, "The Ethics of Cultural Survival," 444.
58. Gayley, "The Ethics of Cultural Survival," 444.
59. Gayley, "The Ethics of Cultural Survival," 445.
60. Gayley, "The Ethics of Cultural Survival," 435.
61. Gayley, "The Ethics of Cultural Survival," 445.
62. Gayley, "The Ethics of Cultural Survival," 451–52.
63. Gaerrang, "Tibetan identity and Tibetan Buddhism in trans-regional connection," 7.
64. Gaerrang, "Tibetan identity and Tibetan Buddhism in trans-regional connection," 7.
65. Gayley, "Reimagining Buddhist Ethics on the Tibetan Plateau," 252.
66. Gayley, "Reimagining Buddhist Ethics on the Tibetan Plateau," 252.
67. Gayley, "The Ethics of Cultural Survival," 438–39.
68. Gayley, "Reimagining Buddhist Ethics on the Tibetan Plateau," 255.
69. Gayley, "Reimagining Buddhist Ethics on the Tibetan Plateau," 258.
70. Gayley, "The Ethics of Cultural Survival," 441–45.
71. Gaerrang, "Development as Entangled Knot," 938.
72. Gaerrang, "Tibetan Identity and Tibetan Buddhism in Trans-Regional Connection," 5.
73. Gaerrang, "Tibetan identity and Tibetan Buddhism in Trans-Regional Connection," 7
74. Gaerrang, "Alternative Development on the Tibetan Plateau," 142.
75. Gayley, "Reimagining Buddhist Ethics on the Tibetan Plateau," 264.
76. Gaerrang, "Tibetan identity and Tibetan Buddhism in Trans-Regional Connection," 7.

77. Fox and Miller-Idriss, "Everyday Nationhood," 538.
78. Fox and Miller-Idriss, "Everyday Nationhood," 542.
79. Fox and Miller-Idriss, "Everyday Nationhood," 542.
80. Gaerrang, "Tibetan identity and Tibetan Buddhism in Trans-Regional Connection," 10.
81. "White Wednesday: The Lhakar Pledge," High Peaks Pure Earth.
82. Shakya, "Wither the Tsampa Eaters?" 11.
83. Okada, "Constructing the Secular," 84.
84. Kolås, "Tibetan Nationalism," 56.
85. Shakya, "Wither the Tsampa Eaters?" 11.
86. Shakya, "Self-Immolation," 24, 36.
87. Shakya, "Self-Immolation," 36.
88. Terrone, "Burning for the Cause," 481–88.
89. Kolås, "Tibetan Nationalism," 55.
90. Smith, *The Cultural Foundations of Nations*, 8.
91. Brook et al., *Sacred Mandates*, 178–81.
92. Goanker, *Alternative Modernities*.
93. Kaviraj, "An Outline of a Revisionist Theory of Modernity."
94. Teeuwen, "Buddhist Modernities: Modernism and its Limits," 4.
95. King, *Ocean of Milk, Ocean of Blood*, 205.
96. Gayley, "The Ethics of Cultural Survival," 439.
97. King, *Ocean of Milk, Ocean of Blood*, 205.
98. King, *Ocean of Milk, Ocean of Blood*, 205.
99. Makley, *The Battle for Fortune*, 17.

## Appendix

1. Shabkar, *The Life of Shabkar*.
2. Pang, "Dissipating Boundaries," 268–71.

# BIBLIOGRAPHY

## Tibetan Sources

*Bod rgya tshig mdzod chen mo.* 2 vols. 1985. Beijing: Mi rigs dpe skrun khang, 2008.

Bstan 'dzin rgya mtsho, Dalai Lama XIV. *Srid zhi'i rnam 'dren gong sa kyabs mgon chen po mchog nas rgya che'i bod mi ser skyab mang tshogs la blang dor byed sgo'i skor stsal ba'i bka' slob phyogs bsdebs.* 3 vols. Dharamsala: Bod gzhung phyi dril las khungs nas dpar bskrun zhus, 2001.

Brag dgon pa dkon mchog bstan pa rab rgyas. *Mdo smad chos 'byung.* 1865. Lanzhou: Cultural Preservation Press, 1982.

'Brug thar dang sangs rgyas tshe ring. *Mdo smad rma khug tsha 'gram yul gru'i lo rgyus deb ther chen mo.* Beijing: Mi rigs dpe skrun khang, 2005.

Dge 'dun chos 'phel. *Deb ther dkar po.* Beijing: Mi rigs dpe skrun khang, 2007.

Don grub rgyal. *Bod kyi mgur glu byung 'phel gyi lo rgyus dang khyad chos bsdus par ston pa rig pa'i khye'u rnam par rtson pa'i skyed tshal zhes bya ba.* In vol. 3 of *Dpal don grub rgyal gyi gsung 'bum,* 316–601. Beijing: Mi rigs dpe skrun khang, 1985.

Gling rgya ba bla ma tshe ring. *Reb gong gser mo ljongs kyi chos srid byung ba brjod pa 'dod 'byung gter gyi bum bzang.* Hong Kong: Zhang kang gyi ling dpe skrun khang, 2002.

'Jam mgon kong sprul yon tan rgya mtsho. *Mdo khams gnas chen nyer lnga yan lag dang bcas pa'i mod byang gi gsal byed zin thung nyung ngu.* In vol. 24 of *The Treasury of Revelations and Teachings of Mchog-gyur-bde-chen-gling-pa,* 125–43. Paro: Lama Pema Tashi, 1982–86.

Jo bo rje dpal ldan a ti sha. *Brom ston rgyal ba'i 'byung gnas kyi skyes rabs bka' gdams bu chos.* Xining: mtsho sngon mi rigs dpe skrun khang, 1993.

Lce nag tshang hum chen and ye shes 'od zer sgrol ma. *Reb kong sngags mang gi lo rgyus phyogs bsgrigs dpal chen khrag 'thung khros pa'i rdo rje'i gad rgyangs zhes bya ba bzhugs so.* Pe cin: mi rigs dpe skrun khang, 2004.

O rgyan 'phrin las rdo rje, Karma-pa XVII, "Phags pa spyan ras gzigs kyi ngo sprod dang sgrub thabs mdor bsdus." In vol. 2 of *Dpal rgyal dbang karma pa sku yi phreng ba bcu bdun pa chen po o rgyan 'gro 'dul phrin las bstan 'dzin kun khyab dpal ldan dbang gi rdo rje dpal bzang po mchog gi bka' slob bzhugs so.* Labrang Sidhbari: Drophen Tsukladk Pentunkhang (Altruism Publication) of Tsurphu, 2006.

Rang byung rdo rje. *Thams cad mkhyen pa rin po che rang byung rdo rje rnam par thar pa tshigs su bcad pa.* In vol. 5 of *Rang byung rdo rje'i gsung 'bum,* 374–414. Mtshur phu: mkhan po lo yag bkra shis, 2006.

Reb gong ba dge 'dun rab gsal. *Bod kyi rtsom rig gyi byung ba brjod pa rab bsal me long.* Lanzhou: Kan su'u mi rigs dpe skrun khang, 2003.

Rta mgrin srungs, ed. *A mdo'i dmangs glu gces bsdus.* Xining: Mtsho sngon mi rigs dpe skrun khang, 2000.

Skal ldan rgya mtsho. *Grub chen skal ldan rgya mtsho'i rnam thar yid bzhin dbang gi rgyal po*. In vol. 1 of *Yab rje bla ma skal ldan rgya mtsho'i gsum 'bum*, 1–99. Lanzhou: Kan su'u mi rigs dpe skrun khang, 1999.

Zhabs dkar tshogs drug rang grol. *Snyigs dus 'gro ba yongs kyi skyabs mgon zhabs dkar rdo rje 'chang chen po'i rnam par thar pa rgyas par bshad pa skal bzang gdul bya thar 'dod rnams kyi re ba skong ba'i yid bzhin gyi nor bu bsam 'phel dbang gi rgyal po*. In vols. 1–2 of *Zhabs dkar tshogs drug rang grol kyi bka' 'bum*. New Delhi: Shechen Publications, 2003.

———. *Snyigs dus 'gro ba yongs kyi skyabs mgon zhabs dkar rdo rje 'chang chen po'i rnam par thar pa rgyas par bshad pa skal bzang gdul bya thar 'dod rnams kyi re ba skong ba'i yid bzhin gyi nor bu bsam 'phel dbang gi rgyal po*. 2 Vols. Xining: Mtsho sngon mi rigs dpe skrun khang, 1985.

———. *Bya btang tshogs drug rang grol gyis phyogs med ri khrod 'grims pa'i tshe rang gzhan chos la bskul phyir glu dbyangs dga' ston 'gyed pa rnams*. In vols. 3–5 of *Zhabs dkar tshogs drug rang grol kyi bka' 'bum*. New Delhi: Shechen Publications, 2003.

———. *O rgyan sprul pla'i glegs bam*. In vol. 9 of *Zhabs dkar tshogs drug rang grol kyi bka' 'bum*. New Delhi: Shechen, 2003.

———. *Legs bshad nyi ma rang shar*. In vol. 12 of *Zhabs dkar tshogs drug rang grol kyi bka' 'bum*. New Delhi: Shechen Publications, 2003.

———. *Chos bshad gzhan phan nor bu*. In vol. 11 of *Zhabs dkar tshogs drug rang grol kyi bka' 'bum*. New Delhi: Shechen Publications, 2003.

———. *Chos bshad gzhan phan nyi ma*. In vol. 10 of *Zhabs dkar tshogs drug rang grol kyi bka' 'bum*. New Delhi: Shechen Publications, 2003.

———. *Ngo mtshar sprul pa'i glegs bam*. In vol. 6 of *Zhabs dkar tshogs drug rang grol kyi bka' 'bum*. New Delhi: Shechen Publications, 2003.

———. *Snying rje sprul pa'i glegs bam*. In vol. 7 of *Zhabs dkar tshogs drug rang grol kyi bka' 'bum*. New Delhi: Shechen, 2003.

———. *Legs bshad kun bzang mchod sprin*. In vol. 12 of *Zhabs dkar tshogs drug rang grol kyi bka' 'bum*. New Delhi: Shechen, 2003.

## English and French Language Sources

Akester, Matthew. *Jamyang Khyentsé Wangpo's Guide to Central Tibet*. Chicago: Serindia Publications, 2016.

Anderson, Benedict. *Imagined Communities: Reflections on the Origin and Spread of Nationalism*. Revised edition. London: Verso, 2016.

Anton-Luca, Alexandru. "Glu and La ye in A mdo: An Introduction to Contemporary Tibetan Folk Songs." In *Amdo Tibetans in Transition: Society and Culture in the Post-Mao Era PIATS 2000: Tibetan Studies: Proceedings of the Ninth Seminar of the International Association for Tibetan Studies, Leiden 2000*, edited by Toni Huber, 173–96. Leiden: Brill, 2002.

Aris, Michael. *Lamas, Princes, and Brigands: Joseph Rock's Photographs of the Tibetan Borderlands of China*. New York: China Institute of America, 1992.

Ary, Elijah S. *Authorized Lives: Biography and the Early Formation of Geluk Identity*. Somerville: Wisdom Publications, 2015.

Barstow, Geoffrey. "Buddhism Between Abstinence and Indulgence: Vegetarianism in the Life and Works of Jigmé Lingpa." *Journal of Buddhist Ethics* 20 (2013): 74–104.

———. *Food of Sinful Demons: Meat, Vegetarianism, and the Limits of Buddhism in Tibet.* New York: Columbia University Press, 2018.

———. "Monastic Meat: The Question of Meat Eating and Vegetarianism in Tibetan Buddhist Monastic Guidelines (*bca' yig*)." *Religions* 10, no. 4 (2019): 240. https://doi.org/10.3390/rel10040240.

Berkwitz, Stephen. "History and Gratitude in Theravāda Buddhism." *Journal of the American Academy of Religion* 71, no. 3 (September 2003): 579–604.

Bhum, Pema. "Heartbeat of a New Generation": A Discussion of the New Poetry. In *Modern Tibetan Literature and Social Change*, edited by Lauran R. Hartley and Patricia Schiaffini-Vedani, 112–34. Durham and London: Duke University Press, 2008.

Blondeau, Anne-Marie. "Padmasambhava et Avalokiteśvara." *Annuaire de l'École Pratique des Hautes* 86 (1977): 77–88.

Brook, Timothy, Michael van Walt van Praag, and Miek Boltjes, eds. *Sacred Mandates: Asian International Relations since Chinggis Khan.* Chicago: University of Chicago Press, 2018.

Brox, Trine. "Changing the Tibetan Way? Contesting Secularisms in the Tibetan Diaspora." In *Tibetan Studies: An Anthology: PIATS 2006: Tibetan Studies: Proceedings of the Eleventh Seminar of the International Association for Tibetan Studies, Königswinter 2006*, edited by Saadet Arslan and Peter Schwieger, 117–42. Andiast: International Institute for Tibetan Studies, 2010.

Bstan-'dzin rgya mtsho Dalai Lama XIV. *My Land and My People: The Original Autobiography of His Holiness the Dalai Lama of Tibet.* New York: Grand Central Publishing, 1997.

———. *Freedom in Exile: The Autobiography of the Dalai Lama.* New York: Harper Perennial, 2008.

———. *Kindness, Clarity and Insight.* Ithaca: Snow Lion Publications, 1984.

Buddhist Digital Resource Center. Accessed January 19, 2023. https://www.bdrc.io/.

Buffetrille, Katia. "Self-Immolation in Tibet: Some Reflections on an Unfolding History." *Revue d'Etudes Tibétaines* 25 (December 2012): 1–17.

———. "The Great Pilgrimage of A-mnyes rma-chen: Written Tradition, Living Realities." In *Maṇḍala and Landscape*, edited by Alexander W. McDonald, 75–132. Delhi: D. K. Printworld, 1997.

———. "The Blue Lake of A-mdo and Its Island: Legends and Pilgrimage Guide." In *Sacred Spaces and Powerful Places in Tibetan Culture: A Collection of Essays*, edited by Toni Huber, 105–24. Dharamsala: Library of Tibetan Works and Archives, 1999.

———. "Reflections on Pilgrimages to Sacred Mountains, Lakes and Caves." In *Pilgrimage in Tibet*, edited by Alex McKay, 18–34. Richmond: Curzon Press, 1998.

Chang, Garma C. C., trans. *The Hundred Thousand Songs of Milarepa.* Oriental Studies Foundation, 1962.

Chatterjee, Partha. *The Nation and Its Fragments: Colonial and Postcolonial Histories.* Princeton: Princeton University Press, 1993.

Cabezón, José Ignacio, and Geshe Lobsang Dargyay. *Freedom from Extremes: Gorampa's*

*"Distinguishing the Views" and the Polemics of Emptiness.* Boston: Wisdom Publications, 2007.

Central Tibetan Administration. "Tibet at a Glance." Accessed August 31, 2022. http://tibet.net/about-tibet/tibet-at-a-glance.

Central Tibetan Administration. "Middle Way Approach: Frequently Asked Questions." Accessed August 31, 2022. http://mwa.tibet.net/faq/.

Dalai Lama and Desmond Tutu. *The Book of Joy: Lasting Happiness in a Changing World.* New York: Avery, 2016.

Dalton, Jacob. "The Early Development of the Padmasambhava Legend in Tibet: A Study of IOL Tib J 644 and Pelliot tibétain 307." *Journal of the American Oriental Society* 124, no. 4 (2004): 759–72.

Dargyay, Lobsang. "The Twelve Deeds of the Buddha—A Controversial Hymn Ascribed to Nāgārjuna." *Tibet Journal* 9, no. 2 (1984): 3–12.

Davidson, Ronald. Tibetan Renaissance: *Tantric Buddhism and the Rebirth of Tibetan Culture.* New York: Columbia University Press, 2005.

de Jong, J. W. *Mi la ras pa'i rnam thar: Texte Tibétain de la vie de Milarepa.* The Hague: Mouton, 1959.

Deroche, Marc-Henri. "On Being 'Impartial' (ris med): From Non-Sectarianism to the Great Perfection." *Revue d'Etudes Tibétaines* 44 (Mars 2018): 129–58.

Dewang, Namkhai Norbu. *Musical Tradition of the Tibetan People: Songs in Dance Measure.* Serie Orientale Roma 36. Orientalia Romana: Essays and Lectures 2, by V. S. Agrawala et al. Roma: Istituto Italiano per il Medio ed Estremo Oriente, 1967.

Dhondup, Yangdon T. "Reb kong: Religion, History and Identity of a Sino-Tibetan Borderland Town," *Revue d'Etudes Tibétaines* 20 (Avril 2011): 33–59.

Doney, Lewis. "Padmasambhava in Tibetan Buddhism." In *Brill's Encyclopedia of Buddhism*, vol. 2, edited by Jonathan A. Silk et al., 1197–212. Leiden: Brill, 2019.

Dorjee, Lobsang, C. B. Josayma, and Migmar Tsering. "Lhamo: The Folk Opera of Tibet." *Tibet Journal* 9, no. 2 (Summer 1984): 13–22.

Dotson, Brandon. "Chapter 3: The Emanated Emperor and His Cosmopolitan Contradictions." In *Faith and Empire: Art and Politics in Tibetan Buddhism*, edited by Karl Debreczeny, 69–81. New York: Rubin Museum of Art, 2019.

Douglas, Kenneth, and Gwendolyn Bays, trans. *The Life and Liberation of Padmasambhava, Padma bka'i thang*, by Yeshe Tsogyal and Terchen Urgyan Lingpa, translated into French by Gustave-Charles Toussaint. 2 vols. Berkeley: Dharma Publishing, 1978.

Dreyfus, Georges. "Proto-Nationalism in Tibet." In *Tibetan Studies: Proceedings of the 6th Seminar of International Association for Tibetan Studies, Fagernes, 1992*, edited by Per Kvaerne, 205–18. Oslo: Institute for Comparative Research in Human Culture, 1994.

———. "Tibetan Religious Nationalism." *Journal of the International Association of Tibetan Studies* 1 (October 2005): 10–14.

Ekvall, Robert B., and James F. Downs. *Tibetan Pilgrimage.* Tokyo: Institute for the Study of Languages and Cultures of Asia & Africa, 1987.

Ehrhard, Franz-Karl. "The Transmission of the Thig-le bcu-drug and the bka' gdams glegs bam." In *The Many Canons of Tibetan Buddhism. PIATS 2000: Tibetan Studies:*

*Proceedings of the Ninth Seminar of the International Association for Tibetan Studies, Leiden 2000*, edited by Helmut Eimer and David Germano. Leiden: Brill, 2002.

Eppling, John F. "A Calculus of Creative Expression: The Central Chapter of Daṇḍin's Kāvyādarśa." PhD diss., University of Wisconsin-Madison, 1989.

Ferrari, Alfonsa. *Mk'yen brtse's Guide to the Holy Places of Central Tibet*. Edited by Luciano Petech and Hugh Richardson. Roma: Istituto Italiano per il Medio ed Estremo Oriente, 1958.

Fox, Jon, and Cynthia Miller-Idriss. "Everyday Nationhood." *Ethnicities* 8, no. 4 (December 2008): 536–63.

Gaerrang. "Development as Entangled Knot: The Case of the Slaughter Renunciation Movement in Tibet, China." *Journal of Asian Studies* 74, no. 4 (November 2015): 927–51.

———. "Tibetan identity and Tibetan Buddhism in trans-regional connection: the contemporary vegetarian movement in pastoral areas of Tibet (China)." *Études mongoles et sibériennes, centrasiatiques et tibétaines* 47 (2016). https://doi.org/10.4000/emscat.2755.

Gaerrang (Kabzung). "Alternative Development on the Tibetan Plateau: The Case of the Slaughter Renunciation Movement." PhD diss., University of Colorado at Boulder, 2012.

Gamble, Ruth. *Reincarnation in Tibetan Buddhism: The Third Karmapa and the Invention of a Tradition*. New York: Oxford University Press, 2018.

Gardner, Alexander, ed. "Map." The Treasury of Lives. Accessed January 19, 2023. https://treasuryoflives.org/map#5/31.82/92.21.

Gardner, Alexander. "The Twenty-five Great Sites of Khams: Religious Geography, Revelation, and Nonsectarianism in Nineteenth-Century Eastern Tibet." PhD diss., University of Michigan, 2006.

Gat, Azar. *Nations: The Long History and Deep Roots of Political Ethnicity and Nationalism*. Cambridge: Cambridge University Press, 2013.

Gayley, Holly. "Reimagining Buddhist Ethics on the Tibetan Plateau." *Journal of Buddhist Ethics* 20 (2013): 252.

———. "The Ethics of Cultural Survival: A Buddhist Vision of Progress in Mkhan po 'jigs phun's *Heart Advice to Tibetans for the 21st Century*." In *Mapping the Modern in Tibet, PIATS 2006: Tibetan Studies: Proceedings of the Eleventh Seminar of the International Association for Tibetan Studies, Königswinter 2006*, edited by Gray Tuttle, 435–502. Andiast: International Institute for Tibetan and Buddhist Studies GmbH, 2011.

———. *Love Letters from Golok: A Tantric Couple in Modern Tibet*. New York: Columbia University Press, 2017.

Gellner, Ernest. *Nations and Nationalism*. 1983. 2nd ed. Ithaca: Cornell University Press, 2009.

Gerke, Barbara. "Engaging the Subtle Body: Re-Approaching Bla Rituals in the Himalaya." In *Soundings in Tibetan Medicine. Anthropological and Historical Perspectives. PIATS 2003: Tibetan Studies: Proceedings of the 10th Seminar of the International Association for Tibetan Studies*, edited by Mona Schrempf, 191–212. Leiden: Brill, 2007.

———. *Long Lives and Untimely Deaths: Life-Span Concepts among Tibetans in the Darjeeling Hills India*. Leiden: Brill, 2011.

Gentry, James. "Historicism, Philology, and State-Building in 17th century Tibet: Observations Apropos of a Text-critical Biography of Padmsambhava." In *Padmasambhava: Historical Narratives and Later Transformations of Guru Rinpoche*, edited by Geoffrey Samuel and Jamyang Oliphant, 223–54. Switzerland: Garuda Verlag, 2020.

Germano, David. "Re-membering the Dismembered Body of Tibet: Contemporary Tibetan Visionary Movements in the People's Republic of China." In *Buddhism In Contemporary Tibet: Religious Revival and Cultural Identity*, edited by Melvyn C. Goldstein and Matthew T. Kapstein, 53–94. Berkeley: University of California Press, 1998.

Goanker, Dilip Parameshwar. *Alternative Modernities*. Durham: Duke University Press, 2001.

Goldstein, Melvyn C. "Introduction." In *Buddhism in Contemporary Tibet: Religious Revival and Cultural Identity*, edited by Melvyn C. Goldstein and Matthew T. Kapstein, 1–14. Berkeley: University of California Press, 1998.

Goldstein, Melvyn C. *A History of Modern Tibet, 1913–1951: The Demise of the Lamaist State*. Berkeley: University of California Press, 1991.

Gomez, Luis, trans. *The Land of Bliss: The Paradise of the Buddha of Measureless Light: Sanskrit and Chinese Versions of the Sukhavativyuha Sutras*. Honolulu: University of Hawai'i Press, 1996.

Google Maps. Accessed January 19, 2023. https://www.google.com/maps.

Gros, Stéphane. *Frontier Tibet: Patterns of Change in the Sino-Tibetan Borderlands*. Amsterdam: Amsterdam University Press, 2019.

Grosby, Steven. *Nationalism: A Very Short Introduction*. Oxford: Oxford University Press, 2005.

Gyallay-Pap, Peter. "Reconstructing the Cambodian Polity: Buddhism, Kingship and the Quest for Legitimacy." In *Buddhism, Power, Political Order*, edited by Ian Harris, 71–103. Abingdon: Routledge, 2007.

Gyatso, Janet. *Apparitions of the Self: The Secret Autobiographies of a Tibetan Visionary—A Translation and Study of Jigme Lingpa's Dancing Moon in the Water and Dakki's Grand Secret Talk*. Princeton: Princeton University Press, 1998.

———. *Being Human in a Buddhist World: An Intellectual History of Medicine in Early Modern Tibet*. New York: Columbia University Press, 2015.

Hadfield, Andrew. "Vanishing Primordialism: Literature, History and the Public." In *The Roots of Nationalism: National Identity Formation in Early Modern Europe, 1600–1815*, edited by Lotte Jensen, 47–66. Amsterdam: Amsterdam University Press, 2016.

Haksar, A. N. D., trans. *Jatakamala: Stories from the Buddha's Previous Births*. New Delhi: HarperCollins Publishers India, 2003.

Hall, Amelia. "How is this Sacred Place Arrayed? Pacification, Increase, Magnetism, and Wrath in the Establishment of an Eastern Himalayan *sbas yul*." In *Hidden Lands in Himalayan Myth and History: Transformations of Sbas yul Through Time*, edited by Frances Garrett, Elizabeth McDougal, and Geoffrey Samuel, 297–314. Leiden: Brill, 2021.

Hartley, Lauren. "'Inventing Modernity' in A mdo: Views on the Role of Traditional Tibetan Culture in a Developing Society." In *Amdo Tibetans in Transition: Society and Culture in the Post-Mao Era. PIATS 2000. Tibetan Studies. Proceedings of the Ninth Seminar of the International Association of Tibetan Studies*, 1–25. Leiden: Brill, 2002.

Hastings, Adrian. *The Construction of Nationhood: Ethnicity, Religion and Nationalism.* Cambridge: Cambridge University Press, 1997.
Hazelton, Barbara. "Bdud 'joms gling pa's *Hidden Sacred Land of Padma bkod.*" In *Hidden Lands in Himalayan Myth and History: Transformations of Sbas yul Through Time*, edited by Frances Garrett, Elizabeth McDougal, and Geoffrey Samuel, 342–45. Leiden: Brill, 2021.
Helgerson, Richard. *Forms of Nationhood: The Elizabethan Writing of England.* Chicago: University of Chicago Press, 1992.
Heller, Amy. "P.T. 7a, P.T. 108, P.T. 240 and Beijing bsTan 'gyur 3489: Ancient Tibetan rituals dedicated to Vairocana." In *The Pandita and the Siddha, Tibetan Studies in honor of E. Gene Smith*, edited by Ramon Prats, 85–91. Dharamsala: Library of Tibetan Works and Archives. 2007.
———. "Early Ninth Century Images of Vairochana from Eastern Tibet." *Orientations* 25, no. 6 (1994): 74–79.
———. "Buddhist images and rock inscriptions from Eastern Tibet, Part IV." In *Tibetan Studies, Proceedings of the 7th Seminar of the International Association for Tibetan Studies, Graz 1995*, edited by H. Krasser, M. T. Much, E. Steinkellner and H. Tauscher, 385–403. Wien: Verlag der Österreichischen Akademie der Wissenschaften, 1997.
Helffer, Mireille. "Tibetan Culture in South Asia." *The Garland Encyclopedia of World Music*, Vol. 5: *South Asia: The Indian Subcontinent*, edited by Alison Arnold, 709–17. New York and London: Garland Publishing, Inc., 2000.
Henrion-Dourcy, Isabelle. *Le théâtre "ache lhamo": Jeux et enjeux d'une tradition tibétaine.* Leuven: Peeters Publishers, 2017.
Heruka, Tsangnyön. *The Life of Milarepa.* Translated by Andrew Quintman. New York: Penguin Classics, 2010.
Hirshberg, Daniel. *Remembering the Lotus-Born: Padmasambhava in the History of Tibet's Golden Age.* Somerville: Wisdom Publications, 2016.
———. "Nyangrel Nyima Wozer." Treasury of Lives. Accessed November 9, 2022. https://treasuryoflives.org/biographies/view/Nyangrel-Nyima-Wozer/P364.
Hobsbawm, Eric J. *Nations and Nationalism since 1780: Programmed, Myth, Reality.* Cambridge: Cambridge University Press, 1990.
Holmes-Tagchungdarpa, Amy. *The Social Life of Tibetan Biography: Textuality, Community, and Authority in the Lineage of Tokden Shakya Shri.* Lanham: Lexington Books, 2014.
Huber, Toni. *The Cult of Pure Crystal Mountain: Popular Pilgrimage and Visionary Landscape in Southeast Tibet.* New York: Oxford University Press, 1999.
Huber, Toni, and Tsepak Rigdzin. "A Tibetan Guide for Pilgrimage of Ti-se (Mount Kailash) and mTsho Ma-pham (Lake Manasarovar)." *Tibet Journal* 20, no. 1 (Spring 1995): 10–47.
Ishihama, Yumiko. "On the Dissemination of the Belief in the Dalai Lama as a Manifestation of the Bodhisattva Avalokiteśvara." *Acta Asiatica* 64 (1993): 53–54.
Jabb, Lama. *Oral and Literary Continuities in Modern Tibetan Literature: The Inescapable Nation.* Lanham: Lexington Books, 2015.
Jackson, Roger. "'Poetry' in Tibet: *Glu mGur, sNyan ngag* and 'Songs of Experience.'" In

*Tibetan Literature: Studies in Genre,* edited by José Ignacio Cabezón and Roger R. Jackson. Ithaca: Snow Lion, 1996.

———. *Tantric Treasures: Three Collections of Mystical Verse from Buddhist India.* Oxford: Oxford University Press, 2004.

Jacob, Christian. *The Sovereign Map: Theoretical Approaches in Cartography throughout History.* Translated by Tom Conley, edited by Edward H. Dahl. Chicago: University of Chicago Press, 2006.

Jacoby, Sarah H. *Love and Liberation: Autobiographical Writings of the Tibetan Buddhist Visionary.* New York: Columbia University Press, 2014.

Jensen, Lotte, ed. *The Roots of Nationalism: National Identity Formation in Early Modern Europe, 1600–1815.* Amsterdam: Amsterdam University Press 2016.

Jinpa, Thupten. "Introduction." In *The Book of Kadam: The Core Texts,* translated and edited by Thupten Jinpa, 1–32. Boston: Wisdom Publications, 2008.

Kamenetz, Rodger. *The Jew in the Lotus: A Poet's Rediscovery of Jewish Identity in Buddhist India.* San Francisco: HarperSanFrancisco, 1994.

Kang, Xiaofei and Donald Sutton. *Contesting the Yellow Dragon: Ethnicity, Religion, and the State in Sino-Tibetan Borderland.* Brill: Leiden, 2016.

Kapstein, Matthew T. *The Tibetan Assimilation of Buddhism: Conversion, Contestation, and Memory.* Oxford: Oxford University Press, 2000.

———. *The Tibetans.* Malden: Blackwell Publishing, 2006.

———. "A Pilgrimage of Rebirth Reborn: The 1992 Celebration of the Drigung Powa Chenmo." In *Buddhism In Contemporary Tibet: Religious Revival and Cultural Identity,* 95–119. Berkeley: University of California Press, 1998.

Karmay, Samten G. "The Cult of Mountain Deities and its Political Significance." In *The Arrow and the Spindle: Studies in History, Myths, Rituals and Beliefs in Tibet,* 432–50. Kantipath: Mandala Book Point, 1998.

———. "Gesar: The Epic Tradition of the Tibetan People." In *The Arrow and the Spindle: Studies in History, Myths, Rituals and Beliefs in Tibet,* 465–71. Kantipath: Mandala Book Point, 1998.

Kaviraj, Sudipta. "An Outline of a Revisionist Theory of Modernity." *European Journal of Sociology* 46, no. 3 (2005): 497–526.

Keyes, Charles F. *Thailand: Buddhist Kingdom as Modern Nation State.* London: Routledge, 1987.

Khoroche, Peter, trans. *Once the Buddha was a Monkey: Ārya-Śūra's Jātakamālā.* Chicago: University of Chicago Press, 1989.

King, Matthew W. *Ocean of Milk, Ocean of Blood: A Mongolian Monk in the Ruins of the Qing Empire.* New York: Columbia University Press, 2019.

Knauft, Bruce M. "Tibetan Buddhist Leadership: Recent Developments in Historical Context." In *Buddhism and the Political Process,* edited by Hiroko Kawanami. London: Palgrave Macmillan, 2016.

Kolås, Åshild. "Tibetan Nationalism: The Politics of Religion." *Journal of Peace Research* 33, no. 1 (February 1996): 51–66.

Kornman, Robin and Lama Chonam, trans. *The Epic of Gesar of Ling: Gesar's Magical Birth, Early Years, and Coronation as King.* Boston: Shambhala, 2015.

Kongtrul, Jamgön. *The Autobiography of Jamgön Kongtrul: A Gem of Many Colors*. Translated and edited by Richard Barron. Ithaca: Snow Lion, 2003.

Kunsang, Erik Pema, trans. *The Lotus-Born: The Life Story of Padmasambhava Recorded by Yeshe Tsogyal*, by Yeshe Tsogyal and Nyang Ral Nyima Öser. Boudhanath: Ranjung Yeshe Publications, 2004.

Lange, Diana. *An Atlas of the Himalayas by a 19th Century Tibetan Lama: a Journey of Discovery*. Boston: Brill, 2020.

Langelaar, Reinier J. "Chasing the Colours of the Rainbow: Tibetan Ethnogenealogies in Flux." *The Medieval History Journal* 21, no. 2 (2018): 328–64.

Lehr, Peter. *Militant Buddhism: The Rise of Religious Violence in Sri Lanka, Myanmar and Thailand*. Palgrave Macmillan, 2019.

Leschly, Jakob. "Guru Chowang." Treasury of Lives. Accessed August 31, 2022. http://treasuryoflives.org/biographies/view/Guru-Chowang/5588.

———. "Orgyen Lingpa." Treasury of Lives. Accessed August 31, 2022. http://treasuryoflives.org/biographies/view/Orgyan-Lingpa/7429.

Leerssen, Joep. *National Thought in Europe: A Cultural History*, Amsterdam: Amsterdam University Press, 2018.

Lopez, Donald, Jr. *The Forest of Faded Wisdom: 104 Poems by Gendun Chophel*. Chicago: University of Chicago Press, 2009.

———. *Gendun Chopel: Tibet's Modern Visionary*. Boston: Shambhala, 2018.

———. *Prisoners of Shangri-La: Tibetan Buddhism and the West*. Chicago: University of Chicago Press, 1999.

MacDonald, Ariane W. "Une lecture des Pelliot Tibétain 1286, 1287, 1038, 1047 et 1290." In *Etudes tibétaines dédiées à la mémoire de Marcelle Lalou*, edited by Ariane McDonald, 190–391. Paris: Adrien Maisonneuve, 1971.

Makley, Charlene. *The Battle for Fortune: State-Led Development, Personhood, and Power among Tibetans in China*. Ithaca: Cornell University Press, 2018.

Mathes, Klaus-Dieter. "Introduction." In *Nonsectarian (ris med) in 19th- and 20th-Century Eastern Tibet: Religious Diffusion and Cross-fertilization beyond the Reach of the Central Tibetan Government*, edited by Klaus-Dieter Mathes and Gabriele Coura, 1–17. Leiden: Brill, 2021.

Mathes, Klaus-Dieter, and Gabriele Coura, eds. *Nonsectarian (ris med) in 19th- and 20th-Century Eastern Tibet: Religious Diffusion and Cross-fertilization beyond the Reach of the Central Tibetan Government*. Leiden: Brill, 2021.

Meiland, Justin, trans. *Garland of the Buddha's Past Lives*, by Āryaśūra, edited by Isabelle Onians. 2 vols. New York University Press, 2009.

Mills, Martin A. "Chapter 16 Who Belongs to Tibet? Governmental Narratives of State in the Ganden Podrang." In *Facing Globalization in the Himalayas: Belonging and the Politics of the Self*, edited by Gerard Toffin and Joanna Pfaff-Czarnecka, 397–418. New Delhi: Sage Publications, 2014.

Nietupski, Paul Kocot. *Labrang Monastery: A Tibetan Buddhist Community on the Inner Asian Borderlands, 1709–1958*. Lanham: Lexington Books, 2011.

———. "Nationalism in Labrang, Amdo: Apa Alo/Huang Zhengzing." In *Studies in the History of Eastern Tibet. PIATS 2006: Proceedings of the Eleventh Seminar of the Inter-*

national Association for Tibetan Studies, Königswinter 2006, edited by Wim van Spengen and Lama Jabb, 179–208. Halle: International Institute for Tibetan and Buddhist Studies GmbH, 2010.

———. "Understanding Sovereignty in Amdo." *Revue d'Etudes Tibétaines* 31 (February 2015): 217–32.

Obeyesekere, Gananath. "Buddhism, Ethnicity and Identity: A Problem of Buddhist History." *Journal of Buddhist Ethics* 10 (2003): 192–242.

———. "Buddhism, Nationhood, and Cultural Identity: A Question of Fundamentals." In *Fundamentalisms Comprehended*, edited by Martin E. Marty and R. Scott Appleby, 231–56. Chicago: University of Chicago Press, 1995.

Okada, Emmi. "Constructing the Secular: The Changing Relationship Between Religion and Politics in the Tibetan Exile Community." *Himalaya: The Journal of the Association for Nepal and Himalayan Studies* 36, no. 1 (2016): 78–95.

Padrón, Ricardo. *The Spacious Word: Cartography, Literature, and Empire in Early Modern Spain*. Chicago: University of Chicago Press, 2004.

Pang, Rachel Hua-Wei. "Dissipating Boundaries: The *Life*, Song-Poems, and Non-Sectarian Paradigm of Shabkar Tsokdruk Rangdrol (1781–1851)." PhD diss., University of Virginia, 2011.

Pang, Rachel H. "The *Rimé* Activities of Shabkar Tsokdruk Rangdrol (1781–1851)." *Revue d'Etudes Tibétaines* 30 (October 2014): 5–30.

———. "*Rimé* Revisited: Shabkar's Response to Religious Difference." *Journal of Buddhist Ethics* 22 (2015): 449–73.

———. "Songs against Meat by Shabkar." In *The Faults of Meat: Tibetan Buddhist Writings on Vegetarianism*, edited by Geoffrey Barstow, 211–21. Boston: Wisdom Publications, 2019.

Park, Jaechan Anselmo. *Thomas Merton's Encounter with Buddhism and Beyond: His Interreligious Dialogue, Inter-Monastic Exchanges, and Their Legacy*. Collegeville: Liturgical Press, 2019.

Pearcey, Adam. "Japa Dongak Gyatso." The Treasury of Lives. Accessed August 31, 2022. https://treasuryoflives.org/biographies/view/Japa-Dongak-Gyatso/12785.

———. "Dongak Chokyi Gyatso." The Treasury of Lives. Accessed August 31, 2022. https://treasuryoflives.org/biographies/view/Dongak-Chokyi-Gyatso/7945.

Pearcey, Adam Scott. "A Greater Perfection? Scholasticism, Comparativism and Issues of Sectarian Identity in Early 20th Century Writings on rDzogs-chen." PhD diss., SOAS University of London, 2018.

Phillips, Bradford Lyman. "Consummation and Compassion in Medieval Tibet: The Maṇi bka'-'bum chen-mo of Guru Chos-kyi dbang-phyug." PhD diss., University of Virginia, 2004.

Pollack, Sheldon. "Introduction." In *Forms of Knowledge in Early Modern Asia: Explorations in the Intellectual History of India and Tibet, 1500–1800*, edited by Sheldon Pollack, 1–18. Durham: Duke University Press, 2011.

Quintman, Andrew. "Mi la ras pa's Many Lives: Anatomy of a Tibetan Biographical Corpus." PhD diss., University of Michigan, 2006.

———. "Toward a Geographic Biography: Mi la ras pa in the Tibetan Landscape." *Numen* 55 (2008): 363–410.

———. "Translator's Introduction." In *The Life of Milarepa* by Tsangnyön Heruka, translated by Andrew Quintman. New York: Penguin Classics, 2010.

———. *The Yogin and the Madman: Reading the Biographical Corpus of Tibet's Great Saint Milarepa*. New York: Columbia University Press, 2014.

Ramble, Charles. "Tibetan Pride of Place: Or, why Nepal's Bhotiyas are Not an Ethnic Group." In *Nationalism and Ethnicity in a Hindu Kingdom: The Politics of Culture in Contemporary Nepal*, edited by David N. Gellner, Joanna Pfaff-Czarnecka, and John Whelpton, 379–413. Amsterdam: Harwood Academic, 1997.

Shabkar Tsogdruk Rangdrol. *The Life of Shabkar: The Autobiography of a Tibetan Yogin*. Translated by Matthieu Ricard and the Padmakara Translation Group. Ithaca: Snow Lion, 2001.

Richardson, Hugh. "The Cult of Vairocana in Early Tibet." In *Indo-Tibetan Studies: Papers in Honour and Appreciation of Professor David L. Snellgrove's Contribution to Indo-Tibetan Studies*, edited by Tadeusz Skorupski. Tring: Institute of Buddhist Studies, 1990.

———. "The Fifth Dalai Lama's Decree Appointing Sangs-rgyas rgya-mtsho as Regent." *Bulletin of the School of Oriental and African Studies, University of London* 43, no. 2 (1980): 329–44.

———. "The Sino-Tibetan Treaty Inscription of A.D. 821–823 at Lhasa." *Journal of the Royal Asiatic Society of Great Britain and Ireland* 2 (1978): 137–62.

———. *Tibet and Its History*. Boston: Shambhala, 1984.

Ryavec, Karl E. *A Historical Atlas of Tibet*. Chicago: University of Chicago Press, 2015.

Roesler, Ulrike. "Operas, Novels, and Religious Instructions." In *Narrative Pattern and Genre in Hagiographic Life Writing: Comparative Perspectives from Asia to Europe*, edited by Stephan Conermann and Jim Rhengans, 113–40. Berlin: EB Verlag, 2014.

———. "Not a Mere Imitation: Indian Narratives in Tibetan Context." In *Facets of Tibetan Religious Tradition and Contacts with Neighbouring Cultural Areas*, edited by Alfredo Cadonna and Ester Bianchi, 153–77. Firenze: Leo S. Olschki, 2002.

Sakyapa, Sonam Gyaltsen. *The Clear Mirror: A Traditional Account of Tibet's Golden Age*. Translated by McComas Taylor and Lama Choedak Yuthok. Ithaca: Snow Lion Publications, 1996.

Samuel, Geoffrey. *Civilized Shamans: Buddhism in Tibetan Societies*. Washington: Smithsonian Institute Press, 1993.

———. "The Gesar Epic of East Tibet." In *Tibetan Literature: Studies in Genre. Essays in Honor of Geshe Lhundup Sopa*, edited by José Ignacio *Cabezón* and Roger Jackson, 358–67. Ithaca, New York: Snow Lion, 1996.

———. "The Epic and Nationalism in Tibet." In *Religion and Biography in China and Tibet*, edited by Benjamin Penny, 178–88. London: Routledge, 2002.

———. "Hidden Lands of Tibet in Myth and History." In *Hidden Lands in Himalayan Myth and History: Transformations of Sbas yul Through Time*, edited by Frances Garrett, Elizabeth McDougal, and Geoffrey Samuel, 51–59. Leiden: Brill, 2021.

Samuel, Geoffrey, and Jamyang Oliphant. *Padmasambhava: Historical Narratives and Later Transformations of Guru Rinpoche.* Switzerland: Garuda Verlag, 2020.

Schaeffer, Kurtis. *Dreaming the Great Brahmin: Tibetan Traditions of the Buddhist Poet-Saint Saraha.* New York: Oxford University Press, 2005.

———. "Tibetan Biography: Growth and Criticism." *Edition, éditions: L'écrit au Tibet, évolution et devenir,* edited by Anne Chayet, Cristina Scherrer-Schaub, Françoise Robin, and Jean-Luc Achard, 263–306. München: Indus Verlag, 2010.

Schwartzberg, Joseph E. "Maps of Greater Tibet." *The History of Cartography.* Vol. 2, Book 2: *Cartography in the Traditional East and SouthEast Asian Societies,* edited by J. B. Harley and David Woodward, 607–81. Chicago: University of Chicago Press, 1994.

Shabkar Tsogdruk Rangdrol. *The Life of Shabkar: The Autobiography of a Tibetan Yogin.* Translated by Matthieu Ricard and the Padmakara Translation Group. Ithaca: Snow Lion, 2001.

———. *Rainbows Appear: Tibetan Poems of Shabkar.* Edited and translated by Matthieu Ricard. Boston: Shambhala, 2002.

Shakabpa, Tsepon W.D. *Tibet: A Political History.* New York: Potala Publications, 1984.

Shakya, Tsering. *The Dragon in the Land of Snows: A History of Modern Tibet since 1947.* New York: Columbia University Press, 1999.

———. "Wither the Tsampa Eaters?" *Himal: Himalayan Magazine* 6, no. 5 (1993): 9–11.

———. "Self-Immolation: the Changing Language of Protest in Tibet." *Revue d'Etudes Tibétaines* 25 (December 2012): 19–39.

Sheehy, Michael. "The Offering of Mount Meru: Contexts of Buddhist Cosmology in the History of Science in Tibet." *Journal of Dharma Studies* 3 (2020): 319–48.

Smith, Anthony D. *Myth and Memories of the Nation.* Oxford: Oxford University Press, 1999.

———. *The Cultural Foundations of Nations: Hierarchy, Covenant, and Republic.* Oxford: Blackwell Publishing, 2008.

Smith, E. Gene. "Jam mgon Kong sprul and the Nonsectarian Movement." In *Among Tibetan Texts: History and Literature of the Himalayan Plateau,* edited by Kurtis R. Schaeffer, 235–72. Boston: Wisdom Publications, 2001.

Smith, Warren. *Tibetan Nation: A History of Tibetan Nationalism and Sino-Tibetan Relations.* London and New York: Routledge, 1996.

Shneiderman, Sara. "Barbarians at the Border and Civilising Projects: Analysing Ethnic and National Identities in the Tibetan Context." In *Tibetan Borderlands,* edited by Christiaan Klieger, 9–34. Leiden: Brill, 2006.

Sørenson, Per K. "Introduction." In *Tibetan Buddhist Historiography: The Mirror Illuminating the Royal Genealogies, An Annotated Translation of the XIVth Century Tibetan Chronicle: rGyal-rabs gsal- ba'i me-long,* edited and translated by Per K. Sørenson, 1–39. Wiesbaden: Harrassowitz Verlag, 1994.

———. *Divinity Secularized: An Inquiry into the Nature and Form of the Songs Ascribed to the Sixth Dalai Lama.* Wien: Arbeitskreis für Tibetische Und Buddhistische Studien Universität Wien, 1990.

Sperling, Elliot. "Les noms du Tibet: Géographie et identité." Translated by Katia Buffetrille. *Monde Chinois: Nouvelle Asie* 31 (2012): 27–32.

———. "Tubote, Tibet, and the Power of Naming." Elliot Sperling. Published April 16, 2011. https://elliotsperling.org/tubote-tibet-and-the-power-of-naming/.

Stroup, David. *Pure and True: The Everyday Politics of Ethnicity for China's Hui Muslims.* Seattle: University of Washington Press, 2022.

Sujata, Victoria. *Journey to Distant Groves: Profound Songs of the Tibetan Siddha Kälden Gyatso.* Kathmandu: Vajra Books, 2019.

———. *Tibetan Songs of Realization: Echoes from a Seventeenth-Century Scholar and Siddha in Amdo.* Leiden: Brill, 2005.

———. *Songs of Shabkar: The Path of a Tibetan Yogi Inspired by Nature.* Cazadero: Dharma Publishing, 2012.

Sullivan, Brenton. *Building a Religious Empire: Tibetan Buddhism, Bureaucracy, and the Rise of the Gelukpa.* Philadelphia: University of Pennsylvania Press, 2021.

———. "The first generation of dGe lugs evangelists in Amdo. The case of 'Dan ma Tshul khrims rgya mtsho (1578–1663/65)." *Études mongoles et sibériennes, centrasiatiques et tibétaines* 52 (December 2021). https://doi.org/10.4000/emscat.5314.

Shawa, Tsering Wangyel. *Tibet: Township Map & Place Name Index.* 1: 1,900,000. Tsering Wangyel Shawa, 2014.

Tambiah, Stanley Jeyaraja. "The Galactic Polity in Southeast Asia." *HAU: Journal of Ethnographic Theory* 3, no. 3 (2013): 503–34.

Teeuwen, Mark. "Buddhist Modernities: Modernism and its Limits." In *Buddhist Modernities: Re-Inventing Tradition in the Globalizing Modern World,* edited by Hanna Havenvik, Ute Hüsken, Mark Teeuwen, Vladimir Tikhonov, and Koen Wellens, 1–11. New York and London: Routledge, 2017.

Terrone, Antonio. "Burning for the Cause: Self-Immolations, Human Security, and the Violence of Nonviolence in Tibet." *Journal of Buddhist Ethics* 25 (2018): 465–529.

———. "10. Nationalism Matters: Among Mystics and Martyrs of Tibet." In *Religion and Nationalism in Chinese Societies,* edited by Cheng-tian Kuo, 279–308. Amsterdam: Amsterdam University Press, 2017. https://doi.org/10.1515/9789048535057-012.

Tibet in Review. "Lhakar Wednesday Movement: Celebration of Tibetan Spirit." VOA Tibetan—English, July 13, 2022. Accessed November 11, 2022. https://www.voatibetan.com/a/1404065.html.

Tibetan Parliament-in-Exile. *Charter of the Tibetans-in-Exile,* 1991. Accessed August 31, 2022, https://tibet.net/wp-content/uploads/2011/06/Charter1.pdf.

Tibetan Youth Congress Central Executive Committee. 2014. "About TYC." Tibetan Youth Congress. Accessed October 4, 2022. http://www.tibetanyouthcongress.org/about-tyc/.

The Tibetan and Himalayan Digital Library. Accessed January 19, 2023. https://www.thlib.org/.

Tsang, Rachel, and Eric Taylor Woods, eds. *The Cultural Politics of Nationalism and Nation-Building: Ritual and Performance in the Study of Nations and Nationalism.* London: Routledge, 2014.

Tsomu, Yudru. *The Rise of Gonpo Namgyel in Kham: The Blind Warrior of Nyarong.* Lanham: Lexington Books, 2014.

Tsurphu Labrang (OHHK). "The Gyalwang Karmapa Rings an Alarm: We Must Preserve

Tibetan Language and Culture." Karmapa: The Official Website. Accessed August 31, 2022. http://kagyuoffice.org/the-gyalwang-karmapa-rings-an-alarm-we-must-preserve-tibetan-language-and-culture/.

Tsurphu Labrang (OHHK). "Addressing 8,000 Newly-Arrived Tibetans in Bodhgaya, Gyalwang Karmapa Urges Tibetans to Unite, To Preserve Tibetan Culture and Religion." Karmapa: The Official Website. January 6, 2012. http://kagyuoffice.org/addressing-8000-newly-arrived-tibetans-in-bodhgaya-gyalwang-karmapa-urges-tibetans-to-unite-to-preserve-tibetan-culture-and-religion/.

Townsend, Dominique. *A Buddhist Sensibility: Aesthetic Education at Tibet's Mindröling Monastery.* New York: Columbia University Press, 2021.

Tucci, Giuseppe, trans. "Tibetan Folk Songs from Gyantse and Western Tibet." 2nd ed. Ascona, Switzerland: Artibus Asiae, 1966.

Tuan, Yi-Fu. "Language and the Making of Place: A Narrative-Descriptive Approach." *Annals of the Association of American Geographers* 81, no. 4 (1991): 684–96.

Turner, Alicia. *Saving Buddhism: The Impermanence of Religion in Colonial Burma.* Honolulu: University of Hawai'i Press, 2014.

Tuttle, Gray. "Challenging Central Tibet's Dominance of History: The Oceanic Book, a 19th Century Politico-Religious Geographic History." In *Mapping the Modern in Tibet, PIATS 2006: Tibetan Studies: Proceedings of the Eleventh Seminar of the International Association for Tibetan Studies, Königswinter 2006,* edited by Gray Tuttle, 135–72. Andiast: International Institute for Tibetan and Buddhist Studies GmbH, 2011.

Vargas-O'Brian, Ivette M. "The Life of dGe slong ma dPal mo: The Experience of a Leper, Founder of a Fasting Ritual, a Transmitter of Buddhist Teachings on Suffering and Renunciation in Tibetan Religious History." *Journal of the International Association of Buddhist Studies* 24, no. 2 (2001): 157–85.

van der Kuijp, Leonard. "The Dalai Lamas and the Origins of Reincarnate Lamas." In *The Tibetan History Reader,* edited by Kurtis R. Schaeffer and Gray Tuttle, 335–47. New York: Columbia University Press, 2013.

van Schaik, Sam. "The Tibetan Avalokiteśvara Cult in the Tenth Century: Evidence from the Dunhuang Manuscripts." *Tibetan Buddhist Literature and Praxis: Studies in its Formative Period, 900–1400. Proceedings of the Tenth Seminar of the IATS, 2003,* edited by Ronald M. Davidson and Christian Wedemeyer, 55–72. Leiden: Brill, 2006.

———. 2011. *Tibet: A History.* New Haven: Yale University Press.

van Spengen, Wim, and Lama Jabb, eds. *Studies in the History of Eastern Tibet. PIATS 2006: Proceedings of the Eleventh Seminar of the International Association for Tibetan Studies, Königswinter 2006.* Halle: International Institute for Tibetan and Buddhist Studies GmbH, 2010.

Verheijen, Bart. "Singing the Nation: Protest Songs and National Thought in the Netherlands during the Napoleonic Annexation (1810–1813)." In *The Roots of Nationalism: National Identity Formation in Early Modern Europe, 1600–1815,* edited by Lotte Jensen, 309–28. Amsterdam: Amsterdam University Press, 2016.

Walton. Matthew. *Buddhism, Politics and Political Thought in Myanmar.* Cambridge: Cambridge University Press, 2016.

Wallace, B. Allan. *Open Mind: View and Meditation in the Lineage of Lerab Lingpa.* Somerville: Wisdom Publications, 2018.

Wang, Michelle. *Maṇḍala of Eight Great Bodhisattvas: The Visual Culture of Esoteric Buddhism at Dunhuang.* Leiden: Brill, 2018.

Wangdu, Pasang, and H. Diemberger. *Dba' bzhed: The Royal Narrative Concerning the Brining of the Buddha's Doctrine to Tibet.* Vienna: Verlag der Österreichischen Akademie der Wissenschaftern, 2000.

"White Wednesday: The Lhakar Pledge." High Peaks Pure Earth. July 4, 2011. Accessed October 5, 2022. https://highpeakspureearth.com/white-wednesday-the-lhakar-pledge/.

Wintle, Michael. "Emergent Nationalism in European Maps of the Eighteenth Century." In *The Roots of Nationalism: National Identity Formation in Early Modern Europe, 1600–1815,* edited by Lotte Jensen, 271–88. Amsterdam: Amsterdam University Press, 2016.

Wylie, Turrell. "The Geography of Tibet According to the 'Dzam-gling-rgyas-bshad." PhD diss., University of Washington, 1958.

Wylie, Turrell. "The Tibetan Tradition of Geography." *Bulletin of Tibetology* 2, no. 1 (1965): 17–25.

Yang, En-Hong. "The Forms of Chanting Gesar and the Bon Religion in Tibet." In *Proceedings of the International Seminar on the Anthropology of Tibet and the Himalaya: September 21–28 1990 at the Ethnographic Museum of the University of Zürich,* 433–41. Zürich: Ethnographic Museum of the University of Zürich, 1993.

Yang, Eveline. "Tracing the *Chol kha gsum*: Reexamining a Sa skya-Yuan Period Administrative Geography." *Revue d'Etudes Tibétaines* 37 (December 2017): 551–68.

Yaroslav, Komarovski. *Visions of Unity: The golden Pandita Shakya Chokden's New Interpretation of Yogacara and Madhyamaka.* Albany: State University of New York Press, 2011.

Yeh, Emily. *Taming Tibet: Landscape Transformation and the Gift of Chinese Development.* Ithaca: Cornell University Press, 2013.

Yongdan, Lobsang. "Geographical Conceptualizations in a Nineteenth-Century Tibetan Text: The Creation of Reponses to the 'Dzam Gling Rgyas Bshad' (The Detailed Description of the World)." PhD Diss. University of Cambridge, 2014.

Zhabs dkar tshogs drug rang grol. *The Emanated Scripture of Manjushri: Shabkar's Essential Meditation Instructions.* Translated by Sean Price. New Delhi: Shechen Publications, 2021.

# INDEX

Achung Namdzong, 33, 56
Amdo: Avalokiteśvara and, 34, 56–57, 94; Dalai Lama's political influence in, 35; ethnic diversity of, 113; folk songs of, 72–76; greater Tibet and, 8; in Gyaltsen's *Clear Mirror*, 28; mapping of, 19, 55–58; Mongols in, 54–55, 113–14; mountain deities of, 2–3; nonsectarianism and, 129–30, 138–40; organization of Shabkar's autobiography and, 57–58; pilgrimage and, 118; Shabkar's legacy in, 15–16; as Tibetan territory, 7, 19, 22, 26, 28–29, 31, 32, 54–60, 178n76; vernacular dialect of, 31, 57, 82, 118; violence in, 113–14
Amitābha, 78–79, 89, 96, 108
Anderson, Benedict, 11–13, 77, 135
Anton-Luca, Alexandru, 69
Anyé Machen: in *Detailed Explanation of the World*, 50; organization of Shabkar's autobiography and, 57; pilgrimage and, 48, 53, 118; praise of place to, 52–53; "Singer of Tibet" epithet and, 57; as soul of Tibet, 2–3; in upper, middle, and lower classification system, 27. *See also* Pomra
Arik Géshé, 15, 130
Aris, Michael, 55
Āryaśūra, *Jātakamālā*, 50, 177n35
Atiśa, 33, 92, 97–98, 104–6
autobiography. *See namtar* genre
Avalokiteśvara: Amdo region and, 34, 56–57, 94; Dalai Lamas and, 13–14, 22, 34–35, 52, 93, 99–101, 108; Gésar and, 85; hidden lands and, 52; introduction into Tibet, 87; Karmapas and, 3, 87, 142; myths of ethnic election and, 5, 88, 93–101; nonsectarianism and, 106–8; oath to tame Tibet, in Gyaltsen's *Clear Mirror*, 28; Shabkar as reincarnation of, 1, 3–4, 20, 78–79, 88, 112; Shabkar's portrayal of, 20, 29, 33–35, 93–101, 107; Songsten Gampo and, 6, 7, 87, 89–90, 93, 96, 99–100; Tibetan opera and, 78–79; Tibetans, terms of address to, 30; as Tibet's patron deity, 6, 7, 12, 13–14, 20, 28, 33–34, 87–93, 95, 97, 106–8, 142; worship of, 3, 87, 89–90, 93, 95–97, 106–7, 114–17, 142

barbarism tropes, 56
Berkwitz, Stephen, 39
Bhrikuti (deity), 89
Bhum, Pema, 64
Bhutanese Legal Code of 1729, 76–77
*bod* ("Tibet"): geographical and historical referents of, 22–24; Shabkar's usage of, 8, 19, 24–29
Boltjes, Miek, 12–13
Bön religion, 129, 130, 132
*Book of Kadam*, 25, 88, 89, 92–93, 96–100, 105
Brook, Timothy, 12
Buddha, 42, 89, 132
Buddhism: Avalokiteśvara myth and, 89–93, 95; countermodern frameworks and, 145–50; environmental understanding through, 27; geographical frameworks of, 43–45, 58–62; hidden lands and propagation of, 52; indigenous literary elements incorporated by, 65; Kublai Khan's conversion to, 7; national framework of, 38–42, 114–15,

Buddhism (*continued*)
147–50; Padmasambhava and, 88, 101–5, 108; state formation and, 110; Tibetan national identity in, 4, 22, 29–30, 32–34, 140–44, 147–50; Tibetan opera and, 78, 83; unity through principles of, 20, 113–15, 119, 125, 141–42; "White Feet" epithet and, 1, 111–12. *See also* Buddhist imagined community; Later Transmission Period; Tibetan Buddhist world model; *specific sects*

Buddhist imagined community: Anderson's imagined community compared to, 11–13; everyday nationalism and, 115–17; mapping and sacred geography of, 16, 19, 36, 58–60; modern/premodern continuity in, 137; myths of ethnic election and, 5, 89–91, 94, 108; nation-state models exceeded by, 5; nonsectarianism and, 39, 129, 133; pilgrimage and, 117, 119–20; religion and nationalism intertwined in, 11–14, 38, 39–40, 147–48; religious values and practices in, 39, 110, 113–15; vegetarianism and, 120–22, 124–28; vernacular literature and, 19–20, 64, 66, 127. *See also* imagined community

Buffetrille, Katia, 118–19

Burma: Buddhist nationalism in, 13, 115; *sasana* concept in, 13, 39, 115; state formation in, 110

cartography. *See* maps and mapping
central Tibet: *bod* usage and, 22, 28–29; folk songs of, 72; Ganden Podrang government of, 7, 8; mapping of, 60; organization of Shabkar's autobiography and, 57

Central Tibetan Administration (CTA): Buddhist elements of, 148; on geographical definition of Tibet, 22–23; on greater Tibet terminology, 23; mapping practices and, 60; Middle Way approach of, 140; nonsectarianism and, 129, 137–38; territorial claims of, 5–7

Chatterjee, Partha, 12

China: Amdo region violence and, 113–14; Buddhist holy site in, 132; Fifth Dalai Lama on, 100. *See also later name* People's Republic of China

Chinese-Tibetan Treaty (821–22), 6, 23

Chögyel Ngakgi Wangpo, 15, 130

Chokgyur Lingpa, 23; *A Brief Inventory of the Great Sites of Tibet*, 8, 28–29, 55

*chölkha sum* (three regions) model, 7, 27

Chöpel, Gendün, 1, 17–18, 22–23, 24, 65, 135–36

chorography. *See* maps and mapping

chosen people narratives. *See* myths of ethnic election

*Chronicle of Péma* (*Padma bka'i thang*), 102–3

Chuzang Monastery, 58

*Collected Songs* (Milarepa), 2, 47, 54, 71, 180n36

*Collected Songs* (Shabkar): cultural identity in, 68–69; geographical organization of, 57, 68; *kāvya* elements in, 67–68; *Life of Milarepa* as model for, 17; sacred geography in, 16–17; Tibetans, terms of address for, 30; "White Feet" epithet in, 111

collective memories: landscape and, 62; myths of ethnic election and, 101; treasure texts and, 91; vernacular literature and, 66

colloquial language. *See* vernacular literature

consuming the nation (Fox and Miller-Idriss), 37, 116, 125

*Copper Island* (*Zangs gling ma*), 102–3, 107

countermodern frameworks, 145, 147–50

CTA. *See* Central Tibetan Administration

cultural nationalism: idea of Tibet as nation and, 5, 36–37; mapping territory and, 36; myths of ethnic origin and election and, 88, 94–95; theoretical framework of, 9–11. *See also* Buddhist imagined community; nationalism; nations; nation-states

cultural Tibet, 5, 22

*ḍākinīs*, 45–46, 48, 49, 70. *See also* deities

Dalai Lamas: First, 105; Third, 100; Fourth, 100; Fifth, 7–8, 23, 34, 87, 89, 92, 93, 100; Ninth, 29, 34, 57, 99; Eleventh,

34; Thirteenth, 135; as embodiment of Avalokiteśvara, 13–14, 20, 22, 34–35, 52, 93, 99–101, 108; myths of ethnic election and, 20; political control of, 35; sectarianism and, 128–29; vegetarianism and, 124–25. *See also* Fourteenth Dalai Lama
Dalton, Jacob, 102
Damdin, Zawa, 149–50
Daṇḍin, *Kāvyādarśa*, 64, 76, 179n7
Dégé kingdom, 55
deities: indigenous practices of worshiping, 117; landscape speaking through, 2–3, 52–54, 62; Padmasambhava's subjugation of, 101, 108; pilgrimage guide genre and, 46–47, 53; praises of place and, 48, 49. *See also* Avalokiteśvara; Pomra
Demo Rinpoché (king), 35
Denma Tsültrim Gyatso, 130
Deroche, Marc-Henri, 130–31
Dezhung Rinpoché, 137
Dilgo Khyentsé Rinpoché, 137
*dohā* genre, 66–67, 179nn18–19
Dokham, 7
Döndrup Gyel, 1–2, 71–73, 180n46
Dongak Chökyi Gyatso, 138–40
Dotson, Brandon, 90
Downs, James, 31, 117–18
Drakgön. See *Oceanic Book*
Drakkar of Loba, 46
Drakkar Treldzong, 27, 33, 57
Drenpa Namkha, 87, 102
Dreyfus, Georges, 6, 90, 95
Drigung Kagyü lineage, 45–46
Dromtön, 92, 93, 105
Dzokchen tradition, 21, 91–92, 106, 108, 131, 139

early modern period: continuity with modernity, 136–37; definitions of, 4, 168n27; imagined communities in, 11
Ekvall, Robert, 31, 117–18
England's vernacular literature, 65–66
ethnic election. *See* myths of ethnic election
ethnicity: national frameworks constituting, 24; place and, 61; religion linked to, 13–14, 114–15, 141; in Shabkar's autobiography, 30, 34, 37–39
ethnographic Tibet. *See* cultural Tibet
ethno-symbolist model of nationhood, 11, 61, 88–89, 90, 94, 101
everyday nationalism, 115–17, 125–28

Five-Point Peace Plan (1988), 6, 23
folk songs: *dohā* genre and, 179n18; in Gésar epic, 86; *mgur* genre and, 66–67; nationalism in nineteenth-century Europe and, 76–77; in Shabkar's autobiography, 20, 64, 71–78, 83; in Tibetan national consciousness, 69, 77. *See also* Tibetan opera; vernacular literature
Fourteenth Dalai Lama: exile into India, 135, 140; Five-Point Peace Plan (1988) of, 6, 23; Middle Way approach of, 140; modernization efforts of, 135; *My Land and My People*, 14; nonsectarianism of, 103, 137–39; Tibetan identity and, 141–42
Fox, Jon, 37, 115–16, 119, 146
fur renunciation movement, 144–47

galactic polity, 19, 39, 40
Ganden Podrang government, 7, 91–92, 148, 149
Gansu Province (PRC), 23, 54
Gardner, Alexander, 56, 59, 60
Gat, Azar, 78, 114
Gayley, Holly, 150
gazetteers (geographical literature), 43–45
Gellner, Ernest, 135
Gélongma Pelmo, 91
Géluk sect: Amdo region and, 55, 129, 138, 140; civil war victory of (1642), 7, 52; nonsectarianism and, 111, 129–30, 138–40; Shabkar's spiritual formation and, 15; Tibetan Assembly representation, 137; Tsongkhapa as founder of, 105
Gendzo (deity), 85
geography. *See* landscape; place; territory
Gésar epic, 64, 84–86, 109
Géwasel, 56
Goankar, Dilip, 149
Gö Lotsāwa, 129
greater Tibet, 5–8, 23–24, 55

Grosby, Steven, 10, 36
*gur* genre. See *mgur* genre
Gurong Trülku, 17
Guru Chöwang, 91, 106
Gushri Khan, 7
Gyatso, Janet, 4, 136–37; *Apparitions of Self*, 14
Gyatso, Kelden, 3, 26, 28, 29, 75, 130, 172n67, 173n71
Gyelwa Gyatso (form of Avalokiteśvara), 97–98

Hadfield, Andrew, 65–66
Hall, Amelia, 177n36
Hastings, Adrian, 37, 66
Hay, William, 42
Helgerson, Richard, 10–11, 65
Herder, Johannn Georg, 76
Heruka, Tsangnyön. See *Life of Milarepa, The*
hidden lands (*sbas yul*), 43, 50–52
Hobsbawm, Eric, 135
Holmes-Tagchungdarpa, Amy, *The Social Life of Tibetan Biography*, 15
Huber, Toni, 118–19
Hui Muslims, 125–26
Hum Chen, *Collection of Histories of Repgong's Tantrists*, 1

imagined community: Anderson's concept of, 11–13; folk songs and, 76–78; mapped territory and, 36, 58–60; myths of ethnic election and, 89–91, 94, 108; nonsectarianism and, 133; Shabkar's establishment of Tibet and, 19; vegetarianism and, 121–22, 125; vernacular literature and, 19–20, 66. See also Buddhist imagined community
India: borders of, 40; British subjugation of, 8; Buddhist geographical framework of, 44–45, 60–61; Buddhist holy site in, 132; Buddhist literature of, 63–64; pilgrimage and, 118; Sikkim incorporated into, 51
indigenous people and means: Buddhist incorporation of, 65, 119–20; deity worship and, 117; folk songs and, 73; *gur* genre and, 67; mapping of Kham and, 56, 59; *namtar* and, 63; Shabkar grounded in, 79; Tibetan opera and, 78
international law, 13. See also Tibetan Buddhist world model

Jabb, Lama, 10, 14, 36, 77, 95, 136, 182n85
Jackson, Roger, 179n18
Jacob, Christian, 10–11
Jacoby, Sarah, *Love and Liberation*, 14–15
Jampa Chödar (epithet), 20
Jamyang Gyatso Rinpoché, 130
Jamyang Khyentsé Wangpo, *Guide to the Holy Places of Central Tibet*, 43
Jamyang Zhépa (Fourth), 130
Japa Dongak Gyatso, 138
*Jātakamālā*, 50, 177n35
Jensen, Lotte, 11, 135
Jetsünpa, 128
Jewish people, compared to contemporary Tibetans, 66
Jigmé Tenpé Nyima (Third Dodrupchen), 138–39
Jokhang temple in Lhasa, 32
Jonang sect, 129

Kadam sect and Kadampas, 91–93, 99, 105, 106
Kagyü sect, 81, 129, 130
Kailash, Mount: kinesthetic dimensions of, 47–48; *maṇḍala* model and, 45; organization of Shabkar's autobiography and, 57; pilgrimage guide on, 45–46; as Tibetan territory, 26–27
Kapstein, Matthew, 90
karma, 114
Karma Pakshi, 93
Karmapas: Second, 78, 93; Seventh, 129; Seventeenth, 141–44; Avalokiteśvara and, 3, 87, 142; nonsectarianism and, 128–29, 137, 141–44. See also Rangjung Dorjé
Karmay, Samten, 86
*Katang* treasure texts, 102
Kaviraj, Sudipta, 149
*kāvya*, 64, 67–68, 71, 179n23
*Kāvyādarśa* (Daṇḍin), 64, 76, 179n7
Kelden Gyatso, 3, 26, 28, 29, 75, 130, 172n67, 173n71

INDEX    217

Kham: *bod* referring to, 22; Dalai Lama's political influence in, 35; in Gyaltsen's *Clear Mirror,* 28; mapping of, 19, 55–58; nonsectarianism and, 138–39; in Shabkar's autobiography, 27, 31; as Tibetan territory, 7, 8, 28–29, 54–60, 178n76
*khampa,* 24
Khedrup Jé Gelek Pelzang, 121
Khenpo Jigmé Phuntsok, 143–47, 149
Khenpo Tsultrim Lodrö, 143–44, 146–47
King, Matthew, 149
Kongtrül, Jamgön, 6, 23; Shabkar's autobiography compared to autobiography of, 83–84; *Twenty Five-Sites of Khams* (*Mdo khams gnas chen nyer lnga*), 4, 8, 55–56, 58–60
Kriki (king), 103, 104
Kublai Khan, 6–7
Kubum monastery, 55
Künzang Déchen Gyelpo, 91

Labrang monastery, 55, 130
Lachi, Mount, 26–27, 30, 53–54, 57, 118
landscape: as body of the Buddha, 132; Buddhism as defining element of, 43–44, 58–62; challenges of navigating, 109; deities of Tibet and, 2–3, 52–54; Indian Buddhist frameworks for, 44–45; kinesthetic dimensions of, 47–48; in *Life of Milarepa,* 43–44; *maṇḍala* organizational model for, 44–47; in pilgrimage guidebooks and gazetteers, 45–47; praises of place and, 48–52; as sites of memory, 2–3, 61; spiritual journey through, 47, 48, 59, 61; vegetarianism and, 120
Lang Darma (king), 56
language: diversity across landscapes, 109, 113; pan-Tibetan identity and, 31–32; Tibetan nation and, 36, 115; vernacular literature and, 65
Larung Gar Monastery and Buddhist Academy, 128, 141, 143, 145–46, 148
Later Transmission Period: Avalokiteśvara myth in, 33–34, 90–91; Buddhism flourishing during, 6–7; early modern period inclusive of, 4; memory of Tibetan Empire and, 28; Padmasambhava myth in, 102, 103; re-importation of Buddhism during, 6–7, 56; religious songs of, 72; Tibetan opera and, 78
Leerssen, Joep, 10
Lepcha people, 52
Lhakar movement, 128, 147
Lhamo. *See* Tibetan opera
Lha Totori Nyentsen, 32–33, 99
Lhatsun Chenpo Namkha Jikmé, 52
*Life of Milarepa, The* (Heruka): classical structure of, 42; emotional register of, 84; local deities absent from, 54; oral conceit in, 80–81; sacred landscape in, 43–44, 50, 61; Shabkar's autobiography compared to, 17–18, 44, 69–71, 82; songs collected separately from, 68, 70, 180n36
Lin, Nancy, 177n35
Lingpa, Jikmé, 14, 15, 120–21, 126
Loba people, 37
Lodrö Rinchen Sengé, 128
*Longchen Nyingtik,* 121
Longchenpa, 128
Lower Tö, 7, 54. *See also* Dokham
Lozang Chökyi Nyima (Third Tukwan), 64, 82, 86, 103

Machak Hermitage, 97
Machen, Mount. *See* Anyé Machen
Machen Pomra (deity). *See* Pomra
Madhyamaka tenet system, 131
Mahāmudrā tenet system, 106, 131
Mahāvairocana, 90
Mahāyāna Buddhism, 78, 83, 119, 131, 138, 145, 148
Makley, Charlene, 149–50
Manasarovar, Lake, 45–46
Maṇḍala of Eight Great Bodhisattvas, 90
*maṇḍala* organizational model, 27, 39, 40, 44–47, 53
Manéné (deity), 85
*Maṇi Kabum,* 88, 90, 92, 96–99, 106, 142
Maṇi Tang temple, 113
Mañjuśrī (deity), 85, 100
Mañjuśrīmitra, 102
maps and mapping: Amdo and Kham regions and, 19, 55–58; cultural nationalism and, 10–11, 37; in early

maps and mapping (*continued*)
modern England, 36, 65–66; imagined community and, 19, 36, 58–60; inclusive of narrative, 59–60; nation visualization through, 58–62

*mgur* genre, 2, 66–67. See also songs of spiritual realization

Middle Way, 140

Milarepa: *Collected Songs,* 2, 47, 54, 71, 180n36; *dohā* genre incorporated by, 67, 179n18; Gyatso and, 130; Mount Kailash and, 47, 50; praises of place and, 48; Shabkar as reincarnation of, 1, 17, 57, 69; Tséringma and, 54. See also *Life of Milarepa, The*

Miller-Idriss, Cynthia, 115–16, 119, 146

Mills, Martin, 4

Mipam, 138

Mongols and Mongolia: Amdo region and, 54–55, 113–14; Buddhist outreach to, 39, 40; nonsectarianism and, 132; in *Oceanic Book,* 50; pan-Tibetan identity and, 6–7; territorial divisions and, 7, 27; unity of Tibetan communities and, 41, 109

Mönpa people, 37, 39, 52, 113, 114

moral communities. See *sasana*

mountain deities, 2–3

Myanmar, 141, 149

myths of ethnic election: Avalokiteśvara myth and, 5, 34, 88, 93–101; Buddhist imagined community and, 5, 8, 89–91, 94, 108; collective identity and, 20, 28, 36, 94; Padmasambhava myth and, 88; political fragmentation and, 90–91. See also Avalokiteśvara; Padmasambhava

Namnang Gangchentso, 97, 98

*namtar* genre: criticism of, 63–64, 82; deities of landscape in, 52; Euro-American scholarship on, 14–15; geographical links to, 43, 48; *rangnam* subgenre of, 63; role in Tibet's national self-imagination, 14–15, 63; Shabkar's autobiography as masterpiece of, 16, 63; Tibetan opera and, 79; vernacular genres merged with, 20, 64, 65, 73, 76, 78, 80, 82–83, 86

Nāropā, 44

nationalism: Buddhist framework for, 32–34, 38–42, 114–15, 140–44, 147–50; everyday, 115–17, 125–28; folk songs and, 76–77; Gésar and, 85; Larung Gar Buddhist Academy and, 143–44; modern Tibetan literature and, 65; myths of ethnic election and, 94–95; *namtar*'s role in, 14–15, 63; nonsectarianism and, 137–40; premodern roots of, 135–36; religious communities and, 114–17; territory and, 59; vegetarianism and, 144–47

nations: Buddhist imagined community compared to, 5; cultural nationalism and formation of, 10–11, 36–37; mapping and visualization of, 58–62; myths of ethnic election and, 20; non-state-centric definitions of, 9–10, 14, 36; territorial basis of, 19, 36; vernacular literature and, 19–20, 66

nation-states: Asian polities in transition to, 55, 135–36; Buddhist national frameworks vs., 38–41, 62, 150; imagined community and, 11–12, 126; limitations of concept of, 9; mapping practices and, 59; *sasana* model compared to, 13, 40

Nepal: Avalokiteśvara and, 89; Buddhist holy site in, 132; ethnic vs. national categorization of, 24; mapping and borders of, 19, 26, 40; Shabkar's pilgrimage to, 57, 58, 118; Shabkar's vegetarianism advocacy in, 125

Ngakgi Wangpo, 15, 130

Ngakwang Trashi (epithet), 15, 21

Ngakwang Trashi Rinpoché, 130

Ngari region, 7, 22, 28–29, 31, 60

*nirvāṇa,* 63

nonsectarianism: Amdo region's diversity and, 55, 114; Avalokiteśvara and, 106–8; of contemporary Tibetan leaders, 129, 137–40; Padmasambhava and, 103–8; of Shabkar, 1, 20, 129–33, 138; threats to, 128–29; "White Feet" epithet and, 111

nonviolence, 142, 148

Nyangrel Nyima Özer, 91, 92, 102, 106, 108

Nyatri Tsenpo, 99
Nyingma sect: myths of ethnic election promoted by, 91; nonsectarianism and, 111, 129–31, 138–40; Padmasambhava and, 87, 101, 102, 105–6, 108; Tibetan Assembly representation, 137. *See also* treasure revealers and treasure texts

Obeyeskere, Gananath, 39, 40, 175n131
*Oceanic Book* (Drakgön), 1, 4, 5, 8, 28, 43; Amdo and Kham mapped in, 55; *bod* usage in, 28; colloquial references to, 167n2; Indian Buddhist geographical framework of, 45; praises of place and, 50
opera. *See* Tibetan opera
orality: Gésar epic and, 85; in *Life of Milarepa*, 80–81; in Shabkar's autobiography, 79–81; Tibetan opera and, 79; vernacular literature and, 78
Orgyen Lingpa, 106
Orgyen Samtenling, 53

Padmasambhava: Buddhism's transmission to Tibet and, 33, 101–5, 108; Gésar and, 85; hidden lands predicted by, 51; myth of, 6, 101–2; nonsectarianism and, 103–8; Nyingma sect and, 91; in *Oceanic Book*, 50, 53; religious songs and, 72; Shabkar as reincarnation of disciple of, 88, 102–3; Shabkar's portrayal of, 20, 102–8; Tibetan deities tamed by, 87–88, 120; Tibetan Empire and, 28; Tibetan opera and, 78–79
pan-Tibetan identity: Amdo region and, 56–57; Avalokiteśvara and, 109; folk song and, 77; historical memory of Tibetan Empire and, 28, 109; language and, 31–32; mapping practices and, 60–61; Shabkar's epithets and, 20–21; terms of address for "Tibetans" and, 31–32. *See also* Buddhist imagined community
Patrul Rinpoché, 138
Pel Nyenmo monastery, 139
Péma Shelpuk (hermitage), 46
People's Republic of China (PRC): Buddhism suppressed by, 148; "greater Tibet" and, 23; Great Western Development program, 145; Hui Muslims in, 125–26; incursion into Tibet (1959), 135; Opening Up and Reform policies, 144–45; Tibetan Autonomous Region created by, 5, 7; Tibetan ethnic minorities in, 37, 140–41, 143–45, 148
performing the nation (Fox and Miller-Idriss), 37, 116–17, 119
pilgrimage, of Shabkar, 1
pilgrimages, 19, 20; Buddhist landscape defined by, 58–59; guidebooks and sacred landscape, 43, 45–47, 53, 61; kinesthetic dimensions of, 47–48; as unifying force, 117–20; "White Feet" epithet and, 111, 112, 117
place: kinesthetic dimensions of, 47–48; in *Life of Milarepa*, 44; mapping practices and, 60; naming of, 57–58; praises of, 43, 48–52, 61, 177n35
political Tibet. *See* Tibetan Autonomous Region
Pollock, Sheldon, 136, 168n27
Pomra (deity), 2–3, 20, 21, 52–53, 57, 68, 79, 85, 120
Potala Palace, 100
praises of place, 43, 48–52, 61, 177n35
PRC. *See* People's Republic of China
printing press and print culture, 12, 77–78, 135
prose style, 50, 71

Qing dynasty, 8, 35, 40, 41, 54, 55
Qinghai Lake, 53, 56–57, 93–99
Qinghai Province (PRC), 23, 54
*qingzhen* dietary codes, 126
Quintman, Andrew, 18, 43–44, 63

Ragya Monastery, 47
Rangjung Dorjé (Third Karmapa), 3, 48, 108, 128
religion: cultural nationalism and, 11, 115, 148; ethnicity linked to, 13–14, 114–15, 141; everyday nationalism and, 116–17; formation of polities around, 12–14, 20, 95; imagined community and, 12–13, 114–15; nation-state concept divorced from, 20, 95, 110. *See also* nonsectarianism

Repgong Valley: counterdevelopment in, 150; geographical framework for, 45; nonsectarianism and, 130; praises of place and, 48–49; regional identity and, 32; in Shabkar's autobiography, 26, 28; Shabkar's legacy in, 1, 15–16, 20; as Tibetan territory, 57

Ricard, Matthieu, 48

Richardson, Hugh, 90

*rnam thar*. See *namtar* genre

Ryavec, Karl, 178n67

Sachen Künga Nyingpo, 93

Sakya Paṇḍita, 6–7, 121

Sakyapa Sönam Gyeltsen, *The Clear Mirror of Royal Genealogies*, 7, 28, 89, 90

Sakya sect, 7, 129

Samantabhadra, 108

Samuel, Geoffrey, 39

Samyé monastery, 101

Sangyé Rinchen, 17, 80

Śāntarakṣita, 101

*sasana* (Buddhist community and teachings), 13, 19, 39–40, 147

Schaeffer, Kurtis, 179n19

Schneiderman, Sara, 24, 37

self-immolation, 140, 148

Sera Jé monastery, 128

Séra Khandro, 15

Shabkar's autobiography: accessibility of, 64, 65, 81; Amdo mapped in, 56–60; composition of, 17; first-person perspective in, 48, 53; folk song in, 71–78; geographical organizational structure of, 18, 42–44, 57–58; Gésar epic and, 85–86; GIS coordinates from, 58; *Life of Milarepa* compared to, 17–18, 44, 69–71, 80–81, 82, 84; *namtar* and vernacular genres merged in, 20, 64, 65, 73, 76, 78, 80, 82–83, 86; nation as concept in, 32–37; oral conceit in, 79–81; pilgrimage guide genre and, 46–47; poetry and prose style in, 50, 71; Qinghai edition, 172n51, 173n80; songs included in, 68, 70–71; "Tibetan" language usage in, 29–32; Tibetan political autonomy in, 35–36; "Tibet" language usage in, 24–28

Shabkar Tsokdruk Rangdröl: appearance of, 1; birth and childhood, 15; *Elegant Sayings: The Self-Arising Sun*, 103; *Emanated Scripture of Compassion*, 121, 124; *Emanated Scripture of Mañjuśrī*, 16, 68, 92; Gésar and, 85; names and epithets, 21–22, 53, 57, 88–89, 110–12; nonsectarianism of, 1, 20, 129–33, 138; as reincarnation of Avalokiteśvara, 1, 3–4, 20, 78–79, 88, 112; as reincarnation of Milarepa, 1, 17, 57, 69; religious vs. nationalistic motivations of, 58, 89, 114–15; singing abilities of, 66, 69, 85; "The Song [called] Laughter of Mañjuśrī and Sarasvatī," 75–76; "The Song of the Six Remembrances of the Lama," 17–18; spiritual formation and education, 15–16, 91, 112, 122, 129–30; Tibetan opera's founder and, 78–79; vegetarianism arguments of, 121–25, 145, 147; "White Feet" epithet and, 1, 21, 110–12, 117, 123. See also *Collected Songs* (Shabkar); Shabkar's autobiography

Shakya, Tsering, 32

Shākya Chokden, 129

Shākya Shrī, 15

Sichuan Province (PRC), 23, 54

Sikkim (Himalayan kingdom), 51–52

"Singer of Tibet, Land of Snows" epithet, 1; folk songs and, 76, 77, 86; landscape and, 61; Milarepa evoked by, 2, 17, 69–70, 88; pan-Tibetan identity and, 2, 21–22, 32, 37; Pomra's bestowal of, 2, 15, 21, 53, 57, 68; Tibetan bardic tradition and, 85, 86, 88–89; "White Feet" epithet as alternative of, 1, 112

Situ Rinpoche, 137

six-syllable mantra in Avalokiteśvara worship, 3, 34, 39, 87, 89–90, 93, 95–97, 106–7, 114–16, 142

Sixteen Spheres meditative practice, 97–99, 104

Smith, Anthony: on collective distinctiveness, 20, 105; ethno-symbolist model of nationhood, 11, 20, 61, 88–89, 90, 94, 101; on nation-state models, 135, 136; non-state definition of nation by, 9, 36; on religious traditions, 13, 62, 148

Smith, Gene, 138
snow as metonym for Tibet, 25, 44
songs of spiritual realization: Avalokiteśvara vision and, 93–94; *Collected Songs* and, 16, 68–69; cultural presence and authority of, 69, 71, 79, 86; folk songs' influence on, 71–78; as genre, 66–67; in *Life of Milarepa* vs. Shabkar's autobiography, 70–71; Shabkar's songs as examples of, 1, 2; typical topics for, 72–73. *See also* praises of place
Songsten Gampo (king): Avalokiteśvara and, 6, 7, 87, 89–90, 93, 96, 99–100; in *Oceanic Book,* 50, 53; Shabkar's portrayal of, 32–33
Sørenson, Per K., 179n18
space. *See* landscape; place; territory
spiritual journey: landscape as part of, 47, 48, 59, 61; Shabkar's teachings in, 114, 131–33; vegetarianism and, 122–23
Sri Lanka: Buddhist nationalism in, 13, 115, 141; countermodern Buddhism compared to Buddhism of, 149; "nation" concept inadequate for, 40; *sasana* concept in, 13, 19, 39, 175n131; state formation in, 110
Stroup, David, 125–26
Sumpa Khenpo, 42
*sūtra* literature, 43, 50, 177n35

Takmo Dzong, 57
talking the nation (Fox and Miller-Idriss), 37, 116, 146
Tambiah, Stanley, 39
Tangtong Gyelpo, 40, 78–79, 83
*Tantra of the Enlightenment of Mahāvairocana,* 132–33
Tārā (deity), 89
Tarē Lhamo, 85
Tayenchi cave at Tsézhung, 57
Tenpo Nomönhen, 4, 42, 50; *Detailed Explanation of the World,* 8, 23–24, 28–29
Terdak Lingpa, 50
territory: Buddhist models for organization of, 27–28, 40–41, 59; hidden lands and, 52; as imagined community, 5; mapping and visualization of, 58–62; in non-state definitions of nation, 19, 36; Tibetan Empire and, 28. *See also specific regions*
*Testimony of Ba* (*Dba' bzhed*), 101, 103
Theravāda Buddhism, 13, 19, 38–39, 147
Three Wise Men of Tibet, 33, 56
Tibet: *bod* and historical referents, 22–24; historical precedents for pan-plateau concept of, 28–29; modernization and, 135–37; Shabkar's references to, 2; snow as metonym for, 25, 44. *See also* Buddhist imagined community; Central Tibetan Administration; cultural Tibet; greater Tibet; Tibetan Autonomous Region; Tibetan Empire
Tibetan Autonomous Region (TAR), 5, 7, 22
Tibetan Buddhist world model, 12–13, 110, 125, 140–41, 149, 194n44
Tibetan Empire: Avalokiteśvara and, 90, 99–100; oral primacy in, 80, 85; reviving memory of, 28, 30; Shabkar's links to, 88–89, 99, 108; in treasure texts, 91; unity of Tibetan communities and, 109
Tibetan opera, 20, 64, 78–84. *See also* folk songs; vernacular literature
Tibetans: *bod pa* and historical referents, 24, 32; as ethnic minority within PRC, 37, 140–41, 143–45, 148; in Shabkar's autobiography, 29–32; vegetarianism and, 126–27, 146–47; vernacular literature and, 64, 65. *See also* myths of ethnic election
Tibetan Youth Congress (TYC), 140
Trashikhyil Hermitage, 1, 82
treasure revealers and treasure texts: Avalokiteśvara myth in, 90–92; Padmasambhava myth in, 87–88, 91, 102–3, 105–8; Shabkar's revitalization of, 89; Tibetan empire and, 99
tripartite classification system, 26–28, 172n51
Trisong Détsen (king), 2, 33, 99, 101
Trungpa, Chogyam, 137
Tsangnyön Heruka. *See Life of Milarepa, The*
Tsari, Mount, 26–27, 44, 57, 111, 118, 119

Tséringma (Five Long Life Sisters), 53–54
Tsering Shakya, 148
Tséring Trashi (epithet), 20
Tsering Wangyel Shawa, 178n67
Tsézhung Hermitage, 58
Tsokdruk Rangdröl. *See* Shabkar Tsokdruk Rangdröl
Tsokdruk Rangdröl (epithet), 20, 25
Tsomen Gyelmo (deity), 53
Tsongkhapa, 104–6, 128
Tsonying Island, 21, 27, 30, 34–35, *35*, 50, 53, 56–57, 93–99
Tuan, Yi-fu, 57
*tulkus* (reincarnations of enlightened figures), 78
Turner, Alicia, 39, 40
Tuttle, Gray, 172n67

upper, middle, and lower classification system, 26–28, 172n51
Upper Tö, 7, 54. *See also* Ngari region

Vairocana (deity), 90
Vajrapāṇi (deity), 85
Vajrāsana (Diamond Throne), 44–45
*Vajravārāhī and Hayagrīva: The Wish Fulfilling Jewel*, 91
Vajrayana Buddhism, 27, 188n11
van Schaik, Sam, 90
van Walt van Praag, Michael, 12–13
vegetarianism: Chinese Buddhism and, 147; everyday nationalism and, 125–28; Shabkar's arguments for, 1, 20, 121–25, 145, 147; Tibetan Buddhist identity and, 120–22, 144–47; Tibetan national identity and, 144–47; "White Feet" epithet and, 111
vernacular literature: collective identity in, 64; Gésar epic and, 85–86; Kadampas and, 92; *namtar* genre merged with, 20, 64, 65, 73, 76, 78, 80, 82–83, 86; nationalism and production of, 18, 19–20, 37, 115; nation-states' rise and, 65–66; vegetarianism and, 121, 127. *See also* folk songs; Tibetan opera
*vimokṣa*, 63

Wang, Michelle, 90
"White Feet" epithet, 1, 21, 110–12, 117, 123
Wintle, Michael, 10–11
Wise Collection, 42, 43
Wü-Tsang, 7, 8, 54–55. *See also* central Tibet
Yang, Eveline, 172n59
Yarlung dynasty, 6, 7, 99, 109
Yongdzin Lama Nyima, 179n23
Yuan dynasty, 54
Yunnan Province (PRC), 23, 54

Traditions and Transformations in Tibetan Buddhism

This series investigates the stability of Tibetan religious culture from its historical beginnings in the sixth century through the modern era as well as how the religious tradition has changed in reaction to historical realities, technological transformation, and social unrest. To facilitate an interdisciplinary approach, the series publishes projects on four interconnected themes: ritual traditions and textual transformations, Tibet in its historical milieu, Tibet and the modern world, and Tibetan Buddhism in diaspora.

*Buddha in the Marketplace: The Commodification of Buddhist Objects in Tibet*
Alex John Catanese

www.ingramcontent.com/pod-product-compliance
Lightning Source LLC
Chambersburg PA
CBHW030825230426
43667CB00008B/1378